M000281554

Cultural Conversions

Religion and Politics
Michael Barkun, *Series Editor*

Other Titles in Religion and Politics

Cultural Conversions

Unexpected Consequences of Christian
Missionary Encounters in the Middle
East, Africa, and South Asia

Edited by **Heather J. Sharkey**

Syracuse University Press

Copyright © 2013 by Syracuse University Press
Syracuse, New York 13244-5290

All Rights Reserved

First Edition 2013

13　14　15　16　17　18　　　6　5　4　3　2　1

Chapter 6, "The Port Said Orphan Scandal of 1933: Colonialism, Islamism,
and the Egyptian Welfare State" © by Beth Baron.

Significant excerpts in chapter 7, "Robert Moffat and the Invention of Christianity in South Africa,"
were originally published in *Popular Politics in the History of South Africa, 1400–1948*, by Paul S. Landau.
Copyright © 2010 Paul S. Landau. Reprinted with the permission of Cambridge University Press.

∞ The paper used in this publication meets the minimum requirements
of the American National Standard for Information Sciences—Permanence
of Paper for Printed Library Materials, ANSI Z39.48-1992.

For a listing of books published and distributed by Syracuse University Press,
visit our website at SyracuseUniversityPress.syr.edu.

ISBN: 978-0-8156-3315-0 (cloth) / 978-0-8156-5220-5 (e-book)

Library of Congress Cataloging-in-Publication Data

Cultural conversions : unexpected consequences of Christian missionary encounters in the
Middle East, Africa, and South Asia / edited by Heather J. Sharkey. — First Edition.
pages cm. — (Religion and politics)
Includes bibliographical references and index.
ISBN 978-0-8156-3315-0 (cloth : alk. paper) 1. Missions—Middle East. 2. Missions—Africa.
3. Missions—South Asia. 4. Christianity—Influence. 5. Christianity and culture. 6. Christianity
and politics. I. Sharkey, Heather J. (Heather Jane), 1967– editor of compilation.
BV2063.C785 2013
266.023—dc23　　2013022123

Manufactured in the United States of America

Contents

Acknowledgments

*I*n April 2008, the contributors to this volume met at the University of Pennsylvania in Philadelphia to participate in a conference on the theme of "Christian Missions and National Identities: Comparative Studies of Cultural 'Conversions' in the Middle East, Africa, South Asia, and East Asia." This event followed from a series of conversations that had started some years before at conferences and symposiums in New York City, Tokyo, Princeton, New Jersey, and Raleigh, North Carolina, as well as through email. This volume is the fruit of that 2008 conference at Penn and of the prior and subsequent exchanges.

At the University of Pennsylvania, many centers and departments contributed funds to make the conference possible. We are grateful to the University Research Foundation, the Middle East Center, the African Studies Center, the South Asia Center, the Center for East Asian Studies, the Graduate School of Education, the Department of Near Eastern Languages and Civilizations, and the Department of South Asia Studies. Later, in the summer of 2011, a grant from the Center for Undergraduate Research and Fellowships (CURF), associated with the Penn Undergraduate Research Mentorship (PURM) program, funded an undergraduate research assistant. This was Ellen Frierson, who did exemplary work in helping to prepare this manuscript for publication.

During the stages of conference planning, James De Lorenzi provided critical logistical support in liaising with speakers and developing the program. Faye Patterson, in the African Studies Center, processed the finances; we are especially grateful to her for volunteering to do so. Kathy Spillman and Roger Allen offered sage advice about organization.

Seven colleagues presented papers that are not included in this volume, but that helped to provide the intellectual context against which this book has developed: Betty S. Anderson, Ellen Fleischmann, Aleksandra Majstorac-Kobiljski, Eugenio Menegon, Charles P. Keith, Firoozeh Kashani-Sabet, and Kathleen L. Lodwick. Still other colleagues served as chairs and discussants, and contributed to lively conversations: Peter Gran, Ronald Granieri, Eve M. Troutt Powell, Cheikh Anta Babou, Jamal Elias, Lee Cassanelli, Thomas M. Ricks, Kathleen Hall, Michael Laffan, and Ignacio Gallup-Díaz. Eric Morier-Genoud offered some important, last-minute suggestions for improving the manuscript.

Several associates of Syracuse University Press lent support at various stages of the process, including Glenn Wright, Annelise Finegan, Jennika Baines, Mary Selden Evans, Erica Sheftic, Kelly Balenske, Kay Steinmetz, and Mona Hamlin. Kay Kodner did meticulous work in preparing the manuscript for publication. Michael Barkun welcomed the volume's inclusion in the "Religion and Politics" series, while two anonymous referees provided detailed reviews that challenged us to strengthen our arguments and unifying themes.

We owe thanks, too, to people at the Presbyterian Historical Society in Philadephia—including Nancy Taylor, Margery Sly, Eileen Sklar, and Lisa Jacobson—for allowing and facilitating the use of archival photographs for both the conference and this volume. Finally, I give personal thanks to Vijay Balasubramanian for his steady and unstinting encouragement.

Contributors

Beth Baron is Professor of History, and co-director of the Middle East and Middle Eastern American Center (MEMEAC), at City University of New York (CUNY) Graduate Center and City College. She is the author of *The Women's Awakening in Egypt: Culture, Society, and the Press* (Yale University Press, 1994) and *Egypt as a Woman: Nationalism, Gender, and Politics* (University of California Press, 2005). With Nikki R. Keddie, she edited *Women in Middle Eastern History: Shifting Boundaries in Sex and Gender* (Yale University Press, 1991). She is also the current editor of the *International Journal of Middle East Studies*.

Stephen C. Berkwitz is Professor of Religious Studies at Missouri State University. His books include *Buddhist History in the Vernacular: The Power of the Past in Late Medieval Sri Lanka* (Brill, 2004), *The History of the Buddha's Relic Shrine: A Translation of the Sinhala Thupavamsa* (Oxford University Press, 2007), and *South Asian Buddhism: A Survey* (Routledge, 2009). He is the editor of the Routledge Critical Studies in Buddhism Series and book review editor for the journal *Religion*.

James De Lorenzi is Assistant Professor of History at City University of New York (CUNY) John Jay College. His work has been published in *Comparative Studies of South Asia, Africa, and the Middle East*; the *Journal of World History*; and most recently, *World-Building in the Early Modern Imagination*, edited by Allison Kavey. He is currently finishing a book manuscript, which is provisionally titled *Being Modern through the Past: Writing History in the Red Sea Region, 1800–1935*.

David M. Gordon, who was born and educated in South Africa, is an Associate Professor of History at Bowdoin College. He is the author of *Nachituti's Gift: Economy, Society and Environment in Central Africa*, which was published by the University of Wisconsin Press in 2006. He has published on a range of topics about southern and central African society and history, including the politics of memory, environmental history, and indigenous knowledge. His current book, a study of the politics of the invisible world in Zambia, is titled *Invisible Agents: Spirits in a Central African History* (Ohio University Press, 2012).

Paul S. Landau is Associate Professor of History at the University of Maryland and a Fellow of the Centre for Historical Studies at the University of Johannesburg. He is the author of *Popular Politics in the History of South Africa, 1400–1948* (Cambridge University Press, 2010) and coeditor of *The African Historical Review.*

Chandra Mallampalli is Associate Professor in the History Department at Westmont College in California and a life member of Clare Hall, Cambridge University. His first book, *Christians and Public Life in South India,* appeared from RoutledgeCurzon in 2004. His second book, *Race, Religion, and Law in Colonial India: Trials of an Interracial Family,* was published by Cambridge University Press in 2011.

Laura Robson received her Ph.D. from Yale University in 2009, and is currently Assistant Professor of History at Portland State University in Oregon. She has published in many journals, including *The Jerusalem Quarterly, Journal of Palestine Studies,* and *Islam and Christian-Muslim Relations.* Her book *Colonialism and Christianity in Mandate Palestine* was published by University of Texas Press in 2011.

Mrinalini Sebastian, who holds a doctorate in English literature from the University of Hamburg, is currently Director of Student Assessment and Institutional Research at the Lutheran Theological Seminary at Philadelphia. She previously served as Fellow at the Centre for the Study of Culture and Society (CSCS), Bangalore, India. Her book *The Enterprise of Reading Differently: The Novels of Shashi Deshpande in Postcolonial Arguments* was published in Delhi in 2000.

Heather J. Sharkey is an Associate Professor in the Department of Near Eastern Languages and Civilizations at the University of Pennsylvania. She is the author of *Living with Colonialism: Nationalism and Culture in the Anglo-Egyptian*

Sudan (University of California Press, 2003) and *American Evangelicals in Egypt: Missionary Encounters in an Age of Empire* (Princeton University Press, 2008). With Mehmet Ali Doğan, she has edited *American Missionaries in the Middle East: Foundational Encounters* (University of Utah Press, 2011).

Abbreviations

AE	*Encyclopaedia Aethiopica*
AHR	Arab Higher Committee (Palestine)
AMEM	American Methodist Episcopal Mission
BDR	Bellary District Records, Tamil Nadu Archives, Chennai, India
BFBS	British and Foreign Bible Society
BM	Basel Mission Archives, Basel, Switzerland
BSA	Bible Society Archives, Cambridge University Library, Cambridge, United Kingdom
BSAC	British South Africa Company
CEOSS	Coptic Evangelical Organization for Social Services, Cairo, Egypt
CMS	Church Missionary Society; also Church Missionary Society Archives, Birmingham, United Kingdom
CO	Colonial Office, National Archives, London, United Kingdom
CUL	Cambridge University Library, Cambridge, United Kingdom
EGM	Egypt General Mission
EMML	Ethiopian Manuscript Microfilm Library, Addis Ababa University, Addis Ababa, Ethiopia, and Hill Monastic Manuscript Library, St. John's College, Minnesota
JEM	Jerusalem and East Mission Archives, Middle East Centre, St. Antony's College, Oxford, United Kingdom

LMJ	London Mission to the Jews
LMS	London Missionary Society
LPA	Lambeth Palace Archives, Lambeth Palace Library, London, United Kingdom
LSE	London School of Economics
MMD	Movement for Multi-party Democracy (Zambia)
MT	*Missions-Tidning* (Stockholm)
MTB	*Missions-Tidning Budbäraren* (Stockholm)
NAM	North Africa Mission
NAZ	National Archive of Zambia, Lusaka, Zambia
NLS	National Library of Scotland, Edinburgh, United Kingdom
OIOC	Oriental and India Office Collection of the British Library, London, United Kingdom
PHS	Presbyterian Historical Society, Philadelphia
PNCC	Palestine Native Church Council
SD	Archives of the U.S. Department of State (State Department), National Archives, Washington, D.C.
SEM	Swedish Evangelical Mission (Evangeliska Fosterlandsstiftelsen)
SJ	Society of Jesuits
SOAS	School of Oriental and African Studies, Special Collections, University of London, United Kingdom
Transactions	*Transactions of the London Missionary Society*
UCZA	United Church of Zambia Archives, Mindolo, Kitwe, Zambia
WFA	White Fathers Archives, Zambia
ZMDG	*Zeitschrift der Deutschen morgenlaendischen Gesellschaft*

Cultural Conversions

1

Introduction

The Unexpected Consequences
of Christian Missionary Encounters

Heather J. Sharkey

Introduction

In the nineteenth and twentieth centuries, Christian missionaries from Europe and North America expanded into Africa and Asia in tandem with Western imperialism. They founded schools, hospitals, printing presses, and factories, which they regarded as vehicles for propagating Christianity. Because missionaries went forth with the idea of changing others, their interactions entailed bids for influence and power and were therefore intrinsically political. Moreover, missionary encounters were sometimes wrenching, because they could transform the most intimate details of who people were and how they fit in among families and neighbors.

The social meanings of missionary "conversions" varied considerably in nature. In some places, individuals and communities embraced Christianity but refashioned it in line with their own cultural traditions and values–thereby contributing in the long run to the emergence of heterogeneous non-Western Christian cultures. In other places, missionaries galvanized anticolonial nationalists and sharpened corporate conceptions of non-Christian identities. This occurred most notably among Muslim, Jewish, Hindu, and Buddhist communities that already had strong literary traditions. Among Eastern and especially Orthodox Christians, missionaries also sharpened non-Catholic and non-Protestant identities. Missionary work sometimes led, more generally, to the reconfiguration of family relations, gender relations, and even relations between young and old. By changing notions of property, mobilizing labor in new ways, and shaping physical environments, missionary work revised economic relations as well.[1] In short, missionary encounters led to transformations that were varied, often ambiguous, and frequently unforeseen, and that had implications for things that were ostensibly far removed from religion.

In examining the social history of Christian missionary encounters, the essays in this volume are tied together by four shared conclusions. First, the history of Christian missions represents a form of world history that goes well beyond the range of professing Christians. Second, Christian missions have exerted far-reaching influences (cultural, political, and economic) that have affected even those who consciously rejected missionary appeals. Third, missionary encounters changed missionaries themselves, and these changes reverberated into the churches and societies that sponsored the missionaries. And fourth, missionaries, their ostensible converts, and local communities were often uncertain about what "conversion" meant (or should mean) in practice, and how it affected (or should affect) earlier loyalties and traditions. Together these essays show that the history of missionary encounters has been a history of the unexpected insofar as the changes set rolling often went far beyond, or even astray from, what the missionaries intended. The essays also examine how the cultural repercussions of conversion were often fraught with ambiguity.

In 1936 the sociologist Robert K. Merton wrote an article, "The Unanticipated Consequences of Purposive Social Action," which one scholar recently described as "the first and most complete analysis of the concept of unintended consequences."[2] Merton emphasized the results of actions that involved both motives and choice, particularly as they related to economic and political decisions.[3] Perhaps for this reason, scholarship informed by his work has tended to associate the "law of unintended consequences" with the actions of nation-states and corporations. An example of this type of action is how coastal U.S. states passed laws about liability for oil tankers in the aftermath of the Exxon Valdez oil spill of

1989, resulting in unforeseen long-term consequences for regulation and oversight.[4]

This book uses instead the term "unexpected consequences," which has currency among biologists, public health specialists, economists, and environmental analysts.[5] An emphasis on the "unexpected" draws attention away from the intent of corporate agents (e.g., the U.S. government, an oil company, or the representatives of a particular mission); removes what Merton called the "purposive" nature of action; and recognizes the multicausal, chaotic, and sometimes elusive forces behind change. In the case of missionaries of European origin, the emphasis on intent (implicit in its foil, the unintended) has the disadvantage of suggesting a kind of central agency among missionaries and a concomitant passivity among the targets of their missions–a suggestion this book is writing *against*. That is, rather than suggesting that missionaries alone acted with an intent that led to unforeseen results, the articles in this volume suggest "a broader set of results 'unexpected' to everyone involved."[6] In this way, the emphasis on the "unexpected" instead of the "unintended" aims to shift the spotlight away from missionaries and onto the manifold changes that surprised everyone caught up in them.

Most studies of missionary encounters focus on individual countries, regions, or missions, or address audiences within discrete area fields. This collection, by contrast, bridges African, Middle Eastern, and South Asian studies and makes connections among diverse Western missionary players–both Catholic and Protestant, as well as British, American, Swedish, Italian, German, French, Portuguese, and Irish. The essays feature local men and women who asserted themselves vis-à-vis missionaries across the globe, including the Arabic-speaking regions of North Africa (from Morocco to Sudan); Egypt and "Palestine" (as the British, after World War I, called the region that is now home to Israel and the Palestinian Territories); South Africa, Zambia, Eritrea, and Ethiopia; and India and Sri Lanka. Missionary encounters appear in these articles as social and political events that involved power plays and quests for meaning and identity.

The contributors to this volume do not consider themselves specialists on mission or conversion per se. Trained in the academic fields of history, religious studies (including Islamic and Buddhist studies), and literature, the contributors combine regional specializations in Africa, the Middle East, and South Asia; interdisciplinary interests in gender studies, environmental studies, and postcolonial studies; and expertise in the history of books, literacy, and mass media. They share the conviction that Christian missionary encounters have claimed historical significance far surpassing the realm of the "religious," suggesting that these encounters have often informed cultural debates about issues as fundamental as who should lead a family, community, or government and how those involved should express their authority. Thus understood, the history of Christian missionary encounters has been deeply political. By taking this approach to the study of missionary encounters, and by showing how the work of missionaries inadvertently jostled or collided with the larger social structures around them, the contributors hope to stimulate further discussion and scholarship across disciplinary and regional lines.

This volume represents part of a continuing dialogue for the contributors, who gathered to present earlier versions of the included essays at a symposium sponsored by the University of Pennsylvania in April 2008. But in fact, the conversations that led to this symposium started much earlier through overlapping circles of academic study and professional activity—in contexts of colleges and universities, at conferences, and through "meetings" in cyberspace, by telephone, and on the printed page.

This chapter is organized in four sections. The first describes new directions in the history of missionary encounters during the past fifteen years, highlighting several master themes that concern the most recent scholarship. The second points to the challenges of identifying the actors in missionary encounters. In the third section, I introduce the articles in this volume and highlight the themes that bind them together. A brief conclusion suggests routes for future study.

New Approaches to Missionary Encounters

Scholarship on colonial missions and their postcolonial legacies is now flourishing. In the 1960s academic interest in, and institutional support for, the history of missions diminished, and several research institutions eliminated faculty lines in the subject. But by the 1980s the field was reviving, while by the 1990s historians and anthropologists were beginning to reshape the scholarly agenda.[7]

During the past fifteen years this fresh scholarship has represented fields like American, British, and French studies, where the focus has generally been on the social impulses that prompted missionary *sending*, as well as fields like Asian, Middle Eastern, and African studies, where the focus has generally been on the consequences of missionary *receiving*. Since 2000 several works have tried to study both sending and receiving by considering the backflow of missionary enterprises for countries that sent missionaries abroad. Such works have considered, for example, the impact of French Catholic missions to Indochina and Madagascar on metropolitan French politics; the influence of Canadian Protestant and Catholic missions to China, Japan, and Oceania on the shaping of Canadian nationalism; and the relationship of British foreign missions to two central stories of modern British history, namely, the "rise and fall of the British Empire and the revival and decline of British religion."[8] Scholars are just beginning to study the most recent manifestations of missionary legacies, such as the impact of immigrants from places like Ghana and Korea, where European and American missionaries once helped to "plant" Christianity, on the United States, where some of these men and women have begun to evangelize among American locals.[9]

Scholars have been viewing these issues through a variety of lenses. These include attention to transnationalism and global connections; the communication and reception of missionary messages, in word, image, and sound, with attention to the means of disseminating, translating, and adapting ideas;[10] the displacement of missionaries from center stage in mission histories in an effort to hear divergent or dissenting voices; the role of women as linchpins of missions and religious communities; ambiguities of conversion and possibilities for hybrid identities; and, finally, failures of persuasion or retention (in contrast to the traditional focus on "success stories") in the political and social dynamics of missionary encounters. The following discussion elaborates briefly on each of these approaches, which inform, to varying degrees, the articles in this book.

Like the "new imperial history" in British studies, which considers the importance of the British Empire for life inside Britain, a defining feature of the "new mission history" has been its emphasis on transnationalism.[11] Rather than treating sites in isolation, this approach recognizes the "economic, social and political linkages between people, places, and institutions crossing nation-state borders and spanning the world."[12] Evincing this attention to transnational linkages, for example, are works that have connected nineteenth-century British missionaries in southern Africa and the Caribbean to churches and societies in Britain and studies of the relationships of American missions in the Ottoman Empire with missions to Native Americans and African Americans.[13] Other works have sought to understand transnational connections by scanning the history of a single mission society as it operated globally in places like India, Polynesia, and Australia, or by bringing new attention to bear on the interrelated histories of imperialism, nationalism, and missionary expansion.[14] Still others have considered the impact of transnational missionary activities on international reform movements, for example, with regard to temperance and women's suffrage.[15] In short, attention to transnationalism illuminates the mechanics of globalization in missionary encounters.

Equally important to recent scholarship has been the recognition that missionary encounters "happened" in literary texts and oral exchanges, as well as in visual, audio, and digital materials that emerged within changing communications landscapes. Aside from seeking out oral histories and printed books, historians and anthropologists have turned to missionaries' handwritten letters and diaries (which one scholar of English literature has called a "genre" of its own),[16] as well as to picture postcards and lantern slides, newspaper articles, moving pictures, radio broadcasts, sermons recorded on cassette tapes or DVDs, and more. Recognizing that the same "tools of empire" (like quinine and steamships) that enabled imperial expansion also allowed missionaries to expand as they did, scholars have likewise opened windows into histories of technology, healing, archaeology, and other "sciences."[17] The influence of Benedict Anderson, who transformed the study of nationalism by introducing the idea of the "imagined community" forged through vernacular print culture, has left its mark, too, by prompting scholars to think more carefully about the translation and publication of texts and ideas and their consequences for collective identities. Thus one recent study has shown how Swiss missionaries promoted new ideas about languages and ethnicities among people in South Africa and Mozambique while fortifying the missionaries' own sense of Swiss national distinction relative to Germany and France. Another has assessed the impact of a group of Yoruba-speaking evangelists in Nigeria who, while working for a British mission society, established foundations for a new Yoruba-language culture of writing by preparing reports for London. A third has considered the role of Scottish missionaries in fostering a new local interest in the Tamil literature of southern India and thereby stimulating the emergence of Dravidian nationalism.[18]

In 1996 a group of historians proposed a kind of "new Latin American mission history" that would move away from the traditional emphasis on Spanish and Portuguese missionary heroism, with its narratives of civilization-through-Christianization and its denigration of "native" cultures. Their mission history aimed to move, instead, toward the recognition of local peoples as historical actors within changing cultures, economies, and societies.[19] Perhaps the lateness of this shift in Latin American studies is itself a commentary on the recent movement of the study of missions from its place as a niche in church history into the mainstream in world history. In any case, this recognition of local agency and autonomy in missionary encounters is now common among historians in general. The move away from narratives of "white, male, clerical heroism"[20]—and away from a focus on men like David Livingstone, the paragon Protestant "missionary-explorer" of Central Africa—has entailed a rejection of the "unvarying story of missionary initiative, followed by indigenous response," which implies that "foreign missionaries acted, but [that] natives could only react."[21] This means, in practice, that historians have begun to tell the history of missionary encounters from different perspectives—such as the perspective of those whom an early-twentieth-century *World Atlas of Christian Missions* called "native staff" (as opposed to "foreign missionaries").

Similarly, historians have been endeavoring to acknowledge the important role that women played in missions even when Christian communities excluded them from clergies and priesthoods. Historians broadly recognize now that the majority of European and American missionaries were women in the late nineteenth and twentieth centuries. In many places, women also appear to have been the majority of *converts* to mission Christianity, and they prompted children and members of extended families to join them. This phenomenon is little studied in recent scholarship, although it goes far back into the history of Christian communities—to women like Helena (d. 328 CE), mother of Constantine (who was the first Roman emperor to convert to Christianity and to legalize the religion in the Roman empire), and Monica (d. 387 CE), mother of Augustine of Hippo (who was educated in his father's Roman religion before eventually embracing his mother's Christianity). In a study of the global diffusion of Christianity, a leading historian of Christian missions contends that women not only have been the "the majority of active believers" in Christian communities and the "backbone" of mission endeavors but also have made Christianity into "predominantly a women's movement."[22]

Approaches to missionary encounters have taken new turns, too, in the study of "conversions"—their nature, causes, and ramifications.[23] As recently as 1999, in a survey article on Christian cultures and missionary influences in southern Africa, one historian pointed to what he called the "endless debate" in African studies "about where to draw the line between what is Christian and what is not." He was referring to debates regarding the status of independent African churches that had broken away or departed from foreign mission-planted churches in organization, leadership, and practice. In the eyes of some missionaries and others, the religious "syncretism" of such churches cast their Christianity in doubt. The same scholar suggested that historians faced a vexing "question of verification" in assessing Christian conversions, given the "leaps of imagination" that were necessary to understand what happened even when missionaries offered descriptions of what they thought they had witnessed in others.[24] The scholarship on missions has moved on from such concerns in two respects. First, among historians of missions there is now wide agreement that people who ostensibly converted to Christianity did so for multiple reasons—in some cases, for example, by adopting Christian identities as "a strategic response to modernization" or social dislocation, or in an effort to assert dignity and status within communities.[25] Second, historians widely acknowledge that conversion to Christianity, or conversion from one form of Christianity to another, did not necessarily nullify earlier beliefs about such things as ancestors, witchcraft, and caste, nor did it necessarily weaken loyalties to neighbors (who may have shared a language but not a religion in common). By extension, Christianity engaged other beliefs just as other beliefs engaged Christianity. In the latter case, this tendency sometimes prompted individuals to call upon Christian ideas for spiritual interventions in this life—rather than in the afterlife, as missionaries hoped.

In short, while historians may have spent time considering Christian "syncretism" or authenticity in the past, mulling over the aforementioned "question of verification" in religious conversions, they are now more likely to consider the ambiguity, hybridity, and internal tensions within religious and other social identities. Historians and anthropologists who study Islam, Hinduism, and other corporate religions have taken a similar turn toward the recognition of plural identities.[26]

Contributors to this volume are particularly attuned to the idea that conversion to mission forms of Christianity was often *painful*. This was particularly true in colonial settings, where power differentials separated colonizers from colonized, and "foreign" missionaries from "native" missionaries and others. Conversions often led to intense social pressures as individuals or groups struggled to justify their embrace of the "foreign" religion, to dispel perceptions of alienation, and to prove their group loyalty or, in a nationalist age, their patriotism. How could one be at once Indian and Christian in a context where *Hindutva* (Hindu-ness) was becoming ever more potent as a nationalist force?[27] Alternately, how could one be Palestinian and Episcopalian in an age of British imperialism? Did conversion signal—or require—an exit from an earlier community? If so, then what claims could (unconverted) relatives, neighbors, and government authorities make on the converted both during their lifetimes and upon death, when issues of inheritance arose?[28]

A final trend in recent studies of missionary encounters entails the examination of failures—including failures to establish lasting institutions, hold members, prevent schisms, or persuade others. Failure stood, for example, at the center of one recent study of Catholic missions in Syria, which tried to understand why one Jesuit-founded congregation for Syrian (Lebanese) men, the Xavériens, emerged in the 1850s but soon withered, whereas a congregation for local women, Les Mariamettes, flourished in the same small towns. By examining why the female order was able to prosper where the male order was not, the author of this study revealed important features of the Syro-Lebanese social landscape relating to families and support networks, economic and career opportunities with the church, and gender relations.[29] Likewise, the study of breakdowns, ruptures, and refusals has enabled contributors to this volume to elucidate how modern Muslim and Buddhist nationalisms emerged in countries like Egypt and Sri Lanka, and how Christian organizations broke off from so-called mother churches or mission-planted churches and asserted themselves in Zambia and Palestine.

Missionaries as Historical Actors

Because this volume proposes to analyze missionary encounters, it is essential at the outset to address two questions. Namely, who were the missionaries in missionary encounters, and how can or should historians represent their roles as agents of transformation? These two questions are easy to pose but hard to answer, because views of missionaries have evolved, even as missionaries have remained figures of controversy.

In the late twentieth century, historians of American missions looked back on nineteenth-century developments and observed the following trend: Protestant missionary societies had commonly reserved the title "missionary" for men, even when these men had wives and other female relatives who performed considerable work for missions as teachers, healers, translators, and more. In the late nineteenth century, following the U.S. Civil War, many American societies began to send single women as designated, salaried "missionaries," though without according the "missionary" title to wives, who were still expected to work for their husbands' missions without remuneration. In the early twentieth century, some societies began to identify both members of husband-and-wife pairs as "missionaries." British and other European Protestant missions followed similar conventions. By the late twentieth century, historians began to note these discrepancies and to account for women as "missionaries" whether their societies—in any given place or time—had accorded them this title or not.[30]

Throughout the twentieth century, historians often assumed that "missionaries," whether male or female, were white people of European origin. Exceptions to this pattern received little attention. Only now, as the twenty-first century opens, are historians beginning to question this assumption as well, to revise interpretations of how missions worked on the ground, and to change terminology accordingly.[31] In 2009, for example, a leading mission historian pointed to these issues. Drawing upon a 1915 tally of Protestant missions worldwide (one of many missionary "atlases" produced in the early twentieth century), she noted that "351 Protestant mission societies were supporting approximately 24,000 'foreign missionaries' [who] worked alongside 109,000 'native' staff members."[32] In other words, according to this count, "natives" in 1915 outnumbered "foreign missionaries" on Protestant mission staffs by a ratio of more than four to one. These proportions recall similar patterns in colonial administrations within the British Empire during this same period.[33]

European and American missionaries called "native" workers by many titles: among Protestants, they were often "lay preachers," "native evangelists," "teachers," "Bible Women," or, in parts of India, *munshis* (meaning language teachers and translators). Among Catholics, they were often "catechists." European and American sources rarely if ever called them "missionaries." In one exceptional case, where an Egyptian Muslim convert to Christianity—a man named Ahmed Fahmy (1861–1933)—became a medical missionary for a British Protestant organization in China, the society in question declared this man to be an "English missionary" for the convenience of their staff directory. Presumably it seemed too awkward to call this Egyptian doctor a "native" in China. However, though his own society listed him as an "English missionary," British consular authorities rejected this man's pleas for British citizenship.[34] His case was an exception that proved the rule of missionary hierarchies and racial ordering.

This convention of restricting the term "missionary" to Europeans and Americans is only now beginning to change. In a history of Christianity in India that appeared in 2008, one scholar acknowledged the work of both "foreign missionaries" and "native missionaries," thereby applying the title "missionary" to men and women of South Asian origin who worked to propagate Christianity on the ground.[35] However, written records by or about "native missionaries" are usually lacking or meager, and this makes telling their histories much harder.[36] Along these lines, another historian argued in 2008, with regard to British missions, that while it may be "almost impossible to restore the full extent of non-western agency in the building of Christian institutions in the British Empire . . . any accurate history must repeatedly look for and acknowledge those acts of participation." "The British missionary enterprise," he contended, "was multiracial and multinational from the first."[37] A major task remaining on the agenda for historians, then, is including these "other" missionaries in narratives of missionary encounters while explaining the differences they made.

The challenge of identifying missionaries pales beside the challenge of assessing foreign missionaries as colonial actors. Here the controversies run deep and hot. Were foreign missionaries agents and beneficiaries of empire? Were they proxies for colonial governments on the ground, and if so, how, and with what effects, did they wield the power that their foreign backing afforded them? Were foreign missionaries Christian universalists, or did they reinforce and uphold racial orders that kept colonized peoples disadvantaged and under European control? Were Christian missionaries benign figures, bringing spiritual solace and social assistance, promoting human rights, and defending colonized peoples against colonial governments? Or were they underminers of peoples and cultures, as well as perpetrators of abuse? Did mission schools uplift people and broaden opportunities, or merely train "natives" to satisfy colonial states' demands for laborers and taxpayers? In short, did missionaries make people free or oppress them?[38]

Examples abound to suggest that the answer to these questions is "all of the above." Historians need only to look to settings like the Congo Free State (1885–1908) and Belgian Congo (1908–1960) to see a system where certain missions enjoyed land grants, tax breaks, and educational monopolies, while serving as "agents of social control" for a colonial government that "viewed Congolese as children" and that wanted Africans minimally schooled to be farmers and miners.[39] As the twentieth century opened, some missionaries in the Congo turned a blind eye when the agents of Belgium's King Leopold perpetrated horrific abuses (such as raping, shooting, flogging, and cutting off hands or ears) to force local people to collect wild rubber for export. Yet some other missionaries in the Congo—including the African-American Presbyterian missionary, William Henry Sheppard (1865–1927)[40]—worked to expose the brutality of King Leopold's rubber-producing system, leading to an international outcry that forced something of a regime change in 1908 and that stimulated new models of human rights activism.[41] Bleak examples can be found, too, in countries like the United States and Canada, where controversies (and lawsuits) continue with regard to the physical and sexual abuse, and cultural denigration, of Native American children who were forced to attend Christian mission schools in government-approved programs of assimilation. (In the United States alone, these mission schools for Native Americans operated from 1869 until the late 1980s.)[42] In many other places missionaries secured churchgoers and potential converts by wresting "orphans" away from extended families and refusing to return them. A historian who studied this phenomenon within nineteenth-century British missions in Palestine declared, in 2007, that one goal of her work was to expose the common missionary practice of "orphan-taking" as a form of human rights abuse.[43]

Scholars in the "secular" academy and missiologists in seminaries are both moving away from celebratory narratives emphasizing missionary "triumphs." But degrees of sympathy toward Christianizing missions vary even among "secular" academics, with some more convinced than others about the "anti-imperialist" nature of white missionaries, for example, or the universalist and humanitarian impulses of their work.[44] Many of the most sanguine "secular" accounts of missionary encounters are written by scholars who are themselves Christians, who come from Christian cultural backgrounds, or who are writing about societies where Christianity was adopted en masse. Yet even among scholars who have been relatively apathetic to or critical of missionary evangelization, there has often been a tendency to accept missionaries as constructive modernizers and to view their "social" (as opposed to "religious") roles with approval. Until recently, this tendency was particularly pronounced in African studies, where historians frequently portrayed the spread of Christianity—like the spread of Islam—as evidence of civilization, progress, and global engagement in regions that once had flourishing local or "traditional" religions (also called "pagan," "animist," or "polytheistic" religions, sometimes pejoratively).[45] In the Western academy, local religions generally garnered little respect, while historians often portrayed those who resisted missionary overtures as reluctant or incapable modernizers.

Blithe denigration of other religious traditions is neither as common nor as widely accepted among scholars today. Some credit for establishing higher standards of cultural awareness within the academy arguably goes to Edward Said. With the publication of his book *Orientalism* in 1982, Said challenged the persistence of denigrating stereotypes toward colonized peoples, illuminated the discursive elements of Western imperialism, and stimulated the emergence of postcolonial studies.[46] He helped to shape the latter field by making marginality a legitimate study within the Anglo-American academy, "foreground[ing] the exclusions and elisions which confirm[ed] the privileges and authority of canonical knowledge systems," and prompting scholars to "recollect the compelling seductions of colonial power."[47] The field of postcolonial studies legitimized the voice of the other.

A postcolonial perspective informs this book. The decline of European empires in Africa and Asia and the concomitant transfers of political power have made it possible to question old social hierarchies and to see missionaries—and missionary encounters—in a new light.[48] Just as important in this postcolonial milieu is the global demographic shift of Christianity away from Europe (where many scholars speak of religion in "decline") and toward Africa and Asia, the two regions at the heart of this book.[49] Given this latter development, then, the postcolonial is in some sense postmissionary.

The Articles: Summary and Themes

The articles that follow are divided into three parts. Part 1, "Christian Contestations," includes articles by David M. Gordon on Zambia, Laura Robson on Palestine, and Chandra Mallampalli on India, which examine Christian communities whose members fashioned identities that were deeply contested and sometimes at odds with those of foreign missionaries and colonial powers. Part 2, "Missionaries, Antimissionaries, and

Doubters," includes articles by Stephen C. Berkwitz on Sri Lanka, Beth Baron on Egypt, and Paul S. Landau on South Africa, which consider some of the missionaries' local critics. These included Sri Lankan Buddhists and Egyptian Muslims who emerged from missionary encounters more conscious of, and committed to, their non-Christian identities, as well as practitioners of local religions in South Africa who remained skeptical of the missionaries' claims until they translated them in ways that made sense vis-à-vis local conditions. Part 3, "Missionaries, Language, and National Expression," includes articles by James De Lorenzi on Eritrea, Mrinalini Sebastian on India, and Heather J. Sharkey on North Africa, which examine how missionary language study, teaching, and printing served as catalysts for ideologies and identities that were largely tangential to religion. After briefly summarizing each article with attention to the role of the unexpected in each, the following discusses the major themes that bind this collection together.

"In Zambia, the activities of Catholic and Protestant missions contributed to the widespread adoption of Christianity," writes David M. Gordon. "But Zambian Christianity took forms that were far removed from what the missionaries had envisaged." Gordon's article, "Conflicting Conversions and Unexpected Christianities in Central Africa," traces developments among the Bemba people, who provided labor for the copper mines that developed after the British South Africa Company (BSAC) seized control of the region in the late nineteenth century. In the early twentieth century, two missions that were active here—the Catholic White Fathers and the Livingstonia mission of the Church of Scotland (Presbyterian)—often behaved as fierce rivals. Yet these two established foreign missions soon faced new rivals: independent African churches whose leaders "employed the spiritual resources and technologies of the Christian missions," such as baptism, "to eradicate the witches that the Christian missions denied existed." A particularly formidable challenge arose in 1953, when a charismatic young woman named Alice Mulenga emerged as a leader of the Lumpa movement and became known as its queen or "Lenshina." This movement organized its rural-dwelling followers into a church that combined congregational worship, hymn-singing, and catechizing with a millenarian focus on purging evil and founding a new Zion. The greatest unexpected consequence of this story, in Gordon's view, is that "the most fervent conflict [arose] not between the European missionaries and Lenshina's followers. It was rather the African educated elite attached to the European missions that felt most threatened and responded most aggressively to Lenshina." The result was an intra-Christian war that roiled Zambia at decolonization and decisively shaped the country's political future.

In "Church versus Country: Palestinian Arab Episcopalians, Nationalism, and Revolt, 1936–39," Laura Robson studies a small but affluent Christian community that found itself caught in the crossfire of anticolonial nationalism. This community consisted of Arabs of Palestine whose forebears had converted from Orthodox Christianity to the Episcopalian Protestantism of nineteenth-century British missionaries. Living in a Muslim majority region, these Arab Episcopalians were a tiny minority (Protestant) of a minority (Christian). Robson catches them at a painful moment in history—the late 1930s—when Arab Muslims and Christians, responding to concerns over Jewish Zionist immigration from Europe, staged what Arabs later called the "Great Revolt." Against this context, the Arab Episcopalian community found itself increasingly at odds with the British Anglican "mother church," whose leaders (arguably influenced by Christian millenarian beliefs) voiced steadfast support for the Jewish "return" to Zion. In this way, unexpectedly, an Anglican-missionary-sponsored church became a center of pan-Arab and anti-British nationalism, while British policies in Palestine increased the vulnerability of Arab Christians vis-à-vis both the Muslim Palestinian majority and the future Israeli state.

Lingering questions about the meaning and consequences of Christian conversion stand at the center of Chandra Mallampalli's essay, "Missionaries and Ethnography in the Service of Litigation: Hindu Law and Christian Custom in India's Deccan, 1750–1863." The pivotal figure is Matthew Abraham, a distillery owner who sold liquor to European troops in the southern Indian garrison city of Bellary. His forebears had been Hindu *paraiyar*—pariahs or untouchables—but had converted to Roman Catholicism three or four generations earlier. However, as Matthew's business prospered, affording him opportunities for social mobility, Matthew converted: first, from Catholicism to the Dissenting Protestantism of

British evangelical missionaries; and second, near the end of his life, to the "higher" Church of England (Anglicanism). When Matthew died without a will in 1842, bitter litigation ensued among his possible heirs. Mallampalli argues that an accumulated local tradition of Protestant and Catholic missionary ethnographies became central to the case, as did the testimony of scores of Indian Protestants and Catholics, who affirmed or rejected the role of Hindu caste and custom in Christian practice. At root, in the case of *Abraham v. Abraham* (1863), was the question of whether "conversion constituted a clean break from Hindu society or a selective appropriation of features from multiple cultural domains"—a question over which Indian Christians in the Deccan remained deeply divided. The most unexpected outgrowth of this affair was arguably that the courts—not the missionaries—became arbiters for assessing conversions, issuing judgments about the nature of Christian family life that left important precedents in India's law books.

In "Hybridity, Parody, and Contempt: Buddhist Responses to Christian Missions in Sri Lanka," Stephen C. Berkwitz explains how and why "Christian missions in Sri Lanka have played a central role in the formation of a modern Buddhist identity." Berkwitz looks at the long sweep of Christian missionaries who arrived in Ceylon, as the island, following European usage, was called until 1972. These included Portuguese Franciscans and Jesuits of the mid-sixteenth and seventeenth centuries; the Dutch Calvinists, British Anglicans, and Wesleyans of the nineteenth century; and members of evangelical American, Korean, and indigenous Sri Lankan churches of the twentieth and early twenty-first centuries. "Missionary encounters, however sporadic and variable, spurred efforts by Sinhala Buddhists in Sri Lanka to accommodate or resist Christianization," Berkwitz observes. Buddhist thinkers expressed their ideas about missionaries in many forms—such as in poetry, royal chronicles, narrative parodies, and sermons—and in many formats, notably on palm leaf manuscripts, later in newspapers and printed books, and eventually on television and in other electronic media. Yet while some Sri Lankan thinkers grafted Christian ideas onto Buddhist notions of the cosmos, thereby converting to Christianity in ways that did not necessarily entail "the rejection of all things Buddhist," others condemned Christian overtures overtly and denounced Christianity as a colonizer religion. At the same time, Buddhist monks initiated an energetic and organized defense of their religion vis-à-vis Christian missionaries. These monks stimulated a Buddhist revival in Sri Lanka that assumed an increasingly ethnic Sinhala nationalist form over the course of the twentieth century. One of the most unexpected results of this discursive history is that, by the mid-twentieth century, Sri Lankan Buddhist nationalists had adopted an exclusivist vision of religious and social identity that undermined the missionary project, limited numbers of converts, and generated tensions between Sinhala Buddhists and the country's Christian minority.

In "The Port Said Orphan Scandal of 1933: Colonialism, Islamism, and the Egyptian Welfare State," Beth Baron presents a case where Christian missionary overtures sharpened and reinforced Muslim identities in Egypt, while at the same time stimulating Muslim social and political activism. The story centers on Turkiyya Hasan, a teenage girl and orphan who lived and studied in a "home for destitutes" that was located in Port Said, a town in the Suez Canal Zone. This home was an initiative of the Swedish Salaam Mission, a loosely organized faith mission, that is, one that lacked a steady stream of revenue and that relied on donations as they came in. Run and staffed by women, this mission drew most of its funds from evangelical Protestant supporters in Sweden, Finland, and the Scandinavian immigrant communities of the United States.[50] On June 7, 1933, a mission teacher beat Turkiyya Hasan, who in turn fled for help. The Arabic periodical press took up the story and the result was a national scandal. In the long run, the uproar over Turkiyya Hasan prompted the Egyptian state to assume greater responsibility for social welfare services among orphans and the poor; led parliamentarians to pass laws restricting missionary interactions with Muslims and minors; and fired up Muslim antimissionary sentiment, with long-term consequences for all Christian missions in Egypt. More broadly, the Turkiyya Hasan affair serves as a reminder that Egyptians—like other colonized people—did not necessarily want or choose to host Christian missionaries, who often came along with the baggage of colonial rule and who enjoyed legal and fiscal immunity.

In "Robert Moffat and the Invention of Christianity in South Africa," Paul S. Landau writes about the fashioning of Christianity out of highveld

South African language and culture during an early nineteenth-century period of dislocation and turmoil. At the center of the story stands Robert Moffat, bumbling along, full of strong opinions, trying to translate the Bible and his own message into a language he did not completely understand. He preached to people who found his constant allusions to death not only unsettling but also vulgar and weird. Eventually he cast his logic in terms of a chiefly "restoration," and became reconciled to the idea of using the word "*modimo*" (ancestor) to render "God," even though this was not his ideal word choice. This discursive maneuver seemed to work in a place where there had been profound political upheavals but where chiefs were still trying to sort out their alliances and to rebuild their power. Moffat would have been astounded by how Christianity developed after him. "Nevertheless," writes Landau, "his actions left a permanent broad-groove imprint on the religious landscape. He created a domain of the unseen based on chiefship, in which an ever-anonymous ancestor, greater than all others, held sway by affecting people's lives like chiefs. And he could do this because of the wounded and fragmented nature of political authority in the 1820s."

In "Missionaries and the Making of Colonial Notables: Conversions to Modernity in Eritrea and Ethiopia, 1890–1935", James De Lorenzi considers the new intellectual culture that Italian and French Catholic and Swedish Protestant missionaries fostered in Eritrea, particularly among Orthodox Christians. "The Eritrean case," he argues, "highlights how the interface between mission education and colonial politics could produce tremendous intellectual heterogeneity, and . . . could foster visions of community beyond nation and congregation." This case also illustrates how mission initiatives transformed cultures of reading and writing—ironically breaking literacy's primary association with religious authority—and in the process "unexpectedly altered the parameters of intellectual inquiry in fundamental ways." Gabra Mikā'él Germu (1900–1969) is one of the intellectuals who features in this story. Educated in both the Orthodox Christian church and in an Italian Capuchin mission school, and apparently an Orthodox convert to Catholicism, Gabra Mikā'él attempted to reconcile the competing identities of his "colonial world" by writing a *History of Italy and Ethiopia*. The manuscript's title was somewhat surprising, however, because the text advanced a view of history that was not Ethiopian but rather distinctly Eritrean, reflecting the recent history of a territory that Italy had wrested from the Ethiopian mainland in 1890. De Lorenzi maps out this changing political and religious terrain, one in which missionary efforts helped to foster a new polyglossia. In the process he reflects on the struggle of Eritrean intellectuals like Gabra Mikā'él to defend themselves against the charge of holding "treasonous Italian sympathies" while challenging both Italian and Ethiopian hegemony in the aftermath of colonial "conversions."

In her article titled "The Scholar-Missionaries of the Basel Mission in Southwest India: Language, Identity, and Knowledge in Flux," Mrinalini Sebastian studies a group of German Pietists who first arrived in Mangalore, on India's southwest coast, in 1834, and who conducted research in "Indology" (the ethno-linguistic study of India) that had much wider reverberations for German and south Indian thought. Influenced by a kind of seventeenth-century Christian utopianism that valued both individual conversion and communal self-sufficiency, the Basel missionaries in Mangalore established compounds where converts could live and work. In the process they initiated some of the earliest industrial projects in the region, such as tile and textile factories, which flourished until World War I. In theory, the Basel missionaries refused to recognize caste among their converts, who mostly came from humble Tulu-speaking communities of toddy-tappers and fishermen. But in 1843, when a Hindu Brahmin named Anandarao Kaundinya joined their fold, the missionaries rejoiced at their high-caste conversion, which seemed to confirm ideas about the relationship between Brahminical, Sanskritic culture and Aryanism that were shaping German thought in this period. Yet just as missionary Indology exerted an influence over German racial thought, so, Sebastian argues, did it influence emerging strains of Dravidian nationalism in south India. Especially influential was the work of the Basel missionary Ferdinand Kittel, who completed the first Kannada-English dictionary in 1894. In 2001, bucking the trend whereby Hindu nationalists have renamed streets and landmarks after local worthies as a way of removing residues of British colonialism, the government of Karnataka state (where Kannada is the official language) installed a statue of Kittel in the middle of Bangalore's main boulevard, the Mahatma Gandhi Road.

In "The Gospel in Arabic Tongues: British Bible Distribution, Evangelical Mission, and Language Politics in North Africa," Heather J. Sharkey examines the work of the British and Foreign Bible Society (BFBS), a publishing mission, founded in 1804, that worked from the premise that scripture-reading could effect inner Christian conversions. Believing that all people should have access to the Bible in their own language, the BFBS started a massive translation effort in cooperation with a multinational array of Protestant missions, and by 1939 it claimed scripture publications in some 734 "tongues." Many of these translations helped to shape new national or regional identities in various corners of the world. By contrast, however, the colloquial Arabic Bibles that the BFBS published in the early twentieth century—appealing to illiterate or barely literate audiences of Muslims and Jews in Morocco, Algeria, Tunisia, Egypt, and Sudan—had a limited and shrinking appeal, so that the BFBS stopped publishing them in the post–World War II era of decolonization. Sharkey considers the political and cultural factors that caused these colloquial Arabic scriptures to flop. Far from increasing the cultural legitimacy of colloquial Arabic in print, she argues, British evangelical support for colloquial Arabic scriptures only strengthened the resolve of Muslim Arab nationalists as they insisted on the primacy of the high literary language instead. What lingers from this story is not just the unexpected, but the unknown. How can one gauge the impact that these colloquial Arabic Bibles may have had in their heyday, given the ephemeral nature of their imprints, the intensely private nature of religious devotion, and the lack of sources left by the humble people who bought and sold them?

Several themes emerge from these essays, and they are worth reviewing in turn.

Missionary history is political. In every case studied in this volume, missionary encounters contributed, almost always inadvertently, to nationalist movements, to struggles for individual and collective identities, and to claims for social authority. Missionaries provided access to educations, technologies (above all printing presses), and ideas, all of which reconfigured worldviews. The history of missionary encounters is thus tightly connected to struggles for power and meaning. Likewise, politics cut across national, sectarian, and communal lines in surprising ways. For example, when Italy seized an enclave in northeast Africa in 1890, thereupon creating the colony of Eritrea, the Italian Capuchins "welcomed colonial rule as a possible boon to their efforts." However, as James De Lorenzi observes in chapter 8, missionaries of another Roman Catholic order, the French Lazarists, "covertly supported local anticolonial resistance movements," so that the Italian authorities expelled them from the colony in 1894 "amid accusations of subversion." Meanwhile and by contrast, missionaries of a Swedish Protestant mission—the Evangeliska Fosterlandsstiftelsen—managed to persist in operating schools despite the colonial government's insistence on their using Italian.

The results of missionary encounters were unpredictable. Missionaries in any one "station" may have imagined that their work addressed a distinct community, but their efforts invariably spilled over boundaries. Consider, again, the Protestant and Catholic missionaries in Zambia. They may have felt a keen sense of mutual rivalry, but their interventions— and their examples of baptism, catechism, and hymn-singing—together provided a common pool of Christian culture on which "independent" churches later drew, for example, by embracing baptism as a technique for the eradication of witchcraft. The Swedish Salaam Mission School in the Egyptian city of Port Said claimed to be educating orphaned or neglected children. But historians today argue that the school left its greatest mark on Egyptian society by triggering an incident—a scandal involving its student, Turkiyya Hasan—that boosted the Egyptian government's welfare policies and the social enterprises of Muslim activists. Likewise, consider the long, layered history of missions in Sri Lanka, to which a motley assortment of Portuguese Jesuits, British Wesleyans, Korean evangelicals, and others have added, and against which Buddhists nationalists now pose their rejoinders. Think, too, of the winding road—and the dictionary—that landed a bronze incarnation of the German missionary, Ferdinand Kittel, onto a traffic island in Bangalore, India's Silicon Valley–like boomtown. Who could have predicted that the mostly Hindu leadership of India's Karnataka state would retroactively embrace the missionary Kittel as a champion of their Kannada language?

Missionaries have not always been clear about their target communities, and they have often worked in a fog. In South Africa, the 1810s and 1820s were decades of massive social upheaval: the Zulu kingdom was expanding under the leadership of Shaka Zulu, and the traumas of war were leading to far-flung displacements. In this place and time, Robert Moffat was groping to find a way of conveying the Bible and Christianity to people whose lives and identities were in great flux. The case of the British and Foreign Bible Society in North Africa is quite different, but the uncertainty about audience also pertains. The Bible Society was a Protestant publishing mission, but it neither sponsored churches nor organized converts. Its agents attempted to distribute Bibles to everyone—Christians, Muslims, Jews, atheists, and others; men and women; peasants and pashas; sex workers and the inebriated. The society appears to have assumed that people, once possessed of some scriptures, might read and contemplate them on their own. But because its agents (who were often transient themselves) sold Bibles so widely, and because the act of Bible-reading (and Bible-thinking) remained so individual and so private, the society could never be certain about who bought their scriptures, what impact their reading had had, and whether or how their efforts fostered distinctly Christian communities.

The fiercest and most anguished battles to arise from missionary encounters were often the ones that involved or occurred among locals. Rivalries between representatives of different Protestant and Catholic missions are well catalogued in the historiography on missions. Much less studied are battles involving local peoples. Yet as the essays in this volume show, battles sometimes roiled the ostensibly converted, and at other times divided the converted and their ostensible patrons. In Zambia, a serious war broke out after decolonization among different kinds of Christians: these included on the one hand Zambian Protestants and Catholics, whose access to mission schooling had propelled them into the ranks of the educated elites, and on the other hand followers of churches like the one inspired by Alice Mulenga (whose peasant-class members enjoyed religious passion, but not much formal education). In Eritrea, men like Gabra Mikā'él became embroiled in wars of words, as they struggled to reconcile their embrace of foreign culture with local belonging, while using printed texts to test an incipient Eritrean nationalism at odds with "Ethiopia." In a Palestine shaped by the post–World War I settlements and the Balfour Declaration (which voiced official British support for the establishment of a Jewish homeland in the region), members of the tiny Arab Episcopalian community struggled to cope with a sense of British betrayal while building a stronger sense of community with the Muslim and other Christian Arabs around them. In southern India, battles over the identity of converts politicized notions of caste and Hindu culture in novel ways.

Conversion is a protracted process, not an isolated event;[51] *it has religious as well as cultural and social dimensions; and it is often painful for converts or their families.* Consider Matthew Abraham, the South Indian distiller, whose relatives battled over inheritance rights following his death. It made things more complicated that Matthew Abraham had converted to different kinds of Christianity, switching from Catholicism, to Dissenting Protestantism, to Anglicanism, while always remaining in some sense (at least according to his brother, the litigant) a "Hindu" by custom. Consider, too, the difficult circumstances that faced the young wife of the convert Anandarao Kaundinya, who features prominently in Mrinalini Sebastian's account of the Basel Mission in southwest India. The conversion of Anandarao to Christianity in 1843–44, and his loss and repudiation of (Brahmin) caste, prompted his family to lament his civil and ritual death and to treat his abandoned wife, Lakshmi, as a widow for the rest of her life. Meanwhile, in the cases of intellectuals like Gabra Mikā'él in Eritrea, and of the Arab Episcopalians in Palestine, ostensible converts often struggled with feelings of cultural betrayal in colonial contexts.

Missionary overtures may not only fail to persuade; they may also backfire. Consider the story of Turkiyya Hasan and the Swedish Salaam Mission in Egypt. Drawing upon the records available in English and Arabic newspapers, missionary archives, and British intelligence reports, historians of Egypt today are likely to remember the Swedish Salaam Mission not for its benevolence in helping orphans and the neglected children of sex workers in the Suez Canal Zone, but rather for the outrage its actions elicited among educated, newspaper-reading Egyptians. This outrage prompted Muslim charity organizations to take action and the Egyptian state to impose legislation restricting missionaries. Consider, too, the case of the Buddhist revival in Sri Lanka. One wonders how many of the authors of the Sri Lankan government's 1956 report entitled *The Betrayal of Buddhism* (a report that traced what it claimed was the long-running role of Christian missions in undermining the integrity of Sri Lankan culture) were themselves graduates of Christian mission schools. Certainly the Buddhist reformer, Anagarika Dharmapala (1864–1933), cited being "humiliated by the denigration of Buddhism by his teachers at Christian schools" as a precipitating factor behind his own brand of religio-nationalist activism.

Missionary encounters had consequences that were unexpected to everyone involved. As Paul Landau points out in his study of South Africa, this volume's central theme of unexpected consequences "expresses more than the inadequacy of historical actors' intentions in shaping the world." Rather, it also "expresses the necessary uncertainty surrounding any historical inquiry into the transformation of a subject" when the spiritual and the unseen—the "domain of religion"—are involved. Ultimately, in examining missionary encounters and cultural conversions, the articles in this volume attempt to address questions not about who did or did not convert and why, but rather about *how* people converted and changed, in ways that missionaries had neither intended nor anticipated, and with lasting significance for individuals and their larger societies.

Conclusion

These essays have endeavored to show the rich possibilities awaiting historians of missionary encounters. In the process, they point the way to future research, and suggest the following agendas. First, historians must continue to question and broaden the category of "missionary," by including the "natives" who introduced new ideas and fostered change at the grassroots level. In 1973, a historian of what was then Zaire (the former Belgian Congo, now the Democratic Republic of the Congo) remarked in passing: "The catechist," trained and deployed by Roman Catholic missionaries during the early twentieth century, "often became one of the most important figures in the village," mediating colonial government policies and acting as advisers to chiefs in rural areas.[52] Is it too late now to go back and trace the steps of these catechists, to understand how they transformed religious, social, and political life in Congolese villages? In retrospect, the catechists' roles were enormous, but are there printed sources or archival documents that once existed and still survive for historians to mine?[53] This leads to the second point: historians must use sources creatively. Poems, popular hymns, newspapers, photographs, and oral histories may be available—so that historians need not restrict themselves to printed books and to the manuscript records of mission societies. Third, historians must try to widen the frame for missionary encounters, in order to include non-adherents and non-Christians, and thereby to identify the intersections of "world Christianities" and world histories.[54] Similarly, historians must recognize the often unofficial roles of women in churches or societies, and consider the involvement of children in Sunday Schools, mission-school classrooms, mission-sponsored farms and factories, and the like. Religion, gender, and age need not figure as barriers.

As a "history of intimacy,"[55] the spiritual dimensions of missionary encounters are likely to remain as elusive as ever. Nevertheless, historians must also continue to grapple with "conversions" and to reflect on the changes that missionary encounters set into motion in private lives and public identities, and among individuals and collectives. Important questions linger. How did the acceptance or rejection of missionary overtures lead to social changes and to different kinds of conversion? Who persuaded whom, and of what? And how did missionary encounters produce ripples that extended forward in time and space? These are some of the questions that scholars need to ask about missionary encounters as they seek to understand the complex, diffuse, and interlocking history of religion, society, and politics.

Part
One

Christian Contestations

2

Conflicting Conversions
and Unexpected Christianities
in Central Africa

David M. Gordon

*I*n the Zambian elections of 1991, Frederick Chiluba and his Movement for Multiparty Democracy (MMD) defeated Kenneth Kaunda, who had ruled since independence from Britain in 1964. Only God's intervention, Chiluba's closest followers believed, had made the MMD victory possible. God had purified Zambia of evil so that Satan would no longer afflict it; the nation was born again. To express his gratitude, Chiluba declared Zambia a "Christian Nation," dedicated to performing the work of God and blessed with prosperity. Zambian Charismatic and Pentecostal leaders were jubilant with his declaration. However, it drew overt criticism from the Catholic and mainline Protestant churches, which had emerged from the many missionary societies that proselytized across Zambia during the previous century.[1] Leaders of these Catholic and Protestant churches felt that Chiluba's declaration was too prophetic, too grandiose, and most of all too focused on spiritual intervention in the world. His was not the Christian nation that the missionaries and their successors had either expected or desired.

In Zambia, the activities of Catholic and Protestant missions contributed to the widespread adoption of Christianity. But Zambian Christianity took forms that were far removed from what the missionaries had envisaged. Zambians selectively adapted some of the spiritual resources, techniques, and technologies of the mission churches and deployed them in ways that they deemed useful—for example, by introducing mission-church-style baptism into witchcraft purification rituals. Out of such adaptive spiritual practices, Zambians created radical new forms of religious devotion.[2] (Note that this study uses the term "spiritual" as it pertains to cosmological, transcendent power that operates beyond the realm of the tangible; and the terms "religion" or "religious" to suggest systematized beliefs, practices, and institutions.)

In this chapter I focus on the northern plateau of Zambia (earlier known as Northern Rhodesia), an area inhabited by the ChiBemba-speaking peoples. Drawing upon archives in Britain and Zambia, on oral sources collected during fieldwork in Zambia in 2005, and on a wealth of studies by historians and anthropologists on the religious and spiritual culture of south central Africa, this essay considers the competing activities, ideologies, and agendas of the region's Catholic and Protestant missions as well as of two religious movements—the Bamuchape and Lenshina movements—that emerged in the 1930s and 1950s respectively. These two movements employed elements of mission Christianity in new ways while addressing one of the great oversights of the mission churches: notably, their failure to acknowledge perceptions of constant threat emanating from malevolent forces, known as *ubuloshi*, roughly translating as "witchcraft."

Indeed, for many people in Northern Zambia, the most pressing spiritual concern was control of *ubuloshi*. Christian "conversions," in the view of many, therefore became a means of applying Christian spiritual resources to the problem of witchcraft. Yet European missionaries did not perceive the threat of witchcraft in the same fashion, and instead viewed the Christian struggle in the light of their own notion of evil. For European missionaries, Christian conversion would combat the sin of immoral behavior; for Zambians, Christian conversion would combat the sin of witchcraft. Christian conversion thus involved a series of cultural misunderstandings, a "dialogue of the deaf" as Wyatt MacGaffey puts it.[3]

The following essay has four parts. The first surveys the political landscape against which the Catholic and Protestant missions to Zambia emerged. The second considers the different means by which Catholic and

Protestant missions sought to make individuals and communities Christian, even while competing with each other. In other words, this section offers a historical ethnography of the colonial mission encounter.[4] The third considers the origins of the Bamuchape movement and the ways in which it promoted a distinct type of "conversion" in the service of combating witchcraft. In its adaptation of Christian spiritual resources (including discourses of "salvation"), the Bamuchape movement established precedents for independent, popular Christian practice that the Lenshina movement later built upon. The fourth part studies the Lenshina movement, its leader Alice Mulenga (known as the queen or "Lenshina"), and the church institutions that she and her followers built. To missionaries and their Zambian protégés, the most radical and threatening aspect of Lenshina's church was that, in her efforts to create a "New Jerusalem," she urged her followers to "convert" or break away from a flawed past that included the missions. Implicitly, too, Lenshina rejected the hierarchical model of Christian authority that the mission-planted churches presented: her religious movement empowered humble villagers more than the mission churches, whose beneficiaries, as one Protestant missionary analyst suggested, belonged to "the incipient African middle class."[5]

The story told here is not ultimately about conversion, although conflicting attitudes toward conversion are central to it. Rather, this is a story about the political infighting that broke out *among* Zambians as a result of the diffusion of Christian religious structures and spiritual concepts. I argue that Christian conversions in Zambia took two major forms: a reformist and didactic form, associated with the Catholic and Protestant missions and with the emergent, educated male African elites (exemplified by Kenneth Kaunda), who stood poised to seize power at decolonization; and a revolutionary and populist form, manifest in the Lenshina movement with its female leader Alice Mulenga, whose members regarded witchcraft as a continuing concern of their modern experience. The Lenshina revolution also challenged the male hierarchies of the new mission-educated elite and the older hereditary rulers. In short, what is so unexpected in this story are the ways Christianity spread as missionaries and their successors deployed—but then lost control of—Christian narratives, with lasting consequences for patterns of leadership, ideology, and political contestation on the Zambian national stage. While this Zambian history unfolds in particular ways, similar prophetic interventions have had profound and unexpected impacts for religion and politics across Africa.[6]

The Catholic and Protestant Missions of Northern Rhodesia

The northern plateau of Zambia was at the center of Zambian political and religious developments before the 1960s. It was home to the Bemba polity of Chitimukulu (The Great Tree), one of the most aggressive politico-military edifices of the nineteenth century. The Bemba were renowned for their involvement in the ivory and slave trade with the east African Swahili and for the defensive wars fought against the invading Ngoni from southern Africa.[7] After conquest at the end of the nineteenth century by the British South Africa Company (BSAC), Catholic and Protestant missionaries competed for influence over the Bemba lands. The Catholic missionary society of the *Société des Missionnaires d'Afrique*, more commonly known as the "White Fathers," was formed in Algiers in 1867 by Cardinal Lavigerie. At the invitation of the Portuguese, the White Fathers established their first missions in central Africa around Lake Malawi. From there, they spread to northern Zambia, under the leadership of Bishop Dupont, who was nicknamed *Moto moto* ("the fire") because of his fiery temperament. Bishop Dupont, following Lavigerie's teachings, sought to spread Christianity through the conversion of kings and the Bemba king, Chitimukulu, was an obvious target.[8] In 1895, Bishop Dupont managed to establish his first Bemba mission on Kayambi Hill, adjacent to one of the Bemba chiefs' villages.

Members of the Presbyterian Livingstonia mission of the Church of Scotland, based in Malawi (then Nyasaland), viewed themselves as the inheritors of the mission of David Livingstone, who had spent his last years in the 1860s and 1870s wandering around the Bemba region. Their first converts were freed slaves, who formed some of their earliest proselytizers. In 1894 Livingstonia opened a mission at Mwenzo, north of the Bemba area. In 1904 they sent an African teacher, David Kaunda, to open up schools in the Bemba areas, which they hoped would spread knowledge of the scripture.[9]

A few years after the British Colonial Office took over the administration of Zambia (then Northern Rhodesia) from the BSAC in 1924, profitable copper mines opened up south of the Bemba heartland. Bemba men formed the most prominent group of migrants to the copper mines, giving the "Copperbelt" towns a marked Bemba character, with ChiBemba as the lingua franca. In part through this process of selective urbanization, the Bemba formed a dominant ethnic group within Zambia, often opposed to their older rivals, the Ngoni from the eastern regions. The western (Lozi) and southern ethnicities (often grouped together as the Bantu Botatwe), on the other hand, became marginal to the centers of political and economic power. The inclusion of Northern Rhodesia with Nyasaland (Malawi) and Rhodesia (Zimbabwe) in the European settler-dominated Central African Federation in 1953 gave impetus to the small but growing nationalist movement in Zambia. By the late 1950s Kenneth Kaunda, son of the African Protestant teacher and missionary David Kaunda, became a key member of the nationalist movement. In 1964 he became the first president of an independent Zambia.

The conversion envisaged by both Catholic and Protestant missions was gradual and reformist. It had to be learned over time and involved the development of a personal relationship between the convert and God for the Protestants, or placing the convert in an established church hierarchy for the Catholics. Both missions sought to provide a new moral environment to ensure that Africans would progressively become better Christians and better people. On the other hand, the African prophetic movements that adopted Christianity to cleanse the evil of witchcraft posed a more radical model of conversion that sought to rapidly transform and revolutionize society. Conversion in this framework harnessed Christianity to local concerns and identities; it critiqued old practices, addressed inequalities that lay behind witchcraft, and promoted a utopian future. Conversion purified the individual and laid the foundations for a new society.

Catholic and Protestant Conversions

The Catholic and Protestant presence on the Bemba plateau spread outward from their first mission strongholds. Despite the stipulations of the

Berlin Treaty of 1885–86 that missionaries should be free to practice in all colonial territories, colonial authorities allocated certain spheres of influence to different missionary societies, resulting in fierce competition. The BSAC administration relegated much of the Bemba highlands to the influence of Catholic White Fathers who were the first mission on the ground. The Livingstonia mission managed to ensure that the BSAC recognized their influence directly north and south of the areas of Catholic influence.[10] To prevent the further spread of the Catholics, Livingstonia sent African teachers, including David Kaunda, to establish schools near the Bemba heartland. Together with Reverend Robert Mac-Minn, Kaunda organized the Lubwa mission station and school in 1913, which was expanded into what became a renowned teacher training center in 1930.[11]

In the early colonial years, the missions made some inroads into the cultivation of a community of local Christians. The Protestants focused on opening schools. They trained and paid a group of African teachers who were their most loyal followers. The Catholics, by contrast, focused on eradicating "pagan" rituals and spreading the sacraments of baptism, confession, and marriage. Their most loyal followers were paid catechists, instructed in Catholic doctrine rather than secular education. This emphasis fit into the broader focus of the White Fathers, and especially Bishop Dupont, who sought to spread Christianity without fundamentally transforming—or "civilizing"—African society, except for replacing indigenous with Catholic beliefs and rituals.

By the late 1920s, competition between the missions came to the fore once again owing to the colonial funding of mission schools. Following the favorable reports of the Phelps-Stokes Commission (a privately funded organization that promoted cooperation between colonial governments and Christian missions) on missionary schools, the colonial government offered financial incentives for missions to expand their educational facilities. The White Fathers realized that if they did not change their orientation and expand schooling they would lose both funding and evangelical opportunities to the Protestants. They increased the number of schools, set up a teacher-training center at Rosa Mission in 1926, and looked for opportunities to establish new missions.[12] Catholic efforts to compete for government education funds and open new schools ignited a new era of competition between the missions. Missionaries of the Protestant Lubwa mission, regarding their role as a bulwark against Catholic intrusion, responded with alarm when they learned of Catholic efforts to open up missions in their immediate vicinity. They wrote, "The Roman Catholics realize . . . that those who get hold of the Bemba have the future of North Eastern Rhodesia in their hands, as far as the native population is concerned. For the Bemba are the most numerous and most virile race in the country, and their language, a live instrument already widespread, is gradually becoming the tongue of the tribes around them."[13]

A few years later, in 1934, the Lubwa missionary David Brown complained that the "the Roman Catholics invaded this year a district hitherto cared for by our Mission alone. They are said to have boasted that in a few years they alone will hold the field . . . though we endeavour to avoid friction, and have instructed our Native helpers to that effect, we do not propose giving way to Rome."[14] The White Fathers had established a mission at Ilondola, barely ten miles from Lubwa. Soon afterward Catholic missions were established at Chalabesa (1934), Mulobola (1935), Mulanga (1936), and Mulilansolo (1936), almost encircling the Protestant Lubwa mission and the Chinsali District.[15]

In spite of their proximity, few formal contacts between the Catholic and Protestant missions existed. Rumors, however, about the evil and corrupt practices of the competing missionaries circulated, both between the missions and within the villages that had a loose and tenuous affiliation to either Catholics or Protestants. In 1937, a Lubwa missionary accused the Catholics of "shady and reprehensible means of proselytizing and thrusting herself on the people. Bribing chiefs and headmen is one of these means . . . one chief, who seized and handcuffed one of our teachers . . . compelled him to sit through a Romanist service."[16] It is difficult to establish the veracity of these claims: the Catholics made similar accusations against the Lubwa mission. But complaints went well beyond the formal reports to the mission authorities, and led to vociferous campaigns across the Bemba highlands. For example, Protestant attempts to counter Catholic influence led to the distribution of ChiBemba-language anti-Catholic documents, such as "Fifty reasons why I have not joined the Church of Rome."[17] The Catholics adopted similar tactics, mostly by increasing the role of the lay apostolate in promoting Catholic loyalty and doctrine.[18] The veracity of the accusations is less important than the attempts to convince the Bemba of the truth of their respective doctrines and the misguided—even evil—beliefs, intents, and actions of their opponents.

Although Catholic and Protestant missionaries wanted to ensure that the converted were well versed in their particular doctrines, they also wanted to make certain that their competitors did not gain a foothold in the villages. Thus, mission rivalries led to two distinct emphases in the ongoing process of conversion: on the one hand, there was a core group of evangelists who would be converted and trained; on the other, there was a populace trained by these evangelists who would have only a loose affiliation to the mission. In the case of the White Fathers, candidates for baptism had to abstain from older practices, ranging from sacred dances and polygamy, and had to memorize the catechism in daily sessions during a three-week intensive training course (even while the early ChiBemba version of the catechism was, according to later missionaries, "full of nonsense and contradictions").[19] Certain young men could then become part of a cohort of paid catechists. They had to undertake a further four years of schooling at the mission and annual retreats to ensure loyalty and discipline.[20] The long period of official catechist instruction was not a broad education and hardly touched on secular matters. Instruction was paternalistic and any autonomous activities discouraged. When it occurred, as in Emilio Mulolani's League of the Sacred Heart (*mutima*) movement in the 1950s, the catechists were excommunicated.[21]

As a matter of formal policy, the Protestants did not have paid African catechists who memorized doctrine, although individual missionaries occasionally made use of such paid evangelists. Instead, they focused on paid "teachers," who were literate and had received a broader education than their Catholic counterparts. According to the 1948 Lubwa Annual Report, the mission derived its "vitality" from the fact that the church and the school were identified as the same. Most of the church classes were given by teachers; the teachers and their dependents formed the most faithful cohort of church followers.[22] They were granted greater autonomy than the Catholic mission elite, in keeping with the Scottish Presbyterian vision of the Livingstonia Mission to establish a self-governing and self-supporting African church.[23] Nevertheless, for both Catholic and Protestant missionaries, it would only be in the late colonial period that these African church leaders began to form an official African clergy.

The different expectations of conversion for Catholics and Protestants led to different emphases. The Catholic missionaries desired a break with "paganism" and, in return, introduced new rituals, such as communal prayer and the administration of sacraments of baptism, confession, and marriage.[24] The Protestant missionaries were more concerned with a secular "civilizing mission" than their Catholic counterparts, placing greater emphasis on transformations in the domestic realm, education, and the moral order of society. The Catholics spread their sacraments as a new spiritual technology, while the Protestants spread "civilization" and scripture.

The elite group of African converts carried the message of their particular missions into their villages, where, away from the direct influence of the mission, a far looser interpretation of mission doctrines prevailed. The missions accepted that for many instructed by the African evangelists and teachers, conversion would be partial and subject to "backsliding." For most converts in the Catholic hinterland, breaking with "paganism" involved relocating village *mfuba* shrines outside of the village and performing *chisungu* initiation rites and *ukupyana* marital succession practices in more secretive settings, especially when a White Father was in the vicinity. The Presbyterian commitment to church autonomy outside the immediate orbit of the mission also eroded Protestant efforts to implement the moral and civil transformation that they envisaged.

At first, Protestant influence proved more decisive than that of the Catholics in the spread of ChiBemba-language religious documents. Because of the late start of the Catholics in the opening of secular schools, most Africans were educated by the Protestants. These African teachers spread literacy and distributed printed books and pamphlets, even to the more remote villages. The translation of the Bible into Bemba by Lubwa clergy, Paul Mushindo and Reverend MacMinn, and its publication, with the completed version arriving at the mission in 1956, was perhaps the most decisive Protestant intervention.[25] Not to be outdone, though, the White Fathers also became influential in the distribution of books. From the late 1920s, they began to match Protestant efforts in the setting up of schools. They also published influential ChiBemba texts, such as the widely read ChiBemba school reader *Ifya Bukaya*.[26] The distribution and dissemination of these texts and of their Christian narratives would, however, not be completely under the control of the missions or their educated teachers.

Bamuchape Purification

For the people of the Bemba plateau, looming behind the conflict between the missionaries was the threat of angry ancestors and unhappy family members. The Bamuchape (the people who cleansed) movement promoted another type of "conversion," a purification that drew on Christian spiritual technologies to rid the world of witchcraft that emanated from the discontented living and dead. The Bamuchape began in colonial Malawi, where their founder Kamwende was said to have died and been resurrected, with a vision to rid the world of witches and witchcraft. In the early 1930s the Bamuchape, mostly young men, traveled from village to village, spreading across much of colonial Zambia, where they identified witches who were forced to drink a purifying potion and offered medicine to combat future acts of witchcraft.[27] Paramount Chief Chitimukulu welcomed the Bamuchape in the hope that they would "take away all the *buloshi* witches in the country."[28]

The local precedents for Bamuchape witchcraft cleansing were the *mwavi* poison ordeals, in the past administered by chiefs with the help of local priests or doctors (*shinganga*: the fathers of magic). But under Indirect Rule and the Witchcraft Ordinance of 1909, the colonial administration did not allow their chiefs to administer the *mwavi* ordeal. The Bamuchape adapted the ordeal instead to ensure that it was within the strictures of the Witchcraft Ordinance. Their medicine worked by persuading people that they were witches—for fear that they would be later revealed, if they did not admit it—rather than by direct accusations. The consequences of admitting to being a witch were relatively minor, as long as one agreed to drink the medicine, which prevented one from committing any future acts of witchcraft. In some cases, there was local pressure and a temptation to accuse people directly, which could result in physical violence against witches. A few of these instances came to the attention of the colonial authorities. Their prosecutions resulted in fines, canings, and imprisonment that ranged from a few months to several years in hard labor. For that reason, the Bamuchape were careful to get the permission of the district officials, who were instructed to allow them to perform witchcraft cleansing, but not to give them written permission for fear that it would be treated as official sanction.[29] For the Bemba, a solution to witchcraft seemed to be at hand and there was an enthusiastic reception for the Bamuchape.

The Bamuchape employed new spiritual resources introduced by the missionaries. They lined people up and instructed them, as if they were giving a church sermon. They claimed to spread the word and power of God—*Lesa*. Most of all, unlike *mwavi*, which was used to identify and administer justice to witches after they had performed witchcraft, the Bamuchape offered a purification that cleansed the evil of past, present, and future. It was a salvation. Their *mwavi* ordeal thus resembled baptism, a spiritual technology adapted to older forms of protection against witchcraft. In August 1933 in the Ufipa district, slightly north of the Zambian border with Tanzania, the head of the Bamuchape preached to a gathering of nearly 2,000 people:

> Your Missionaries came to the country some 50 years ago; they tried with all their best to save the people and teach you not to kill one another yet without success. But we feel sympathy for you have lost dear friends, some of you standing here, not because God took them away—but by being poisoned by these witchcraft [*sic*], whom you will see today. We follow God's law that *"Thou shalt not kill."* This commandment is being observed and fulfilled by us more than any religion. For they all fail to save people—but we do . . . I know that some of your Christians argue, but I tell you some of your native ministers of religion have been found in possession of a skull of a European Lady. I do not know where they

killed this lady, and took her skull. So you must not trust the Christians, they are the people who are hiding in this religion, and are the great witchcrafts more than any one else.[30]

The Bamuchape, then, claimed to promote the salvation that the Christians promised but were unable to deliver because they harbored their own witchcraft. They employed the spiritual resources and technologies of the Christian missions to eradicate the witches that the Christian missionaries denied existed.

The missionaries and the Bamuchape were similar in many regards, most of all in their insistence on a transformation, or "conversion," that rejected old practices. For the Bamuchape, the permanence of purification was questionable: there was no heaven or hell, and no millenarian vision attached to purification. Spiritual interventions were pragmatic and focused on this world, not on the afterlife of the missionaries. A new identity would be achieved by the cleansing of old forms of evil magic. The most fervent Christian missionaries and their local agents had burnt the shrines and other "idolatrous" objects; or, at the very least, they insisted that such shrines be situated well away from the villages that they visited.[31] The Bamuchape were far more successful in the purification of such objects, however. Outside the villages, the piles of "charms" that the missionaries had tried to eradicate for decades, mostly horns (*nsengo*) containing potent medicine (*muti*), piled up.

Even while the Bamuchape responded to spiritual insecurities, they fomented greater turmoil. In the 1930s, around the same time that the Catholics established several missions, the Bamuchape began to visit villages in the Chinsali District. A three-way competition among religious agents, with their concomitant strategies of conversion, now existed: Protestants, Catholics, and Bamuchape. At first, the Catholics proved the most stubborn, dogmatic, and combative. They prohibited the Bamuchape from visiting villages where they held sway; this earned them the reputation of being witches, a reputation that at least some White Fathers cultivated to enhance their power and authority.[32] Competition between these movements combined with other colonial transformations led to feelings of spiritual disempowerment and insecurity. The people of the Bemba plateau needed a resolution cast in familiar terms, yet more convincing, forward-looking, and permanent than the cleansing of the Bamuchape. They sought out a process of conversion that reconciled the purification and witchcraft eradication of the Bamuchape with the fostering of a permanent Christian identity.

Lenshina and the New Christians

In 1953 a new movement attempted a comprehensive conversion that combined the Bamuchape's concern to cleanse witchcraft with the mission processes of teaching about and against sin. It began when a young woman and a mother of six, Alice Mulenga, fell sick, died, and was resurrected. Upon awakening, she claimed that she had been sent back to life by God who had instructed her to baptize her people and to eradicate witchcraft. Although Alice Mulenga received visions in a similar fashion to the story of the Bamuchape leader, Kamwende, she more decisively attached these revelations to the Christian doctrines espoused by the nearby Lubwa mission (the story of her revelation closely mirrored *The Pilgrim's Progress*) and to the popular sacraments administered by the White Fathers. At first, Lenshina began to preach on behalf of the Lubwa mission, but the missionaries did not allow her to preach in the chapel.[33] So she established her own "Lumpa" church, a church that "went beyond" other churches and hastened all to salvation. Soon she became known as "Regina" (or Lenshina), meaning "queen." From 1954 to the early 1960s stories of Lenshina's resurrection and her communications with God spread across northern Zambia. Upon hearing the good news, many Zambians made the pilgrimage to the striking church that Lenshina's followers were building at Zion (or "Sione"). Lenshina and her deacons baptized them with names from heaven (*ishina lya mulu*) and they learned to sing the distinctive and beautiful Lumpa hymns, which formed the most popular genre for the transmission of Lumpa ideas.[34] They then went out to more remote villages to spread Lenshina's message and teach her hymns. By the mid-1950s almost all of the villages in Chief Nkula's area had Lumpa churches in which new congregants sang Lenshina's hymns.[35] Between 60,000 and 100,000 people claimed some sort of affiliation to the Lumpa church, far more than the combined membership of the Catholics and Protestants, and including nearly 90 percent of the population in the Chinsali District where Lenshina had her headquarters.[36] Lenshina's deacons began traveling to the urban areas. Men wearing long white robes, calling themselves the "twelve disciples of Lenshina," arrived in the Copperbelt in 1956.[37]

Lenshina's church can be explained in terms of a series of political, economic, and social factors. Conflict over the advent of the white settler-dominated Central African Federation in 1953 led to the suspicion of colonial motives, even while the coronation of the "Regina," Queen Elizabeth II of the United Kingdom, was "celebrated" across the colony. The Catholics had embarked on an aggressive program of proselytizing through Catholic Action groups in the name of the Legion of Mary, their own "Regina." There was a local outbreak of smallpox with unusual severity.[38] The village economy was under continued structural strain and change brought about by the migration of young male labor to urban areas, in turn offering new challenges and sometimes opportunities to rural women.[39] All of these factors contributed to spiritual insecurity; yet none of them explains the form that the Lumpa church took and the distinctive spiritual resources it mobilized.

Lenshina's followers combined aspects of Catholic, Protestant, and Bamuchape conversion. Not only did she insist on doing away with the sins of the past, but her acts of purification held some similarity to Catholic confession and communion. Indeed, her name "Regina" frequently appeared in Catholic Latin liturgies.[40] Her emphasis on a new moral order and the transferal of the morality of heaven to earth resembled Protestant conversion, especially of the more radical evangelicals. Conversion for Lenshina's followers also drew on notions introduced by the Bamuchape, especially the purification rites. Yet it differed from the onetime purification offered by the Bamuchape: Lenshina wanted to create a new community of Christians. The followers of Lenshina had begun to associate witchcraft with the Christian notion of "sin" directly. Missionary insistence on the pervasiveness of this "sin," then, only further encouraged frenzied attempts to eradicate it. At the same time, Lenshina's notion of evil was also more doctrinaire and moral than the witches and angry ancestors with whom the Bamuchape were concerned. By 1957 Lenshina had developed a set of rules that dictated familial and moral practices. These included outlawing adultery, polygamy, and insults to others.[41] The eradication of evil for Lenshina was part of a moral *and* spiritual program. It would change social practices and end witchcraft, leading to heaven on earth.

At first the center of Lenshina's movement was the temple (*itempile*), a grass-fenced enclosure around the tree where Lenshina had first had her visions. Here Lenshina, or at least her agents, preached, baptized, and distributed medicines and remedies that ensured good health, fertility, and a prosperous harvest.[42] A small hut to one side was reserved for marriage ceremonies.[43] Just outside the temple, people deposited the *fyabupe*, the bad things, which spread misfortune, so that they could be purified by Lenshina.[44] Many of these bad things had been part of a ceremonial life that had previously ensured fertility and good harvests: "horns [*nsengo*], beads, lion claws, medicine pouches . . . ceremonial battle axes (*mbafi*) and ceremonial hoes (*tulonde*)."[45] Lenshina rejected old forms of supernatural intervention; even if previous ceremonial and ritual acts had previously acted against witchcraft, Lenshina claimed they were witchcraft. Instead of sacred relics and ceremonies that the chiefs claimed ensured agricultural prosperity, Lenshina blessed the seeds before planting and crops before harvesting.[46] In one of her hymns, she even named her church the "house of seed."[47] Her movement appropriated Christian practices to solve pragmatic and everyday issues such as health and prosperity, which were subject to spiritual malaise.

The rivalry between Lenshina and the other churches encouraged polarization and increased the radicalism of Lenshina's message. Lenshina's followers claimed the Catholics spread evil and were witches. It was, after all, the "Romans" who had killed Jesus. The Lumpa withdrew their children from schools.[48] When the White Fathers appeared in the villages, Lenshina's adherents cried, "Mulwani aisa ee utufunya kuli tata" ("The enemy is coming to chase us from our father").[49] Catholic rosaries, crosses, and medals were objects of witchcraft—in a similar fashion to the *babenye* relics of chiefs and *chisungu mbusa* of young girls. Lenshina had to purify all such objects.[50]

In part owing to such acts, which the White Fathers viewed as provocation and antagonism rather than an attempt to purify their evil (just as the White Fathers had attempted to purify the Bemba's magic through their baptism), the White Fathers crusaded against Lenshina in a far more aggressive fashion than the Church of Scotland had done. They produced a pamphlet titled "Mwitina Bena Itempele" ("Do not fear the people of the temple") and undertook "Rosary Campaigns."[51] At Chalabesa mission, they celebrated the "heroic examples" of Christians who "attacked the Regina-sect messengers, forbade them to delay and preach in their villages and beat their own children who followed the crowds to Kasomo [Lenshina's headquarters]."[52] Catholic Action programs and a new youth movement organized Corpus Christi processions to counter the influence of Lenshina's church.[53] By 1957, the Catholics attempted to temper their response: a circular letter called on the missionaries to "calm down in our direct attacks . . . we should be less negative and more positive."[54] The Protestant missionaries initially embarked on a campaign to ensure that Lenshina and her followers clarify their relationship to the mission and suspended the church membership of Lenshina and her close associates. By 1956, however, they had decided to limit any large-scale campaign, because it "seems to increase ill-feeling."[55] Instead they tended to focus on spreading literacy and scripture, especially the Bible, the first complete printed copies of which were just arriving at the mission.

Despite these efforts, the most fervent conflict was not between European missionaries and Lenshina's followers. It was rather the African educated elite attached to the European missions that felt most threatened and responded most aggressively to Lenshina. When a Bemba priest, Fr. Pascal Kakokota, was accused of witchcraft by a Lumpa adherent, Joseph Mumba, he took the complaint to the Native Authority Court and then to the colonial Boma, resulting in the imprisonment of Mumba. After leading a protest against Mumba's imprisonment, Lenshina's husband, Petros Chintankwa, was sentenced to two years in hard labor for "inciting violence," bringing about the first open conflict between the Lumpa and the colonial administration.[56] Paul Mushindo, the longtime Lubwa mission teacher and evangelist, was also a target for witchcraft accusations and an ardent opponent of Lenshina.[57] A few former teachers who had become disillusioned with the mission, such as Robert Kaunda (the elder son of David Kaunda) and Sandile Rain were at first attracted to Lenshina's movement. Yet church members accused them of embezzling church funds and even of witchcraft.[58] Lenshina refused to acknowledge the significance of the Bible, or at least subordinated it to the hymns that God had taught her directly. She distributed written documents, "passports to heaven," circumventing the power of the teachers. The Lumpa movement attacked the hegemony of the teachers.

The millenarian temperament of the Lumpa increased with the completion of Lenshina's church at Zion in 1958. The magnificent church, modeled on the Catholic Ilondola mission (except built with dimensions one foot longer), had been financed through church donations and business, especially trade with the Copperbelt towns, and proudly built by Lenshina's local followers. Its completion and opening was meant to herald a New Jerusalem and perhaps even the return of Jesus Christ. On one level it did herald a new enterprise. People from across the country came to Lenshina's Zion and settled there. The village was becoming a town, free from chiefly interference and colonial taxation. Yet even in this new utopian community, there were problems, jealousy, and conflict. People still fell sick and died. Witchcraft was still evident and Jesus had not arrived. The problem, for the followers of Lenshina, were the "sinners," those who still committed acts of witchcraft. Efforts to eradicate witchcraft intensified and the Lumpa church took on more of a millenarian focus. After 1958, then, Lenshina's church transformed from a Christian witchcraft cleansing movement to a millenarian movement that sought an absolute end to witchcraft and sin and the rise of a new order, a New Jerusalem.

The missionaries had trained a community of converts who were paid to evangelize, to spread the influence of the missions, and to gradually bring about a Christian modernity under their leadership. For Lenshina, conversion entailed a break from the past and the creation of a new society, purified of spiritual evil, and freed from the missions and their hierarchical modernity. This was a radically different program to the emphasis on personal salvation, confession, and membership of a church hierarchy found in Protestant and Catholic missionary discourses and practices. Lubwa missionary W. V. Stone perceived the difference:

It would be a sin to deny that our orthodox Christianity has not produced wonderful fruit and is still producing it . . . all that a *Christian layman* can be . . . he takes his full part in the Courts of the Church, where time and again his lead is more spiritual, more Christian than that of us Ministers; he imbues the school with his spirit . . . introduced to white man's knowledge and religion . . . they become leaders in all parts of life . . . a school like Lubwa lays the Christian foundations on which we hope and pray that the *incipient African middle class* will build its ethos in the next generation. . . .

But when we look at *people proper*, the *ordinary villager*, a very different picture presents itself. They belong to a *People Movement*, but it is not the Church. They have with their own hands erected simple Churches in nearly every village, they gather enthusiastically three times a week at worship . . . Alice has succeeded into bringing into being a People's Movement . . . her success marks our failure. . . . It leaves one with the feeling that nowhere has the missionary succeeded in really integrating Christianity in the daily life of the people.[59]

In its appeal to quotidian and vernacular issues, Lenshina's "people's movement" was revolutionary and uncompromising in its efforts to eradicate spiritual evil. It identified the kingdom and, as indicated in this popular Lumpa hymn, offered a choice between being saved or lost:

Subileni bonse, umwine ale isa

Iseeni mumwimbile
Tapali mfumu iyacila ine kamo
ine neka
Iseeni mumwimbile
Uwashama eka, Uwashama eka
Ewuka filwa kupalama kwi sano

Nelyo wa filwa, iwe
Ukalola kwi

Believe, all of you, the owner is coming
Come together and praise

There is no king who surpasses me
Come together and praise
The unfortunate one
Who fails to come to the Kingdom of God
When you have failed,
Where will you go?[60]

Conclusions

Through the first half of the twentieth century, two different forms of conversion emerged: the reformist and didactic on the one hand and the prophetic and revolutionary on the other. The former was hierarchical, text-based, doctrinaire, and led by missionaries and educated elites. It emerged out of a vision of what European missionaries felt Christian conversion should be like (even if Christianity had not had such a reformist influence in the recent history of their own societies). The latter was revolutionary, populist, oral, millenarian, and led by prophets. It emerged out of attempts to adapt Christian spiritual resources to the eradication of spiritual evil, witchcraft, which became more prevalent with the missionary insistence on the pervasiveness of sin alongside colonial transformations and insecurities. Both visions aimed for a new universal order of converts. However, the reformists insisted on individual subordination to a hierarchical community of educated Christians that would guide a sometimes confused people toward good through the promise and threat of a spiritual afterlife. The revolutionary insisted that individuals be cleansed of their spiritual evil, their witchcraft, as a basis for the radical and rapid creation of a New Jerusalem in this life.

Both visions would appear repeatedly in Zambia, a reformist impulse that legitimized an authority that strived for progress and improvement, with a revolutionary agenda that sought to cleanse evil. The radical conversion, involving a reinvention of the self, represented a revolutionary element in the Zambian political imagination. Two strands of such radicalism, popular nationalism and popular Christianity, came into conflict in the 1960s. At the time of independence in 1963–64, a war fought between the revolutionary nationalists and revolutionary Christians in northern Zambia led to the defeat of both of them.[61] The war not only subdued popular Christianity but also repressed the revolutionary element in nationalist discourse. Reformism became the basis of Zambia's postindependence political program, Kenneth Kaunda's Christian socialist doctrine of "Humanism," which aimed to create a new civilization by subordinating Zambians to a progressive postcolonial state led by educated elites. The reformists, however, were never hegemonic. The revolutionary agenda continued to be expressed by (and contained within) Zambia's many Christian movements. The electoral defeat of Kaunda and the declaration of the born-again Christian nation in 1991 was a striking and explosive example of such resurgent Christianity.

The first Zambian president, Kenneth Kaunda, grew up at the Presbyterian Lubwa mission and his father, David Kaunda, was one of its founding missionaries. Here was a significant representative of the "teachers," the educated elite who guided Zambians toward "development" and "progress." Yet Kenneth Kaunda's mother and elder brother were keen members of Lenshina's church; for a brief period, they too were proponents of its revolutionary spiritual programs and promises. The Kaunda family history, then, encapsulates the conflicting conversions of the missionaries and the prophets, a crucible for Zambia's future political imagination.

3

Church versus Country

Palestinian Arab Episcopalians,
Nationalism, and Revolt, 1936–39

Laura Robson

In my final years at primary school, I became aware of the troubles
in my country, the open rebellion of the Palestinians against the
pro-Zionist policies of British rule. There were demonstrations and
strikes. The girls in my school stayed away, protesting against Jewish immigration and the Balfour Declaration. When I was in the
top class, I joined them. We started from the square of the Greek
Orthodox church, where the boys also assembled, and walked down
the main street, passing the Latin convent, to the bus station, where
we were joined by men and women from the surrounding villages,
wearing their *kaffiyehs* (headscarfs). We sang about our homeland.
 —Najwa Kawar Farah, *A Continent Called Palestine:*
 One Woman's Story

Introduction

In 1936 a major rebellion broke out in Palestine that would last three years,
claim thousands of lives, and go down in history as the most important
anticolonial uprising in the interwar Middle East. *Al-thawra al-kubra,*
"the Great Revolt," represented the biggest Palestinian Arab rebellion yet
against the mandate state and its policy of promoting a "Jewish National
Home" in Palestine. The revolt constituted itself simultaneously against
British colonial occupation and a Zionist movement that Palestinian

49

Arabs regarded as colonialism's protégé, and it quickly became a defining moment in the formation of a specifically Palestinian national consciousness based on both a sense of territorial belonging and an opposition to European Jewish settlement and state formation. Historians have come to regard the revolt as a watershed in Palestinian history. It was one of a chain of events that included the 1948 war (known to Palestinians as *al-Nakba*, the catastrophe), which resulted in the creation of the State of Israel and the dispossession and dispersal of the great majority of Palestinian Arabs; the 1967 Arab-Israeli war that led to the Israeli occupation of the West Bank, the Gaza Strip, and the Golan Heights; and the first intifada (which unfolded in ways uncannily similar to the Great Revolt). Together, these events have defined the modern history of the Palestinian people.[1]

Caught within the currents of the 1936–39 revolt were members of the small but prominent Arab Palestinian Episcopalian community, products of late nineteenth- and early twentieth-century missionary encounters. For these Palestinian Arab Episcopalians, the revolt sparked a major reevaluation of the meaning of religious identity, their community's commitment to the Palestinian nationalist movement, and their relationship with their British parent church. In response to the revolt, Palestinian Episcopalians began to use their leadership organization, the Palestine Native Church Council (PNCC), as a mouthpiece for expressing nationalist sentiment in both Palestine and England. Over the protests of their British coreligionists, Palestinian Episcopalian leaders used their churches as venues for expressing support for the Palestinian cause and tried to drum up international support for the Palestinians through their international Anglican connections. During the years of the revolt, the PNCC and its churches became public supporters of Palestinian nationalism, vocally opposing their spiritual leaders in England who backed the project of a Jewish state.

Eventually, the upheaval surrounding the revolt soured the relationship between Palestinian Arab Episcopalians and the British Anglican institutions in Palestine, to the extent that some began to consider conversion to Islam as a mark of their commitment to the Palestinian Arab national cause. This course of action was a drastic one, as nearly all

Palestinian Episcopalians had originally converted not from Islam but from Greek Orthodox Christianity. Many more were so disillusioned by the actions of the British and the resultant branding of the Palestinian Episcopalian community as traitors to the Arab cause that they began to plan for emigration. By the 1940s, then, the small but prominent community of Palestinian Arab Episcopalians that had been a feature of the Palestinian landscape for less than a hundred years was rapidly dwindling.

The Great Revolt, and the brutal colonial response to it, placed Palestinian Arab Christians committed to both an emerging Palestinian national identity and a British-based Episcopalian church in an impossible position. During the course of the revolt, the British missions saw their Palestinian Episcopalian protégés turn church institutions into venues for the promotion of Palestinian nationalism. The missions then watched Palestinian Episcopalians succumb to conversion and emigration as they became radically disillusioned with and under suspicion for their church's associations with an imperial state that supported the project of a Jewish National Home in Palestine.

The Origins of the Palestinian Arab Episcopalian Community

Nineteenth-century European missionaries looked on the "Holy Land" as particularly fertile soil for proselytizing. With the rise of evangelical approaches to Protestantism and the messianic and revivalist messages of the "awakenings" in Britain and the United States during the early nineteenth century, interest grew in taking the Christian message back to its place of origin. The American evangelical Protestant missionary Levi Parsons traveled to Palestine in 1820, declaring, "With the spirit of Moses I can lead the armies of Israel to the spiritual Canaan."[2] In 1826 the Anglican Church Missionary Society (CMS) sent its first missionary to Jerusalem. Fifteen years later the Church of England collaborated with the Evangelical Church of Prussia to set up the first Protestant bishopric in Palestine. Then, in 1887, the bishopric dissolved its partnership with the Prussian church and became purely Anglican. The new Jerusalem and East Mission focused on education, opening dozens of schools throughout

Palestine and building St. George's Cathedral Church and School in Jerusalem.

Early mission efforts were focused primarily on the conversion of the Jews, an idea promoted by evangelical "revivalists" hoping to assist in the fulfillment of biblical prophecy. To this end, the first bishop appointed to the Jerusalem post was Michael Solomon Alexander, a former rabbi and convert to Protestant Christianity. But the Jews of Palestine proved unamenable to conversion, and as proselytizing to Muslims was a punishable offense under Ottoman law, these early Protestant missionaries turned their attention elsewhere.[3] The local Arab Christian populations, they reasoned, also needed saving. These communities were mainly Greek Orthodox, a church whose rituals and liturgies had, to evangelical Protestants, an unmistakable whiff of popery about them.

By the late nineteenth century these missions had assembled a small but influential community of Palestinian Arab converts, almost all from Greek Orthodox backgrounds. These newly minted Episcopalians soon wanted to take a stronger role in their new church.[4] In 1905 Palestinian priests and members of the congregations drew up a set of regulations for an Arab church council, which was called the Palestine Native Church Council (PNCC) in English and the Council of the Episcopal Evangelical Church (*majma' al-kanisa al-injiliyya al-usqufiyya*) in Arabic. Its membership comprised all the Palestinian priests, lay catechists of the Arab congregations, lay delegates elected by pastorate committees, and "visitors" nominated by the CMS. The council met with all its members annually and had a rotating standing committee for issues that came up between meetings. The CMS undertook to provide monetary support for the council, with the idea that the PNCC would eventually become financially independent of its parent body.

Even at this early date, the PNCC took on a specifically Arab character that prefigured its later emergence as a vehicle of Palestinian Arab nationalism. The regulations of 1905, for instance, explicitly excluded non-Arab congregations—not only the English-speaking congregations of expatriate Europeans and Americans but also the tiny number of "Hebrew Christians" (Jews who had converted to Christianity at the behest of European missionaries). The all-Arab character of the PNCC and the Palestinian

Episcopalian community was strengthened during World War I, when the forced evacuation of all British residents in Palestine left the fledgling church wholly in the hands of its Palestinian clergy and lay leaders. When British mission personnel returned after the war, the PNCC continued to take a major role in the administration of church affairs, including running a number of Episcopalian schools and encouraging the ordination of more Palestinian Arab clergy.

By the 1920s the community had emerged as a highly influential component of elite Palestinian Arab society. Palestinian Arab Episcopalians represented a privileged group whose members had often benefited materially from an English education and whose leaders came from within the Palestinian Arab middle and upper-middle classes. Lay readers and representatives in the PNCC were mainly professionals—teachers, journalists, doctors, dentists, and civil servants. Many of them were involved in education, particularly in the running of Anglican schools like Bishop Gobat's and St. George's, and many of them had studied abroad. The PNCC itself sometimes funded study at the renowned American University of Beirut for aspiring Arab clergy.[5] Some members were actively engaged in nationalist political activity at the highest levels, and Arab Episcopalians owned two of the most widely read newspapers in the country, *al-Karmil* and *Mir'at al-sharq.* The community "number in all 9 clergy and about 3,000 laity," the British archdeacon W. H. Stewart wrote in 1936, "but [their] weight and standing in the business life of the country is much greater than their number alone would indicate."[6] Anglican mission efforts had produced a small but highly visible and successful community of Palestinian Arab converts.

Nationalism, Arabism, Zionism:
The Mandate State and the Outbreak of Revolt

The meaning of the European missionary presence changed when the British entered Palestine as colonial rulers. The British army occupied Palestine in 1917, during the later stages of World War I, and a British military administration took over the country from the Ottomans while European colonial bureaucrats were parceling out the Middle East among themselves in the peace negotiations. In 1920 Britain appointed its first High Commissioner for Palestine and began the reorganization of the colonial state; the League of Nations finalized Britain's possession of the mandate for Palestine three years later. By this time, Britain's support for the Zionist movement and for the construction of a "Jewish National Home" in Palestine—first confirmed in the Balfour Declaration of 1917 and eventually formalized in the text of the League's mandate—had already caused major hostility, resentment, and rebellion among Palestinian Arabs.

A number of incidences of anticolonial and anti-Zionist violence occurred in the first decade of the mandate, including the *Buraq*/Western Wall riots of 1929. But from 1936 to 1939, rebellion rose to new heights in the form of a general revolt that came to be known as *al-thawra al-kubra*, the Great Revolt. It began in April 1936 with a general strike in protest of mandate policy on land and Jewish immigration in Nablus, and quickly spread throughout the country. A body of prominent urban notables and nationalist politicians known as the Arab Higher Committee (AHC), headed by the Grand Mufti of Jerusalem, Hajj Amin al-Husayni, formulated the strikers' demands (independence, an immediate end to Jewish immigration, and the stoppage of land sales to the Jews) and presented them to the mandate state. Although the AHC represented the primary Palestinian nationalist leadership and constituted the main point of contact between Palestinian Arabs and the mandate government, it was not able to exercise much control over the rebel bands in the Palestinian countryside who were spearheading the strike and military operations outside the major cities.

The AHC called off the strike in October. The British Peel Commission, charged with the task of examining the causes of the demonstrations and recommending the future direction of Palestine, arrived in November to begin making inquiries.[7] In July 1937, the commission published a report recommending the partition of Palestine into an Arab and a Jewish state, a proposal that infuriated Palestinian Arabs.[8] In the fall a British commissioner named Lewis Andrews was assassinated in Nazareth and serious violence broke out across the country. The British government responded by disbanding the AHC and driving its members into exile, along with any other nationalist leaders they could identify.[9] Consequently, rural peasant leaders now took over the direction of the uprising, which began again almost immediately.

This development marked a major shift in the nature and direction of the Palestinian nationalist movement. Before the revolt, the nationalist leadership had tended to focus on Palestinian elite politics and high-level negotiations with the mandate state. This revolt came mainly from below; it mobilized the Palestinian rural poor, rather than the middle-class elites and notables who had until then been the primary face of the nationalist movement. The revolt arose more or less spontaneously, without organizational direction from the national political leadership. And it spread through wide swaths of the country astonishingly quickly. By 1938 the British had lost control of major parts of the Palestinian countryside.

Although the shift of political momentum from the notables and the professional classes to the rural peasantry in 1936–39 caused a loss of influence for the elite populations to which most Palestinian Christians belonged, there is little evidence of the sudden emergence of a deeply felt sectarian divide between Muslims and Christians in the context of the revolt.[10] But for Palestinian Episcopalians, the revolt raised serious problems because of their community's high degree of contact with the British through church and missionary institutions. As a result of the constant interaction and mutual dependence between Palestinian Episcopalians and their British coreligionists, the Palestinian Arab Episcopalian community began to face suspicion from their fellow nationalists. And as the revolt continued, the leadership of the Anglican church in the metropole responded with public expressions of support for the Zionist project in Palestine, causing major disillusionment among Palestinian Episcopalians and prompting them to turn their church institutions into venues for the public expression of nationalist sentiments.

The Church as a Nationalist Venue

Palestinian Episcopalians strongly sympathized with Palestinian nationalist aims, and the strike led the PNCC's leaders to begin to use the council as a mouthpiece to express Arab Episcopalian support for anti-Zionist and anti-British action. In June 1936, three months into the general strike, the PNCC took on its new role with a letter to the Archbishop of Canterbury, Cosmo Lang. In this missive, the council's leaders expressed Arab anger over the missteps of the British mandate government and the injustices of the British treatment of Arabs in Palestine, noting the peaceful relations that had existed between Arab and Jewish communities in Palestine before the British mandate. They praised Islam as having a long record of good treatment of its Jewish minorities, contrasting it with the history of European oppression of Jews. The letter requested that Lang use his powers to help stop Jewish immigration into Palestine, saying that if the influx of Jewish immigrants was not ended, Christians in Palestine would be violently driven out of Palestine as the Armenians and Greeks had been expelled from Turkey. Finally, they wrote that the anti-Arab and pro-Zionist policies of the British government had given rise to a newly strengthened anti-British feeling throughout Palestine.[11]

In the same month, Shibli Jamal and 'Izzat Tannus—both leading nationalist activists associated with the Husayni family's *majlisi* political faction,[12] as well as prominent members of the Palestinian Episcopalian community—paid their own way to London to accompany Jamal al-Husayni on an unofficial delegation to the British government to "argue our just case to the British Government and, also, to tell our story to the British people who had never heard of it before from the right people."[13] Imil Ghori, an Orthodox Christian who had taken a major role in the Husaynis' political organization, joined them in London, and the four men presented themselves to various British officials as a representative body "entrusted with the task of presenting the Arab Case before the British People."[14] While they were in London, Jamal and Tannus contacted a number of Anglican missionaries and churchpeople in an attempt to drum up support for their cause. The PNCC and the Palestinian Episcopalians' international Anglican connections had become a potential network for the dissemination of nationalist material.

The response from the Anglican church leadership in England was lukewarm at best. Lambeth Palace (the official residence of the Archbishop of Canterbury) responded to the PNCC's letter by noting, "The Oriental is apt to think that he has a much larger measure of political power and influence than in fact he has. [The Archbishop of Canterbury] does not think that he can do anything more than draw the Colonial Secretary's personal attention to the contents of the Arabs' letter."[15] By contrast, the Arab Episcopalian community had the sympathy of many British missionaries in Palestine, in both the CMS and the bishopric, on the subjects of Zionism and Jewish immigration. The CMS's secretary Wilson Cash wrote to the PNCC's chairman, Reverend Ilyas Marmura, after receiving a copy of the council's letter to Canterbury, "I think you have presented the case fairly, honestly, and with great restraint. . . . As you know my sympathies in this controversy have all along been pro-Arab, and the present situation is the natural outcome of the policy developed over a period of years."[16] The Anglican bishop in Jerusalem, Francis Graham Brown, was himself opposed to the project of a Jewish National Home. In a letter to the Jerusalem and East Mission in October 1936, he wrote, "Does not [Jesus'] teaching of a spiritual Israel, really deny the basis of a 'National Home' in Palestine? In other words, the establishment of a 'National Home' in Palestine cannot be made to depend on the prophecies of the Old Testament, but rather on other grounds."[17]

But despite their sympathy, the use of a church forum to promote a nationalist political stance worried British CMS members, who saw in it a warning that the PNCC might leave the Church of England altogether. As CMS official Eric Bishop wrote in 1936, "I think that many of them feel the injustice of the Government (British NOT Palestine) and the League of Nations so keenly that it would not take very much for a number of them to decide to cut their connection, not with Christianity, but with the Church of England, just because it is the Church of *England*."[18] British Anglicans in Palestine, though many of them sympathized with the Palestinian Arab cause, were anxious that this new political activity on the part of the PNCC not interfere with the project of building a global Anglican church headed by England.

Pro-Zionism at the Metropole and the Arab Episcopalian Reaction

In the summer of 1937, the House of Lords opened a debate on the report of the Peel Commission, which had recommended partition as the only possible solution for the conflict in Palestine. The Archbishop of Canterbury Cosmo Lang addressed the House on July 20. In his speech, he expressed support for the idea of partition, based on sympathy for Jewish victims of anti-Semitism in Germany and on a theological interpretation of the Jewish return to the Holy Land. He also stated his belief that parts of the city of Jerusalem should be included in the new Jewish state.

This speech caused an immediate uproar among Palestinian Arab Episcopalians, who naturally saw it as a betrayal. The community now redoubled its efforts to use its Anglican connections and church venues to promote the Palestinian cause in the West. A PNCC meeting in Jerusalem recorded that the standing committee had read a letter from their chairman, Reverend Marmura, and his congregation at St. Paul's Church in Jerusalem protesting Lang's address, and stated that the committee "was sorry for the painful effect the words of His Grace have had on the Arabs, and especially on the Christians, not only from a national point of view, but also from a religious point of view . . . all those who help in circulating this thought are met—especially by the Christians of Palestine—with abhorrence."[19] A group of Arab Episcopalians, joined by a priest from the Orthodox church of Jerusalem, visited Bishop Francis Graham Brown to protest the archbishop's speech, objecting particularly to his use of the term "minority" to describe the Palestinian Arab Christians: "the delegation asked His Lordship to inform the Archbishop of Canterbury that the Christian Arabs are a part of the Arab community and do not wish to be thought of as a minority in the country."[20] The Women's Arab Society, of which the Arab Episcopalian writer Matiel Mughannam was a leading member, published a letter protesting the speech in the Jaffa-based newspaper *Filastin* on July 24 and also sent a delegation to the bishop to express opposition to the archbishop's statements.[21] Marmura, in his capacity as chair of the PNCC, wrote to Lang demanding the abandonment of the partition scheme, which he described as "disastrous" to all Arab Christians in Palestine who would be abandoned to Muslim or Jewish overlordship. He took the opportunity to propose a new political solution, a modified British mandate overseeing radically restricted Jewish immigration. "Such a scheme," he wrote, "is the only safeguard for the preservation and liberty of Christians in the Holy Land."[22]

Prominent Palestinian Episcopalian intellectuals turned their efforts toward the production of English-language political tracts explaining the Palestinian position to the Western powers.[23] The prominent doctor and ethnographer Tewfiq Kana'an, in a pamphlet on "The Palestine Arab Cause," linked the nationalist position specifically to the Arab Christian communities. "We Arab Christians of Palestine," he wrote, "who were mostly educated in British schools and who are attached to the British people more than are any other Palestinians, admiring British justice, British manners and British policy, are those at present who hate most bitterly the unchristian policy of Great Britain."[24] 'Izzat Tannus deplored the slowness of the Palestinian Arabs in producing propaganda aimed at a British audience: "This is a frank admission of our backwardness in the very important field of information and propaganda. I must admit again that it was wrong of the Arab people of Palestine to depend only on their indisputable natural rights to their country and on the Covenant of the League of Nations which decreed their self-determination."[25]

Arab Episcopalians also cultivated their ties with highly placed members of the nationalist movement. In 1937 Hajj Amin al-Husayni asked Marmura to serve as the representative of the Palestinian national cause at the London celebrations of the fiftieth anniversary of the Jerusalem diocese, where Marmura tried to present the Arab Christian point of view to the Anglican policymakers in the metropole.[26] The leaders of the PNCC were repositioning themselves and their churches as representatives and outposts of the Palestinian nationalist movement, responding to the outrages of British colonial rule.

Although Arab Episcopalians were of course most deeply affected by this turn of events, Lang's comments also aroused protest from British Anglicans in Palestine. Graham Brown wrote to Lang to report on the disturbances his speech had caused, taking particular exception to the archbishop's derogatory comments about Hajj Amin al-Husayni and to his support for including Jerusalem in a proposed Jewish state.[27] He also collaborated with his education adviser Mabel Warburton, American chaplain Charles Bridgemen, and Archdeacon W. H. Stewart to produce a memo detailing the bishopric's position on the idea of partition. "The Jewish problem of Europe," the memo stated, "must be solved

by the Christian powers at their own expense and not at the expense of
Palestine." The authors were generally opposed to partition; if partition
did occur, they said, it must recognize current ethnic boundaries, reject
forced population transfers, and provide a mandatory area "large enough
to accommodate those who do not wish to remain in either the proposed
Arab or the proposed Jewish state," as well as protecting the interests of
Palestine's Christian institutions.[28] Many leading British Anglicans in Palestine thought that Zionism and a potential Jewish state threatened Christian interests in the "Holy Land."

The anti-Zionist position of the bishopric and the CMS was also
based in sympathy for their Arab congregants. Graham Brown wrote to
Lang in 1937, "Christian Arabs are under no illusion as to their possible
ultimate fate. Although they realise that under an Arab National Government it might mean for them submergence or at least discrimination and
persecution, yet they would prefer an Arab regime to a Jewish one. . . . If
the Mandatory can see its way clear to render real service to the Christian
minorities, and pursue a long-term and unselfish policy, all will be well; if
not, it were better to leave the Christian to get along as best they can with
their masters."[29] There was no illusion on the part of Graham Brown or
the CMS, as there was on the part of some British colonial officials, that
Arab Christians were any less opposed to Zionism and a possible Jewish
state than their Muslim counterparts.

Lang himself, on the other hand, demonstrated a very limited grasp
of the damage he had caused to the Palestinian Arab Episcopalian community: "I fear it is impossible for me to correct all the misunderstandings
of my words which constantly occur in all parts of the world. . . . If the
Arabs are so afraid of the Jews and their financial power, it surprises me
that they are not more ready to think favourably of a definitely Arab State
from which they would be able to exclude the Jews which they certainly
could not do if the Mandate in its present form, or even a modified form,
were maintained. As for the Jews, I read [Chaim] Weizmann's speech
at Zurich [accepting, as a spokesman for the World Zionist movement,
the Peel Commission's proposal for partition] very carefully and I was
impressed by its ability and statesmanlike outlook."[30] The Anglican leadership in the metropole harbored no sympathy for the small community

its mission efforts had founded; indeed, Lang considered support for the Zionist movement to be his Christian duty.

The End of the Revolt

In the fall and summer of 1938, Arab rebel bands took control of much of the Palestinian countryside as well as some urban areas. The seriousness of the situation had led British officials in London to dismiss the High Commissioner, Sir Arthur Wauchope, who had resisted the imposition of military law and tried to leverage his personal relationships with both the Arab and the Jewish leadership to stop the violence. Wauchope's replacement, Sir Harold MacMichael, had served previously in the colonial administrations of the Sudan and Tanganyika; he proved much more willing to exercise his emergency powers. Under his guidance, the mandate government now responded to the revolt with what Ted Swedenburg has called "the classical savagery of colonial counterinsurgency"[31]—brutal strategies of collective punishment, mass hangings, the destruction of whole villages, and sweeping arrests.[32] The Palestinian Episcopalian community naturally suffered from the violence; their churches and homes suffered serious damage, and one of their clergymen at Bir Zayt, Butrus Aranky, was murdered in the spring of 1938. During this period, the PNCC's meetings began to feature frequent references to the violence and chaos. In one meeting in Jaffa, Butrus Nasir "thanked God for preserving the Palestine Native Church Council and the church and for guiding them through the dark clouds by the light of the Christian hope."[33]

The brutal crackdown eventually succeeded in ending the revolt in March 1939. More than 5,000 Arabs had been killed and 15,000 wounded; 200 Britons and 400 Jews also lost their lives. In May the British government issued a new White Paper that met some of the demands of the Palestinian Arabs; it called for a sharp reduction in Jewish immigration, limitations on land sales to Jews, and steps toward the eventual establishment of an independent Palestinian Arab state. The rebellion had not achieved all its political goals, but it had forced the British away from accepting the Peel Commission's proposal of partition.

Disillusionment and Disenfranchisement

For Arab Episcopalians, the end of the revolt and the support of many members of the missionary societies and the Jerusalem bishopric could not undo the damage inflicted by Lang's speech and the mandate government's brutality. The community was now under suspicion for treachery and covert pro-Zionism, despite the longstanding nationalist orientation of the PNCC and its vocal opposition to Lang's position. Arab Episcopalians were also permanently disillusioned with the Anglican church leadership, feeling that the Archbishop of Canterbury had betrayed them and that their parent British institutions could no longer be trusted.

British Anglicans in London tended to represent any anti-Christian feeling that emerged in the context of the revolt as a manifestation of a primitive sectarianism endemic in Palestine.[34] Palestinian Episcopalians rejected this explanation. They told their British coreligionists over and over that although they had never before viewed themselves as a disadvantaged minority vis-à-vis the Muslim community, the policies of the British government, combined with the attitude of the Anglican leadership in the metropole, had now combined to discredit their community in the eyes of their fellow citizens.

Ilyas Marmura accused Lang of having permanently and irreversibly damaged the position and standing of Palestine's Episcopalians. "Your advocating to give more of Jerusalem to the Jews was, however, unfortunate," he wrote, "from the point of view of the Christian Arabs who have been strongly opposed to Zionist policy. They with the Moslem Arabs have always been under the impression that the leading Christians in England were opposed to the political leaders who were in favour of Zionism. All the Arabs of Palestine, Moslems and Christians were disconcerted and indignant." Demonstrating a shrewd apprehension of Anglican priorities, Marmura added, "I am afraid that the Anglican church both British and Arab has lost its prestige which it has been gaining both among Arab Christians and Moslems as against Catholicism. However, that cannot be revoked."[35] Another Palestinian Episcopalian told the bishop that "the position of the Christians vis-à-vis the Moslems was worse now than in

Turkish times . . . the present government offered no prospect of 'protecting' the Christian interests."[36]

This theme recurred again and again. "I don't think it wise," the Palestinian Episcopalian and prominent civil servant Nicola Saba wrote to the CMS, "to end this note without some reference to the sufferings our congregations have to undergo on account of the theory now and anon expounded by certain dignitaries of the Church of England relating to the return of the Jews to Palestine. Although, as individuals, we do not believe that this doctrine agrees with our interpretation of the New Testament, there can be no doubt that, being in communion with the Church of England, we are as a body suspected of holding the same view. What makes it worse for us is that some of the missionary workers in Palestine stick to what is termed to be the declared doctrine of the Church of England. We are therefore not only looked upon as enemies of our own country, but as spies or agents for the British Government, who is solely responsible for the enforcement of the Balfour Declaration, thereby breaking its promises to the Arabs of whom we form a part."[37] Even some British Anglican missionaries in Palestine recognized the problem. In a conference on "Moslem Evangelism" held in 1936, they noted, "In many people's minds missionaries are regarded as political agents and are therefore now associated with the move to make Palestine a National Home for the Jews. A popular word for Protestant Christians is 'Inglesi' [English]."[38] Palestinian Episcopalians had always considered themselves to be an indivisible part of a Palestinian Arab polity; but now, the policies of both the mandate government and the British Anglican church had opened up a major breach between the Arab Episcopalian community and their Palestinian fellow citizens that appeared to be irreversible.

Some Palestinian Episcopalians responded with anti-British activity within the church. When the bishop tried to restart talks on a church constitution in 1938, the PNCC refused to participate on the grounds that "the present state of affairs in the country do not enable the Council to continue discussing the subject for the purpose of taking a resolution."[39] Members of the PNCC began to protest holding council meetings at the British Institute.[40] Jiryes Khoury, a town clerk in Haifa who took an active role in the PNCC during the 1940s, promoted the idea of breaking away from the Anglican church to form an Arab Protestant church outside the Anglican fold.[41]

These political maneuvers continued right up until the end of the mandate. In April 1947 the PNCC under the direction of its new chair Najib Quba'in (later to become the first Palestinian Arab bishop of Jordan, Lebanon, and Syria) unanimously agreed to send a telegram to the United Nations in New York, deploying Palestine's Christian history to call on Christians to support the Arab cause: "The PNCC meeting in Nazareth beseeches the U.N.O. in the name of Christianity and from the city of Christ to do justice in giving the Arabs of Palestine their National rights, to terminate the British mandate, to declare Palestine an independent country and to form a democratic Government immediately." At the PNCC meeting at Nazareth and at the United Missionary Conference in Beirut that same year, Quba'in and the other PNCC leaders demanded that the CMS turn over all its work (including schools, churches, charities, hospitals, and orphanages) to the PNCC, which would rename the CMS Mission the "Mission of the Church"; they appointed Habib Khoury, a retired government inspector, chair of a new committee on running all the church schools.[42] Nicola Saba and Suleiman Tannus ('Izzat Tannus's brother) lobbied the CMS to transfer its land, offices, and personnel to the PNCC and appoint a Palestinian Arab assistant bishop.[43]

But for many Arab Episcopalians, the damage was done. Rather than engage in further political activity through the church, they began to consider the more radical possibilities of conversion to Islam or emigration out of Palestine. One of Graham Brown's Palestinian Christian friends told the bishop that the idea of "accepting Islam was being much discussed . . . in his own house in the last week, Christians had said it was their opinion that they must face the possibility."[44] Marmura seconded this worry in a letter to Lambeth Palace, relating that that there was a movement of Arab Christians toward converting to Islam as a mode of joining in the nationalist movement: "Out of despair of obtaining justice and hearing from the greatest Christian government [they] urged Christians to unite with Moslems under the banner of Islam." He ascribed the idea of conversion to the policies of the British government, but also to the unwillingness of international Christian institutions to intervene on behalf of their coreligionists in Palestine. "They are shamed by their Moslem neighbors," he wrote, "that no Pope, Archbishop or Bishop has raised his voice against the Zionist ambitions, whereas all the Moslem kings and princes and religious leaders have done their utmost to help the Arab cause."[45] Although firm evidence is lacking on the question of precisely how many Palestinian Episcopalians may have converted to Islam, the frequency with which this theme occurs suggests that conversion to Islam had genuinely become a possible response to the situation in which the community found itself.

Even more appealing, at this stage, was the possibility of emigration. "The other possibility," Graham Brown's Palestinian friend told him, "emigration to some Christian country, was what he himself envisaged as the preferable course. Were America open for immigration, many of the Christians would go there happily. Another possible place was the new Lebanese Republic."[46] Nicola Saba, whose wife and children had lived for some years in London, tried to persuade the Arab Episcopal communities in the southern parts of Palestine to sell their lands and possessions and move en masse to Brazil.[47] The longstanding European connections, the Western schooling, and the multilingual educations many of these Arab Episcopalian leaders and congregants had received meant that emigration to Lebanon, the United States, or Europe was quite often a real possibility, one that became more attractive as Palestine descended into violence and the position of the Palestinian Arab Episcopalian community continued to decline.

Emigration became a central theme in the Palestinian Arab Christian historical narrative after 1948, when Christians began to emigrate out of the Palestinian territories at a rate twice that of the general population. In Jerusalem, the Christian population fell by more than half between 1948 and 1961, a trend that accelerated after the 1967 war and Israel's takeover of the West Bank and Gaza.[48] Christians now constitute less than 3 percent of the Palestinian Arab population in the occupied territories, down from more than 10 percent during the mandate period.[49] In Israel proper, the proportion of Christians in the Arab population fell from a high of 21 percent in 1950 to approximately 9 percent in 2003.[50] Many emigrants relocated to Jordan, particularly Amman, or to the Gulf states;

Palestinian Christians also formed large expatriate communities in Latin America (especially Chile and Honduras), Australia, and Canada.[51] Some went to Europe or the United States; by 2000, nearly three-quarters of the 1.2 million Arab-Americans counted identified themselves as Christian.[52] While these numbers include other Arab Christian communities, they are important for gauging the disposition of Palestinian Arab Episcopalians in the years following the revolt, and suggest that many began to consider emigration as the only possible response to their disillusionment with their church and their damaged standing within Palestinian society.[53]

Conclusion

For Palestinian Episcopalians, the revolt and the international debate over Palestine during the crucial years of 1936–39 led to a reexamination of their community's ties with both the Palestinian nationalist movement and their British parent church. The revolt set off a chain reaction with a number of unexpected consequences: the Palestinian use of Anglican church institutions and international fora as venues for an impassioned defense of Palestinian Arab nationalism; the British Anglican declaration that the protection of the Zionist cause was a Christian duty; alienation between Palestinian Episcopalians and the British missionary institutions that had converted them; and, eventually, at least a few Arab Episcopalians abandoning their faith altogether and converting to Islam as a declaration of Palestinian Arab identity, and many more emigrating to other Christian countries halfway around the world.

As a consequence of the momentous events of 1936–39, the Palestinian Episcopalian community, which had represented such a prominent and important part of Palestine's emerging middle classes, eventually dwindled to nearly nothing. Through the actions of its church leadership in the metropole and its ties to a seriously discredited mandate government, the British Anglican presence in Palestine undermined the political and social standing of its converts to the degree that they often felt obliged to abandon either their faith or their country. In the end, a century of Anglican missionary activity actually led to a substantial diminution of the numbers of Christians in Palestine.

4

Missionaries and Ethnography in the Service of Litigation

Hindu Law and Christian Custom in India's Deccan, 1750–1863

Chandra Mallampalli

> I am a Protestant Christian of the London Mission. I am a member
> of the class called Native Christians. Persons dressed like me are
> called by people Native Christians. . . . Our manners are like the
> Hindoos, but we conform to our religion in other matters. I do not
> conform to Hindu law in any matter.
>
> —Testimony of Plaintiff's 22nd witness, Jacob, son of
> Isaac, a Christian, aged 40 years, a book binder, and
> residing at Bellary

*I*n 1820, in the south-central plateau region of India known as the Deccan, Charlotte Fox, a woman of mixed British, Portuguese, and Indian ancestry, married Matthew Abraham.[1] Born a Roman Catholic *paraiyar* (the term applies to the many "untouchable" groups in South India and has entered the English lexicon as "pariah"), Matthew Abraham converted to Protestantism as an adult—first joining a Nonconformist church, later embracing Anglicanism. In Bellary, a town that was one of the Ceded Districts placed under British East India Company control, Matthew owned and operated a distillery and sold liquor to the European troops that were stationed in its cantonment.[2] His business flourished, and so did the family: Charlotte and Matthew had two sons, named Charles Henry and Daniel Vincent. In time, Matthew turned to his younger brother, Francis Abraham, for help in managing the distillery and enlisted him as a partner. But when Matthew died without a will in 1842, conflict arose between Charlotte and Francis as to who should be head of the household and therefore inherit Matthew's property and assets. Their arguments fundamentally hinged on assumptions about the definition of families under "English" and "Hindu" law.

This battle reached the courts in 1863 and resulted in a famous legal case: *Abraham v. Abraham*. Charlotte argued in court that by marrying her and adopting her English customs, Matthew, her Tamil *paraiyar* husband, had assimilated into her world—and into the world of the "East Indian" (also known as the "Anglo-Indian" or "Eurasian") community. English law should therefore decide the case in her favor. Francis rejoined that the family, while Christian, continued to adhere to some aspects of "native society," most notably the practice of undivided Hindu families. According to the Hindu law of inheritance, he reasoned, Francis and the two sons should inherit Matthew's wealth, while Charlotte, as a widow, should be entitled to mere maintenance in the family home. The two sides called nearly three hundred witnesses to testify concerning the family's cultural habits and those of families "similarly situated." The result was a massive production of ethnography about "native Christians," East Indians, and persons of "pure Hindoo blood." *Abraham v. Abraham* also involved Christian missionaries—or rather, it called upon the large, diverse, and at times contradictory body of "knowledge" that Protestant and Catholic missionaries had produced about "natives" of the region. This knowledge, which missionaries had often produced in the absence of (and not for the sake of) conversion, in turn reflected different perceptions of what conversion looked like and meant, and how (if at all) an individual's conversion changed or should change such things as familial caste customs.[3]

Most striking about the witnesses called by each side in court was the predominance of Protestants among Charlotte's witnesses and of Catholics for Francis. Charlotte's witnesses stressed the radical difference between East Indians (as mixed Indian-European hybrids) and all aspects of "native" or "Hindoo" society (including the habits of Native Christians). They insisted that Matthew Abraham, in spite of his "pure Hindoo blood," had *become* an East Indian by converting to Protestantism and assimilating into Charlotte's world. Francis's witnesses, by contrast, consisted largely of low-caste converts to Catholicism as well as other Indians who observed caste practices. Like his brother, Francis had become a Protestant as an adult. In court, however, he drew upon his family's Catholic origins in order to make a case for his enduring Indianness. He freely admitted that he had embraced many European customs, but maintained that he and Matthew were "Hindoo Christians" who shared property like brothers of a Hindu undivided family.

Again, the arguments each side produced in court were not invented ex nihilo but drew from a history of missionary encounters with South Indian society. Early nineteenth-century British evangelicals to South India tended to regard conversion as requiring the severance of converts from "idolatry" and "superstitions."[4] In some instances, they also called upon converts to renounce their caste identity in the name of their new Christian one.[5] Catholics to a greater degree appreciated continuities between Catholicism and local culture. This approach is traceable to the work of the seventeenth-century Jesuit missionary Robert de Nobili (1577–1656), who embraced the culture of Tamil Brahmins and honored their caste traditions in his work among them.[6] Later Jesuits in South India continued de Nobili's culturally accommodating missionary policy in spite of facing opposition from the Vatican.

Pleaders for Charlotte and Francis organized and simplified missionary encounters in ways that advanced their own legal agendas. In the process their arguments often seemed to "distill" discrete Protestant and Catholic views of conversion, suggesting a Catholic emphasis on ritual and sacrament, along with tolerance toward extant tradition, versus a Protestant tendency to emphasize word over ritual (i.e., a logocentrism) and to encourage converts to break away from prior, ostensibly non-Christian, customs. Yet, the actual history of missionary practice and discourse in the Deccan was far more complex and indeed more ambiguous than the witnesses' testimony would suggest.

Herein rest the most unexpected aspects of this Abraham affair as it related to missionary encounters in the Deccan. Through their ethnographic production of "knowledge," missionaries inadvertently provided ammunition for those waging battles over issues of law, family, custom, and caste. The Abraham case made witnesses into "experts" with the power to advance their own individual, often idiosyncratic, understandings of the social transformations that religious choices set rolling. Equally unexpected was the way the Abraham case made law courts—and not missionaries—into arbiters for gauging the meaning and extent of conversion, with consequences for social identity and legal status.

This study considers, in turn, two pools of sources—two sites of knowledge production—that factored into this Abraham family feud. It considers, first, the extensive contemporary writings produced by (and in some cases also about) three missionaries (two Catholics and one Protestant) who were active in the Deccan, whose social circles overlapped, and whose lives directly or indirectly impinged upon the Abraham family. The study examines, second, the District Court records of *Abraham v. Abraham* (1863) and the 104 witness depositions preserved therein. These records make it possible to reconstruct the case of *Abraham v. Abraham* in light of missionary ethnographic production. The essay concludes by assessing the verdict, or more accurately, the verdicts that were issued on the case and the uncertainties they reveal about family life and Christian culture in a very complicated, quickly changing, social terrain.

The Missionaries and Their "Knowledge"

Three missionaries have a bearing on this Abraham family story. The first was John Hands, a British London Missionary Society (LMS) missionary in Bellary, who played a direct role in converting Matthew from Catholicism to dissenting (non-Anglican) Protestantism. The second was Jean Antoine Dubois, the distinguished French Catholic missionary to Mysore. The third was Patrick Doyle, an Irish Catholic missionary to Bellary, who knew the Abrahams and sustained a relationship with Francis in particular. Doyle is the one missionary in this story who became directly involved in the family dispute: he eventually tried to effect an out-of-court settlement between Charlotte and Francis. While there is no record of Hands ever meeting Doyle (for indeed Doyle arrived in Bellary in 1840, by which time Hands had already returned to England), Hands did write about his meeting with Dubois during one of his visits to Mysore. Hands, Dubois, and Doyle shared the dream of making converts—albeit with varying degrees of optimism—but the work of all three required practical adaptations to the local, pluralistic societies of the Deccan.[7]

Hands, Dubois, and Doyle followed a common pattern of redirecting their missionary vision into what is fashionably referred to as "knowledge production."[8] To one extent or another, they compiled information about Indian society. While it is tempting to regard this as being only in the service of conversion, the following discussion will show how knowledge production often occurred in the absence of conversion or in response to Indian resistance. Dubois, as Nicolas Dirks has observed, was responsible for bringing ethnographic data about caste to the attention of the East India Company.[9] He also wrote a highly polemical (and pessimistic) tract on the futility of trying to convert Hindus to Christianity.[10] In one of the Madras district gazetteers, Doyle authored a section on Sandur, one of the princely states near the Ceded Districts in which Bellary was located. And Hands, while not an ethnographer in any formal sense, translated portions of the New Testament into Kannada and provided sketches of the Hindu and Islamic heritage of various *taluks* (units of revenue collection, comprising a district) in reports that he sent to the LMS Secretary.

The following section briefly summarizes the ethnographic writings of Hands, Dubois, and Doyle, which in turn informed the types of knowledge that witnesses invoked in *Abraham v. Abraham*. Next, the essay will examine the court testimony, particularly depositions that comment on the nature of Hindu and Christian identities vis-à-vis cultural habits and rituals. From this we can observe how the "official knowledge" generated in court simplified more complex negotiations of difference articulated even by missionaries like Hands, Dubois, and Doyle who were professionally committed to the idea of conversion.

John Hands and the LMS in Bellary

In 1810 John Hands initiated the work of the London Missionary Society (LMS) in Bellary, after his earlier effort to start work in Srirangapatnam (just outside of Mysore) had foundered.[11] In 1811 Hands applied for and eventually obtained a plot of land in order to establish a school for the education of "country born and native youth."[12] The land was in close proximity to the Bellary Fort, inhabited primarily by British soldiers and their families, and to Bruce Pettah, a township occupied primarily by Indian shop owners.[13] In addition to these two parts of Bellary, Hands also conducted services at a church in Cowl Bazaar, a commercial area where Indians enjoyed tax-exempt status for the services provided for the troops.

Shortly after arriving in India, Hands committed himself to the study of Kannada. By 1811, he was holding services in Kannada; by 1812, he had finished a Kannada grammar and a partial translation of the New Testament.[14] Hands's work consisted of both congregational and itinerant preaching. At his church in Bruce Pettah, Hands oversaw both Kannada- and Tamil-speaking congregations. While he preached to the Kannada group, he employed Indian catechists to conduct services among the Tamils. The Tamil Christians consisted primarily of camp followers. Many had migrated from Madras and its vicinity to find a livelihood by serving Bellary's cantonment.[15] Although Hands was a Dissenter, he preached occasionally to the "English congregation" at Trinity Church, the Anglican Church in the Fort.[16] Hands thus labored among residents of the Bellary Fort, Bruce Pettah, and Cowl Bazaar, corresponding to Europeans and East Indians, Indian shop owners, and service providers.[17]

Missionaries of the LMS tended to regard the Kannada parishioners as being of a higher class than the Tamils. This is evident not only in references to Tamil "servants" and "camp followers" but also in the moral critique leveled by John Reid, the missionary who in 1828 replaced Hands in Bellary. Reid described the Kannadas (or Canarese) as possessing "more candor and more decision in them" and as a people who, "if brought under the influence of divine grace, would be a noble race." By contrast, he described the Tamils as deceitful and driven by self-interest.[18] This distinction echoed Reid's persistent complaints about the depraved spiritual condition of Bellary's population as a whole and of the "duplicitous native character."[19]

British colonial officials in Bellary, as in other districts ruled by the East India Company, were well aware of the potentially disruptive consequences of missionary work. During the 1820s, Thomas Munro, the Principal Collector of the Ceded Districts, had to dismiss one of his Sub Collectors, John Allen Dalzell, for engaging in evangelistic activities in his capacity as a government servant. According to Munro, Dalzell had been distributing "Canarese [Kannada] versions of parts of the New Testament, and . . . Tracts in the same language on moral and religious subjects. They were distributed to the Reddies/Potails/Curnams (i.e., Panchayat members/village heads/accountants), Merchants, and Rayets (*ryots*, or individual cultivators of land) with whom he had intercourse."[20] Quite likely, Dalzell had received these materials from Hands (or other LMS missionaries), though Munro did not mention Hands in his minutes.

While Dalzell did not use direct compulsion, he used something very much like it. According to Munro, this amounted to "open interference, official agency, the hope of favors, the fear of displeasure [even though] the people, he says, 'could have no difficulty in distinguishing between a matter of authority and of option.'" Munro concluded that "there can be no real freedom of choice, where official authority is interested deeply, and exerted openly . . . [and when most people perceive him] to serve the general measure of conversion."[21]

As principal collector, Munro's chief responsibility was to assess lands and create conditions for the steady collection of revenue. His sensitivity to the plight of *ryots* and advocacy for their land tenure rights is well documented. What we see in these minutes, however, is a highly nuanced statement about the use of state power for purposes of religious conversion.[22] This illustrates Munro's commitment to "noninterference" in cultural or religious affairs within the newly acquired Ceded Districts.

This climate of sensitivity made Hands and his associates more aware of the implications of introducing a missionary agenda into any presumably neutral activities, especially those receiving state assistance. Sometime around 1812, he tried to introduce more explicitly Christian instruction in his school. This elicited a strong reaction among the students and their families, and many of them withdrew in protest.[23]

The highly charged nature of religious conversion also made Hands and his LMS colleagues keen observers of religious customs and students of the historical landscape. They included in their travel accounts historical details of each region. They usually enclosed these details, however, in an evangelical narrative that described the "pagan" local history giving way to the light of Christianity. In some instances, LMS missionaries seemed content merely to gain an audience with someone of notoriety or status, such as the raja of Mysore. This pattern is evident in accounts of their visit in 1817 to Mysore and the neighboring town of Srirangapatnam. Before 1799 when the East India Company had conquered this region, Mysore was a Hindu domain ruled roughly for forty years by the Muslim Haider Ali and his son, Tipu Sultan. After the company defeated Tipu, it reinstated the Wodeyar dynasty by designating as king Krishnawodeyar III, then only age four. During his seventy-year tenure, Mysore was a tributary regime of the East India Company.

En route to Mysore, Hands, accompanied by the Reverend William Reeve (also with the LMS), stopped in Harpenahalli to interview its raja. Reeve's account of this visit highlights the ritual authority of the raja and the extensive courtesies the raja extended to them upon arrival. The raja offered to sponsor a hunting trip for them, providing "dogs, guns, horses, etc." and offered to provide servants to "lead them in the fields of sport and amusement." Seated in an English chair and "surrounded by his courtiers and principal officers of state," the raja chatted with the missionaries, but seemed more interested in the "arts and sciences" of the West than in hearing about the gospel.[24] After their conversation, the raja offered to host them for another several days, but they declined. Upon leaving, the raja "took them by the hand" and presented them with "the usual presents of rose water, beetle nut, spices, etc."[25]

While in Srirangapatnam, Hands described in detail the mosques constructed by Tipu Sultan along with the mausoleum of Tipu's father, Haider Ali. Only twenty years before, the British had finally captured and killed Tipu, imprisoned his sons, and taken control of Srirangapatnam and Mysore. Hands visited the palaces, mosques, forts, and gardens once belonging to Haider and Tipu. These he described in greater detail than one might expect in a letter directed to his LMS headquarters. Hands marveled at the towering minarets and domed structures, while also noting the *madrasas* in which Muslim boys were taught the Koran. Because most of the boys spoke Kannada, Hands took it upon himself to tell them about the Christian gospel.[26]

Hands then went to the palace of Haider Ali and the tombs of Tipu, Haider, and Haider's wife. Captain Moorehouse, the superintendent of a gun carriage manufactory in Mysore, accompanied him. The details with which he described the courtly spectacle conveyed his own sense of awe:

> Each of these courts is open in the front, and has galleries in the inner side, where Hyder sat to give audience, transact business, and amuse himself with those exhibitions which form so considerable a part of the amusements of Indian princes. Some of the walls, ceilings, and pillars, are painted in a very fanciful style. Of the apartments some still retain a portion of their original beauty, but parts thereof are fallen down, and, probably, a few more years will bring the whole of it to the ground.[27]

Hands maintained a similar tenor of appreciation in his elaborate descriptions of the tombs. This, however, he followed with commentary on the "transitory nature of all earthly glory" and on the judgment that had fallen upon Haider and his lineage.[28]

Throughout his visits to various sites including mosques, Hands stressed his readiness to share his Christian message, both orally and through the distribution of tracts. Upon his second visit to Haider's mosque, he gave a copy of Henry Martyn's Persian New Testament to his host, and to the schoolmaster a Hindustani New Testament. Later he would lament that the raja of Mysore, Krishnaraja Wodeyar III, to whom he also gave copies, could read neither Persian nor Hindustani.[29]

Upon meeting the raja, Hands again provided thick description of palace life and architecture. Along with references to the rare trees in his garden and the ornately sculpted chambers of the palace, Hands detailed the boxing matches, ram and buffalo fights, and other "barbarous spectacles" that captivated audiences at the palace complex.[30] He was observant enough to make note of the Hindu festival of Dasara, which, he stated, "is in no part of India celebrated so expensively as at the court of the Mysore Raja."[31] The raja received them seated on a throne richly ornamented with pearls and precious stones. Here again, after seeming to lose himself in the details of the raja's courtly decor, Hands criticized the raja for being more drawn to the "pleasures of the zenana [the women's quarters]" than to higher pursuits. He blamed the raja's coterie of "unprincipled and crafty Brahmin" advisers for steering the substantial state revenues toward the construction of their pagodas and patronage of their ritual authority.[32]

These travel narratives illustrate how LMS missionaries to the Deccan, in spite of being committed to the goal of converting Hindus and Muslims, paid attention to their surroundings and were mindful—in however shallow or prejudiced a manner—of the histories of these regions. Theirs was not a tunnel vision that lumped all of the "unsaved" together, but rather their view was one that partook, at least to some degree, in the give and take of ritual honor, hospitality, and status differentials within both Hindu and Islamic polities.

But what do we make of Hands's reference to the "unprincipled and crafty Brahmins"? From where did he derive this impression of their role in corrupting regimes and perhaps even in impeding the spread of the gospel?

John Hands meets J. A. Dubois

John Hands was stationed at Bellary, which as a dry zone did not recognize caste distinctions or Brahminical authority to the extent of the more fertile agricultural districts. According to the *Madras Gazetteer*, Brahmins of Bellary did not occupy a separate neighborhood or *agraharam*, were more secular in their outlook, and often employed Muslims as household servants.[33] Hence, occasional references of Hands and Reeve to "crafty Brahmins" possibly drew upon a discourse from Mysore or other princely domains, where Brahmins enjoyed the patronage of the state and enhanced its ritual authority. It was to Mysore, after all, that Hands was originally commissioned before being transferred to Bellary.

While in Mysore, Hands met the French Catholic missionary Jean Antoine Dubois. Dubois came to India after the outbreak of the French

Revolution with the aim of propagating Catholicism among South Indians. Initially, he worked with the Pondicherry Mission, but after the fall of Srirangapatnam he went to Mysore. It was in Mysore primarily that Dubois developed his views on Indian caste, the role of Brahmins, and the futility of attempting to convert the Hindus. Dubois's anti-Brahminical discourse, while not the first of its kind, appears to have directly influenced Hands.

Jesuits had been working in Mysore since 1649, when the Italians Leonardo Cinnami and Fortunato Serafini had arrived at Srirangapatnam from Goa. Like the Jesuits of the Madurai Mission (located in present-day Tamil Nadu state), these Jesuits employed a strategy of cultural adaptation. They embraced the customs and veneer of learned Brahmins (as spiritual teachers) in order to find their niche among the elites of Mysore.[34] Over the next century, they and their successors experienced varying degrees of tolerance from the Wodeyar kings who ruled Mysore. During the middle of the seventeenth century, Jesuit missionaries reportedly made some 1,700 converts, chiefly among Tamils (only a quarter were Kannada-speaking).[35] Their reports also described instances of persecution by the Wodeyar state. Some, like Cinnami, were expelled and others imprisoned. By the turn of the eighteenth century, Jesuits had become keen observers of Wodeyar politics by way of such mixed experiences.

Sanjay Subrahmanyam has noted how Jesuits became students and chroniclers of other "non-religious" spheres of activity in Mysore. "Lacking the intellectual stimulus of the Madurai mission," he wrote, and "lacking too the extensive religious activity which characterized the coastal missionary settlements, the Jesuit in Mysore occupied himself with collecting and digesting the rumours of the bazaar, which in turn centred above all on the military and political activities of the region, in order to construct a form of 'political ethnography.'"[36]

Again, this was not knowledge in the service of conversion, but in its absence. The religious impenetrability of Mysore society resulted in greater effort by Jesuits to understand its politics, perhaps to secure a more stable existence.[37] This scrutiny of the state resulted in the Jesuits' negative regard for the role of Brahmins. According to the account of Joachim Dias, who lived in the Hassan district of western Mysore, Brahmins wielded considerable influence as advisers of kings and as those who controlled fiscal records and information about military stores. It was chiefly in their administrative, not ritual, roles that Brahmins, according to Dias, held most of their power in eighteenth-century Mysore.[38]

In contrast to this earlier Jesuit tradition, Dubois stressed the ritual and philosophical power of Brahmins. It was in their role as guardians of custom, embodied in the caste order, that they most impeded the spread of Christianity.[39] Dubois's narrative carries a somewhat paradoxical relationship to the Jesuit strategy of cultural adaptation. He credits, on the one hand, early Jesuit accommodations to local customs, but criticizes, on the other, Brahmins for making such accommodations necessary. Brahmins had solidified custom by means of their knowledge, ritual authority over other castes, and access to state power.

Dubois's treatise on Hindu customs and practices stresses the Brahminical orientation toward the body and its cleanliness. This consciousness pervades restrictions concerning contact with corpses or other articles such as dishes, clothing, or cooking vessels, which could be polluted through the mere touch of lower-caste members or non-Hindus.[40] Even cotton "is unfortunately subject to contract impurity from the touch of persons of an inferior cast [sic], and particularly by that of pariahs or Europeans. A Brahman who piques himself on his delicacy, shews in a case of this kind, a thousand squeamish tricks, and in the intercourse of life is obliged to move under perpetual constraint."[41] Hindu homes underwent daily purification rituals because of defilement from occasional visits from outsiders. Contact with a *pariah* was among the worst sources of pollution and accounted for their constant efforts to retain physical distance from them.[42] Dubois extended this ethnography concerning Brahminical practices into his treatment of other castes and into his appraisal of Jesuit missionary policies.

By virtue of their accommodating approach to Indian culture, the first Jesuits, according to Dubois, had made tens of thousands of converts within various districts of South India. Eventually members of other Catholic orders, suspicious of Jesuit accommodations to "idolatrous superstitions," reported them to the Vatican. Pope Benedict the XIV (1675–1758) invited the Jesuits to explain their cultural policies. Unconvinced by their account, he ordered them to desist from all "superstitious practices." Afterward, huge numbers of converts abandoned the faith and Christianity became steadily less tolerated by Hindus and Muslims alike.[43] Tipu Sultan, Dubois reports, gave secret orders to escort 60,000 Christians to Srirangapatnam to undergo mass circumcision and conversion to Islam. Dubois lamented that all had apostatized and none had become martyrs.[44]

This account, while initially conveying sympathy for Jesuit methods, devolved into a polemical assault on South Indians for being addicted to their customs and impervious to foreign influence. The chief culprits behind this adherence to custom were Brahmins:

> An Hindoo, and above all, a Brahmin, by his institutions, his usages, his education and customs, must be considered as a kind of moral monster, as an individual placed in a state of continual variance and opposition with the rest of the human race. . . . The crafty Brahmins (in order that the system of imposture that establishes their unmolested superiority over the other tribes, and brings the latter under their uncontrolled bondage, might in no way be discovered or questioned) had the foresight to draw up between the Hindoos and the other nations on earth an impassable, and impregnable line, that defies all attacks from foreigners.[45]

The impact of Brahminical authority and knowledge upon the spread of Christianity for Dubois was clear. Brahmins infected every layer of society with caste feeling and animosity, the antithesis of Christian love. Only those who thrived beyond the pale of Brahminical influence would consider becoming Christian. Hence, converts did not hail from the more "respected" classes, but only from among those outcasts who had played the most servile and marginal roles in society. Dubois even went so far as to cast doubt on whether such conversions were genuine.[46]

Dubois's explanation of the state of Indian society needs to be situated within a Catholic tradition of local knowledge production. Though he criticized Indians for their adherence to custom, he was critically engaged with caste as a dimension of Indian life, as were Jesuit missionaries of the Madurai mission. This focus on caste is also what placed him in an ambiguous relationship with Protestants. Protestants shared his antipathy for local customs and "idolatrous superstitions," but never reached Dubois's conclusion that they made conversion "impracticable."

Protestant evangelicals saw in Hindu "idolatry and superstition" a reflection of the "popish customs" of Catholicism. The veneration of images, wearing of the *tali* (the sacred thread worn by Brahmins and other upper castes), and smearing of ashes on the forehead were customs seen among Tamil Hindus and Catholic converts alike. The LMS missionaries adopted an alternative cultural policy that was logocentric (centered upon the written and spoken word, in contrast to ritual or sacrament) and intent on extricating converts from their original matrix of beliefs and customs.

In his 1824 rebuttal of Dubois, James Hough, the chaplain to the East India Company in Madras, contrasted the simplicity of Protestant worship with the pomp of Catholic festivals and ritual.[47] He criticized Dubois for "indulg[ing] their proselytes in their use of superstitions" while at the same time maintaining that the "Hindoo's prejudices are insurmountable."[48] Protestants, he argued, struck the correct balance by translating the Bible into Indian languages and training Indian catechists, while also insisting that converts abandon all vestiges of "paganism." Hough's arguments echo those of John Hands, who during his 1822 visit to Goa lamented the heritage of the Inquisition and the ornate ritual of Catholic worship. "To one who has seen the spacious and glittering temples of Goa, the gaudy vestments of its priests, and the pomp and parade of its worship," he writes, "it cannot appear surprising that such numbers of poor Hindoos, who are so fond of noise and show, should have been brought over so quickly from Paganism to Popery."[49]

As much as he shared this Protestant antipathy for Catholic ritual and accommodation, Hands took great pleasure in meeting Dubois during his 1817 visit to Mysore. He found in Dubois someone who had diagnosed the illnesses of Hindu society in ways that confirmed his own Protestant convictions. For Hands, solidarity in the plight against Hindu intransigence formed the basis of interfaith cooperation. While Dubois had not yet published his tract concerning the state of Christianity, he must have disseminated his views by other means, because Hands recounted them clearly in his 1817 journal: "He regards the obstacles which oppose the progress of

Christianity insuperable, and imagines the Hindoos are entirely rejected of God."[50]

Hands described Dubois as a "venerable looking old man, with a long flowing beard," who "appears to possess much more liberality than is usually found in the Church of Rome." Dubois had "adopted most of the customs of the Hindoos, in respect to dress, diet, etc."[51] When Hands visited Dubois's church in Sahur Ganjam (near Mysore), he observed his observance of local customs:

> He entered the church in a pair of wooden clogs; thus conforming to the prejudices of the Hindoos, who consider it as very unsuitable to enter a place of worship with shoes or sandals on. I expected that I should have been required to take off my shoes; but this was dispensed with. About 200 persons, men, women and children, were present. A chair was placed for l'Abbe on an elevation, in front of the altar, which was decorated with flowers, candles, and all the vanity of popish finery.[52]

Because of his grasp of the Kannada language, Hands consulted Dubois for advice regarding his own translations of New Testament texts into Kannada. He and Dubois disagreed, however, over the importance of Bible translation for the conversion of Hindus. Hands supplied Dubois with tracts, four gospels in Marathi, and abundant information about the progress of Protestant missions in various parts of India. This indicated that the two had sustained a substantial conversation about conversion.

This sketch of Hands's work in Bellary and his travels to Mysore and Goa illustrates the eclectic participation to which he was inevitably drawn as a resident of this complex region. Instead of remaining enclosed within a tightly sealed "mission compound" and fixated on his own agenda, he was compelled to become an avid observer of kings and their courtly lives, of linguistic groups, of class and racial differences, and of Roman Catholic influence in South India. Yet, one more aspect of Hands's work requires discussion, namely, his conversion of Matthew Abraham.

One might ask why the conversion of this Roman Catholic *paraiyar* should occupy a significant place within the larger story of Hands's involvement in Bellary. Minimally, it illustrates Hands's interest in converting not only Hindus and Muslims but also "nominal" Indian Catholics to Evangelicalism. More significantly, his role in making Matthew Abraham a Protestant ended up playing a pivotal role in deciding the case concerning his property. Among the issues raised in *Abraham v. Abraham* (1863) was which knowledge base, Protestant or Roman Catholic, would form the basis of Christian personal law in India.

Hands and the Abraham Family

When he was not preaching to various congregations in Bellary or paying visits to neighboring towns, John Hands met individually with persons interested in learning more about the Christian religion. A few of the converts he mentions in his reports to the LMS went on to become catechists or evangelists. Hands made no mention, however, of Matthew Abraham the distiller, who met with him routinely to receive religious instruction. In fact, we must note the striking contrast between Matthew's conversion narrative, derived from legal records, and other conversion narratives recorded in the writings of Hands and other LMS missionaries. All of them tell stories of transformation; but while some describe a shift from paganism (or "Romish" ritualism) to Christian piety and an account of suffering for the gospel, Matthew's story is that of a *paraiyar* Roman Catholic who converts to Protestantism and rises economically as a Bellary entrepreneur.

To illustrate the contrast, we need only examine the account of Samuel Flavel, who came from a *sudra*[53] Hindu family from Malabar. Flavel spent much of his life working as a butler for various English officers and eventually came into contact with the LMS in Bangalore and Bellary. He followed a series of officers to different regions of South India, Ceylon, and Mauritius. In Ceylon, a Tamil camp follower had left behind a Tamil translation of the Bible. Flavel read the text with great interest, but never seems to have found any missionary to expound its meaning.[54] Filled with conviction from his study of the Bible and newfound faith in Christ, he combined his work as a butler with his new role as a preacher of the word.

A prominent theme in the account of Flavel's conversion is the hostility he encountered from Roman Catholics. During his preaching

engagements in South India, Flavel seems to have encountered more hostility from Catholics than from Hindus or Muslims. While in Mysore,
he was physically assaulted by Catholics who resented his encroachment
upon their domains. Their hostility was so severe that he required the
intervention of local authorities. Flavel knew of Dubois and cited his towering influence in Mysore as a chief reason for why he eventually left the
region.[55] In search of another place where he could conduct his baptisms
without fear of reprisals from Catholics, he went to Bangalore where he
came under the influence of Stephen Laidler of the LMS. He then went
to Bellary where he met John Hands.

After reaching Bellary in 1827, Flavel became acquainted with its
Tamil camp-follower population. Hands invited him to the pulpit and formally entrusted the LMS Tamil congregation to his care.[56] Many of the
Tamil parishioners were camp followers and members of a native cavalry
regiment stationed at Bellary. They came from different castes and religious origins:

> [The Tamil church members] were chiefly servants and camp followers.
> Some of them had been Heathens, and others of them Roman Catholics,
> differing from the Heathen, in naught that tends to elevate and purify:—
> no very promising material of which to build God's holy temple. The
> Church and Congregation were to form the nucleus of Samuel's future
> labours; but the Farriers and Musicians of the Native regiments stationed
> here, with that "mixed multitude" from the different classes of Indian soci-
> ety, ever found in our Military cantonments—the Hindoo, the Moham-
> medan, the Romanist, and those empty professors of a purer creed, who
> exhibit scarcely a purer morality,—were to share, as time and strength
> might be afforded him, in his self-denying efforts for the good of souls.[57]

The conversion narrative of Flavel is marked by its sharp distinctions between adherents of the true Protestant faith and those of Roman or Hindu
"paganism." In spite of these distinctions, we gain a sense of Bellary's "mixed
multitude" and the need for this native convert to come to terms with it.

In contrast to Flavel's classically Evangelical conversion narrative, that
of Matthew Abraham, gleaned from sparse references of witnesses provided in the court case, is oriented chiefly to his cultural transformation

from being a "Native" to supposedly becoming an "East Indian." Here, indeed, is where the depositions recorded from *Abraham v. Abraham* become most valuable.

The depositions suggest that, as a single adult, Matthew Abraham met with Hands regularly in the chapel at Cowl Bazaar. He eventually joined the Bellary Mission Church of the LMS, a dissenting or non-Anglican church. Occasionally he was asked like Flavel to "conduct a religious service for a short period (on a week day) in the Mission house for the servants in the Tamil language."[58] While no explanation is given for why Matthew eventually abandoned these duties and left the mission church, these events seem to have coincided with Flavel's arrival in 1827 and Matthew's mounting duties as a vendor of *abkari* (i.e., liquor and other intoxicating substances) that began the same year.[59] In any case, depositions show that witnesses in court registered Matthew's turn or "conversion" to the Protestantism of the LMS mission as more of a process, not an event, and moreover as a process leading to a change of community that gained expression as much through dress and comportment.

The most frequent references to the conversion of both Matthew and his brother Francis to Protestantism came from Charlotte's witnesses. These references, however, were framed not merely as a change in religious convictions, but as one facet of their assimilation into Bellary's East Indian community. One witness, Frederick Seymour, for instance, knew Matthew's father while he was employed as a Mess Butler and became acquainted with Matthew just as he was coming under the influence of the LMS:

> When I first knew Matthew Abraham he was undergoing religious instruction under Mr. Hands and others, and I constantly met him in the Chapel in the petta [abbreviation for the section of town called Bruce Pettah]. Mr. Hands was a Dissenting Missionary. Matthew Abraham was then in his noviciate and was dressed in plain linen clothes, and was constantly seen at the Chapel. His appearance at the time did not indicate the possession of any property whatever. His father was generally called Abraham. He was pointed out to me as the father of the Convert from the Roman Catholic faith who used to attend the chapel.[60]

Seymour's testimony is significant because he knew Matthew before and after he "joined" the East Indian community. He dated his conversion around the year 1813, but offered no explanation as to what his motivations might have been. Just before he spoke of Matthew's work with Hands, Seymour had discussed Matthew's father's drinking habit, disease, and dismissal from his job with the cantonment mess. From this we may only speculate that Matthew's movement into Protestantism may have had something to do with a sense of shame in his father and a desire to shape a very different future for himself.

The LMS missionary, William Howell, had been a member of a mission church at Madras. He worked in Bellary until he was appointed in 1822 to start a Telugu Mission at the neighboring district of Cuddapah.[61] As a retired missionary, Howell testified in court about Matthew's appearance and customs. For witnesses such as Howell, Matthew's adoption of Western clothes was just as radical a break from his past as becoming a Protestant Dissenter.[62] Most likely, Matthew adopted the Western dress between 1818 and 1820.[63] Implied both in the questions posed to Howell and his replies were cultural assumptions about Protestant identity, which included frequent references to work ethic and dress:

> Q. What were Matthew Abraham's character and habits, with reference to business, were they such as would naturally lead to the acquisition of property?
>
> A. He was a man of steady character and well adapted to habits of business so as to become a man of property.
>
> Q. Do you recollect Matthew Abraham's leaving off the Native costume, and assuming the European dress?
>
> A. Yes, I do recollect very well.
>
> Q. What was it that led him to take this step?
>
> A. His intention in doing so was, I think, to make a respectable appearance to move into the society of Europeans.
>
> Q. Did he afterwards formally renounce the Roman Catholic religion, and embrace the Protestant faith; and under what auspices was this done?
>
> A. Yes, under the Missionaries of the London Missionary Society.

Q. Was any point raised on the occasion of his marriage with reference to the East Indian Community of Bellary? If so, please to state what it was and how it was disposed of?

A. There was an objection raised, but it was overruled, by the East Indian community at Bellary agreeing to admit him and his wife into the Society.

Q. With what class of the community did he thenceforward identify himself, and to what customs and usages did he conform in all matters without exception?

A. He identified himself as an East Indian and followed all the customs and usages etc., of the East Indian community without exception.[64]

Much is revealed in the above exchange not only about the defining values of Bellary's East Indians but also, by implication, what "Indian" characteristics must look like. Testimonies such as Howell's constructed a binary that defined East Indians (and Europeans) by values of industry, thrift, individualism, and Western dress and Indians by social inertia, caste consciousness, and "native" religiosity and dress.

Depositions from Charlotte's witnesses also focused on whether conversion constituted a clean break from Hindu society or a selective appropriation of features from multiple cultural domains. In keeping with a Protestant tradition stressing discontinuities with local custom, the examination embraced an "all or nothing" approach:

Q. Do people, who are in their own persons converts from one system to another of a totally opposite nature, usually keep up the most marked and characteristic feature of the old system that they have abandoned, in the most important affairs of life, and conform to the new one only in minor points; or does their zeal as converts generally induce them to cast off every vestige of the former, and to adhere rigidly to the latter in all things?

A. With reference to caste converts to Christianity, I do not think they do abandon all their former customs and practices.

Q. Have you ever known or heard of a class or individual in this country who, while adhering to the social customs and usages of a totally distinct class, (whichsoever) in all the other circumstances of life, still avowedly adheres to Hindoo Law, as such, in one solitary matter?[65]

Charlotte's case therefore rested on critical distinctions between core and peripheral aspects of Hindu customs. If Francis were "Hindu" in the eyes of the law, he would have to have demonstrated a comprehensive adherence to "Hindu" customs and habits.[66]

Further complicating this exploration of "native customs" among converts was the issue of race. The Abraham brothers were, in the eyes of the court, persons of "pure native blood," who married women of "mixed blood." Charlotte argued that her East Indian community included people like Matthew, who were racially Indian, but culturally English. The questions advanced by her attorney suggested that the desire to assimilate was actually stronger among persons of pure Indian ancestry.

> Q. Are they [East Indians] or are they not members of a class whose strongest desire is to assimilate themselves to European manners, customs and usages in *all* matters, without exception and to avoid even the semblance of similarity to natives, in any matter whatsoever?
> A. I believe that is the case.
> Q. Is this feeling weaker or stronger in persons answering to the description given in No. 2 of these Interrogatories, who happen to be the children of parents of pure native blood and are thus interlopers, as it were, in a class composed principally of persons of mixed European and native blood?
> A. I believe it is.
> Q. Do even natives consider such persons, as belonging to their own body, or do they regard them as belonging to a totally distinct community from themselves?
> A. I believe they consider them belonging to their own body.[67]

By this reasoning, Matthew's status as an "interloper" in Charlotte's community made him all the more eager to embrace English customs and all the less likely to have abided by the Hindu law of inheritance.

Patrick Doyle: The Case for Continuity

From 1840 to 1877, Patrick Doyle conducted extensive missionary work among Telugu-, Tamil-, and Kannada-speaking people in and around

Bellary District. In spite of the breadth of his impact in the Ceded Districts, his work is largely overlooked in literature on Indian Catholicism. In fact, relatively little is known about Catholic origins in Bellary. This is largely because Bellary, a hinterland district, is located roughly the same distance from Goa to the west and Mysore to the south, two regions receiving more attention because of their more active Catholic orders. From the little written about Bellary's Catholics in the government gazetteers and other sources, it appears that well before the nineteenth century, French Jesuits from Mysore and Portuguese Franciscans and Carmelites from Goa had both visited Bellary.[68]

While it is uncertain to which order, if any, Doyle belonged, we know that in 1837 Bellary was transferred from the jurisdiction of Goa to that of the Vicar Apostolic of Madras. The transition was a turbulent one and Doyle's involvement in the ordeal displayed his loyalties to Madras. Shortly after Doyle's arrival, the newly appointed archbishop at Goa tried to bring Bellary back under his jurisdiction by sending Fulgence Perozy (who had been the priest at Bellary since 1828) to the chapel in Bellary's Fort. Doyle intervened by locking up the chapel to keep Perozy out. When the case went to court, Doyle successfully proved that the East India Company had given the site of the Fort chapel to the Catholics of Bellary, who had financed it with local resources.[69]

With very few assistants, Doyle covered an immense area on horseback, which included Bellary, Kurnool, Cuddapah, and Mugdal. He conducted mass at chapels in the Fort, in Cowl Bazaar, and in the neighboring *taluk*, or tax district, of Adoni. Shortly after he arrived, he started a school in Cowl Bazaar.[70] According to his own report of 1845, there were 2,400 Catholics in Bellary. In the neighboring district of Cuddapah, Doyle had registered 200 baptisms.[71] So popular was Doyle among his converts that he was referred to as "Dayananda" (father of mercy).[72]

Doyle arrived in Bellary in 1840, only two years before Matthew Abraham's death. By then, Matthew had made yet another conversion, from being a Protestant Dissenter under the LMS's tutelage to joining the Church of England. While Doyle's contact with Mathew was at best minimal, he maintained a relationship with Francis. Francis had financed the education of the son of his cousin, Chouriah, at a Catholic school in

Bellary. He used to send money to a Catholic priest, most likely Doyle, to be allocated for the boy's education. Doyle knew of the rupture between Charlotte and Francis, and was asked after the suit was filed to help reconcile their relationship.

In spite of having joined the Church of England as an adult, Francis drew heavily upon his family's Roman Catholic roots.[73] Because Catholic missionary practice tended to be more embracing of caste customs, Catholic converts tended to retain many of their former practices. As such, they were ideal witnesses for Francis in his attempt to show that many Christians continued to abide by the Hindu law of inheritance. Of the 104 witnesses whose depositions are included in the case records, roughly half are Roman Catholics who came from various South Indian communities of land cultivators (such as the Kapus) and who had converted en masse to Catholicism. Francis's witnesses also included clusters of Protestants; but unlike Charlotte's predominantly European or East Indian Protestants, Francis's Protestants were Tamil converts from Madura. These included Vellalars, who tended to retain their high-ranking *jati* (birthgroup or subcaste) identity even as Christians.[74]

A typical deposition for the defense consisted of a set of questions relating to the witness's Catholic identity. One after another, *vakils* (native pleaders employed in the courts of the *mofussil*, or countryside) asked witnesses how long they and their ancestors had been Catholic, what religion they had belonged to before conversion, and whether they had continued as Christians to abide by the customs and usages of their ancestors. Most claimed to have retained many of the customs of their ancestors, including their inheritance practices.

Murrya Sowriah Pillay, a Roman Catholic Vellalar from Madura, stated that he and his family gave up some of their Saiva practices, which were associated with worship of the god Shiva or Siva, but retained others:

1. How long have you and your ancestors been Christians?
   A. From five generations. I mean 200 years. Since then we have been Roman Catholic Christians.
2. Before your ancestors became Christians, to what religion did they conform?

A. They belonged to the Siva sect.

3. Do you conform to the same usages as your ancestors with reference to the acquisition and division of property, or in consequence of your having changed your religion do you observe any new usages?

A. When my ancestors were in the Siva sect, it was customary for them to divide the property into 3 parts if a person has 3 children. Now during the time we are Christians, we divide in the same manner.

Under cross-examination by the plaintiffs, Murrya Sowriah revealed the complex social location of his family after their conversion:

1. To what particular class or community do you belong, and by what designation is that class or community called?

A. Although we belong to the "Coralla Vumsum" of the Vellala class, yet in consequence of our belonging to the Roman Catholic faith, we are named and called by the names of any of the 12 apostles in the Christian religion.

2. In case you and your community, though Christians, actually do conform to Hindoo law and Hindoo customs and usages, as such, in the acquisition, inheritance and division of property, do you not also avowedly and from preference conform to Hindoo law and Hindoo customs and usages, as such, in all other matters besides, in which they are not directly opposed to the Christian religion?

A. We have renounced all the customs adopted by a Hindoo Siva follower and still divide property according as our ancestors did.

3. Do you keep up caste and caste usages, and do you entertain caste feelings like Hindoos?

A. We act according to caste rules.[75]

Murrya Sowriah stated that he had never been to Bellary and hence did not know which customs persons of his class observed there. The fact that he had been deposed in a different civil court shows the lengths Francis's pleader had gone to locate Christians who maintained the customs of Hindu undivided families. Murrya Sowriah's testimony, however, also indicates the importance of caste for Francis's case. Even if all other "religious" traditions were abandoned upon conversion, the continued observance of caste customs seems to have coincided with the observance of traditional inheritance practices.

Govindu Rayannah, a Catholic cultivator, was examined in the civil court at Guntur, a Telugu-speaking district nearly five hundred miles from Bellary. In contrast to Murrya Sowriah's testimony, which stressed the persistence of caste, Govindu's testimony highlighted religious and bodily practices. After responding to the usual set of questions posed to the defendant's witnesses, he commented on the role of his priest and catechist and how he worshipped:

15. Did you see persons of this country, who have adopted the Christian religion, dress like Europeans and conform to their manners, divide their property in conformity with the English Law?

A. I did not see.

15. Did your padre give you any name connected with your religion?

A. My priest baptized me after my birth, and gave me the name Rayannah, which is my caste name.

15. How do you offer prayers to God?

A. We pray to God sometimes in a sitting posture, and sometimes in a kneeling posture; daily we offer prayers for 2 hours.

15. When you offer prayers to God do you keep anything on your head, and have any book in your hands?

A. We keep head cloths on our heads, but no books in our hands.

15. On what day of the week do you pray to God?

A. We pray in the morning and evening daily. On Sundays we abandon all other work and offer prayers, besides in the morning and evening, in the afternoon also.

15. Who solemnizes marriages, etc. in your houses?

A. Our padre employs a man of our class on pay; he is called catechist. He solemnizes our marriages.

15. Are there any marks of religion exhibited over your houses?

A. We mark our walls with *chunam* [lime powder made from burnt shells] and red mud, and place marked sticks on the roof [i.e., a cross].[76]

These questions reflect the colonial judiciary's fixation on bodily practices as indicators of social belonging. Earlier in his testimony, Govindu had stated that he and his family divide property like other members of his caste. Most likely these questions sought to establish a line of continuity between Catholic forms of worship and traditional inheritance practices.[77]

As the first witness called by Francis, Patrick Doyle provided detailed ethnographic data about his converts and their inheritance practices. His deposition's rich content reflects not only the vast scope of his knowledge about local customs but also the Catholic quest for cultural continuity:

> My duty lay amongst Native Christians, as well as amongst Europeans. My experience in respect to the Law of Inheritance, which Native Christians followed has been chiefly amongst the Telugoo Christians in Bellary, Kurnool, and Cuddapah Districts. They followed the same Law of inheritance as the other native inhabitants of the country who are not Christians. In Ramdroog in the Goollum Talook of this District, a man named Adonee Anthoneyappah, a Christian ryot, made a division of his property in that manner with his nephew. I mean in the same manner as the other Native inhabitants of the country. The nephew was the elder brother's son. The division was made in a friendly way in my own presence. One Chintalachervoo Chinnappah in the village of Ondadapully in Coilacoonta Talook in the Cuddapah district, divided his property in the same way with his nephew, i.e., his brother's son; but as he was a minor, the division was made with his brother's widow. In this case, the widow and her son were not Christians. This also occurred before me. I know several instances of persons of pure native blood who are Christians and wear the English dress, but I do not know how their property was divided.[78]

After providing details about how various "native Christians" had divided their property in his presence according to local customs, Doyle responded to questions under cross-examination. These pertained specifically to caste distinctions observed by Telugu Christians:

> The Telugoo Christians I have referred to are Christians of high caste, of the Soodra caste. They wear the Native dress as the other inhabitants do of their villages. They do not wear the marks. They speak the Telugoo language as their mother tongue. In all respects, not opposed to matters of the Christian Religion, they live like Hindoos. In matters not opposed to Christianity, they keep up caste and caste usages.

R. Would a Telugoo Christian of the caste you have spoken of eat or
   drink out of a vessel used by a Christian of the Bender caste?
A. I do not know what you mean by a Christian of the Bender caste.

   I know a class of Christians by the name of "Boyawandooloo."
These Christians are included amongst the Telugoo Christians that I
have spoken of. These Telugoo Christians embrace a great many castes,
and amongst them a man of higher caste will not eat or drink with one of
lower. They will not draw water from the same well as a pariah. It makes
no difference whether the pariah is a Christian or not. The Telugoo
Christians will only intermarry with persons of their own caste. They
will not intermarry with Christians of other castes. The Native Christians of whom I have spoken, do observe the same prohibited degrees of
consanguinity with respect to marriage as Hindoos do.[79]

Citing numerous instances in which Telugu Christians divided their property like undivided Hindu families, Doyle concluded, "Native Christians
follow the same Law of Inheritance as the other native inhabitants of the
country."

Doyle also described the role of the village panchayat in Undadapalli
(Cuddapah District) in executing divisions of property among Christian families. He claimed that he was present when the panchayat was
formed and at least on one occasion was handed their written decision.
Several key insights can be gleaned from his deposition. First, that Indian
Catholics and other members of their respective *jatis* often occupied overlapping domains, adhered to similar customs, and resorted to common
mechanisms for dispute resolution. Second, that Doyle himself as a Catholic priest seems to have found a niche at the nexus of these overlapping
domains and local authorities. Finally, that the colonial courts served as
arenas in which litigants utilized and produced knowledge as they fought
for their own interests.

The Verdict

On June 1, 1858 the Bellary District Court issued a decree in Charlotte's
favor. The court determined that the Abraham brothers neither considered themselves to be undivided Hindu brothers nor displayed objectively

characteristics of such a bond. The court rejected the evidence of Charlotte's East Indian witnesses, considering them to belong to a "different class" than that of Matthew and Francis. The judge ordered that accounts be taken, and that an allowance be paid to Francis for his share of the shop and earnings at the distillery, but that the ownership and profits of the distillery and the houses go to Charlotte and her two sons.

Upon appeal, the appeals court, known as the Sadr Adalat, viewed the evidence in a manner more sympathetic with Francis's cause. The Sadr Adalat was persuaded by Francis's evidence concerning his exertions on the family's behalf, before and after Matthew's death. The court noted Francis's willingness to manage the business during Matthew's years of ill health and his joint ventures with Matthew in Kurnool, where they had incurred huge debts. Such actions demonstrated that Francis was acting instinctively, as an undivided brother, and not merely as a paid, subordinate agent. The court also sought input from Brahmin *pandits* or scholars, who declared the brothers as belonging to a class—"natives of pure Hindoo blood"—that observed the Hindu law of inheritance.

Upon appeal by Charlotte and one of her sons, Daniel Vincent Abraham, the Judicial Committee of the Privy Council overturned the decision of the Sadr Adalat and concluded that Hindu law should *not* apply to the Abrahams, based upon the evidence. Converts, it held, would not have to follow Hindu law, but could do so if they could demonstrate retention of the characteristics of undivided families. This Francis failed to demonstrate. On the contrary, the Abraham family, their Lordships contended, "lived in all respects like an East Indian family." That being so, how could Hindu law ever apply?[80] Based on a rereading of the evidence submitted in court, the Privy Council reversed the decision of the Sadr Adalat, essentially reinstating the decision of the Bellary District Court to award Charlotte her husband's property. The Privy Council, however, altered one important aspect of the District Court decree: it awarded Francis half the profits of the distillery since the time of Matthew's death and also did not hold him responsible for the costs of the appeal.

In her book titled, *Outside the Fold* (Princeton University Press, 1998), Gauri Viswanathan discusses *Abraham v. Abraham* along with many other important cases in nineteenth-century India that concerned the rights of converts. Viswanathan's main aim in this book is to show how religious conversion functioned as a form of cultural criticism and as a subversion of colonial authority. Colonial courts, whenever possible, she argues, attempted to minimize the disruptive effects of conversion by treating converts as if they never had adopted a new religion. By contrast, I see in *Abraham v. Abraham* evidence of how Roman Catholic and Protestant witnesses simplified what was actually a much more complex history of missionary involvement in the Deccan for the sake of pressing a particular claim in court. They used history and information in ways that could help them.

In her attempt to advance her evocative thesis, it is only reasonable that Viswanathan would regard Francis as the winner of this suit. This, after all, would illustrate the court's interest in keeping this convert within the orbit of Hindu Law. However, Viswanathan's interpretation of the verdict differs from my own and is, moreover, technically incorrect. She bases her analysis on a secondary compilation of Privy Council Decisions,[81] not on the original documents of the case, and not on the official publication of Privy Council decisions (namely, *Moore's Indian Appeals*). From these more authoritative sources, it is clear that the Privy Council reversed the decision of the Sadr Adalat (which did rule in Francis's favor) and ruled in favor of Charlotte. In short, in the case of *Abraham v. Abraham* there was not one judgment but three. In this third ruling the Lordships clearly recognized the Abraham family as falling under English customs, thereby confirming an argument that stood at the center of Charlotte's case. Even so, the Privy Council's award of half the profits to Francis significantly mitigated this judgment, which is arguably what Francis wanted to achieve from the outset.[82]

Considering this case in all its complexity, what is the historian's verdict?

From the perspective of missionary studies, *Abraham v. Abraham* yields insights not into missionary practices, but into the way witnesses in this case simplified and distorted formalized knowledge in order to serve the immediate agendas of Charlotte and Francis. It yields insights, in other words, into the political deployment of "knowledge." Witnesses in the court could not account for the everyday adaptations, adjustments, compromises, and variations among missionaries as they interacted with Deccan society. For indeed, upon scrutiny, the stories of Hands, Doyle, and Dubois show instances of Protestant accommodation to the local landscape and Catholic antipathy for custom—challenging simplified ideas about "the Protestant" and "the Catholic" missionary approaches. Clearly missionaries, when they were not successful at converting or changing Indians, could assault Indian customs as did Dubois, or could find other ways of involving themselves in south India's pluralistic landscape, among Christians as among Hindus, Muslims, and others.

Who deserved control over Matthew Abraham's business and assets, and who was the real head of his family? These immediate questions drove the case of *Abraham v. Abraham* as it pitted Charlotte and Francis against each other. Yet the case had a significance for modern India that went far beyond this one family's argument, for it broached questions about defining and gauging conversion for the sake of determining, interpreting, and applying personal laws.[83]

Part Two

Missionaries, Antimissionaries, and Doubters

5

Hybridity, Parody, and Contempt

Buddhist Responses to Christian Missions in Sri Lanka

Stephen C. Berkwitz

*I*t is widely recognized that Christian missions in Sri Lanka have played a central role in the formation of a modern Buddhist identity.[1] These missions began with Portuguese Franciscans in the mid-sixteenth century, continued with Jesuits in the early seventeenth century, were followed by Dutch Calvinists and then British Anglicans and Wesleyans in the nineteenth century, and continue to this day through the efforts of evangelical American, Korean, and indigenous churches. Prior to the arrival of Christian missionaries in the island, Sri Lanka had long been a multi-religious society made up of Buddhists, Hindus, and Muslims. However, Christian missionaries undertook a new project in the island—seeking to convert people from so-called heathen religions to the "True Religion" of Christianity.[2]

This series of missions in Sri Lanka introduced not only different forms of Christianity but also new conceptions of religious identity. Missionary encounters, however sporadic and variable, spurred efforts by Sinhala Buddhists in Sri Lanka to accommodate or resist Christianization. The Buddhist religion has had a presence in Sri Lanka since at least the third century BCE. Literary and archaeological evidence suggests that Buddhism was quickly established and spread through the efforts of ancient kings and monks in the island. The well-known sixth-century history called the *Mahāvaṃsa* (Great Chronicle) asserts that long ago the Buddha predicted that his religion would be established and preserved in Sri Lanka.[3] The same text asserts that only Buddhist kings would be fit to rule over the island. But when the Portuguese, Dutch, and British successively governed the littoral regions, and later the entirety of the island, from the latter part of the sixteenth century up to 1948, the privileges and patronage afforded to Buddhist institutions were interrupted. With colonialism came Christian missions, which spurred various Buddhist responses to the efforts to displace the native religions and convert local people to one or another form of Christianity.

Numerous historical records and studies have told this story of Christian missions in Sri Lanka. Depending on an author's own religious affiliation, Christian missions may appear as coercive and imperialistic forces in displacing local religions or as heroic and virtuous agents in uplifting a native civilization.[4] There has been, in other words, little nuance when it comes to analyzing the motives and effects behind Christian missions in Sri Lanka. Nevertheless, Buddhists responded in a variety of ways to Christian missions in colonial and postcolonial Sri Lanka. Their responses ranged from conversion and varying degrees of assimilation to outright rejection and hostility. Rarely, however, did missions effect the complete abandonment of previous religious and cultural affinities in Sri Lanka. Nor did the Buddhist opponents of Christianity completely succeed in eradicating its presence and influence in the island. More frequently, Christian missions gave rise to new intercultural conversions wherein Sinhalas adopted certain elements and presuppositions from another religion in the process of defining and practicing their own.

The move to posit a range of Buddhist responses to Christian missions in Sri Lanka adds some nuance to views that generally hold the Sri Lankan reaction as uniformly and consistently hostile to missions.[5] Although the historical associations between colonial power and Christian missions have generated widely negative views of the latter among Sinhala Buddhists, a closer examination of some written sources reveals that Buddhist responses to encounters with Christian missionaries were more varied and complex than commonly thought. Although Buddhist writings on Christianity tend not to differentiate between the various forms of this religion, the perception of Christianity as a "foreign," proselytizing religion has nevertheless spurred different responses among Buddhists.

Three Sinhala-language works from the seventeenth, eighteenth, and twenty-first centuries respectively convey to us something of the range of responses expressed by Buddhists in their encounters with Christian missions. These particular responses invoke hybridity, parody, and contempt as strategies to adapt or refute the discourse of Christian missionaries at different points in history. These responses do not exhaust the range of possible reactions to missionary activity, but they illustrate different methods of engaging with Christian conversion efforts.

This study aims to advance three arguments through the close study of Sinhala Buddhist discourses about Christianity. First, the Christian missionary encounter in Sri Lanka not only has been protracted, dating from sixteenth-century Portuguese initiatives, but also has been constantly evolving, reflecting the entry of successive foreigners into the Sri Lankan scene. Second, conversions between Buddhism and Christianity in Sri Lanka may have been neither absolute nor culturally effacing in practice, although the discourses surrounding conversions have often hardened with time. Indeed, Buddhists in Sri Lanka have increasingly adopted Christian missionaries' exclusive notions of religious identity while rejecting the possibility (and desirability) of maintaining hybrid identities. Third and finally, "Protestant Buddhism," to the extent that such a thing exists in Sri Lanka today, allows for what may be called "critique with mimesis": the harsh rejection of Christian missionary religion accompanied by the imitation of certain Christian missionary techniques (for example, the inauguration of social welfare projects by monks). In the end, the most unexpected consequence of this history may be that the gradual adoption of Christian missionary–style attitudes toward conversion among Sinhala Buddhists has, since the mid-twentieth century, been working to the detriment of Christians and Christian converts on the island today while allowing for the more strident expression of Buddhist nationalism.

Hybridity and the *Kustantīnu Haṭana*

The period of Portuguese colonialism in Sri Lanka (1506–1658) is remembered today by Sri Lankans with much bitterness.[6] It appears in the popular imagination as a one-sided story of destructive military campaigns and intolerant missionaries. Clearly, the actions of Portuguese missionaries displayed some fundamental cultural incongruities with the island's Buddhist population. The first Franciscan missionaries to arrive in Sri Lanka in the 1540s rejected a gift of money from the lowland Buddhist king, whose position made him the traditional patron of local religious institutions; they also rejected the traditional religious pluralism of the island in order to effect the exclusivist transformation of people's interior lives.[7] Religious and cultural clashes were sure to follow. The Council at Goa in 1567 rejected conversions by force, but it confirmed that the Portuguese crown had the duty to spread the Catholic faith.[8] In time, Portuguese authorities in Sri Lanka acted to restrict non-Christian religious activity in the lands that they controlled, offering inducements such as exemption from taxes to encourage people to convert to Catholicism.[9]

Not surprisingly, accounts of Catholicism in Sinhala sources from the late sixteenth and seventeenth centuries are generally unflattering. The *Rājāvaliya* (Lineage of Kings), a chronicle composed around the late seventeenth century, depicts the conversion of Sinhala Buddhists to Catholicism in opportunistic terms. It claims that many women of low birth consorted with Portuguese men and converted to Christianity out of greed for wealth.[10] Certainly, the reasons for Sinhalas to convert were many, and not all of them related to sincere religious convictions. But the *Rājāvaliya* clearly implies that conversion was, strictly speaking, always self-interested. Another Buddhist text from the period, the *Cūḷavaṃsa* (Minor Chronicle), depicts Buddhist converts to Christianity in a similar fashion. "The infamous *Parangis*, the infidels, the impious ones . . . rich in cunning, endeavored by gifts of money and the like to get their creed adopted by others, led a life without reverence for the doctrine [of the Buddha]."[11] These Buddhist representations of Christian missions highlight the idea that conversion was achieved through bribery and accepted by those greedy for worldly gain. In such a view, there is no legitimate religious reason for a Buddhist to convert to Christianity. And while there is historical evidence that colonial governments did offer tangible benefits and rewards to converts, the above remarks from the Buddhist sources must be read as polemical.[12]

In contrast to the highly negative portrayal of Christian missions in some colonial-era texts, there is another Buddhist response wherein Christian identity and religious symbolism is assimilated with local Buddhist imagery in a hybrid fashion. A renowned Sinhala court poet named Alagiyavanna (b. 1552) complicates our picture of Buddhist responses to the Portuguese missions. Alagiyavanna originally served King Rajasiṃha I, the last independent, lowland Sinhala king, who emerged as a fierce opponent of the Portuguese presence in the island. Alagiyavanna composed traditional poems that praised the Sinhala king, the Buddha, and the institutions of the Buddhist religion up through the king's death and the resurgence of Christian missions in the first decade of the seventeenth century. Sometime around 1612, he apparently converted to Christianity and began to work for the local Portuguese *Vedor da Fazenda*, or revenue official, and assisted in the compilation of the *Tombo*, or land register. An account of his conversion was recorded decades later by the French Protestant traveler Jean Baptiste Tavernier (1605–89):

[A] very accomplished man and good native philosopher, named Alegamma Motiar, as one might say master of philosophers, after having conversed some time with the Jesuit Fathers and other priests of Colombo, was inspired to become a Christian. With this object he went to see the Jesuit Fathers, and told them that he desired to be instructed in the Christian faith, but he inquired what Jesus Christ had done and left in writing. He set himself then to read the New Testament with so much attention and ardour that in less than six months there was not a passage which he could not recite, for he had acquired Latin very thoroughly. After having been well instructed, he told the Fathers that he wished to receive holy baptism, that he saw that their religion was the only good and true one, and such as Jesus Christ had taught, but what astonished him was, that they did not follow Christ's example, because, according to the Gospel, he never took money from anyone, while they, on the contrary, took it from everyone and neither baptized nor buried anyone without it. This did not prevent him from being baptized and from working for the conversion of the idolaters afterwards.[13]

Tavernier's praise of Alagiyavanna clearly also contains more than a trace of the French Protestant's disdain for the Jesuits in Sri Lanka. The fact that he received and related this account about Alagiyavanna's conversion—a story he probably heard when visiting Goa in the 1640s—says much about the importance to which the Portuguese attributed Alagiyavanna's embrace of Catholicism. It may also say something about the overall lack of success that Christian missions had in Sri Lanka if no other important convert could be made in the interval of two or three decades.[14]

The case of Alagiyavanna, the Sinhala Buddhist poet turned Catholic assistant to the Portuguese colonial administration, remains a fascinating and little-studied subject that sheds more light on the transformation of religious culture and identity in the early stages of European colonialism in Asia.[15] For the present purpose, it suffices to say that Alagiyavanna's apparent embrace of Catholicism prevents us from viewing Buddhist responses to Christian missions in Sri Lanka as uniformly negative. Identified as a Catholic convert in Portuguese references to native assistants on the *Tombo*, Alagiyavanna is a complex figure. He composed learned poems in praise of Buddhist personages and institutions before penning the *Kustantīnu Haṭana* (War Poem of General Constantino) around 1620 near the end of his life. Earlier works such as the *Sävul Sandeśaya* (Message of the Cock) and *Subhāṣitaya* (Words Well Spoken) celebrate Buddhist kings and institutions in the panegyric verse characteristic of classical Sinhala Buddhist poetry. With his adherence to formal poetic conventions and his frequent lifting of phrases taken from earlier works, Alagiyavanna clearly styled himself as a classical court poet deserving of fame and praise.[16]

However, with the death of Rajasimha I in 1593, the royal court soon fell and the inland Sitāvaka kingdom was overrun by Portuguese-led forces. It is unclear what Alagiyavanna did during these years immediately after the king's death. Local traditions hold that Rajasimha's patronage of Hindu Brahmins and alleged persecution of Buddhist monks drove Alagiyavanna south to the town of Matara for a time.[17] His composition of the poetic work *Subhāṣitaya*, which contains general moral advice and a robust defense of Buddhist teachings, is dated to 1611, although this date has been called

into question.[18] His conversion around 1612 coincides with his work on
the *Tombo*, which is evidenced by his appearance in Portuguese records in
1615.[19] Other evidence points to the fact that Alagiyavanna lost his title and
his lands under the Portuguese captain-general Nuno Alvares Pereira after
1616. He made an effort to reclaim them, and appears to have had them
restored by the next captain-general Constantino de Sá de Noronha, the
figure after which *Kustantīnu Haṭana* was composed.

This complicated, incomplete history aside, Alagiyavanna's *Kustantīnu
Haṭana* represents a work that assimilates the Christianity of the Catholic
religious orders into Buddhist cultural forms. Whereas modern Sinhala
scholars have argued over whether Alagiyavanna was a sincere Christian
and the actual author of the anonymous *Kustantīnu Haṭana*, these debates
miss a larger point. The author of the text, likely Alagiyavanna,[20] retains
the conventions of classical Sinhala Buddhist poetry to express devotion
and praise to the Christian God and to Portuguese leaders. His adoption
of Catholicism is qualified—even mixed, as it were—so that it resembles
something quite different from what the Jesuit missionaries intended for
him to adopt. For example, the poem opens by substituting praise for the
Holy Trinity, Christ, and the Virgin Mary in place of, but in the manner
of, conventional worship shown to the Three Jewels of Buddhism:

> I venerate with reverence the one God (*eksura*) who is of three kinds,
> Namely the Father (*piti*), Son (*put*) and Spirit (*vīdi*),
> Who exists without revealing any division,
> Like the word, the letter, and the meaning.

> I venerate the noble Lord Jesus Christ (*yēsus kristu surindun*),
> Who is a treasure that is full with the virtue of loving-kindness,
> And who bestowed the lotuses of his resplendent feet (*siripā*),
> Upon the heads of the beings (*sat*) in the entire world.

> I venerate with devotion the Noble Lord (*surindun*) who issued forth,
> From the womb of the Virgin Mary (*kanni mari*),
> In the manner of the flames of fire that issue forth,
> From a sunlight stone.[21]

It had long been customary for Sinhala Buddhist works to open with expressions of reverence to the Three Jewels of the Buddha, the Dharma (Teaching), and the Sangha (monastic community). Alagiyavanna's praise for Christian figures changes the content but maintains the standard opening formula in Sinhala Buddhist literature.

The *Kustantīnu Haṭana* cannot be read simply as a "Christian" text. At first glance, it might seem like one when it describes how Constantino de Sá worships the Christian deity before heading off into battle: "And venerating with esteem the feet of the Majestic God who is three in one, and who created the beings in the entire Three Worlds with loving-kindness and compassion."[22] But this description of God borrows freely from Buddhist notions of the cosmos—that is, the "Three Worlds"—and from moral virtues normally associated with the Buddha himself. And the very next verse compares de Sá to Lord Vishnu, borrowing a common convention in Sinhala Buddhist poetry to symbolize the captain-general's power. In fact there are numerous instances where Portuguese commanders are compared to Indic gods, such as the following verse where de Sá describes himself in terms of Hindu-Buddhist mythology:

> Entering the center of the battle without fear.
> Displaying strength and courage,
> Like [the gods] Skandakumar and Vishnu,
> I will display my might before you.[23]

By depicting a Portuguese general as referring to Indic gods to boast of his martial prowess, the poet continued to employ non-Christian images in his poetic work. Alagiyavanna goes further when he explains how the native upcountry king was able to escape the treachery of the Sinhala rebels who sought to conquer him. He attributes the king's escape to the "power of the Three Jewels of Buddhism," the "influence of the [native] gods," and the "power of the merit" earned by the king in acts of good karma.[24] By crediting the good fortune of the Buddhist king to his sincerity in adhering to the Buddha's religion, Alagiyavanna implicitly recognizes the validity of Buddhism.

Alagiyavanna's personal conversion to Catholicism did not preclude recognizing the integrity of the Buddhist tradition. Instead it inaugurated a novel form of cultural conversion, wherein Catholic figures and discourse were rendered into something more indigenous and familiar through the use of Sinhala poetic conventions.[25] While the Portuguese missionaries aimed for the natives' exclusive adoption of the Christian faith, even a celebrated convert like Alagiyavanna maintained an assimilative approach whereby Catholicism was fashioned more along Buddhist lines. Indeed the inclusive, hybrid religious view in *Kustantīnu Haṭana* appears to belie Tavernier's portrayal of Alagiyavanna as a zealous missionary himself, a portrayal that may well have reflected an exaggerated, self-congratulatory view of earlier events among Jesuits in Goa. The hybridity of *Kustantīnu Haṭana* demonstrates that even accommodation and conversion to Christianity need not have entailed the rejection of all things Buddhist or an exclusive identification with the religion of the European missionaries.[26] As a response to missions, hybridity could in fact be a form of resistance, as it destabilized the authority of Christian knowledge by undermining and revaluing European definitions of religious difference.[27] As a symbol of successful conversions, Alagiyavanna was celebrated. But the *Kustantīnu Haṭana* suggests that he embraced a more complex religious identity than was recognized by Europeans.

Parody and the *Vaḍu Tīrthaka Maḷasohonpreta Kathāva*

A quite different response to Christian missions in Sri Lanka is evidenced in a story called *Vaḍu Tīrthaka Maḷasohonpreta Kathāva* (translated as "Story of the Carpenter-Heretic Cemetery Ghost," subsequently referred to as "The Carpenter-Heretic") from the latter eighteenth century. Composed by an unknown author at a time when the Dutch had gained colonial control over much of Sri Lanka, this text contains a much less charitable view of Christianity. A number of short stories like "The Carpenter-Heretic" offer parodies of Christianity and its missionaries that misrepresent the religion and depict it in a negative light. It is significant that these stories ignore the Dutch and continue to cast the Portuguese as the foes of Buddhists. This may be due to the fact that the Portuguese encounter was unprecedented and marked by considerable destruction.[28] The Dutch were somewhat less intolerant of Buddhist institutions than their Portuguese predecessors, although they too sought to promote Christianity in the island.

Ongoing encounters with Christian missionaries and their converts led Sinhala Buddhists to develop more knowledge of Christianity. And while converts assimilated new and old traditions in varying degrees, other Sinhalas countered the encroachment of missions indirectly. Some people composed works in the Sinhala language that parody and critique the Christianity of the colonizers. Such texts contain what Young and Senanayaka have described as covert resistance that was not told to missionaries but was circulated "behind their backs."[29] The evidence of such stories, parodies, and jokes is scant compared to what must have been a fairly common response to missionary efforts to spread the Gospel and convert the natives. But in the extant texts, we find some recurrent themes in which Christian figures are portrayed as demonic and malevolent beings. The narratives frequently employ similar distinctions between the allegedly immoral followers of Christ and the virtuous followers of the Buddha: carnivores versus vegetarians, drinkers versus teetotalers, worldly heretics versus world-renouncing sages.[30] In "The Carpenter-Heretic," the son of a carpenter—obviously representing Jesus—is depicted as an immoral fraud, one of a group of "rascals who enjoy drinking toddy and eating beef while propagating a religion that deceives people into believing they are gods."[31] While in Portugal, the heretic convinces the people that he and his disciples are gods, and that they should give them liquor and meat from slaughtered goats, sheep, and cattle. The king of Portugal, depicted here as a vassal to a great Indian king, is persuaded by his overlord to expel the heretic. Thus, the carpenter-heretic is said to have left Portugal with his disciples, wandering as a thief and a charlatan through many countries. They arrive in the ancient Indian city of Sāgala, and decide to dress up in black cloaks and jackets and pretend to be *arhats*, or enlightened Buddhist saints.

The text then describes how the carpenter-heretic and his disciples behave like a band of thieves, breaking into animal pens and stealing goats and cattle. They slay the animals and devour them while drinking the fermented toddy from coconut trees. One of the band, deprived of his fellow rogues' drink and meat, turns them in to the authorities. The carpenter-heretic is executed by hanging, and then his corpse is nailed down through the hands and feet for several days before being buried. Demonic forces, concerned that the heretic's death will prevent people from being misled into immorality and rebirth in hell, bellow out from the sky and falsely claim that the carpenter-heretic has risen from the dead and ascended to the heavens. The rogue who betrayed him and the other wicked disciples were tricked into believing that their leader had been born again and was ascending to heaven.[32] The other inhabitants went to check out the noise, but upon finding the grave fully intact, returned to their houses. The implication here is that those people who remain deluded by ignorance and malevolent forces accept the claims of divinity for the carpenter-heretic. Significantly, most people do not fall for these illusions.

The *Vaḍu Tīrthaka Maḷasohonpreta Kathāva* presents us with a Buddhist response to Christian missions that relies on parody to undermine missionary claims about the divinity of Jesus Christ. Instead of making an effort to facilitate the adoption of Christianity in a local setting, it twists Christian narratives around in order to resist missionary efforts at converting the native population. The text in question begins to take on the appearance of, in James C. Scott's words, a "hidden transcript" used by a restricted group to confront and negate the ideologies of the colonial-missionary project by offering a counterideology for those who were constrained by laws and policies that promoted Christianity over Buddhism.[33] Written in Sinhala on probably no more than a few palm leaf manuscripts, the story nevertheless gives material form to a Buddhist discourse designed to challenge Christian claims about the truth of the Gospels and the benefits of accepting the Christian God. Hugh Nevill (1848–97), the British civil servant who collected or had copied over 2,000 palm leaf texts in Sri Lanka, speculated that the *Vaḍu Tīrthaka Maḷasohonpreta Kathāva* contains a "corrupt account" of the story of Christ, with mistakes due either to imperfect recollection or to distortions in some sort of "heretical gospel."[34] Nevill did not see this text as an insult to the Gospel, presumably because it deviates so far from the Christian account. Nevertheless, the fact that someone composed a text equating a figure resembling Jesus with a thug sent by Māra, the legendary Buddhist God of Death, to spread false views and immoral conduct surely indicates an attempt to undermine the central narrative in the missionaries' discourse—namely the divinity of Jesus Christ.

This particular story, however imaginative, is not unique. There are a number of other tales from eighteenth- and nineteenth-century Sri Lanka that also portray Jesus and his Christian followers in demonic terms. Involved in efforts to lure people away from Buddhist truths and virtue, these figures come to represent missionaries who made and were making disparaging claims against Buddhism in order to show the natives the way to the Christian God. Between around 1830 and 1870, the exclusivist religious convictions of the British in Ceylon, along with the demands for stories about the conversion of the heathens, led many Methodist, Anglican, and Baptist missionaries and churchmen to write and speak more negatively about Buddhism, rejecting the spirit of earlier British accounts that recognized its moral virtues.[35] A monk writing about Buddhist concepts in the nineteenth century repeated much of the story from *Vaḍu Tīrthaka Maḷasohonpreta Kathāva* in a renewed attempt to undercut the claims of missionaries who sought to demonstrate the falsity of the Buddha's Word. Thus, the monk Bentara Atthadassī (d. 1865) explained in his treatise that Christianity was the invention of Māra, the God of Death and foe of the Buddha, and that Jesus was simply a rustler-cum-heretic with an appetite for beef and liquor and a mission to deceive the witless by making them into Christians.[36] Further, his alleged ascension into heaven was merely an illusion cast by Māra, making the risen savior of the Christian religion into little more than a *preta*, or vengeful ghost.

The circulation of such stories that parodied Christian narratives reflected a new stage in Buddhist responses to Christian missions in Sri Lanka. Beyond the ambiguity and ambivalence found in hybrid narratives such as *Kustantīnu Haṭana* that recast Christian images and figures in terms of local cultural expressions and literary conventions, the "Carpenter-Heretic" story challenged the legitimacy of Christian narratives indirectly through a parody of the story of Jesus. While Jesus is not specifically

named in the text and Christian religious orders are nowhere clearly identified, the depiction of a false *avatāraya* (divine incarnation), accompanied by disciples wearing black cloaks and jackets coming from Portugal,
amounts to a deliberate caricature of the Christian god and the missionaries who advocated faith in him. Parody as a form of Buddhist response
to Christian missions foreshadowed increasing Sinhala resistance to the
methods employed for converting natives to Christianity.

Contempt and the *"Mē Mama Karana Avasan Kathāvayi"*

Sinhala Buddhist contempt for Christian missions has become a common response in the latter colonial and postindependence eras. Although
the British colonial presence in Sri Lanka formally ended in 1948, Christian missions have continued in various forms up to the present. The text
chosen here to illustrate this stance, titled *"Mē Mama Karana Avasan
Kathāvayi"* (This Is the Last Talk I Will Give), is the transcript of a sermon
delivered by a popular Sinhala Buddhist monk, Venerable Gangodawila
Soma (1948–2003), about three months before he died. Soma enjoyed a
meteoric rise in Sri Lanka by employing a charismatic speaking style to
address contemporary social problems and religious needs on his own television program and in numerous newspaper essays. His caustic criticism of
Sinhala politicians, Tamil separatists, foreign NGOs, and Christian missionaries attracted a great deal of interest and support among the Sinhala
Buddhist public.[37] He blamed such actors for the moral and economic
decline of the nation. And while novel in some ways, Soma's Buddhist
nationalist discourse drew inspiration from an older tradition of antimissionary polemics in Sri Lanka.

The history of this discourse is rooted in the Sri Lankan Buddhist
revival of the late nineteenth and twentieth centuries. The intensive British colonization of Sri Lanka, which was then called "Ceylon," involved
deposing the island's last Buddhist king in 1815 and then establishing an
island-wide infrastructure of schools, hospitals, and roads to facilitate the
development and governance of the country in subsequent years. Increased
denunciations and challenges by Christian missionaries eventually caused
Buddhist monks to launch a more energetic and organized defense of their

religion beginning in the 1860s. A group of monks accepted an invitation to engage in a series of public debates with missionaries who believed that missionary tracts had proven the truth and superiority of Christianity. These debates were held in sites around the southern and central parts of the island between 1865 and 1873. Local Christian converts argued the case for Christianity, while a handful of monks held forth on behalf of Buddhism. Venerable Mohottivatte Gunananda was among the leading spokesmen who contested the missionaries' claims, and he argued in a lively and energetic style reminiscent of the missionaries themselves. Gunananda and the other monks, supported by a mainly Buddhist audience in the thousands, met the missionaries' rhetoric head-on, raising counterobjections and challenging them to prove their own scriptural claims.[38] Local newspaper accounts published celebratory accounts of the monks' defense of their religion and the widespread acclaim they received from those in attendance.

Despite what by most accounts was a triumphant effort by the monks, Christian missionaries continued to augment their influence through the establishment of missionary schools. The English education offered at such schools was often held necessary for social advancement in colonial society governed by the British.[39] The perceptions of the advantages given to Christian missionaries and the heated rhetoric that many of them employed to convince Buddhists of the supposed falsehoods and inferiority of their religion sparked a broader Buddhist revival. (In this regard, there are striking parallels with other parts of the colonial world, such as Egypt, where Christian missionary activity stimulated Muslim nationalists in response.)[40] The revival in Sri Lanka was characterized by a more aggressive defense of the tradition and the gradual conflation of Buddhism and Sinhala identity in nationalist thought. Missionaries became implicated in colonial British efforts to "disestablish" Buddhism as the primary religion in the island, taking over the social and welfare activities previously managed by the monks and encouraging the adoption of Western culture in the forms of language, manners, and dress.

Nationalist sentiments were mobilized by Sinhala leaders like the Buddhist layperson Anagarika Dharmapala (1864–1933) who, humiliated by the denigration of Buddhism by his teachers at Christian schools, later

began to argue for the reform of Buddhism as the means for creating a progressive and prosperous modern society.[41] Although Dharmapala praised
the ancient heritage of Sinhala Buddhists, as evidenced in their long literary and archaeological history, the type of Buddhism he promoted was
distinctly modern and reactionary. He emphasized puritan values of discipline, hard work, and punctuality, while charging monks with the duty
to revive Buddhism at home and abroad through active social service and
preaching.[42] Dharmapala popularized the image of Christian missionaries
as working hand-in-hand with the British administrators to turn the country's Buddhists into subservient drunkards who adopted Christian names
and customs at the expense of their country's great traditions.[43]

Dharmapala's cultural critiques and his mission to utilize Buddhism
in efforts to regenerate Sinhala society and the nation have had profound
impacts throughout the twentieth century and into the twenty-first. After
Independence in 1948, Sinhala-dominated political parties began mobilizing popular support by initiating policies that ostensibly sought to
redress the alleged bias shown toward the island's religious and ethnic
minorities under British rule. Despite comprising a religious majority of
over two-thirds of the population, Buddhists felt that their religion was
under threat and in need of protection. In 1956 the "Buddhist Committee
of Enquiry" issued a public report that claimed that the Buddhist religion
had been betrayed by the colonial rulers and was in dire need of revival.
Among the findings and statements issued, the report claimed that given
the privileges afforded to Catholics in the country there was a real threat
that Sri Lanka would become "an Eastern outpost of the Vatican" if Buddhists were not allowed to practice their religion freely and without hin-
drance.[44] Obstacles to Buddhist practice were identified as the low number
of lucrative government posts assigned to Buddhists, the denigration of the
native Sinhala language in schools, and the advantages given to Christian missionary schools. Spurred on by this report, Buddhist nationalists
in the 1950s worked successfully to nationalize private Christian schools,
evict Catholic nuns from nursing positions, and secure more civil service
and military positions for Buddhists.[45] Again, this activity by Sinhala Buddhists reflects similar responses among nationalization movements vis-à-
vis Christian missionaries elsewhere, such as Sudan.[46]

The underlying message of the 1956 report on the "betrayal of Buddhism" was that foreign rule and Christian missions had conspired to bring about the decline of Buddhist culture in Sri Lanka. It faulted the British for ignoring their responsibility to protect and promote the Buddha's religion just like the country's previous kings had done for centuries. It asserted that favoritism had been shown to a minority of Christians, with unfair advantages given to their schools and with lands from Buddhist temples seized for plantations under European owners and for sites where new churches could be built.[47] The Buddhist nationalists behind this report, as well as the ones persuaded by its findings and recommendations, began to campaign more vigorously for a Buddhist revival with state support. Some prominent monks like Walpola Rahula argued in favor of a natural unity among Buddhism, the Sinhala people, and the state—an argument that made room for the participation of Buddhist monks in political affairs.[48] The Constitution of 1972 (as well as subsequent versions) effectively recognized Sri Lanka as a Buddhist state by stating that the government must give Buddhism "the foremost place" and must strive to protect and foster the religion.[49]

Activists justified the special position granted to Buddhism by law as a necessary measure to protect the religion against forces seeking its demise. They regularly identified Christian missions as hostile toward Buddhism. And following this line of thinking, to the extent that missionaries succeeded in converting Sinhala Buddhists, they also worked to undermine the cultural foundations and sovereignty of the nation. In this context, at the turn of the twenty-first century, Ven. Soma espoused similar ideas on the dangers of Christian evangelism to Buddhism. His sermons, newspaper articles, and television appearances frequently condemned the use of liquor, cigarettes, and other vices that he linked with wicked conduct promoted by Christians in order to undermine Buddhist morality and win converts.[50] The sermon "Mē Mama Karana Avasan Kathāvayi," which Soma delivered on September 13, 2003 at the famous Temple of the Tooth Relic in Kandy, contains a summary of his many objections to Christian missions. His arguments against the negative effects of missionary activity in Sri Lanka illustrate a widely held stance of Buddhist contempt for Christian proselytization in Sri Lanka today.

Soma opened his sermon by asserting how the forces of Christianity continue to try to subjugate Buddhism in Sri Lanka by converting Buddhists to their religion.[51] He then links such activity to the island's long history of colonialism. He describes how the British, unlike the Portuguese and the Dutch, realized that killing, enslaving, and intimidating the Sinhalas would not work to convert them to the Christian faith.[52] Instead, he argues, British missionaries encouraged policies to restrict Buddhist practice and encourage immoral behavior in order to weaken the commitment of the Sinhala Buddhists to their religion. Soma explains that British prohibitions against Buddhist sermons and rites eventually led to a rise in immoral conduct (*durācāraya*) and the corresponding loss of the people's "Sinhalaness," their Buddhist identity, and even their humanity.[53] Such a project for Soma represents the missionary method that supported colonial goals by subjugating and converting a nation. In this sense, much like Anagarika Dharmapala before him and the contemporary "Hindutva" movement in India, Soma explicitly tied Christian missions to the rise of immorality and the extension of foreign domination in Sri Lanka.[54]

By drawing on this colonial history, Soma's sermon implicates all subsequent missionary activity in postcolonial Sri Lanka as part of a broader effort to rob Sinhala Buddhists of their morality, their welfare, and their freedom. According to him, this stratagem was devised by missionaries to weaken the moral resolve and self-control of Sinhala Buddhists, making them more susceptible to conquest and conversion. Like generations of Buddhist nationalists before him, Soma understood that the country's distinctive heritage lies in its historical relationship to the Buddhist religion. Dharmapala and many of his ideological heirs understood that "country, nation, and religion" cohere and reflect what for them is a basic social fact wherein the territory of Sri Lanka belongs primarily to the Sinhala Buddhist ethnic group.[55] As a result, an attack on any one of them is seen as an attack on the others. Within this framework, attempts to convert Buddhists are equivalent to attempts to conquer the country and the nation. Soma remarks in "Mē Mama Karana Avasan Kathāvayi" that contemporary Christian groups have established health organizations and NGOs that seek to extinguish Sinhala Buddhists within the next fifty years.[56] As dire as this prediction may sound, it is consistent with a message that held

the survival of the country, nation, and religion in doubt, and that compared the future of the Sinhalas with other indigenous peoples whose cultural heritage and very existence is threatened.[57]

At the center of the threats to country, nation, and religion lies the
activity and basic logic of Christian missions. Soma's contempt for missionary work is based on the conviction that, like the European missionaries who denounced Buddhism and sought to convert Sinhalas in colonial
eras, modern Christian organizations continue to seek converts who will
reject their nation and religion by any means necessary. He describes in
his sermon how Christians prey on hospital patients by visiting them,
inquiring after their health, promising to pray for them, and distributing pamphlets in order to convert them.[58] Soma depicts such activity as
unethical since it takes advantage of people who are innocent and weak.
At the same time, however, he advocates for Buddhists to visit and inquire
after patients too, as this would generate more respect and appreciation for
Buddhism. Herein one finds some evidence of grudging admiration for
the tactics of missionaries, although Soma clearly finds their overall work
contemptible.

This example of critique coupled with mimesis has been a longstanding feature of modern Buddhism in Sri Lanka. Described previously by
Gananath Obeyesekere as "Protestant Buddhism," a significant strand of
modern Sri Lankan Buddhism has vociferously protested the influences
of Protestant Christian missionaries while at the same time adopting many
of their ethical ideas and organizational methods.[59] This terminology is not
unproblematic, however, as it suggests that modern Buddhist reforms were
modeled chiefly after Protestantism, despite their vastly different views on
divinity, ritualism, monasticism, and iconography.[60] Nevertheless, Buddhist reformers like Dharmapala who often criticized missionaries also
drew selectively from their examples (among other influences—including
those from within the Buddhist tradition itself). For instance, attempts by
Buddhists like Dharmapala and Soma to value social service by teaching the general public how to develop the nation and how to suffuse
their everyday lives with moral restraint were specifically modeled after
Christian missionaries who engaged in the same kinds of behavior.[61] This

adoption and adaptation of certain features of Protestantism stops short of assimilation, however, since the modern ethos of what some have called "Protestant Buddhism" among the urban Sinhala Buddhist middle class typically rejects any sort of Christian identity or doctrine.

For his part, Soma maintains that Christian efforts to convert Sinhala Buddhists are unethical. His final sermon, like many of his earlier talks and essays, functioned both to raise awareness of missionary activity and to denounce it. The threat posed by Christian missions is said to be grave, largely because their methods are cast as devious and unethical. According to Soma, the Christian religion is not obviously superior to Buddhism, and thus the missionaries must resort to bribing poor Buddhists with money in order to convert them to the "darkness" of the "blind faith" of Christianity.[62] Near the end of his sermon, Soma's condemnation of the aims and the methods of Christian missions is strong and unyielding. He implies that all mission work is disingenuous, concerned more with converting people than with truly helping them. The apparent lack of disinterested giving among Christian missionaries conflicts with Buddhist values of selfless generosity and the wholesome regard for others. To portray mission work in this manner is to render it ethically suspect and inferior to Buddhist acts of compassionate giving. Soma asserts that the final aim of the Jehovah's Witnesses and other Protestant sects is to turn the country's Buddhist-dominated government into a Christian Kingdom of God.[63] Soma urges active resistance to all attempts by Christian missionaries to undermine and exterminate Buddhism in Sri Lanka, calling for steps to prevent Christian interests from supplanting Buddhist ones in the government of the country.

Three months after delivering this sermon, Soma died of apparent heart failure while he was in Russia to receive an honorary degree from a little-known theological institute. The unusual circumstances of his death, combined with his antimissionary rhetoric, sparked a sharp increase in incidents of violence, vandalism, and intimidation directed against Christian churches and worshippers in Sri Lanka. Although anti-Christian activity has decreased in recent years, skepticism and contempt directed against Christian missionary activities remain high in the country.

Diverse Encounters and Responses

The three texts examined above demonstrate that Christian missions in Sri Lanka have generated a variety of responses, most of which were likely unexpected. Christian missionaries among the Portuguese, Dutch, British, and, more recently, Americans and Koreans expected to achieve conversions or at least cooperation with local Sinhala Buddhists on achieving similar goals of societal development. Instead, we have seen how Buddhists from the seventeenth through the twenty-first centuries have transformed and often resisted the Christianity of the missionaries, through adaptation, parody, and outright condemnation. Through efforts including handwritten palm-leaf manuscripts; printed pamphlets and newspaper accounts; and sermons conveyed orally and reproduced in books, newspapers, and even on video available on television and the internet, Sinhala Buddhists have adapted and critiqued Christianity in as many, if not more, forms of communication media as Christian missionaries have used themselves. The long history of Christian missions in Sri Lanka has yielded intercultural conversions in which Buddhists and Christians have often emerged from encounters with new understandings of their religions and themselves.

The focus on Buddhist responses to Christian missions in Sri Lanka reveals a considerable degree of complexity and variability in how Sinhalas adapted or resisted the messages of the missionaries. Sinhala Buddhists have, over the centuries, sought to assimilate Christian forms with local religious forms, engaged in subtle forms of resistance to missionary claims about the exclusive truth and superiority of Christianity, and openly condemned the goals and tactics of missionaries as unethical. Hybridity, parody, and contempt are all in their own right responses to missions that resist the definitive substitution of Christianity for Buddhism. Over time, as Sinhala Buddhists have become more willing and able to reject the logic and strategy of Christian missions, their responses have become more forceful and direct. Furthermore, the type and degree of Buddhist resistance to missions varies. While Catholic and mainline Protestant churches generally receive more acceptance due to their long history in the island and their adaptation to local norms and customs, newer evangelical churches are routinely denounced for their allegedly loud services, aggressive methods of proselytization, and appeals to new converts to break their ties with their local culture and social relationships. Recent estimates suggest that between 6 and 8 percent of the total population is Christian, the majority of whom are Catholic, but anecdotal reports suggest rapid growth in newer evangelical and Pentecostal churches.[64] These reports suggest that throughout the history of Christian missions in Sri Lanka, at least some Sinhala Buddhists have responded by converting and assuming new, exclusively Christian identities.

Contemporary Buddhist responses to Christian missions revolve around traditional views linking Buddhism and the state, and conversely those that link Christian missions with the colonial imposition of foreign rule.[65] From the Buddhist nationalists' perspective, the Christian religion is the antithesis of Buddhism. It is viewed as being "foreign" rather than native, it sanctions the killing of animals and drinking liquor instead of denouncing these acts as immoral, and it relies on so-called blind faith in a supreme deity rather than on insight and wisdom guided by the Buddha but developed through one's own rational analysis. Yet despite the assertions of radical difference in the religion promoted by Christian missions, Buddhist nationalism and much of modern Buddhism in Sri Lanka owe their forms and existence to historical efforts to evangelize the Christian faith.

Among the far-reaching effects of Christian missions in Sri Lanka have been moves by Buddhists to change the terms of conversion or to resist it outright. Whether or not they have actively sought converts, Christian missionaries have introduced and reinforced more discrete and exclusive notions of religious identity. When applied to Buddhism, such notions are likely the consequences of the long history of polemical debate and proselytization that signaled to Sinhala Buddhists that one could not simply appropriate parts of the new Christian religion while retaining one's commitment to a more permeable and syncretic form of Buddhism. As a result of the missions and other colonial projects, such as census taking, religious identity became an either/or proposition.[66] Indeed, the politics of postcolonial religion tends to view hybridity with suspicion. In contrast to Alagiyavanna's experiment with fluid religious identities in *Kustantīnu Haṭana*, later experiences with missions and the colonial exercise of power led to the formation of more rigid religious identities in Sri Lanka. Christianity gradually became something that was associated with foreign powers and rejected, despite the enduring presence of some Sinhala Christian communities in parts of the island.

Buddhist responses to Christian missions in Sri Lanka remain overwhelmingly negative, but they tend to operate on many of the same premises about religious identity—ideas gleaned from missionaries over the centuries. Buddhist identity has thus become a distinct social marker, a way of referring to individuals that allows for them to be counted and used to define the nation. This same discrete Buddhist identity can further be mobilized to arrange for the protection of the nation from the forces perceived to threaten its continued existence. Perhaps the overriding Buddhist response to Christian missions in Sri Lanka has been the fashioning of a Buddhist identity that mirrors the notion of religious identity employed by Christians, in order to resist conversion efforts by appropriating aspects of the missionaries' own logic of religious identity. Efforts to clearly define what it means to be Buddhist, and to stake out a claim for the religion as an unassailable aspect of the local cultural heritage, propelled many of the responses to Christian missions. These efforts enabled Buddhists to reject the aims of Christian missions while drawing upon many of their assumptions about religious identity in order to develop a new sense of what it means to be "Buddhist," and only Buddhist, in the modern world.

6

The Port Said Orphan Scandal of 1933

Colonialism, Islamism, and the Egyptian Welfare State

Beth Baron

*O*n the morning of June 7, 1933, a fifteen-year-old Muslim orphan girl named Turkiyya Hasan refused to rise for the headmaster of the Salaam School in Port Said. This school was an enterprise of a nondenominational and internationally staffed Protestant mission that was originally known as the Swedish Mission, because its first leaders and many of its missionaries were Swedish or Swedish-speaking Finns, but which became commonly known as either the Swedish Salaam Mission or simply the Salaam Mission (from the Arabic word *salaam*, meaning peace). A resident in the mission's Home for Destitutes, which was an orphanage associated with the school, Turkiyya Hasan may well have felt enervated by the extreme heat that day and frustrated by the missionaries' relentless pressure to convert to Christianity. Some of her friends had already done so, persuaded by the message or the possibility of employment with the missionaries. The matron did not take Turkiyya's refusal to stand for prayer lightly and reprimanded her. When that did not work, the matron hit her with a stick, resulting in a ruckus, as the girl screamed and the matron rebuked her. What happened next is not exactly clear: the girl fled the school and was taken to the police or the police later came to the school and removed her. In any case, news of the beating of the orphan girl spread like wildfire from the port city to the capital, unleashing a firestorm.[1]

The caning of Turkiyya became a national scandal, generating a long paper trail of press stories, confidential consular reports, government circulars, and missionary accounts. Combined, the different accounts create a general picture of what happened that June morning. Juxtaposed, they show the contrasts in various understandings of the event, as multiple versions of the "Port Said Missionary Incident" or "The Criminal in the News" circulated through disparate networks. To some the matron's response was understandable, for they saw Turkiyya as an unruly girl who deserved a little slap; but others saw the girl as the victim of a brutal beating that constituted a crime. "Saving" Turkiyya thus had very different connotations to the missionaries who were concerned about her soul and the Egyptians who intervened to extricate her from the orphanage and safeguard her religion. The affair provides an unparalleled opportunity to examine the encounter between missionaries and Muslims in Egypt and the issue of conversion.

Some scholars claim that missionaries to the Middle East quickly abandoned the effort to convert Muslims because the social barriers (notably, attitudes informed by Islamic doctrines of apostasy) were too steep. Instead, they argue, missionaries turned most of their energies to running schools and hospitals, modernizing and not proselytizing to their protégés or clients. The consensus seems to be, at least for regions such as Anatolia, Lebanon, and Palestine, that missionaries focused their efforts on Eastern Christians.[2] Yet missionaries in Egypt attempted to convert Muslims as well as Copts, whether stealthily or in the open, and were given great leeway to do so under the British occupation. Many justified their proselytizing by citing the Egyptian Constitution of 1923, which affirmed freedom of religion and belief, as grounds for changing religions.[3] Muslims often took freedom of religion to mean freedom to practice, not freedom to change.

This study accepts the definition of Lewis Rambo, who identifies conversion not merely as an event but as a "process of religious change that takes place in a dynamic force field of people, events, ideologies, institutions, expectations, and orientations."[4] In early twentieth-century Egypt (as in countries like India), conversion was never just a matter of a transformed personal conviction. Rather, it remained a practical matter of law, for religious identity had consequences for public legal identity or "personal status" with regard to matters of marriage, divorce, inheritance, and so on.[5] In Egyptian Islamic society, the prevailing assumption was that non-Muslims could convert to Islam but that Muslims could not convert out. By challenging this precept, Christian missionaries undermined a foundational assumption. The fact that Christian missionaries were able to evangelize among Muslims like Turkiyya Hasan with such impunity led many Muslims (and Copts) to perceive Christian missionary activity as an extension of Western imperial aggression in the lands of Islam.

Here then were the major unexpected consequences of the Port Said orphan scandal of 1933. The Turkiyya Hasan affair touched a raw nerve among Egyptians who were weary of half a century of British colonial presence. Lively press coverage forced the Egyptian government to take action, articulating and implementing a plan for a welfare state that would guarantee the well-being and cultural integrity of vulnerable groups such as orphans.[6] Public outrage was fueled by and in turn energized an organization known in Arabic as *Jam'iyyat al-Ikhwan al-Muslimun*, and variously known in English as the Society of Muslim Brothers, the Muslim Brotherhood, and the Muslim Brethren (henceforth called here "the Muslim Brothers"), which had been founded five years earlier to rejuvenate Islamic practice in a modern context.[7] The Muslim Brothers grew to become the heart of a Sunni Islamic mass movement, spawning branches throughout Egypt, Syria, Palestine, and elsewhere in the Middle East and beyond.

Prelude: The Brewing Storm

Turkiyya Hasan was born toward the end of World War I, in about 1918, the year the Salaam Mission in Port Said moved to its new home in the Arab district on the edge of the prostitutes' quarter. Press accounts give her name variously as Turkiyya Hasan, Turkiyya Hasan Yusuf, and Turkiyya al-Sayyid Yusuf, and government documents transliterate her name alternately as Turkia, Turkya, and Turkiya. The founder of the orphanage, Maria Ericsson, refers to Turkiyya's mother and sister in correspondence in 1932, though a mother is nowhere in evidence in the summer of 1933.[8] Under Islamic law, a girl with a mother but without a father would in any case have been considered an orphan. Confidential sources in the United States refer to a sister and brother, but no male relative appeared in any other sources.[9] Little is known of Turkiyya's early years or when exactly she entered the mission's Home for Destitutes. It might have been as late as 1928, at about the age of ten, for a reporter in the newspaper *al-Siyasa* mentioned that in five years the missionaries at Port Said had failed to convert her.[10]

A storm had been brewing for some time at the Salaam Mission, for Turkiyya was not the only girl pressured by missionaries to accept Christianity. A case involving four siblings—three females named Aida, Nabawiyya, Fathiyya, and a male named Abduh Niman—created an uproar. Aida had converted to Christianity in 1931 on a visit to Zaytun, a town outside Cairo where missionaries kept a refuge for those female converts who could not return to their own homes and families or did not have them.[11] She became a teacher and urged her sisters to follow her path in order to have a means to earn a steady income. When the sisters refused, the siblings were separated: Nabawiyya was sent by the missionaries to the Salaam School in Dikirnis; Abduh was shipped to the Qalyub Orphanage for Boys, which fell under the auspices of the American Mission of the United Presbyterian Church of North America; and Fathiyya was consigned to the Salaam Mission's Home for Destitutes in Port Said.

Fathiyya faced heavy pressure to convert in this "home" and its associated school. She later reported that one of the tactics used by the missionaries to undermine the Muslim girls' faith was to place a Qur'an in the girls' bathroom. "We took it, but next day we found another one."[12] Despite such tactics and beatings, Fathiyya continued to resist appeals to convert and asked Turkiyya to help her escape. Fleeing the Home in May 1931, she took refuge in the police station, where she met Muhammad Effendi Khalil. A hastily arranged marriage gave the young woman protection and the young man a bride (without having to pay a high dowry).

The relentless appeals to Turkiyya to convert increased after Fathiyya's flight. Her recalcitrance reached the Salaam Mission founder Maria Ericsson, who was then fundraising in North America. The onetime surrogate mother used her moral authority to try to persuade Turkiyya from half a world away to accept Christ. In a letter penned in Flint, Michigan, and dated September 8, 1932, Maria recalled the youthful Turkiyya, who "used to try to teach visitors to say words in Arabic" and was "so earnest in making them repeat the words."[13] Maria, who had left for North America in the summer of 1931, flattered the girl by saying, "What a joy it would be to me to see you. I suppose that you have grown so that I would not know you," and let her know that "my heart is with you all the time."[14]

After the warm opening, Maria got down to business, pressing her former ward: "My dear Turkya, will you be among those who are washed in the BLOOD of the LAMB? Are you ready when the Lord your Saviour comes? He is coming soon. It was for me that Jesus dies on Calvary, that is what my heart sings, can you join me in this song?"[15] In her effort to convince the teenage girl to accept Christ, Maria Ericsson moved from images of singing to cries of agony, urging the teenager to believe in Him, to learn to love Him, not to fight against Him any longer. "Do not try to silence His voice speaking in your heart. The dear Lord is coming back very, very soon, and oh, what cries of agony there will be from all who rejected HIM." Shifting from persuasion to fear as a tactic, she continued, "For then the great day of HIS wrath is come; and who shall be able to stand? . . . even the might[y?] kings on earth shall not know how to escape from His judgement." She pointed Turkiyya to several specific passages in the Bible—every girl in the orphanage would have been given one to study—and then ended her letter with images of joy and love, signing as "your praying motherly friend."[16]

Not persuaded, Turkiyya tucked the letter away, along with a subsequent one from Finland, home of Anna Eklund, cofounder of the Salaam Mission, which had congratulated her on her new Christian name, Louisa.[17] But Turkiyya refused to go to Zaytun during Easter in 1933 to be baptized and take the name. She also refused to join in prayer at the dining table, causing a cutback in her servings of food.[18] In the meantime, she watched a battle unfold between missionaries, Muslims, and residents in Port Said over one of the older converts.

Like Turkiyya, Nazla Ibrahim Ghunaym had a mother but no father. She had attended a missionary school in Zaytun, and after graduating she took up work as a teacher in the Salaam School in Port Said. A convert from Islam to Christianity, she joined the Evangelical Church (which was the largest Protestant church in Egypt, and one founded by American Presbyterian missionaries), and married an Egyptian evangelist. Although she was now pregnant, her Muslim relatives (or mother) demanded her return, claiming that her conversion had been forced and her marriage invalid. The case pitted the authority of Islamic courts against those of religious minorities, Islamic prohibitions against apostasy against the notion of religious freedom, and a government seeking to prove its nationalist credentials against the colonial British presence.[19] Whatever the merits of the case and differences in the dispositions of the two young women— Nazla chose to convert and Turkiyya chose not to—the Salaam School and Home in Port Said came under close outside scrutiny. Under attack, the missionaries went on the offensive to save the girls in their care.

The Government Investigates

Competing accounts circulated about events that took place in the Salaam Mission School in Port Said on the morning of June 7, 1933, between Turkiyya Hasan and Alzire Richoz, the Swiss matron left in charge that day while the acting school director was away. News that the matron of the Salaam School had beaten an orphan girl in an attempt to convert her to Christianity spread quickly from the Mediterranean port city to the capital, sparking an investigation by the police and the Parquet (as the public prosecutor's department was known). The press buzzed: *Al-Jihad* took credit for breaking the story and positioned itself as the vanguard of the journalistic corps investigating missionary abuses. Reports in *al-Jihad* on June 12 claimed that a woman missionary had attempted to force a Muslim girl of fifteen to convert to Christianity.[20] The next day, Turkiyya Hasan's picture appeared on the front page of *al-Ahram*, the Egyptian Arabic daily with the largest distribution, showing her standing near the desks of members of the Parquet.[21] Articles in the newspapers *al-Balagh*, *al-Siyasa*, *al-Jihad*, *Kawkab al-Sharq*, and *al-Wadi* attacked the government for leniency in dealing with missionaries and negligence in defending the official religion of the state. *Al-Sha'b*, a government organ, retorted that the government was taking measures, and that the press might do better to advise Muslim parents not to send their children to such schools and to encourage wealthy Muslims to establish alternative educational institutions. The paper added that in the absence of proof of coercion to embrace Christianity, the government could not close missionary schools.[22]

The government had faced a series of missionary scandals in the early 1930s and had promised results, but had little to show for the effort. It claimed its hands were tied by the Capitulations, the set of legal and fiscal privileges enjoyed by foreign nationals and their protégés, and by the post-1882 British occupation of Egypt, which protected missionary activity. Although Prime Minister Isma'il Sidqi had abrogated the 1923 Constitution, the protection of freedom in religion still held; missionaries could proselytize in Egypt, just not with force. The government had a rough time cracking down on missionary activity, but it also had little desire to do so, for missionaries provided a range of social services on the cheap. But the Egyptian government wanted to resolve the Turkiyya Hasan affair quickly before it spun out of control.

The letters that Turkiyya had saved became crucial evidence in the investigation and critical in persuading government officials about the need to rein in the Salaam Mission. The Egyptian minister of interior pointed to the letters in a conversation with A. W. Keown-Boyd, the head of the European Department in the ministry, saying, "You have told me often that the missionaries do not press or incite Moslem children to change their religion. Here are documents which prove that they use both cajolery and intimidation."[23] Keown-Boyd then turned to George Swan, head of the Inter-Mission Council, a group comprised of representatives of many (but not all) of the evangelical organizations in Egypt that acted as a liaison between missionaries and the government. Keown-Boyd told Swan that the Ericsson letter "has done your cause more harm with responsible and reasonable Egyptians than any of the calumnies published against you."[24]

Turkiyya testified in the inquiry that the head of the orphanage had beaten her for refusing to embrace Christianity. Physicians examining her found bruises and scratches that required observation in the hospital for three days. The matron of the orphanage, Miss Richoz, and the director of the school, Alice Marshall, admitted that Turkiyya had been beaten. Yet they asserted that it was because she had acted "ill-behaved and impolite" and had been justifiably disciplined. They denied that they pressed her to embrace Christianity and maintained that they gave her and other students a choice in religious beliefs. When cross-examined on these statements, Turkiyya admitted that she had made a scornful remark to the headmistress, but insisted that the matron's desire to convert her was one of the reasons for the beating.[25]

The missionaries pushed for an interpretation of events that emphasized Turkiyya's unruly behavior and not their own. But either way, the matron was in deep trouble, for both forcible conversion and physical punishment in schools by those not authorized (in this case only the headmistress was authorized to use force) were illegal, though the latter was a less serious charge. The accusation of forcible conversion undermined the entire missionary enterprise and had broad ramifications, threatening the work of missionaries throughout Egypt and beyond.

An accommodation was quickly reached between the caretaker government (at the time Sidqi, the prime minister, was abroad receiving medical treatment) and the missionaries. After interviewing Turkiyya Hasan, Alice Marshall, and Alzire Richoz, the Parquet concluded that this was a case of school discipline rather than force in religion. Keown-Boyd then presented the Inter-Mission Council, of which the Salaam Mission was a member, with a choice: either the matron would leave the country or she would stand trial for having contravened the laws against corporal punishment in schools. The executive committee of the Inter-Mission Council advised her to leave but had no power to enforce its recommendation. The government gave the missionaries a few hours to decide whether to fight the charges or leave the country. With the clock ticking, Richoz packed her bags and proceeded to Palestine, taking refuge in the Swedish mission there, hoping perhaps that when the storm died down she could return to her post.[26]

A week after the "missionary incident," on Wednesday, June 14, the Minister of Interior, Mahmud Fahmi al-Qaysi, responded to questions in the Chamber of Deputies of the Egyptian Parliament. He reported that the government had come to an agreement with the relevant authorities that the matron of the school should leave Egypt and that she had left. He also announced that the remaining Muslim girls in the Salaam Mission orphanage would be sent immediately to government institutions or Islamic associations to be maintained and educated at government expense. And, with great pleasure, he reported that the government had allocated seventy thousand pounds for new institutions and refuges to provide orphans and destitute children with a sound upbringing.[27]

The government's plan—getting the matron out of the country, promising to extract the other Muslim girls, and setting aside funds for new orphanages—aimed to quiet the affair. But with the caning of Turkiyya, the missionaries had overreached, and the Egyptian public, already incensed over earlier missionary scandals, was not placated so easily. Rather than bring the matter to closure, momentum continued to build, and Turkiyya became the poster child for the growing antimissionary movement. Overnight the spirited fifteen-year-old girl became a hero. On the evening of Wednesday, June 15, after the minister of interior had delivered his parliamentary remarks hoping to quiet dissent, Turkiyya addressed a large assembly at the home of one of her Port Said supporters. She discussed the methods of missionaries, urging her listeners to intercede on behalf of the young and calling upon them to build refuges and schools. Those gathered donated 300 pounds to the cause and formed a committee to establish a Muslim orphanage.[28]

A week later Turkiyya traveled to Cairo with an escort to be feted by the press. A large crowd sent her off from the train station, presenting her with bouquets of flowers to celebrate her resistance to the missionaries' entreaties and threats. In the capital, she visited the offices of *al-Balagh*, *al-Siyasa*, and *al-Jihad*, the triad of papers that had covered the story most closely and reported her visit in articles on June 22 and 23.[29] At *al-Siyasa*, she explained her reasons for rejecting Christianity: she could not believe that Jesus was the son of God, for as the Qur'an said, God is one, and she was ready to die for her beliefs.[30] At *al-Jihad*, she gave details of her life in the Salaam Mission and the cruelty she experienced to force her to convert.[31] The press kept the affair alive.

Concerned Americans:
The Presbyterians and the Port Said Consul

Although the Salaam Mission had Swedish founders, it evolved into an interdenominational and international Protestant operation with a strong American component. The mission's founder lived in the United States, four Americans resided in the compound, and American funds kept the mission afloat. American Presbyterians, whose mission was the single largest missionary enterprise in Egypt, but who provided no funding for and had no institutional connection to the Salaam Mission and its enterprises, kept a close watch on the affair, concerned about its widening repercussions. They stood to lose the most if the antimissionary movement mushroomed. "I am writing to give you some account of a storm of an anti-missionary agitation through which we are at present passing," C. C. Adams, the head of the American Mission in Egypt, wrote to Presbyterian officials in Philadelphia on June 26. He recounted the version that had reached him of events in the school. "One of the Muslim girls, named Turkiyah, refused to stand up as usual to join in the daily prayers of the school." American missionaries, like the Swedes, mandated that all students regardless of their religious backgrounds participate in Christian prayer sessions, and Turkiyya had contravened the rules. "When the head mistress, a Swiss lady, a member of that Mission, remonstrated with her the girl became unmanageable and broke out into disrespectful language and screaming and created such a scene that the missionary, perhaps in exasperation, used a small rattan cane on the girl's legs." Here a naughty girl exceeds the bounds of good behavior, and a matron, pushed to her limits, uses minimal force. "The girl struggled to get possession of the cane and in doing so received some scratches."[32]

Adams's account of the incident diverges from the one recounted by Turkiyya to the police and circulating in the Egyptian press. The head of the American Mission emphasized the girl's responsibility for the punishment and minimized the extent of the inflicted damage to the girl. Like other missionaries, he argued that the "discipline which was administered for disobedience and insubordination was thoroughly deserved," while admitting that, "the manner of it was unwise." Adams had little problem with the disciplining of the girl (all the missionaries occasionally faced insubordinate children), but admitted that the situation was complicated. "And the unfortunate part about it was that it all arose because of the refusal of the girl to take part in Christian religious exercises and has given color to the charge which is now being broadcasted indiscriminately against all mission work of an attempt at forcible conversion."[33] In short, he objected to the spin that Egyptian observers put on events, linking the discipline to forced conversion.

Throughout this episode, American and other missionaries were keen to distinguish between required school activities, which included prayer and Bible study, and compulsion in religion, which they denied. They maintained that they gave students a choice in religion, exposing them to the gospel but not forcing them to accept it. Missionaries stressed the difference between illegitimate attempts to forcibly convert and legitimate discipline. At the same time, they sidestepped the parameters set on corporal punishment in Egyptian schools, under which only designated personnel had permission to cane students. The principal had the authority to cane Turkiyya; Alzire Richoz did not have this privilege.

Two weeks after the incident in the Salaam Mission school, and in light of continued media furor and public outrage, the U.S. Legation in Cairo sent a request to the American consul in Port Said to report on the "so-called missionary incident."[34] Through one of the American missionaries affiliated with the Salaam Mission, the American consul, Horace Remillard, asked Alice Marshall, the acting principal and a British national, for a written statement. She would not give one, for the Swedish Legation in Cairo had "bound the Mission to secrecy," but she offered to meet with Remillard to answer questions, providing that the account be kept confidential. They met on Monday, June 26, nineteen days after the caning.[35]

In Marshall's narrative of events, as recorded by Remillard, Miss Richoz reprimanded Turkiyya "for not standing up in the presence of visitors as she had been taught to do and as was done by the other pupils with her at that time." The response to the reprimand was "violent, abusive and blasphemous language," at which point Richoz threatened corporal punishment. The girl "dared her teacher" (knowing perhaps that she was not authorized to cane her), "refused to hold out her hand to receive the blows," and struggled with Richoz, who struck the girl "with the stick over one shoulder while holding her wrists."[36] This account deletes any religious context, such as an obligatory morning service or prayer, for the caning.

Marshall reconstructed events for Remillard's report that she herself had not witnessed, but she was on hand for the follow-up. Marshall noted that Turkiyya's brother and sister "called for an explanation" but "seemed to be satisfied that the punishment had been justly administered." (This is the only time we hear of a brother, who may have been a brother-in-law.) The evening following the caning, Thursday, June 8, a police officer came to the mission to take the girl away. Two days later, the chief of police notified Marshall that the matter was being taken up at the national level with the Departments of Interior and Justice. After giving testimony to the Parquet, Turkiyya traveled to Cairo, where June 13 she met in the Ministry of the Interior with Keown-Boyd, Swan, and Judge Booth, who gave her the ultimatum about Miss Richoz.[37]

Remillard's own assessment was that assertions that the girl was beaten "because she refused to be baptized" were without foundation. But he admitted that the mission "appears embarrassed" and saw Richoz's actions as "unwise." As a result of "inflammatory" articles in the press, the mission received veiled threats, which it reported, and the police assigned the compound protection.[38] The credibility of the missions in Port Said had definitely suffered as a result of the affair. Muslim attendance at Sunday service of the American Peniel Mission (another small, independent, and interdenominational mission active in Egypt) was down drastically, from fifty or sixty to two or three.[39] Still, the incident might not have drawn attention, according to the Mission, "had it not been for a certain Doctor Soliman . . . who is inimical to the Mission for reasons of personal jealousy."[40] He had been behind the "secret influence" used to propel the event into a national and religious issue.[41] But Remillard reported that Marshall was anxious about divulging Dr. Soliman's name, for "it would lead to certain trouble, with the Mission at a disadvantage from lack of tangible evidence."[42] In spite of credible proof, the story made the rounds, and was the lens through which the Salaam School missionaries understood the affair.

The Swedes, the Mysterious "Dr. S," and the Muslim Brothers

Keeping Turkiyya in the news fueled anger over an affair that Egyptian government officials, British colonial officers, and Americans consular and missionary observers all hoped to quickly put behind them. They saw the affair as unfortunate but isolated. However, those affiliated with the Salaam Mission saw the whole event as staged and part of a larger conspiracy. "The members of the Swedish Mission now suspect that the girl may have been instructed by parties outside to make such a scene in order to bring about what has happened," Charles Adams wrote to the head of his board in the United States, the same day that Remillard wrote to the head of the American Legation something along the same lines.[43] Although Adams dismissed the suspicion as farfetched, his British counterpart, Swan, head of the Inter-Mission Council and the Egyptian General Mission based in Zaytun, supported the claim. "There is before us abudant [sic] evidence to show that the incidents at Port Said were originated and continued by a malicious and evil-minded man, who was seeking to satisfy thereby his own personal aims, and have since been exploited for political purposes."[44]

A history of the Salaam Mission written by Helmi Pekkola in the wake of the orphan scandal and published in Finnish in 1934 refers to a mysterious "Dr. S." Pekkola's history draws on a Swedish manuscript by Erica Lindstrom, a teacher in the mission; Maria Ericsson's short book, *The Swedish Mission Story*, published earlier; and letters, stories, and presentations by the mission's cofounder, Anna Eklund.[45] According to Pekkola, Dr. S had been deeply implicated in the controversy surrounding Nazla, which had set the stage for the Turkiyya Hasan affair. He had been married to a German woman who had left him and saw Nazla, who with her husband Zaki had rented an apartment in a building he owned, as a replacement. In spite of Nazla's pregnancy, he had sought "to charm" her for "he wanted to have Nazla for himself."[46] In this version of events, Dr. S conspired with Nazla's mother and informed the police that Nazla was underage; the authorities subsequently brought her in for questioning. After pressure and a few sleepless nights, she signed a paper "not knowing what she did," renouncing her faith in Jesus Christ. This voided her marriage, since a Muslim woman could not marry a Christian man. Nazla quickly sought to reverse this and turned to the missionaries for help, taking refuge at the Salaam Mission. She later fled to Cairo, where she gave birth (possibly in the American Presbyterian Mission's Fowler Orphanage), but the baby did not survive more than a few days. In the words of Pekkola, the "distress and strain experienced by the mother had left its marks on the baby, making it too weak for this evil world." Later Nazla and Zaki were spirited out of the country where "in their new homeland they are able to continue the service of their Lord and Master."[47]

Seen another way, Dr. S could have been trying to save Nazla and return her to her Muslim faith, not to seduce her, as the missionaries asserted. "Doctor S's plans with regard to Nazla hadn't worked out," wrote the Finnish mission historian, "and in his rage he decided to bring down the whole hated Mission."[48] According to Pekkola, Dr. S found an ally in trying to bring down the Salaam Mission. "One of the pupils at the Salaam Mission girls' orphanage was to become a very helpful henchman to him." That pupil, "T," as the mission historian called Turkiyya, had apparently visited Dr. S frequently in the spring of 1933. And "with his advice she secretly collected photographs and letters that her friends had received from the missionaries," placing these in a suitcase for safekeeping.[49]

In hindsight, the missionaries saw T as a "difficult-to-educate bad-mannered girl," who had always been "a source of grief and sorrow to the Mission." In this version of events, T provoked the matron in a premeditated act. One day in early June, "she organized a scene/had a fit. She got mean, and got even more upset from the scolding, until she was physically punished." The context of the "fit" is not mentioned, but the consequences are: "That is when she ran away, taking with her the photographs and letters she had collected, that she in advance had stuffed in a suitcase and hidden." She ran to Dr. S and with him "went to the other enemies of the Mission and told that she had been hit because she did not let herself be forcefully baptized."[50] The evidence in Turkiyya's suitcase had a large impact on the court of public opinion, for the letters were published. The Egyptian press carried photographs of students and teachers alongside letters from missionaries such as the one from Maria Ericsson to

Turkiyya—which the mission chronicler described as "heartfelt words of advice and consolation to the young Christians."[51] The press accused the Salaam Mission of hypnotizing children, kidnapping them, and taking them to Finland, where Anna Eklund was born and many of the mission supporters lived.[52]

Nordic missionaries focused on a plot with twists and turns that ultimately missed the main point. This was more than the story of a despondent husband or jilted lover trying to destroy a foreign institution in revenge, a tale that made the rounds of foreign missionaries in Egypt and reached Keown-Boyd. He warned Swan "not to think in terms of Dr. Mohammed Suliman who plots and plans the destruction of the Salaam School partly from bitterness of soul caused by the light morals of his German Christian wife and perhaps partly to fill his clinic."[53] Keown-Boyd wanted Swan to focus on defusing the crisis instead.

Dr. Muhammad Sulayman, who was disparagingly called "Dr. S" by the Finnish mission historian, headed the delegation that escorted Turkiyya to Cairo and took her on a tour of daily newspapers. His political affiliations rather than his romantic inclinations provide the key to understanding the scandal. Sulayman was a member, among other organizations, of the Port Said branch of the Muslim Brothers, a society founded in 1928 by Hasan al-Banna in the nearby canal city of Ismailiyah to strengthen Islam in the face of British occupation, Westernization, and missionary inroads. The origin and spread of the Muslim Brothers is closely linked to missionary activity in the Suez Canal Zone and Egyptian Delta region, for it became the main grassroots organization trying to combat Christian evangelizing. The Muslim Brothers in Port Said and nearby towns had placed the Salaam Mission in its sights and watched the place carefully for opportunities to rescue girls. Gossip about an Egyptian notable's marital distress missed the main point and the genuine concern of Muslims about the conversion of minors.

The Salaam Mission historian acknowledged that Sulayman was a member of a league started to support and defend Islam and that "[t]hese kinds of leagues of the most zealous Mohammedans have been forming everywhere in the last few years."[54] She was probably referring to the League for the Defense of Islam, an organization that was founded June

23 as a result of the Turkiyya Hasan affair, but was oblivious of his links to the older organization. Most of the foreign missionaries in Egypt did not link evangelical activities to the rise of Islamist organizations such as the Muslim Brothers and see the larger picture.

The Muslim Brothers went under the radar of British and other foreign officials, as did publications sympathetic to their cause, such as *al-Fath*. Edited by Muhibb al-Din al-Khatib, an Islamic activist from Syria and Muslim Brothers member, *al-Fath* gave a dramatic account of the events of June 7. In this version, under the headline "Criminal in the News" (a reference to the school matron), Miss Richoz picked a quarrel with Turkiyya, hit her with a bamboo/rattan cane, and humiliated her in front of her friends. Then "she threw her down on the big bench, leaned over her back, pulled her hair taut and banged her head." What for the Americans were a few scratches looked to many Muslims like "evangelical brutality." When asked for the reason for her actions, Richoz replied that she did this because Turkiyya deviated from the routine. Turkiyya claimed that the matron perpetrated these offenses "to kill the devil" that stood between her and Jesus.[55]

According to *al-Fath*, under this pressure Turkiyya feigned acceptance of Christianity, and when the missionaries tried to appoint her as a nurse in a missionary hospital, she escaped. Dr. Sulayman was "in a position to learn of her story" and "had the merit to lift the curtain" on the crimes committed under the name of "peace" at the Salaam School. Earlier, another girl had tried to flee from "that hellish place" and asked Dr. Sulayman for help; but he was unable to aid her legally because she had no family with whom he could intercede and the state intimidated her to stay in the home. The Muslims of Port Said started an organization, the Society of Islamic Awakening (*Jam'iyyat al-Nahda al-Islamiyya*), to rescue poor Muslim boys and girls from missionaries like the unnamed girl who solicited help from Dr. Sulayman. The group requested guardianship of orphans "like that victim"; in the wake of the Turkiyya Hasan affair, the government decided to build its own refuge.[56]

Upon her return from the press circuit in Cairo, Turkiyya began working in the Ophthalmic Hospital in Port Said. But the town was simply not big enough for her to avoid chance meetings with missionaries and converts form the Salaam Mission. When they attempted to woo Turkiyya back into the fold, her sister Amina (who had not figured prominently in the story until then) complained to the Parquet. She asked to have contacts between the missionaries and Turkiyya severed completely.[57] Government officials moved Turkiyya from Port Said to Cairo, where she was enrolled in a nursing course at the King's Hospital at their expense. Her handlers in the Ministry of Interior hoped that upon completing the course she would take up employment as a nurse in the same hospital.[58]

Conclusion

There are numerous holes in the story of the Turkiyya Hasan affair and contradictions in the reports: Was Turkiyya beaten badly? Was she beaten to force her conversion or her compliance with school regulations? Did the beating occur during prayer or a school visit? Did she accept Christianity only to later recant? Did she flee the Salaam Mission or was she taken out by the police? We may never know exactly what happened in the Salaam Mission in Port Said that June. It is clear, however, that the contradictory versions reveal a wide gulf in the way foreign missionaries and Egyptian Muslims perceived aims, activities, and agendas.

In Cairo, Turkiyya disappeared almost completely from the public eye and the historical record. But the caning in the Salaam Mission continued to reverberate, setting in motion a train of events that had consequences way beyond Port Said and the set of actors involved in the scandal. The affair that Turkiyya had sparked spurred the spread of Islamist societies in Egypt, undermined the privileges of missionaries, and toppled a government. This was no small feat for a fifteen-year-old girl.

The missionaries were tone deaf and did not hear the concerns of the Muslims they had come to "enlighten" and "save." Those affiliated with the Salaam Mission saw some good emerge from the affair. As with past persecutions, this one generated "testimonial of Jesus Christ" for governments, heads of states, and "all the people to hear." The missionaries believed in an ultimate victory, that God, "in his grace," would "let the light of gospel shine in the darkness of Islam for the salvation of many."[59] They certainly believed in their good intentions of enlightening and saving those in darkness. But those in the "darkness of Islam" did not see matters in the same way. They mobilized under the banner of the Muslim Brothers and similar associations to fight the missionaries, rescue their victims, and strengthen Islam.

The missionaries' good intentions produced unintended and unforeseen consequences that would have a lasting impact on Egyptian society and politics. The effort to convert Turkiyya Hasan set off an antimissionary movement that reached a crescendo in the summer of 1933. The affair was the beginning of the end for American and other missionaries in Egypt, who slowly retreated from most of their outposts in Egypt, leaving in their wake a vibrant Islamist movement, which was born in large part in opposition to them and in their image.

7

Robert Moffat and the Invention of Christianity in South Africa

Paul S. Landau

We like to feel that, in considering a problem in an interdisciplinary framework, every practitioner has essentially the same aim. A historian, a political scientist, a demographer, a sociologist, a literature person, all come together in a classroom. They recognize a common heritage, a vision of representation, explanation, and potential improvement. Each may comprehend his or her own tenets better than others, it is true; the barber trims his cigar with his shears. Together, however, they hope to explain and diagnose a problem, narrate its trajectory, sketch out a plausible solution. They want to bring to visibility, and legibility, that which is initially encountered as inchoate. If they hold fundamental disagreements—say, on the nature of the soul, morality, or human agency—those are put aside.

This already tentative scenario vanishes like smoke as soon as a theologian enters the mix. One does not have to agree with Nietzsche that theology is fundamentally antithetical to modern thought to recognize that the interdisciplinary meeting will no longer share a common aim. Theology cherishes the existence of the unseen, and it understands the unseen as what is kept away from reason by design. The facticity, the absolute reality, of the unseen cannot be challenged, as that is why theology and theologians exist. Man's traffic on the margins of this discipline is nonetheless of the greatest importance. Theologians offer themselves as guides to what they simultaneously demand is unknowable. In contrast, those in the humanities and social sciences like to think their subject matter can, in principle, fully be known. As for theology—to paraphrase Wittgenstein, for that which cannot be spoken about—it is better not to speak.

There are several detours around the conflict, and these paths are well-trodden. One of the most common is to pretend to restrict the subject matter to matters *also* of interest to theology. We may all safely agree that missionaries exist; perhaps we might say we are discussing missionaries. We may say we are talking about "beliefs," as if we are collectors of stories and fables. We only must avoid noting the truth value of those beliefs. Then there is the close pursuit of source criticism since Bultmann, which, by its cold and thrilling logic, suffices for a while. A relentless focus on evidence can pare down the subject matter until theology loses interest in it. A third ruse is for social historians to salute religion and reference God but actually, in their analysis, to ignore them. Religion becomes an inert text that stands apart from the tangible engines of human behavior. Finally, some scholars deal with theologians in a kind of intellectual antechamber. The texts that theology grasps as closest to the nub of things, they treat rather as scrims on which people in the past projected representations of their actual condition.

The theme of this volume, "unexpected consequences," therefore expresses more than the inadequacy of historical actors' intentions in shaping the world—although this also holds true. It expresses the necessary uncertainty surrounding any historical inquiry into the transformation of a subject—the spiritual, the unseen, the domain of religion—that cannot be cleanly defined. The efforts of historians of religion are bound to have "unexpected consequences." If we are honest, we must admit that no conclusion about human behavior in the domain of religion will be entirely satisfying to everyone. The history of religion is an ineluctable partnership between the Comptean and the Clergyman, who, while pretending to operate within common parameters, actually drive at very different outcomes.

Below, drawing on two chapters from a book about South Africans' political behavior, broadly conceived, I discuss the very early development of religion as a subject. I think about it as a new field for mediating debate and ambition in South Africa, a veiled and abridged dialogue rendered according to compromises never fully articulated. I view the missionaries as theologians, and precolonial South African men and women as pragmatic doubters. Most often in modern historical literature, the reverse is assumed. Missionaries are framed as harbingers of positivist thought, exponents of the logic of causation, bent on revising the natives' unconsidered trust in superhuman forces. Protestant missionaries are taken as the social scientists, however prejudiced; Africans are seen as the theologians. Much of the urge to frame the encounter in that way derives from a presentist view. Surely Africans were then as they appear now, distant from the real levers and switches of power, satisfied to pantomime their operation; surely the missionaries, as rearward extensions of nineteenth-century European thought, represented causal logic.

But I wish to suggest the opposite. The early encounters between missionaries and Africans previewed all later engagements between those who trusted their navigational capacities in the world of the visible, and those exegetical scholars with master texts who were certain of their own correctness. Africans repeatedly fell back on what they could speak about from experience, while evangelists touted their knowledge of what could not be seen.

My specific focus alights upon the pioneering efforts of the Reverend Robert Moffat (1795–1883) to learn highveld southern Bantu speech, called "the Sichuaan" at the time, and his efforts to select a vocabulary for communicating his knowledge of the unseen. For him and, he hoped, for his interlocutors, that vocabulary, along with a mandated, attendant set of practices, would constitute Christianity.

Moffat, the father-in-law of the famous missionary and explorer David Livingstone (1813–1873), was a formidable intellect. He created himself as a soldier of orthodoxy and an advance agent of colonial control. He wished to prevent the proliferation of uncorraled theocratic domains of power in South Africa, be they European, African, or "Griqua." *Griqua* as an identity indicated people's allegiance to two mixed-race or *métis* settlements in the borderlands of the Cape Colony. Moffat tried to tear apart the web of Griqua Christian agents, which was spreading across the highveld. At other times, he attacked the African highveld chiefs' arrogation of supremacy, characterizing their power as an affront to God. He translated and published a vernacular Bible beginning in 1829 and 1830, and sought to require that it be read by all highveld non-European Christians. Ultimately all black schoolchildren in South Africa up to the 1930s either read his translations or others influenced by them. South African Christianity was to a large extent designed by Moffat. Only it never was entirely such; not eventually, and even, it turns out, not at the beginning.

Robert Moffat (at Large)

Robert Moffat was a young man of twenty-two years when he arrived in South Africa in 1817, an employee of the London Missionary Society (LMS). He first settled in a parish in Stellenbosch, a conservative, rural Boer town. He assisted in the small church and learned the local version of Dutch, forming a lifelong fondness for the Boers as a people. Then he moved to purge the LMS as an organization in South Africa (as the society called the African subcontinent) in order to remove wayward preachers, white men who let down the evolving bourgeois white standard.[1] Cape Town was throwing off its shore-leave reputation for whoredom and slavery. Moffat, acting together with George Thom, effectively compelled James Campbell to visit South Africa on behalf of the society in London and to appoint a local supervisor after him. That man turned out to be John Philip, the famous Exeter Hall antislavery advocate, who ultimately was not a dependable ally of Moffat's program. In the near term, however, Philip confirmed the firing of several missionaries, including that of James Read, the pioneering missionary to Dithakong, on grounds of adultery (for Read) and for taking common-law indigenous wives.

Read was Moffat's largest target. He had supervised the very first printings of "Sechuana," as the Sichuaan language would be called, in a spelling book made at Griquatown in 1819. Around this time Moffat decided to evict Read personally from Dithakong, the chief town among African farmers called "the Bachapees" (or *batlhaping*, which means "people of the place of fish"). Unfortunately the Cape Colony refused to permit missionaries to travel freely beyond the border in 1820, in reaction to the Berganaar rebellion of *métis* settlers against conscription, which (not entirely without reason) was blamed on European missionaries. While he waited for the border to reopen in Griquatown, Moffat "purge[d]" the Griqua-town church, expelling many venerable members.[2]

Once the ban on transborder travel was lifted in 1821, Moffat wasted no time and set out via wagon and yoke to Dithakong, to personally replace Read and begin a new mission at the Kuruman River. His delega-tion included a good number of *métis* people, indispensable men without whom he could not have done the job, yet he was opposed to "Griqua evangelism," thinking it a disguise for "Griqua imperialism."[3] The line between religion and politics itself became the central issue. In fact, Read had already quit preaching at Dithakong when he became aware—shortly after arriving and confessing his adultery—that his parishioners thought he was alluding to himself when he used the word he had designated for God, *modimo*. He then handed his preaching work to his assistant, a *métis* man named Hendrick.[4] It had been John Campbell of the LMS who in 1813 initiated the containment of *métis* ambiguity with the new national name, "Griqua." Now Griqua-ness was in Moffat's view seeping out and growing with and through Christianity.

Moffat beheld a world of dangerous and crosscutting loyalties. There were Griqua churchgoers, but then there were also pro-LMS "Baster" and "Bastaard" (*métis*) churchgoers, who disdained the Griqua name. They were pursued by highveld chiefdoms as allies, who yet traded gunpowder and arms to non-Christian "mountain" (*bergenaar*) communities in open rebellion against the colony. There were Engelbrechts, Hendrickses, Bar-ends, and other powerful Griqua Christians who demanded parity with "European" Christians and intermarried with them. Moffat's position was *avant la lettre* in the growing annals of racism in South Africa, in that he set himself squarely against *métis*- and Southern Bantu–speaking Chris-tian, proselytizing, court-based power-holders—allied with, or ensconced in highveld chiefdoms. He opposed autonomy among the denizens of the highveld, unless that authority was traditional, ethnic, and customary, by his own calculation.[5]

If Moffat was against emergent, autonomous political power, he was for something else. We might call his program "establishment Christian-ity." The word "establishment" connects it to other domains of institution-alized practices reformers wished to establish, not only in the Cape Colony but also broadly in the British Empire. Yet the word "establishment" only begins to explain its place in Moffat's program, which was proactive. In evicting Read from Dithakong, Moffat decided to ignore the very strenuous protests of Dithakong's chief, Mothibe, because, Moffat wrote, it was important to "teach the people . . . to submit to the powers that be." These powers would very soon include institutions of administrative overrule.[6] Moffat next purged the Dithakong church of its *métis* "council," acting much as he had in Griquatown. He wore his long beard uncut, like an Old Testament patriarch, for this work.

Such is one context for the analysis of Robert Moffat's language work, discussed below: his insistent political program, seeking to remove Africans from the vicinity of the levers and switches of earthly power.

Moffat and Pifo: Creating God's Kingdom, Part 1

Nearly all early observers, whatever their differences, felt that the people of the highveld, the population of farmers in South Africa's elevated interior, had no "religious worship" before Christians came among them. There was no special domain of the sacred, no false idols to smash. When asked to whom Rev. John Campbell "prayed," and told, "a Great Being" (*mogolo*), they replied that "they did not know him, for they had never seen him."[7] Robert Moffat agreed, "They have no religion," they were "entirely ignorant of a . . . Creator." Most observers would second Moffat in his observation that for highveld people, anything "beyond what they see and feel they consider vanities of vanities."[8]

Moffat and other early South African missionaries asserted that this was wrong. The world was made by an external Power that must be respected according to their established Christian rules, and known by their canonical narratives and texts.[9] The truest domain into which all people were headed could not be seen, and existed for people after the visible body was rendered silent and still. It was "up," or "in the air," all around us, and yet beyond us. Like *where*, the question of *when*, if applied to God's domain, was displaced from visibility and ordinary language. The biblical era was "long ago," when the ancestors were men; but there was no easy gloss for "long ago." The same words are also given as "very great," with "*golo*," great, repeated, as "very-greatness" (*bogologolo*). Long ago was a location outside the boundaries of cyclical time, outside "the mind," and ipso facto great or "very great." God created the stars like the earth and its denizens in the "very great" era, when the world operated differently from the present.

Complicating the placement of this space, *when* had a second answer, in addition to "long ago." This was "very soon." The Bible was divided between record and prophecy. Disobeying its commands brought misfortune in life, right now, and also later, and also after death. What was coming soon for everybody, and for you, with the Grim Reaper, was an encounter with the great-greatness time and a father up above, poised to judge, theretofore unknown. No wonder many people ducked away when missionaries approached, muttering, "I only know how to drink milk."[10]

In the 1820s there was no clear concord on how the omnipotence and omniscience of God were to be depicted or named or firmly located as a separate space. Moffat preferred a version of "Great One" while other missionaries had other solutions: perhaps the name of a past chief, or distant hero; perhaps a neologism (like "Jesu," God's son); a Methodist pioneer favored "Jehovah." Moffat was suspicious of "ancestor" as it gained ground beneath him. For one thing, the word "ancestor"—*modimo*—had been the Rev. Read's first choice for God, back in Dithakong. For another thing, *modimo* unalterably belonged to the highveld's own past, and so had a preexisting coloration and set of contexts. All these things weighed on Moffat, but he could scarcely act in a determined or determinative manner, because he had yet to learn the language sufficiently to preach in it.

In the austral fall of 1827 Moffat decided to remedy this situation. After an arduous journey—for virtually all travel was so—he arrived at Letswaing (or Chuin or Chwaing Pan), 96 miles northwest of Vryburg, today called "Tswaing Rural Area" on Google's satellite maps. He spent time also in Kongke, "about 20 miles west" of Chuin, and rendezvoused there with an old acquaintance of his, a minor chief named Bogachu. Robert Moffat came "alone" to this part of the country, the salt pans, a hundred miles from anywhere: meaning, he came with no other Europeans, and no interpreter.[11]

Set where the veld was sparse but wide open for grazing, several "captains" or small chiefs had small encampments, akin to large, seasonally inhabited "cattle post" homes in peacetime. They were too small to draw the notice of hostile patrols sent by Mzilikazi or MmaNtathisi, two infamous chiefs who presided over militarized states. Moffat stayed close to a few other smaller chiefs: Bogachu, his "cousin" Lekomenyane, and others supposedly of the dead chief's name, *Seleka*—like *Seitshiro*, a scion of the venerable people-of-*rolong* association—and, finally, Pifo and his large household, who stemmed from the chiefdoms of the Marico called place-of-*rotse* (later rendered "BaHurutshe"). A dozen miles from Kongke lay a settlement called Setabeng, where Chief Gonntse held court. Gonntse was a scion of the *Seitshiro* chiefdom of the *Ratlou* inheritance—both were names of former chiefs, as were the words selected by some missionaries for "God." The men of Chuin lived 4 miles away from the nearest springs, to which they sent the women to fetch water; this was convenient, they told Moffat, because they (the men) had found the kind of brush they preferred for their beloved kraal fences.

Moffat thus encountered, in Chuin and its neighboring settlements, a masculinized environment of roughly ranked peers. Moffat greeted Pifo

> with peculiar feelings, reflecting, as I did, on the events which have scattered and pealed that once industrious and interesting tribe *to which he belonged.* "Where are the Baharutse?" was my first question. "Destroyed by the Mantatees, and a few scattered," was his reply, *with the emphasis of heart-feeling.*[12]

The odd emphases, the italics here, are Moffat's. Pifo worked for Diutlwileng, the regent chief at Kaditshwene, of the oldest place-of-*rotse* nexus on the highveld—he was the former ambassador to Mothibe at Dithakong. Moffat's encounter with Pifo was his first experience of emotional bonding in his Chuin retreat, with "peculiar feelings," and "heart-feeling," and with no mediating vocabulary.[13]

The 1820s in the Cape borderlands were a period of violence, associated on the highveld with slave raids, guns and horses, and opportunistic incursions and expansions by competing chiefdoms. This was called the

Difaqane, likely deriving from the same root as *Mfecane*, a word familiarly associated with the expansion of the Zulu kingdom in the east. As in previous times of mobilization and warfare, male pursuits and male concerns with cattle and power ascended nakedly over women and agriculture. In keeping with this principle, during Moffat's two-month stay in the salt pans, a man murdered his wife with his spear, and the full court of senior men thought Moffat was joking around when he asked them to punish the killer; and Bogachu, the effective chief at Setabeng, assaulted his wife with an axe, wounding her badly in the leg.

As Moffat became close to these men, incidents involving gunfire and killing helped bind him to them severally: his witness of an attack on the oxen by a lion, in which Moffat and the *métis* wagoneer fired their rifles in its direction; his repeated hunting trips with Bogachu and Lekomenyane; and his killing of a hippo and the disposition of the meat. These men showed Moffat "unwonted kindness," and Moffat adopted Bogachu and Lekomenyane and his allies, including Pifo, as his own companions. They were the closest thing to friends, among the people of the highveld, that the missionary ever had.[14]

The men in the Chuin salt pans were not tribespeople unaware of the changing world around them. Indeed, they were men of the borderlands. While none of them could translate for Moffat, Bogachu and his men spoke a little bit of Dutch, and Lekomenyane wished to go to work "for white men," and may have been on furlough from such work. Both Lekomenyane and Bogachu hunted proficiently with firearms and knew how to handle gunpowder, smoked tobacco in pipes, and wore hats. They had had several opportunities to learn about Christians and Christianity, even before Moffat's arrival.

In 1824 the Cape Colony unilaterally extended its northern boundary to the Orange River, and so too its racist pass laws. Bogachu was perhaps still negotiating his subchiefdom's future within the neighborhoods of the *Tshidi, Ratlou, Ngwaketse,* and *Seleka* ruling houses, not to mention with the apparently friendly forces of English imperialism and Christianity. He is described in a particularly clumsy "linguistically correct" ethnic formula by Isaac Schapera: he belonged to "the royal family of the BaRolong-booSeleka (Sehunêlô's people)," and elsewhere Schapera implies he was the son or brother of a *Seleka* chief.[15] There is room to doubt it. The name "Bogachu" recurred in at least one other chiefdom outside the people-of-*rolong* orbit. A youth of fourteen named Bogachu appears in the records of the Methodist church in 1817, and his status then was not a "person of Seleka" but that of a visitor to the region from somewhere else. If this was the same person, his realignment would hardly have been unique.[16]

Bogachu and his peers were thus figures of hybridity (even *métissage*), at home in the borderlands. But they also headed competing *rolong* (place of *rola*) chiefly houses, rooted on the highveld and in its history. These houses picked up the pieces of place-of-*rotse* and crocodile (*kwena*) chiefdoms littering the highveld, in the ongoing, larger effort to build new towns or town sections under chiefs' rule. Bogachu and his colleagues represented the intersection, in the 1820s, of Cape evangelical connections, armed Boer and *métis* vanguards, and ranked alliances of men on the highveld.

Moffat, after his encounter with Pifo described above, spent his first days visiting a place-of-*rotse* ("Harutsi") blacksmith, and on Sunday, April 8, 1827, he gathered "the people" to preach. In contrast to his interesting discussions with Pifo or with the blacksmith, when Moffat preached, "everything was turned to ridicule," until Moffat ended the mockery and spoke directly about death and dying, which sent the audience away. "They rehearse my crooked speeches with violent bursts of laughter," he reflected later. His relief was to repair to Pifo's compound:

> [A] couple of hours at the house of Piho the Moharutse. It afforded me much pleasure to be enabled to tell him and his domestic a few of the truths of divine revelation. I made him a present of some beads . . . [I assured him] that at some future period, perhaps not very distant, a mission would be commenced at Kurecheune [*sic*], which appeared to afford him the utmost pleasure, [and] he remarked that the scattered Baharutse would collect.[17]

Herewith is the (re)invention of "to collect" as a salvational concept. Moffat found meaning with Pifo, in the midst of otherwise failing, humiliating, nonengagement, by saying, in passable highveld speech, that he hoped to help effect the restoration of a great "Harutse" kingdom. As he grew to understand more around him, however, he was disturbed not only by the obvious disapproval with which people greeted his words but also by several deliberate distortions of his emphases. "I was much grieved to hear them making a kind of diversion of some part of the discourse, particularly that which related to a future state of reward"—to Heaven, in other words. "I went and placed myself among them, and resumed the subject in a way of argument; when they changed their tone, especially when I dwelt on the article of death, to them a subject . . . the most unpleasant."[18]

This was the cycle he usually encountered. Moffat typically felt "low" and "down" afterward. While "Our Lord" translated most simply as "Kosse a choane" ("our chief," according to Samuel Broadbent, a contemporary interlocutor), he was also the chief of the dead, or of what happened to you when you died. If the "where" question was answered by "up above," the "when" question was not only "soon," but "after you are dead." The question of "when" was thus ever an oppressive one for most people, as it entailed death.[19]

A couple of days later (on April 17), Moffat felt "better," somehow, and turned something of a corner. He began to show an interest in subjects "of a worldly nature," and complained of drowning in "a superabundance of names," "despairing of ever becoming perfect." In other words, only now did Moffat hammer at the barrier of real fluency, before entering the world of *thinking* in the language; and despite his protestations, interaction in the language afforded him "considerable pleasure" (to hear the news that some *métis* traders were coming, and that the *Ngwaketse* chief had driven away "the marauders"). In this short period he transcended his racism. He permitted Bogachu especially to occupy the status of equal, even friend, with Moffat "deferring" to him on the "subject" of religion, maintaining a "silence" on it with him, and refraining from hard judgment. Moffat only learned how to speak and think by engaging in this way, by *not* trying to "convert" another as he had, for instance, Jonker Afrikaner.[20]

Moffat was frustrated that he had no one to tell him the "real meaning" of words, but it would have been hard for him to form such attachments if there had been a translator by his side. With no such assistant, and of course no glossary in his pocket, he was forced to write down words and phrases he picked up in conversation. Then he listened "to hear them in another conversation," understanding from the context of what one conversation had in common with another, until finally he used the phrases himself in a third interaction. Only when he was forced to operate in this way, purely contextually, in a world of speaking and hearing, did highveld ideas begin making sense, as it were; and only then did they threaten to displace his mother-tongue's exclusive claim on his being, and frighten him.

It was important not to give up. Moffat continued to learn and to preach, to dwell on death and individual salvation, ending as usual on the "certainty of death." Sometimes however he decided not to drive away his audience so quickly. About a "dozen" women, the wives of headmen and chiefs, stayed round him at one juncture, while Moffat spoke not only of the past (*bogologolo*), of sin and of death awaiting, but of something else that was "coming": something else that was "near" or "close at hand."

Beyond *Ha-rotse*: Creating God's Kingdom, Part 2

As the weeks passed, Moffat's mood went up and down, depending on visitors, letters, and other things. He aimed bad sermons at indifferent people, and noted that they parroted back what he wanted to hear: if they were asked "what their wish would be on their deathbed, they of course answer, 'to go to heaven,'" just as they would say anything for a "piece of tobacco." With chiefs he fared better. The people-of-*Ngwaketse* chief, Sebego, came to visit Moffat, and Moffat was able to talk with him freely. In the company of Pifo, Moffat brought up the subject of the "poor Baharutsees," his recent topic, and spoke earnestly. Sebego was initially rather cold. He asked Moffat what attraction he saw in that "poor and dispersed people." Moffat said, or "rejoined," that "that was one of the reasons for my desiring to fix a mission among them." Here we must bear in mind that Moffat actually intended no such mission:

> I sympathised with them in their distresses, and if the Wankets [*Ngwaketse* chiefship] were in similar circumstances, I should feel the same towards them, and cheerfully go and live among them, for the sake of restoring them to their former comfortable condition.[21]

In a sense, Moffat was no longer talking about Kaditshwene, which was in fact a twin-court arrangement, but was instead talking about kingdoms in general. In this way the previous "pleasure" and then empathy discovered in his interaction with Pifo was removed and rendered abstract.

In reaction to this discourse, Sebego, the *Ngwaketse* chief, "put his hand on his mouth (a token of wonder), and turned to his brother Mangala," and said that Moffat had "a heart." Moffat could scarcely avoid noting the contrasting disinterest in people's reactions when he spoke about "divine things." The lesson was to steer clear of the immortal soul, away from death and personal culpability for sin. Instead, it was better to connect to available emotions about real belonging, and real peace, in this time of turmoil and famine. On Wednesday, April 30, Moffat again and for the final time visited Pifo. "I always feel some degree of pleasure in my visits to his house. He has lost a wife and four children, who were killed by the Mantatees; his cattle were also all taken." Pifo's yearning for the old order, and for his old life, stoked by Moffat's displaced nostalgia for his own family, created their fragile common ground.[22]

> He always seems to hear divine things with interest, but nothing so much arrests his attention, and cheers his spirits, as to tell him that the Makoas [whites] love the Baharutse, and that they will be one day in possession of the land of their forefathers.

Forefathers were, of course, ancestors. And "ancestor" was how the Reverend Read, and now perhaps Moffat, would refer to God.

Perhaps it is unkind to Moffat to call these interactions "experiments" in evangelism, because it was only when operating without translating, through the words of others, that Moffat freed himself and understood what was going on around him. Still, he acted as if he were mastering a new method, working up a nostalgia for a lost *temporal* propriety, and he provoked desires that could never again be met in the nineteenth-century world. It is significant that the Kaditshwene people in their ruin were everywhere known merely as (of) or (place of) *rotse*, as people from "Baharutse country," as it was often put, and rarely under the name of subsequent ancestors or chiefs.[23] Because *ha-rotse* irredentism might be generally expressed, it preconditioned power, chiefship, and up-aboveness, and colored Moffat's depiction of Christianity's promise of what was to come.

The oral creation of what was coming, a kingdom that was also somehow the great ancestral domain, a life of peace and prosperity, postulated no *named* ancestor, no historical chief. If Moffat could seize on the realm of restorationist fantasy, and provoke the feelings of nationalism he noted in Pifo, he might yet take this unnamed ancestor, or chief, ensconced in *rotse* or what we may call "prestige-place-association nostalgia," and turn it into Christianity. There remained the problem of the Reverend Read's "ancestor," *modimo*, a word that in the common plural—*badimo*, "ancestors"—still meant "Satan," an artifact of the early engagement of Moffat's contemporaries with *métis* men. Could this singular form for a word (mis) translated as Satan come to mean God? In a time of uncertain authority, it was impolitic to talk in the specifics, by name, about one's ultimate ancestor, especially in contradistinction to one's actual, current situation. To do so was to speak the language of insurgency. The polite thing in the rough-and-ready politics of new state formation and warfare in the 1820s was to discuss the identity of one's ancestors in vague terms. In speaking of history one just said "them."

Therefore there was no reason for Moffat's highveld friends, farmers, and herders of the borderlands to correct the missionaries' misuse of "ancestor" as an anonymous entity. After his return from Chuin and Kongke, Moffat translated some of "Mr. Brown's catechisms," and next a "selection of passages of scripture by the same author," with this freedom.[24] Then he applied himself seriously to Luke, which was probably printed in 1829, and then again in a large run by a Cape Town press in 1830. Psalms and other material came out in small printings under his name in the 1820s and 1830s, and the entire New Testament was done in 1840. The term "ancestor" ("Molimo," i.e., *modimo*) was deployed in it for Deity.[25]

Thus at the moment of the ancestors' greatest mutability at the edge of the borderlands, in the 1820s and 1830s, the term "ancestor" ceased naming a chief of the past, any chief designated or referenced, and slipped into permanent singularity and generality. My surmise is that it was Bogachu, Lekomenyane, and Pifo who pushed Moffat finally to accept and to embrace this usage of "ancestor," as God, as he learnt Sechuana. As they themselves adjusted their genealogical claims, joining and rejoining one another's fraternal societies, and rendering their greatest ancestors anonymous, Robert Moffat built his theology on the same equivalence and anonymity. Notwithstanding the central role of African men, the move constituted a basic depoliticization of a fundamental aspect of popular political mobilization. Ancestry and patriarchy were tightly woven into the language and attitudes of the people toward the state, their chiefdoms. Now this language would be uttered in ceremonies with mainly transcendental effects.

The making of Christianity from the inside was just one aspect of Moffat's program. Along with like-minded missionaries, he installed the mechanisms to guarantee his monopoly on the status of "Christian" and its perceived worth, at least until the close of the century. In the end, his seizure of "text," of the high ground over this domain that South African and London presses offered his ideas, was not determinative. The nineteenth- and twentieth-century consequences of his actions in creating religion as a discrete form certainly would have astounded Moffat. Nevertheless his actions left a permanent broad-groove imprint on the religious landscape.[26] He created a domain of the unseen based on chiefship, in which an ever-anonymous ancestor, greater than all others, held sway by affecting people's lives like chiefs. And he could do this because of the wounded and fragmented nature of political authority in the 1820s.[27] The primacy of the unseen arrived in a period of crisis and instability.

It is noteworthy that Moffat concentrated on translating Isaiah before other parts of the Old Testament:

> Your country lies desolate
> Your cities are burned with fire:
> In your very presence
> devour your land (1:7)
> . . .
> Deep from the earth you shall speak
> From low in the dust your words shall come
> Your voice shall come from the ground like the voice of a ghost
> And your speech shall whisper out of the dust. (29:4)[28]

Moffat recognized the power of nostalgia, for riches, for rain, and for the kingdoms of one's ancestors, to give content to an imaginary Christian space-time. He wished to move toward the "king" (or "chief," -*kosi* and variants) idea, because the distressed state of the highveld made this possible. The blueprint was to extol no particular chiefdom, not Mothibe's or Mengwe's or Tshawe's or any real ancestor's, but all of them: a domain when the rains came regularly, and the chiefship of ancestor(s) was powerful, and the cattle were plentiful and fat. In compensation, Moffat would forever stress the *ethereal nature* of his chiefship, his ancestor and father, the moral nature of God's domain, despite the implications of his vocabulary.

No chief successfully opposed him. Nonetheless as a social space with its own signifying order, Christianity still lay too close to the domain of chiefs for their comfort. As South African chiefs built and rebuilt their chiefdoms in the 1830s they by and large rejected it. In the language of Moffat's Christianity, the sinners were those left behind (*lathega*), consigned to the fate of those who could not keep up; they were as the stray heifer (*timelo*) and the refusers (*gana*) who kept themselves apart (*ikepa*). To be saved would be to be gathered, to be collected like cattle and people under a just king. Strays therefore pledged themselves to incorporative chiefs, peopled the fledgling churches, and flocked to Moffat at Kuruman. Christ was the herder (*modise*) and annointer, rectifying sinners, offering them an eventual home. A great chiefdom was coming, restored to perfect glory, connected to their time: the great time. All one had to do was wait.

Christianity as purveyed by Moffat in the decades after the *Difaqane*, as the turmoil of the 1810s–1820s was known, demanded an end to the speaking of political words in the world and of public speech about patrimony and ancestrally oriented unity. Church was the only proper place for collective unity and aspiration; all other situations for mobilizing people with the same or similar ideas were declared "fraudulent" and had to be shut down by the state. Christianity only expanded in rural South Africa when real-world alternatives were permanently wrecked. Mass Christianity thus dates from the middle of the 1870s on, with the widespread destruction of ancestral unities, men's alliances, and chiefship itself. But that is another story.

Part
Three

Missionaries, Language,
and National Expression

8

Missionaries and the Making of Colonial Notables

Conversions to Modernity in Eritrea and Ethiopia, 1890–1935

James De Lorenzi

W ork," Pr. Ezechia da Iseo explained, "is a necessity."[1] The Capuchin resident of the Italian colony of Eritrea offered two explanations for this unequivocal assessment in his 1914 textbook for the local mission schools. His first was providential: work is necessary because God desires mankind to tend to his creation and live by its products. His second was rather worldly: work is necessary because it is only through labor that one "makes oneself useful to the nation and humanity."[2] Though unrelated to salvation, this second point had tremendous significance for da Iseo (1880–1947) and his fellow missionaries in Eritrea, since it increasingly defined their role in the social and economic order of the Italian colony. With the help of da Iseo's bilingual Italian-Tigrinya textbook, *Manuale d'industrie, arti e mestieri*, teachers in the colony's Catholic mission schools instructed their Eritrean students not only in catechism but also in the Italian language and skilled trades, thereby developing a suitably trained and productive workforce. As his superior and close colleague Msgr. Camillo Carrara (1871–1924) explained on another occasion, graduates from the mission schools benefited not only Christ and the church but also the *Colonia Eritrea*, since they became "competent and useful citizens, so much so that in public offices, the natives who occupy the best jobs are those who have left the Catholic mission."[3] Thus Carrara, da Iseo, and their colleagues had two overlapping goals: to save Eritrean souls while producing colonial subjects.

Some mission school graduates did not live up to these expectations. The young colonial clerk Gabra Mika'él Germu (1900–69), an alumnus of an Italian school, had indeed put his mission training to work by serving in the colonial administration as a secretary and translator. Yet in his private writings, he suggested that the relationships among faith, work, education, and loyalty were far more complex than da Iseo's words implied. Using his education to draw upon printed Italian books, manuscripts in local languages, and the rich oral traditions of his elders, Gabra Mika'él produced a unique Amharic history entitled *Tārik 'iṭālyānā 'ityop̄yā* (*History of Italy and Ethiopia*) that outlined in rich detail the complex ambiguities of the colonial situation in Eritrea.[4] His work described Italian soldiers, traders, and missionaries, and also indigenous conscripts (*'askari*), nobles, Catholics, and anticolonial rebels—but in Gabra Mika'él's narrative, the roles of villains and heroes were ambiguously cast, and he often blurred the line between colonial collaboration and anticolonial protest. In short, he suggested that appearance and affiliation could be deceiving in the Italian colony. He most evocatively hinted at this fact in a passage describing the Ethiopian military victory at Adwa, where he wrote that the brave Ethiopian soldiers' "hearts burned like fire" as they faced down their *farangi*, or foreign, foes.[5] Perhaps Gabra Mika'él intended this subtle turn of language to remind his readers that although he was an Italian-speaking, Catholic-school graduate employed by the colonial state, and though his scholarship depended on the cross-cultural outlook imparted by his mission education, these outward facts nonetheless concealed a smoldering inner patriotism. His mission education may have led to colonial service—to the ennobling work that Carrara envisioned—but it did not necessarily lead him to abandon his love of country.

Gabra Mika'él was but one of many early-twentieth-century Eritreans and Ethiopians who were profoundly influenced by their encounter with *farangi* missionaries and their institutions. Some mission-school graduates went on to become the region's most illustrious scholars and reformers, intellectuals remembered today as pioneers of change.[6] Gabra Heywet Bāykadāñ (1886–1919), for example, became a theorist of under-development and an outspoken critic of Ethiopia's nobility and land ten-ure system, and Walde'ab Walda Māryām (1905–95) taught in a mission school before becoming a prominent Eritrean nationalist in the postwar period.[7] Other graduates became leading figures in the region's grow-ing indigenous evangelical Christian congregations, leading the way as pioneers of faith.[8] Tāye Gabra Māryām (1860–1924), born in Ethio-pia but educated in Eritrea, was an eminent historian, theologian, and linguist who briefly taught Ge'ez at Berlin University, while Onésimos Nesib (1850–1931), an emancipated slave, led missions in Wallagā and produced the first Oromo translation of the Bible. Gabra Mikā'él's case illustrates a third, less recognized outcome of mission education, the one desired by da Iseo and Carrara—service with the Italian colonial state. Though associations with mission institutions could be brief, they were very often formative.

Like their counterparts elsewhere in Africa and Asia, many of these mission-educated intellectuals eventually became proponents of modern-ization and national emancipation, in keeping with Benedict Anderson's influential arguments about the links between vernacular print culture and the emergence of a national imagination.[9] But we should be wary of seeing a sense of national community as a natural outcome of these developments, or of overlooking what Partha Chatterjee calls "the twists and turns, the suppressed possibilities, [and] the contradictions still unresolved" that these complex intellectual encounters entailed.[10] The Eritrean case highlights how the interface between mission education and colonial politics could produce tremendous intellectual heterogeneity, and importantly, how it could foster visions of community beyond nation and congregation. This chapter considers this topic by examining the role of mission education in the emergence of a cohort of colonial notables in Eritrea, using the life and work of Gabra Mikā'él to suggest that mis-sionaries like Carrara brokered a "conversion to modernity" in Eritrea and Ethiopia with some surprising outcomes.[11]

Catholic and Protestant Missions in Northeast Africa

In the final decades of the nineteenth century, Northeast Africa entered into a period of intense and prolonged crisis. Against the backdrop of chronic drought, famine, and epidemic catastrophe, local Muslim and Christian polities faced a new set of formidable European challenges to their sovereignty after 1869, when the Rubattino Shipping Company purchased the Red Sea port of 'Āsab from two local sultans. Though Ethiopia's Christian rulers managed to check European expansion with their dramatic defeat of the Italians at Adwa in 1896, other large-scale challenges to European conquest were ultimately less successful. In Sudan, the millenarian Mahdist state collapsed following military defeat by the British in 1898, and in Somalia, the anticolonial jihad led by sheikh Muhammad Abdulle Hasan—better known to European journalists as the "Mad Mullah of Somaliland"—abruptly ended with its leader's death in 1920. By that time, the region had been violently partitioned into French, British, and Italian colonies and protectorates, and immigrant settlers, urbanization, and the world economy began reshaping the contours of everyday life. It was a tumultuous period in which local processes of change collided with global patterns of imperial expansion, in a region astride the intersecting frontiers of Africa, the Middle East, and the Indian Ocean rim.

These dramatic developments were especially evident in the new Italian colony of Eritrea, the most direct legacy of the Rubattino purchase. After acquiring 'Āsab in 1882, the Italians expanded to Massawa in 1885, claimed the coastal regions between the two ports, and then annexed Asmara and the northern edge of the highland plateau in 1889. These territories were then united in 1890 to form Italy's first African colony, Eritrea, *la colonia primogenita*. The Italian colonial project had three principal goals: to create a territory of settlement for Italian emigrants, to produce raw materials for export to the metropole, and to develop a colonial conscript army to fight Italy's foreign wars. To achieve these aims, the Italians pacified the territory through military campaigns, punishing resistance and executing and exiling uncooperative local elites. They also enacted laws that dismantled the highland land tenure system and expropriated communal and private property in the name of the state.[12]

And through the colony's native policy, the *politica indigena*, the colony's governors and administrators aimed to make the region's disparate social groups into colonial subjects by awarding privileges to cooperative elites and previously marginalized religious and ethnic groups.[13] Substantial debate surrounds the impact of these developments.[14]

Missionaries played an important role in this colonizing process, though the Bible advanced well before the flag.[15] The Church Missionary Society led the earliest nineteenth-century missions to the region, working among the local Orthodox Christians between 1830 and 1842 as part of its larger strategy of mission to Eastern Christians. By midcentury, Italian Capuchins, French Lazarists, and the Swedish Evangelical Mission (SEM, Evangeliska Fosterlandsstiftelsen) had established themselves at points along the coast and in the highlands, building churches, schools, medical stations, and small mission presses. However, the formal creation of the colony in 1890 transformed the context of these ongoing mission projects. While the Italian Capuchins welcomed colonial rule as a possible boon to their efforts, the French Lazarists covertly supported local anticolonial resistance movements and were expelled from the colony in 1894 amid accusations of subversion.[16] From that point on, Italian Capuchins led the Catholic missions in Eritrea, first under Michele Da Carbonara (1836–1910), and then under Carrara and his successor, Celestino Cattaneo (1864–1946). The imperial contest had spilled over into the Catholic mission field.[17]

Unlike the Lazarists, the Lutheran SEM managed to establish itself in the Italian colony, though some adaptation was necessary. One particularly pressing issue was the Italian language, the new colonial lingua franca that few of the Swedish missionaries could speak. The SEM leadership resolved this dilemma by requesting aid from an Italian Protestant organization, the Waldensian Evangelical Church, which began sending representatives to the colony.[18] The former Jesuit and Protestant convert Benedetto Giudici (1862–1926) arrived in 1902 and taught at an SEM school for several years, while Alessandro Tron (1887–1966) arrived in 1909 and worked in Asmara and Belessa for many years.[19] Other Italian Protestants occasionally came to work for the SEM mission: the evangelical doctor Nicola de Pertis (1884–1931) arrived through the recommendation of a Waldensian colleague in Rome, and he ran an infirmary and nursing school in Asmara for a number of years.[20] These Italians earned the esteem of many of their Swedish colleagues: in the estimation of Karl Rodén, a veteran SEM pastor, they were stirring beacons of truth in "ignorant, dark, and superstitious Catholic Italy."[21]

As Rodén's words suggest, there was some mutual hostility between the Catholic and Protestant missionaries in the new Italian colony. In the Swedish gazette *Missions-Tidning* (Stockholm), SEM writers occasionally derided their Catholic rivals in typically evangelical terms, and these sentiments were sometimes reciprocated by the Capuchins and their allies. Bishop Carrara, for example, explained in a mission history that he cried "bitter tears" over the fact that the colony had been "invaded" by "fanatical and unrelenting" Lutherans, who were disseminating Protestant literature that was "harmful and deadly beyond words." In his view, it was particularly shameful that SEM activities in the colony, and especially in the capital, Asmara, threatened to overshadow the hard work of his Capuchin colleagues. "It is this that injures and demeans," he wrote, "[that] before the Swedish Protestant Mission, the poor Catholic mission is like a begging pauper [*mendica pezzente*] facing a powerful, haughty, and daring matron."[22]

Yet despite the simmering adversity and doctrinal differences, there were some fundamental similarities between the two European missions. Both, for example, focused on schools as key institutions of ministry. For the Swedes and their Italian coworkers, conversion was inseparable from the development of vernacular literacy—after all, as one SEM publication proclaimed, "one cannot be a good evangelical Christian unless one can read one's own Bible."[23] With this in mind, the SEM opened schools in Asmara, Kunama, Belessa, and Hāzzagā, and it claimed more than 3,500 converts by 1917.[24] Surveying the schools in 1925, an Italian inspector conceded that they were "extraordinarily satisfactory."[25] Like the Protestants, the Catholic missionaries also saw a close link between education and salvation. As one father told his colleagues, "catechism, catechism, always catechism" was the key to cultivating sincere and enduring faith.[26] To this end, the Capuchins opened schools in Hamasén, Āddi Qayeh, Bogos, and Ākkala Guzāy, and by 1914 the Catholic mission claimed just over 20,000 converts.[27] For both Protestants and Catholics, the mission schools were also important centers for the training of indigenous pastors and clergy. Education and the road to salvation were closely linked.[28]

Profane motives also contributed to the missionaries' interest in schools, especially as the Protestants and Catholics became caught up in the contentious politics of the Italian metropole. In a perceptive study of this period, Uoldelul Chelati Dirar notes that the post-Risorgimento political debates concerning the ideal relationship between the church and state had significant repercussions for missionaries in Eritrea.[29] Some Catholic intellectuals argued that faith was a defining feature of Italian national identity, implying that Catholicism had a central place in the Italian civilizing mission. This sentiment was clearly shared by some missionaries on the ground: Carrara, for example, told a governor that he and his colleagues were "conquering a people through the splendors of faith and Christian civilization."[30] Against this view, anticlerical Italian liberals argued that the church was by definition subordinate to the state, implying that in colonial contexts, Catholicism should simply be a vehicle of *italianità*, a mere policy instrument to be used as needed. Each of these views suggested a different vision of missionary activities in the colony, and as a result, both the Capuchins and the SEM were caught amid clashing models of what the colonial project entailed.

The Capuchins resolved these tensions largely through Carrara's productive model of native education, using their schools to demonstrate how their spiritual mission supported economic growth in the colony. His own work described such key trades as salt- and bread-making, butter- and cheese-making, printing, engraving, photography, smelting, tailoring, and carpentry, and he offered appendices that dealt with the postal service, telegraph operation, Morse code, and pearl diving.[31] In additional to this practical knowledge, the Italian textbooks celebrated the Italian nation and its civilizing mission in Africa, and their curricula aimed to foster Italian sympathy by training students in the Italian language and spreading its national form of Christianity, Roman Catholicism.[32] Some missionaries also publicly voiced their support for Italy's colonial conquests abroad.[33] Over time, Eritrea's colonial administrators came to recognize the value of the Catholic missionaries and rewarded them accordingly.

In 1907 Catholicism became an official religion of the colony, alongside Orthodox Christianity and Islam, and by 1923 the Capuchins took over the remaining state-run schools. As Jonathan Miran has observed, these were groundbreaking developments in terms of the reconciliation of church and state in Italy, early steps in a longer process of reconciliation that culminated in the Lateran Accords of 1929.[34] For the Italian Capuchins, then, support for native education in Eritrea was both spiritually uplifting and politically pragmatic.

The SEM had less success convincing Italian administrators of its value to the colony, despite significant effort. A recurring concern was the fact that as predominantly non-Italian foreigners, the Swedes were insufficiently patriotic and possibly even subversive. Several SEM publications indirectly addressed this issue by attempting to show their support for the Italian civilizing mission. For example, a 1912 Tigrinya reader included biographies of Italian royalty, penned by the Waldensian Giudici,[35] and a 1917 Tigrinya teacher's manual contained an Italian preface explaining that "the instruction of natives is a duty of the civilizing mission," and that SEM schools fostered "salvation in Christ for the next life, and the light of civilization for the present one."[36] Yet despite these efforts, the SEM became embroiled in a number of controversies with the Italian authorities. In the 1890s they clashed with administrators over their missions to local Muslims, and in 1910 governor Ferdinando Martini claimed they violated the official language policy by teaching French and German in their schools and, further, that they used "Protestant propaganda" to incite the local population.[37] Though there were occasional moments of calm, the situation generally deteriorated over the next two decades. The SEM missionaries were expelled and refused reentry to the colony between 1915 and 1919,[38] and at that time, the Swedish mission historians lamented that their once-amicable relations with the Capuchins no longer continued.[39] The colonial government forced the SEM to change its name to *Missione Evangelica*,[40] and expulsions and school closures continued for the next decade.[41] Many Eritrean evangelicals and mission school graduates began emigrating to Ethiopia to find work with the reform-minded Crown Prince Tafari Makonen, the future emperor Haylé Selāsé,[42] and this led the colonial governor to accuse the SEM of promoting Ethiopian ties in

Eritrea.[43] Further expulsions followed in the early 1930s, and after the Italian invasion in 1935 and the creation of the unified Africa Orientale Italiana in 1936, most SEM missionaries left the region altogether until the postwar period.[44]

Although their political fortunes may have differed, the Italian and Swedish missionaries collectively brokered fundamental changes in local intellectual life. The emergence of a new form of cross-cultural literacy and learning was one major development. Prior to the creation of the mission schools, language instruction took place in traditional Orthodox Christian and Muslim schools, where students studied local languages like Amharic and Tigrinya, and at a more advanced level, scholarly languages like Ge'ez and Arabic.[45] Beyond its reflection of the indigenous linguistic landscape, this traditional system also reflected the fact that for both Muslims and Christians, literacy remained the highly specialized skill of scholars and religious leaders.[46] Importantly, this pattern began to change with the arrival of the Protestant and Catholic missionaries. At mission schools, Eritrean students learned to speak and read local languages (Amharic, Tigrinya, and Tigre) and European ones (Italian, French, German, and Swedish), and in some cases, graduates continued their studies in Europe or Ethiopia. As the scope of literacy evolved and polyglossia increasingly took on a cross-cultural character, the ability to read and write ceased to be exclusively associated with religious and political authority.[47]

Another consequence of the Protestant and Catholic missions was the emergence of print. In 1863 the Italian Lazarist Lorenzo Biancheri imported a press and established a mission press at Massawa, but the machine and type were destroyed after his death in 1864.[48] The SEM established presses in 1885 at 'Emkullu and then Asmara, and in the following decade the Capuchins began printing books at Karan and, after 1917, Asmara. These presses were responsible for producing the first widely available printed vernacular texts in the region. Their products were quite similar, especially when compared to the output of their counterparts in Ethiopia.[49] The European presses focused on scripture, textbooks, mission histories, calendars, bilingual dictionaries, and grammars in European and local languages. The SEM also published vernacular

Bibles, hymnals, and a version of *Pilgrim's Progress*, while the Capuchins produced missals, catechisms, a concordance of the Gregorian and Ethiopian calendars, and various hagiographies, such as a life of the nineteenth-century Ethiopian Catholic martyr Gabra Mikā'él.[50] Occasionally, highly unique works appeared. For example, the SEM produced the eclectic Tigrinya reader *Berhān Yehun*, which included sermons, a mission history by pastors Salomon 'Aṣqu and Zar'ā Ṣeyon Musé, and a historical study of Menilek II by Gabra Hewyet Bāykadāñ.[51] Eritreans were involved in these publications in various ways: they worked as typesetters and bookbinders, and suitable mission students and alumni sometimes went on to work as authors and translators, like Walde'ab Walda Māryām, who produced a syllabary, *Bairu Okbit*, and aided in the Tigrinya translation of *Pilgrim's Progress*; and Gabra Krestos Takla Hāymānot (1892–1932), who collaborated with the Swedes on a guide for teachers.[52]

Mission publications reached local readers in several ways. Libraries were one important source of books. In 1906 the Italian traveler Renato Paoli found a well-stocked Swedish mission library in Asmara and noted its diverse contents, and in 1908 Pier Ludovico Occhini found that the Capuchin mission station in Karan included a library.[53] Printed books were also given away at no cost: the evangelical Zar'ā Ṣeyon Musé found mission publications in a town square in the late nineteenth century.[54] By the first decades of the twentieth century, there was also a mission-run bookstore in the Aksum/Adwa border area, and according to the estimation of one Swedish employee, the demand for printed books was very high.[55] It is also likely that Eritrean readers had access to the burgeoning print trade in nearby Ethiopia, especially after Tafari Makonen sponsored the publication of Amharic newspapers and books, occasionally featuring work by Eritrean intellectuals.[56] When the Ethiopian intellectual Ḥeruy Walda Śelāsé completed two bibliographic surveys of the region, he listed several Eritrean works in his findings, suggesting that books flowed across the colonial border with some regularity.[57] For the first time, printed books began to take their place alongside the region's long-established Muslim and Christian manuscript traditions.

In a provocative analysis of this period, Irma Taddia and Uoldelul Chelati Dirar suggest that colonial rule "revised ways of writing and thinking" in Eritrea by contributing to a general "informalization" of literacy and knowledge.[58] Their analysis suggests a number of additional intellectual trends fostered by missionaries and their institutions: the transformation of Amharic from a regional language into a bureaucratic lingua franca and *yamesyon qwānqwā* (mission language);[59] the erosion of the established "official traditions" of Muslim and Orthodox Christian scholars; and the growth of epistolography as a mode of private communication.[60] In conjunction with the growth of cross-cultural literacy, the new educational institutions, and the growing availability of foreign and local books, these more subtle developments encouraged an eclectic approach to knowledge—one rooted in an increased access to texts and ideas with foreign provenance. In short, while contemporaries like Walde'ab Walda Māryām may have seen Carrara's schools as essentially making "sheep . . . graze before slaughtering," they also unexpectedly altered the parameters of intellectual inquiry in fundamental ways.[61]

Mission Education and the Emergence of Colonial Notables

These developments paralleled changes in the social landscape of Eritrea that emerged from the range of indigenous responses to colonial rule. In the immediate aftermath of the Italian conquest, a number of local elites led armed struggles against the Italians. Some did so to restore their property and political authority, while others aimed to defend Ethiopian sovereignty from the Italian threat. Banditry and raiding were similarly overt acts of defiance, as were the armed revolts and assassinations that took place during the period of the Ethiopian invasion (1935–41). Avoidance protest was another common if less dramatic response, and many nobles and intellectuals fled the colony for independent Ethiopia to continue challenging Italian power with the support of new patrons.[62] But it is also true that many Eritreans grudgingly resigned themselves to the new context of Italian rule, choosing to live with colonialism instead of challenging it overtly.[63] This pragmatic response took many different forms: migration to the cities for casual work in the colony's subsidized industries, possibly as a supplement to income from agriculture or trade; voluntary or coerced service as a colonial soldier, or *'askari;* or accommodation to parameters and possibilities of the colonial system as a community, as with the urban Khatmiyya Sufis of Massawa and its environs.[64]

For Catholic and Protestant mission alumni, living with colonialism often entailed a career as an interpreter, soldier, clerk, tax collector, or minor bureaucrat. Many biographies of the time document these choices. For example, 'Asresu Baraki (1892–n.d.) studied Ge'ez, Tigrinya, and Amharic at a Swedish school before working for the Italians, first at the Hamasén Commissariat and then as a district chief for nearly two decades. For his lifetime of service, he was inducted into the *Ordine coloniale della stella d'Italia* in 1935.[65] His contemporary Gabra Baraki (1902–n.d.) had an equally illustrious career: born in Asmara, he studied at both the SEM and Catholic mission schools before becoming a cashier with the colonial health department. He went on to work with the rationing department until 1935, after which he served as a military interpreter and finally as a district chief and commander after 1939.[66] Similar too was the administrative service of Hadegu Gilagabra Habteşion (1894–n.d.), who studied at the Catholic mission school in Asmara before beginning a career in the colonial bureaucracy that culminated in the grade of *Coadiuatore di governo*.[67] 'Asfaha Walda Mikā'él (1914–97) had a peripatetic decade in colonial administration that took him from Eritrea to Rome and Ethiopia.[68] Kantiba Gilāmikā'él, the son of a noble from Godayef, attended a European school before leading *'askari* campaigns against the Mahdists and eventually becoming a telegraph operator in Ethiopia.[69] These connections were so extensive that in 1914, the Capuchin mission historian noted that Asmara's indigenous Catholic community was entirely composed of *'askari* and laborers dependent upon the government.[70]

Mission education was also an avenue to less illustrious colonial careers in the professions and skilled trades. Gabra Heywet Mebratu Desta (1916–n.d.), for example, learned Tigrinya, Amharic, Arabic, and Italian in the mission schools, and then found work as a state archivist.[71] 'Embay Gere'amlak (n.d.) studied at both the Catholic San Michele school in Saganeti and the Institute for the English Language in Asmara before becoming a police inspector.[72] Similar is the case of Omar Sefaf Idris Asana (1900–n.d.), who attended the Saganeti school before becoming a police chief on the Dahlak islands off the Eritrean coast.[73] Gerenkiel

Baraki (n.d.) attended the schools of the Capuchins and Comboni Fathers before working as a film operator in Asmara and Massawa,[74] and 'Almedom Mesghenna (1923–n.d.) attended a Swedish school before becoming a teacher in Asmara.[75] The Capuchin Alberini Appolonio (1885–n.d.), director of both a trade school in Saganéti and a professional school in Asmara, reported that he trained the sons of local *capi* as telegraph operators and typists.[76]

Taken together, these diverse biographies suggest that missionary activities in Eritrea fostered the emergence of a new kind of mission-educated colonial notable, a social group that stood apart from the region's traditional elites, scholars, and religious leaders through occupation and ties to the new intellectual culture of the era. Mission graduates developed a valuable combination of multilingualism, literacy, and technical skill that could lead to new, albeit limited, kinds of careers. To be sure, these possibilities were deeply curtailed: though culturally distinct from other Eritreans, colonial notables still confronted the very real racial hierarchy of colonial society, which confined them to the lower echelons of the bureaucracy. But their wages, intellectual orientation, and professional experience still set them apart from their countrymen, and their Italian employers cultivated this sense of difference for practical reasons. Eritrean employees ran the colony on the cheap, and their incorporation into the urban economy reduced the possibility of mass resistance by creating a new cadre of salaried dependents who had little to gain from movements to restore the privileges and wealth of traditional elites.[77]

In recent years, scholars have reconsidered the role of these kinds of intermediary figures in colonial Africa and Asia. Transcending an older approach to colonial history that focused on collaboration and resistance as an analytic model, historians Benjamin Lawrance, Emily Lynn Osborn, and Richard Roberts have argued that indigenous employees were crucial to the functioning of the colonial state. In their view, these local intermediaries performed the critical function of "bridging the gap" between the colonizer and the colonized: they translated state ordinances and courtroom testimony, mediated between local elites and European administrators, staffed state bureaucracies, and filled the ranks of colonial armies.[78] Yet their intermediary role very often led to a political paradox. Because they gained a qualified kind of power from this "bargain of collaboration," these individuals very often sought to gain respectability within colonial structures rather than destroy them.[79] In the eyes of postcolonial nationalists, then, the intermediary came to represent the comprador or collaborator par excellence.

The category of the intermediary is a useful tool for examining colonial society in Eritrea. On the one hand, it goes beyond the analytic framework of collaboration and resistance, which privileges the category of comprador and suggests that mission converts and colonial notables were simply "Italianized" Eritreans with a colonized consciousness—national traitors who uncritically accepted the logic of domination for their own short-term gain.[80] On the other hand, mediation also reveals the unexpected political impact of Protestant and Catholic missionaries, whose educational institutions gave many of the colonial notables their defining linguistic and cultural profile. We can bring these various themes together by returning to the life and work of Gabra Mikā'él Germu—a mission school graduate, a colonial clerk, and a prolific scholar. His career and writings offer us a rare but detailed glimpse into the emerging intellectual world of the colonial notable and the role of mission education therein.

A Notable History?

Gabra Mikā'él's own biography rehearses themes common in the lives of other colonial notables.[81] He was born in 1900 in a rural village near Asmara, and in his youth obtained a traditional Orthodox Christian education that included Amharic, Tigrinya, and Ge'ez language training. He continued his studies at an Italian Capuchin school, where he acquired sufficient skill in Italian to find work as a translator and clerk in the colonial bureaucracy. At some point in the 1920s, he began using his wages to collect manuscripts and books, and during the 1930s he wrote his history of Ethiopia and Italy. During the postwar British administration, Gabra Mikā'él formally entered public life as the editor of Eritrea's Tigrinya-language newspaper, *Nāy 'Éretrā sāmonāwi gāzéṭā* (*Eritrean Weekly News*), to which he made a variety of contributions on political and historical subjects. Puglisi's biographical dictionary describes him at this time as an "influential" journalist and political leader.[82] Over the next few decades, Gabra Mikā'él continued his public writing, private scholarship, and manuscript collecting, though he appears to have had little contact with the growing circle of scholars at Haile Selassie University and the Institute of Ethiopian Studies in Addis Ababa.[83] Upon his death in 1969, the institute acquired his library of books and manuscripts, and they are preserved there to this day.[84]

Gabra Mikā'él was an extremely prolific scholar. His shorter historical works include a biography of Bāhtā Hāgos, the leader of the largest nineteenth-century revolt against colonial rule in Eritrea, and a biography of Gabra 'Ezi'ābhér Gilay, an Eritrean intellectual whom the Italians accused of treason and espionage.[85] He also wrote a long, detailed religious work called *Yemeṣehaf maker* (*Book of Counsel*).[86] But for the purposes of understanding the worldview of the colonial notable, his most important work is his *History of Italy and Ethiopia*, contained in his historical notebook *Zemeṣehaf Zegabra Mikā'él Germu* (*Book of Gabra Mika'él Germu*). Opening with a *longue durée* chronology of European imperialism from the Spanish conquest of the Americas up to the Italian occupation of Ethiopia in the 1930s, the history narrates European imperial designs on Northeast Africa, the growing conflicts between Ethiopia and the Sudanese Mahdists, the beginning of Italian rule in Eritrea, and the various indigenous responses to colonial rule. Gabra Mikā'él abruptly concludes the work in 1896, on the eve of the Ethiopian defeat of the Italians at Adwa.

Among the most striking features of *Italy and Ethiopia* are its novel historical arguments. At a time when most Ethiopian intellectuals lauded Emperor Menilek II as the hero of 'Adwa and the savior of the Ethiopian nation, Gabra Mikā'él instead casts him as a naïve opportunist who only reluctantly recognized the foreign dangers his advisers and rivals could plainly see, and as a ruler who abetted the colonial project by seeking to enlist Italian allies in his local power struggles.[87] It is one of the first articulations of a narrative now common among Eritrean nationalists.[88] But Gabra Mikā'él also proposes that many patriotic Ethiopians and Eritreans struggled to preserve local sovereignty, even when their rulers did not. In some cases, he describes the resistance of nobles who led campaigns and revolts against the Italians, such as *ras* 'Alula, who in 1887 ambushed an Italian battalion at Dogʿāli, where "within twelve hours time the five hundred soldiers of Colonel Da Cristofero were mown down by the merciless hand of the brave Abyssinians."[89] In the estimation of Gabra Mikāʾél, "it was a battle that left the Italians with much fear, deep sorrow, and great terror."[90] Similar is his discussion of Debeb 'Araya of Massawa, a relative of Emperor Yohānes IV who briefly supported the Italians before refusing an order to bring his soldiers to Asmara and Saganeti. Agreeing with his soldiers "to shed their blood for their country rather than betraying it," he intercepted colonial communications to plan an ambush of some Italian troops. Gabra Mikāʾél's most dramatic example of resistance to colonial rule is his extended discussion of the 1894 revolt led by Bāhtā Hāgos—a figure vilified by Italian colonial administrators, overlooked by Ethiopian intellectuals and historians, and later celebrated by Eritrean nationalists.[91] Gabra Mikāʾél narrates the failed revolt as a tragedy, describing Bāhtā's capture of the Italian officers, the support he received from both Eritreans and Lazarist missionaries, and his ambush and eventual death at Saganeti after a battle with the Italian troops. These acts of resistance—acts that challenged Italian claims to moral, political, and military superiority— made leaders like Bāhtā, *ras* 'Alula, and *degazmač* Debeb worthy of history.

This last point is key. Like many of the mission-educated *'askari*, teachers, clerks, and translators of colonial Eritrea, Gabra Mikāʾél was an individual whose social status was clearly linked to colonial subjecthood, and who could plausibly be accused of harboring treasonous Italian sympathies.[92] This potential suspicion is subtly addressed in *Italy and Ethiopia*, since Gabra Mikāʾél's work features a variety of "collaborationist" colonial notables who nonetheless exemplify patriotic resistance. Most obvious among these is the last example of Bāhtā Hagos, a Catholic who like Gabra Mikāʾél worked for the colonial state for an extended period of time, but who nonetheless became a potent symbol for Eritrean anticolonialists and nationalists.[93] But equally patriotic are the two Eritrean Catholic priests who aided him in his efforts, *'abba* Taklahāymānot and *'abba* Keflemaryām, and more generally the Lazarist missionaries who supported the rebellion by colluding with the French consul at Djibouti. Similar too are the various Eritrean notables who revealed their true patriotic sentiment after a period of initial collaboration with colonial rule, such as Debeb and Mengešā. As a colonial subject in a similar intermediary position, Gabra Mikā'él was fully prepared to accept the tensions between the ideals of Eritrean patriotism and the pragmatic reality of living with colonialism: like many of his historical subjects, he was an individual whose patriotism was masked by an outward appearance of cultural conversion. It is thus possible to see *Italy and Ethiopia* as an attempt to legitimize and document the unclear political status of the emerging colonial notable group—and by extension, a broader community of Eritreans who were in some way distinct from Ethiopians. Absent the genealogies and biographies that documented the *zer*, or roots, of his more traditional contemporaries, Gabra Mikā'él used his mission education, cross-cultural literacy, and printed books to describe a truth that had yet to be told, his own history.

Conclusions

Gabra Mikā'él's tale suggests three points. First, the mission field in Eritrea (and Ethiopia) is sufficiently complex to defy easy categorization. Although some Italian missionaries, like Carrara, publicly voiced their support for the colonial project, others, like his Capuchin colleague *Apollonio*, had a more nuanced view of the relations between Eritreans and Italians.[94] Even Carrara periodically presented a more pessimistic view of the colonial project, as when he lamented that the Italian settlers and soldiers in the colony had "a sinister influence on the natives" through their unchristian behavior.[95] The situation is equally complex in the case of the SEM. Although dominated by Swedes, the organization had a small but important cohort of Italian Protestants who periodically assisted the mission in its relations with the increasingly hostile colonial state. And finally, both the Catholic and Protestant missionaries were highly dependent on their indigenous colleagues, who worked as evangelists, translators, teachers, and scholars, and who publicly represented the missions in the wider world.[96] This complexity belies both the missionaries' occasionally heroic characterizations of their work and also their categorical designation as colonialists or cultural imperialists. Some missionaries were European, some were not; some were ardent supporters of the colonial project, others were more critical.[97] In light of this complexity, it is perhaps more helpful to think of mission institutions like churches, schools, hospitals, and printing presses as cross-cultural meeting places than as European or even colonial outposts.

A second point is that the impact of missionary activities reverberated far beyond these institutions and the local congregations they sustained. While the emergence of indigenous evangelical and Catholic traditions and communities is of course a key dimension of Eritrean and Ethiopian mission history, the career of Gabra Mikā'él illustrates how the repercussions of mission institutions were as much intellectual and political as they were religious. Contacts with one or both of the missionary organizations,[98] whether for a brief interlude in a night course or for a more extended period of education or worship, was an important career move for many colonial notables, as their biographies attest. Whether mission alumni obtained practical training as a baker, tanner, typist, or clerk, or whether like Gabra Mikā'él they developed European language skills that prepared them for a range of intermediary roles, these facts were at best only tangentially related to the Europeans' specific vision of salvation and lifelong congregational affiliation. The same can be said for the broader informalization of knowledge set into motion by the mission schools and presses, and for the subtle forces of globalization they fostered. Colonial notables read books with foreign origins, spoke European languages, and often traveled abroad to fight Italian wars and occasionally study in European institutions, and the outcomes of this could never be as limited as Carrara hoped. At the same time, the argument that missionaries were mere brokers of a hegemonic colonial culture, and that their pupils were simply Italianized collaborators, is undercut by the extent to which missionary languages, literacy, and books were adapted to suit a range of purposes.

Finally, these developments laid the foundations for new forms of communal identity that clearly went beyond faith. As Gabra Mikā'él's history makes clear, the colonial notable group that emerged in the colonial period was a crucial transitional cohort of Eritrean intellectuals, ones who surely saw themselves as distinct from their contemporaries in profession and outlook. It is this worldview that is subtly on display in Gabra Mikā'él's history, but it is highly significant—and perhaps surprising—that the author chose to use the term "Ethiopia"—not "Eritrea"—in his title and throughout this work.[99] The contrast between his title and the specifically Eritrean historical dynamics he describes highlight the extent to which this new group affiliation was in a dynamic, formative stage. Though his arguments would become familiar to later generations of Eritrean nationalists, he did not yet imagine himself to be a member of an inherently limited community, but instead saw himself as part of a greater Ethiopia.

9

The Scholar-Missionaries of the Basel Mission in Southwest India

Language, Identity, and Knowledge in Flux

Mrinalini Sebastian

Introduction

In 1834 the Evangelical Missionary Society of Basel, Switzerland—commonly known as the Basel Mission—sent its first three missionaries to the Malabar coast of southwest India.[1] They arrived in Mangalore, a small town where no other Protestant mission was yet active but where there existed a smaller Catholic community (the product of missionary initiatives that dated from the sixteenth century).[2] Within a few years, Basel missionaries were working in many parts of the Tulu- and Kannada-speaking regions that are now part of India's Karnataka state; its stations by the 1850s stretched northward to the Dharwad district. The Basel missionaries also extended their work into Malayalam-speaking communities as well as the tribal communities inhabiting the Nilgiri Hills, in what is now western Tamil Nadu. For decades the Basel missionaries retained cordial relations with the colonial officers who consolidated Britain's hold over India. However, with the outbreak of World War I, relations turned hostile between British colonial forces and the Basel missionaries, who were mostly of German and Swiss origin. British authorities deported many German missionaries of the Basel Mission at that time and interned some others in India. The British also imposed

176

heavy regulations over the mission's activities.[3] For these reasons, it makes sense to date the heyday of the Basel Mission's work in southwest India to the period from 1834, when work began, until 1914, when war intervened.

Over the course of several decades, the Basel missionaries tried to introduce Indian people to their faith and to organize converts into communities. Today, the presence of a small but flourishing Protestant community in the towns where they worked attests, in part, to their efforts. Nevertheless, from the beginning, the work and impact of the Basel missionaries went well beyond the realm of evangelism. The Basel missionaries opened schools and a printing press. They developed tile factories and weaving units that flourished for over a century, providing a livelihood for their converts as well as for non-Christians in the vicinity while introducing new modes of industrial activity. At the same time, they produced substantial works of linguistic and ethnographic research. This research, in turn, influenced a German intellectual culture of "Indology" in which theories of language and nation figured prominently. This research also transformed local and regional notions of community and ethnicity in southwest India. It was in the latter sphere, by influencing perceptions of cultural and ethno-linguistic identity among Tulu-, Kannada-, and Malayalam-speakers across the religious spectrum, that the Basel missionaries had their most enduring—and most unexpected—impact. The Basel missionaries of the late nineteenth century are acclaimed in southwest India for the work they did in "modernizing" Kannada and Malayalam and in collecting, categorizing, and recording the oral traditions of Tulu, a language previously not rendered in script.

This history of the Basel "scholar-missionaries" of southwest India challenges the assumption that the impact of Christian missionaries in the non-Western world may be immediate, concrete, and measurable. It suggests, on the contrary, that a missionary impact may be long-lasting, diffuse, and—especially when occurring in the realm of ideas—palpable but yet resistant to measurement. Certainly the case of the Basel missionaries in southwest India suggests how missionaries, and the things they seemed to represent, were able to bring inter- and intracommunity relationships into states of crisis. The history of the Basel missionaries also shows how missionary scholarship was able to exert important influences on Western institutions of higher learning while generating new interest among local peoples in local intellectual and cultural legacies.

This research draws upon the records stored in the Basel Mission's archives in Switzerland and upon nineteenth-century missionary publications. It also benefits from a rich body of secondary sources in English and German. After surveying the work of the Basel Mission and the Protestant culture of Pietism that inspired it, the essay pursues two major lines of inquiry. These two lines of inquiry intersect repeatedly, thanks to certain figures who appear in the narrative that follows and whose life experiences, missionary careers, and writings bring them together.

The first line of inquiry considers the reconfigurations in communal identities, which the activities of the mission induced. It analyzes the responses in India and among the mission's German-speaking supporters in Europe to the conversion of a young Brahmin named Anandarao Kaundinya (1825–1893), who was a student in one of the Basel mission schools. While this particular case was not of great significance to the "native" Christians who had already converted, it created unrest among other Indian groups, including Muslims and Hindus, and led to the formation of new local coalitions. The litigation that ensued, which involved British colonial authorities, also led to the passage of landmark laws that became applicable throughout India.[4] Above all, the case of Anandarao shows that missionary-negotiated events such as conversion had communal-level consequences, implicating missionaries in a series of local transformations that were far beyond the control of the mission agency.[5]

The second line of inquiry considers an academic presupposition of the late eighteenth and nineteenth centuries about the inextricable relationship between languages and nations, and assesses its bearing on the scholarship of the Basel missionaries in southwest India.[6] It considers more closely examples of Basel missionaries whose studies of the Kannada, Malayalam, and Tulu languages were influenced by, and influenced in turn, Indological studies in contemporary German universities such as Tübingen. In the long run, missionary writings not only became a primary source for linguistic scholarship in South India but also provided a model for constructing or consolidating language- and culture-based identities.

A particularly vivid example of this trend was the writings of Ferdinand Kittel (1832–1903), a Basel missionary-scholar, hailed as a language "modernizer," whose work has indirectly informed identity debates—and identity politics—in the Indian state of Karnataka today.

The Basel Mission: Its Religious and Intellectual Context, in Europe and India

In 1780 a group of prominent "Swiss and German clergymen, community leaders, business owners, and academic theologians" established the German Society for Christianity as a means for gathering to study and discuss the Bible.[7] This group, which was in many ways a precursor to the Basel Mission, drew inspiration from Pietism, which had become a prominent religious movement following the end of the Thirty Years' War (1618–1648). Pietists demanded spiritual rebirth from an individual while professing deep care for the well-being of the collective. This combination of individualism and communalism became a hallmark of most of the Protestant missions that emerged in northern Europe during the eighteenth and nineteenth centuries.[8]

Pietism also left its mark on Christian scholarship, both in fields of history, philosophy, literature, and education and also on a European university culture that was itself in a state of ferment.[9] University scholars were undertaking a quest for academic freedom and intellectual innovation even as advocates of Pietism were suggesting their radical shift to personal and communal popular piety. At the University of Halle in what is now Germany, these developments converged.

Though scholars generally trace the beginning of the Pietist movement to the thought of Philipp Jakob Spener (1635–1705), it was August Hermann Francke (1663–1727), a professor at the University of Halle, who articulated a practical model for missionary work. For Francke, *Erziehung*, or the upbringing of a child through Christian education, was an important responsibility of the community of believers.[10] He integrated the study of languages and scientific knowledge within a new system of education that would provide also for the education of girls, the poor, and orphans. In this way, Francke's institutional complex at Halle brings to mind the ideal Christian city imagined by the writer Johann Valentin Andreä in his seventeenth-century work called *Christianopolis* (1619).[11] Significantly, too, Francke's educational complex included a printing press, which later became the central mechanism used by the missionaries for the spread of Christian values and educational ideals in most mission contexts.

The University of Halle was also one of the first institutions in Europe to show an academic interest in Oriental cultures. At Halle, Christian Wolff, a prominent philosopher of the German Enlightenment, faced stiff opposition from Francke and a few others because of his views on the merits of some non-Christian religions. Wolff's views on Chinese ethics, in particular, cost him his university job; in the words of Mark Larrimore, the "striking absence of any suggestion [in his published work] that the Chinese needed to learn about Christianity" appears to have provoked his critics the most.[12] Nevertheless, Wolff's writings about China—or about an imagined China—did succeed in influencing evangelical Pietist discourses about the Orient in ways that anticipated by over a century the Orientalism that Edward Said so famously analyzed.[13]

In any case, at Halle, the environment of debate over other philosophies and cultures helped to shape plans for training missionaries to work in the "Orient." However, the institution that Francke set up in Halle trained missionaries who eventually went not to China but to India. This happened in 1706 when Bartholomäus Ziegenbalg and Heinrich Plutschau ventured to start a station in Tranquebar, on India's southeast coast, where there was already an established Danish fort and trading settlement.

More than a century passed until 1815, when a group of idealistic German-speaking Protestants founded the Evangelical Missionary Society, soon to be more commonly known as the Basel Mission, after the town where it was centered. Its founders aimed to go out and evangelize, not merely to promote Bible study. From the outset the Basel Mission trained missionaries who sought employment with other European missionary agencies, such as the London Missionary Society and the Church Missionary Society, both British organizations. But soon the Basel mission's administrators (the "Committee") in Basel decided to send missionaries independently to various parts of the world: first to Russia, then to the

Gold Coast in Africa (1828), and finally, in 1834, to southwest India (which is, again, when the mission to Mangalore began).

The Basel Mission's debt to Pietism was clear in its desire for spiritual and worldly transformation through conversion; its minimizing of denominational differences among Protestants; and its demands for spiritual "rebirth" as the sine qua non for missionary candidates.[14] In southwest India, the Basel Mission's Pietistic rejection of social distinctions among the pious gained expression, too, in its commitment to fight against local caste practices and to reject caste distinctions within the church—positions that amounted to a call for radical social transformation. Attesting to the influence of Francke's pedagogical philosophy as articulated at Halle, the boarding schools of the Basel Mission in South India combined work, scientific knowledge, and spiritual learning. Finally, like Ziegenbalg, who founded the early mission to Tranquebar, some of the first Basel missionaries sent to southwest India were keen observers and excellent linguists. They were proto-ethnographers who collected information on the plants, peoples, and cultures of the many places where they sought to spread the Christian gospel.

In sum, Pietism exerted an influence on the Basel Mission in four areas. These were its adherence to the concept of "rebirth" and "true discipleship"; its cultivation of the "mission compound" as a self-sufficient community of the faithful; its commitment to transforming the convert in both spiritual and worldly arenas; and its strong support for the provision of "Christian" education across the social spectrum.

Although the Basel Mission evinced an egalitarian social ethic in many ways, a noticeable class distinction separated the Committee from the missionaries that it fielded. That is, its administrators were generally pastors and merchants who came from the elite ranks of the city of Basel, whereas many of the missionaries themselves were from the artisanal and farming villages of southern Germany.[15] This obvious hierarchy between the elite Committee and its humble delegates notwithstanding, argues Jon Miller, the two groups succeeded in engaging in "class collaboration for the sake of religion"—something that was another unique feature of the early Pietist movement.[16]

Miller also suggests that, in formulating early policy for the Gold Coast, the administrators and the missionaries of the Basel Mission agreed on three principles that should guide the mission's practical "pursuit of its evangelical goals": first, preaching the gospel in the local language; second, making education, especially Bible education, a central concern; and, third, creating an economically self-sustained community of Christians by teaching "modern husbandry and craft skills."[17] These principles informed the Indian context as well, thereby attesting to the linkages in policy and practice that connected mission endeavors in different fields.

Training as seminarians for the Basel Mission, missionaries were able to acquire solid educations (which would have otherwise been impossible, given their humble origins) and thereby achieve upward mobility. In the early phase of the mission's work in India, some of the Basel missionaries arrived as university graduates as well. The academic ethos of the German universities instilled in them an interest in philology and Indology. To India, they brought skills and presuppositions about the study of languages, and they also produced knowledge, in collaboration with local intellectuals (most of whom were their language teachers or *munshis*), which in turn transformed the nature of academic disciplines in Europe as in India. The second half of this essay will examine the work of these scholar-missionaries in greater depth.

Significantly, unlike many other missions that were ready to compromise on issues of caste, the Basel Mission insisted on not allowing caste practices to creep into their churches. It undoubtedly helped in their efforts to resist caste that most of their converts came from comparable caste backgrounds, that is, from groups that depended on fishing and on "toddy-tapping" for the production of coconut palm wine. This resulted in a Christian community that was not, for the most part, divided along caste lines. Forming mission compounds or settlements for newly converted Christians, often close to the church, and establishing industrial units and other job-generating enterprises along with schools and hospitals, transformed the topography of towns by demarking certain spaces for "mission people" and by ensuring that earlier caste distinctions would not dominate communal life. In short, the establishment of mission compounds in southwest India allowed for the erasure of old cultural practices and the inscription of new ones.

Yet a note of caution is warranted here. The Basel missionaries may have disavowed "caste" as a feature of communal life within their Christian communities, but awareness of and attention to the phenomenon did not entirely vanish from their consciousness; their attitudes were ambivalent. This ambivalence reflected less of the local or regional caste politics with which the subcontinent had long since been identified and more of the Basel missionaries' transnational search for a comparative framework that could comprehensively explain caste, religion, and culture in a world that was shrinking through travel, conquest, and commerce. In the story of Anandarao Kaundinya, whose conversion is central to the analysis here, the "caste" issue, which was resolved at some level because of his conversion, returned at times very subtly as a race issue, as we shall see later. This return of caste as race was only possible in an academic milieu where assumptions and theories about the relationships among languages, ethnicities, and cultures were pervasive. The European network of institutions, academic as well as religious, through which such discourses about race, language, and caste circulated, drew sustenance from its "knowledge" about non-Western cultures.

Reconfiguring Communal Identities: The Case of Anandarao, the Brahmin

Reaching Mangalore in October 1834, Samuel Hebich, Christian Leonhard, and Johann Christoph Lehner initiated the work of the Basel Mission in southwest India by establishing a mission base as well as schools for the local people. This was a time in modern Indian history when populations were still barely conscious of themselves as "communities" needing to contend for rights and privileges. By contrast, six decades later as the nineteenth century was ending, many such communities in India were beginning to negotiate with each other and with the colonial government for their collective civic advancement. In retrospect, it is clear that European and American Protestant Christian missions played an important role in transforming the relational webs that connected different groups of people. Revisiting the moments of interaction between the Protestant missions and the "natives" provides insights into the community-level transformations that transpired in the Indian subcontinent over the course of the nineteenth century.

In the eyes of the Basel missionaries, everyone, including Catholics and the Orthodox Christians from Kerala, needed "conversion," an experience of spiritual rebirth that would bring them close to Christ. The missionaries often engaged in debates and public disputations with Brahmins, heads of Lingayat Matts (monastic institutions of the Veerashaiva sects), Catholic priests, and Muslim leaders, elaborating and defending the truth of Christian faith. The early reports of the mission show that there was a general atmosphere of hospitality in most of the places they visited, though occasionally some groups were less willing to interact with them. But most listened to the missionaries, often agreed with them, and went on to say that they would nevertheless continue following the ways of their ancestors.

Whether it was in Calcutta or in Mangalore, an encounter with the Protestant missionaries during the eighteenth and nineteenth centuries always drove the local communities to make statements about their practices, beliefs, and sacred texts in an effort to defend themselves and their ancestors against the missionaries' claims. That is because for missionaries, the point of disputation was to prove the veracity and superiority of Christianity over all other religions.[18] Religious disputations naturally elicited much writing about what the different communities believed in, and especially analyses of their respective "sacred texts." Sadly, many of the polemic writings coming from the missionaries (of all denominations) had the objective of proving the falsity of "idolatry." Many Hindu pundits, therefore, took it upon themselves to explain how worshipping an image did not necessarily exclude a concept of the divine. Still others, like Ram Mohan Roy (1774–1833), began to argue that Hinduism is foundationally a monotheistic religion.

In 1834, when the Basel missionaries began their work, Mangalore was a small port town along India's southwestern coast. Yet it was also a cosmopolitan space that had experienced a range of cultural influences over many centuries.[19] When the first Basel missionaries arrived, there were 651,000 Hindus, 46,000 Muslims, and 20,000 Catholics in the province (then called "Canara") where Mangalore was located.[20] The Basel Mission's archives preserve an autobiography by Anandarao Kaundinya, the young Brahmin whose conversion became the catalyst of communal unrest in 1844. Its preface contains this nuanced description of the inhabitants of Mangalore at the time:

> The population of this city is 40,000 and consists of people of all kinds of race, tribe, caste and language [sic].[21] There are seven languages here, whose tones are mixed with one another. There are Englishmen, who work as the civil servants and serve the provincial administration, but also as officers who command the regiments of black, native soldiers; there are Parsis, Gujaratis, Moplas, old Muslim men, who move around as the main tradesmen in the Bazaar, speaking Gujarati and Hindustani; there are the children of the Portuguese and the native Catholics, who speak Konkana like the Sarasvata-Brahmins and the other Konkanis; there are the actual Kannadigas, Tamil-speaking soldiers and workers, who have moved here with their regiments and their masters from the East; the majority of the population consists of the Tulu-people, whose language is Tulu, who have also come from many of the earlier mentioned castes and tribes. As can be expected, there is no single religion that the people of this coast knows and practices. There are many religious communities staying here next to one another.[22]

This account suggests that the town, given all its diversity, offered a congenial space for the new Basel missionaries. The missionary Hermann Gundert (1814–1893), a graduate of Tübingen University who authored the first Malayalam-English dictionary in 1872, reflected as much when he wrote that in Mangalore there was a "mixture of all castes."[23] Apart from the Brahmins, Muslims, and Roman Catholics, there were also three prominent though relatively humble groups whose members spoke Tulu, the town's most widely spoken language, and who shared the practice of matrilineal succession. These were the Bunts (who were often landowners), the Billavas (toddy-tappers), and the Moghaviras (fisher folk). The Bunts, Billavas, and Moghaviras worshipped the Bhutas, deities who played a crucial role as protecting and, at times, punitive spirits.[24] Indeed, the cultural and social lives of the Bunts, Billavas, and Moghaviras revolved around the worship of these Bhutas. Like the other mission agencies in India, the Basel Mission had hoped to convince the more "respectable classes" about the "truth" of Christianity. But in southwest India it was mostly people of the "lower castes"—and especially the Billava and Moghavira people— who found Christianity most appealing.

It was against this social context that the conversion of the Brahmin student, Anandarao Kaundinya, occurred in 1844. Even today, the Protestant Christians of South Kanara retain the story of his conversion in their collective memory, while his story has also been the subject of reports, narratives, judgments, and critical writings.[25] Anandarao belonged to the first batch of students to emerge from a local school run by English missionaries. Since he was one of the first Brahmins ever inclined to convert, the missionaries saw him as a messenger to the "respectable" classes and hoped that he would draw many other Brahmins and upper-caste people to Christianity. Yet this hope was never fulfilled. What his conversion—or his apostasy—did do, however, was to galvanize upper-caste communities in the face of Christian missionary activity.

Anandarao's Conversion: The Event and Its Consequences

Born in 1825, Anandarao Kaundinya belonged to a prominent Saraswat Brahmin family in Mangalore. Orphaned at a young age, he was married to the daughter of a local judge. The relatives who looked after him took a special interest in educating Anandarao in the different schools of Indian philosophical thought. His companions remembered him as a student who constantly opposed the Bible. Nevertheless, in 1844 he embraced Christianity. His own early representation of his conversion experience seems to follow the familiar progressive trajectory of being aware of his sins, asking for forgiveness, and acknowledging Jesus as his savior. In a letter written in English shortly after his conversion to Inspector (Director) Hoffmann of the Basel Mission, he wrote:

> At the sixteenth year of my age I went to the Mangalore English School
> to acquire some knowledge of the English language and of other things

which I thought would be useful for me. After some time when I began to understand what I read in the school and as I had some instructions of the word of God there I received them as useful and good but without heart.

Eight months ago I felt sick of the fever for nearly 2 ½ months. At this time I was minded of my future life and how one is to be saved. This gave me no rest in my heart all the time but I knew not that it was of the infinite mercies of our Lord and Christ Jesu, who shed his blood on the cross for all the world.[26]

The Basel missionary Hermann Moegling (1811–1881), who became Anandarao's mentor, gave another account of his conversion. According to this account, Anandarao had learned to pray during his illness. But his actual transformation began when he read a story about a Greek king who had "his son's and his own eye gouged out, in order to maintain the law."[27] This story, which was used to illustrate God's mercy for all, had encouraged Anandarao to initiate a conversation with Moegling about sin and salvation.

When Anandarao's fifteen-year-old[28] wife Lakshmi disclosed his intention to other members of the family, a highly emotional scene unfolded. Relatives placed Anandarao under close watch and forbade him from meeting the missionaries again. However, the Collector of Mangalore, a British official named Blair, intervened by sending a letter to his father-in-law asking Anandarao to be sent to meet him. After his conversation with Blair, Anandarao decided to go to the house of the missionaries, although he "was almost intimidated and had become undecided concerning the moment of his public conversion to Christian faith."[29] He finally made up his mind and decided to stay with the missionaries in spite of the efforts of his father-in-law and other relatives to persuade him to return.

Two other Brahmin classmates of Anandarao also wanted to become Christians. For these three Brahmins (Anandarao, Bhgavanta Rao, and Mukunda Rao) who had decided to stay with the missionaries the symbolic moment of rupture from their earlier community was marked by the act of eating. For the Brahmins, eating food cooked by others, and eating along with Christian foreigners, amounted to losing their caste: "Only late in the evening did the three Brahmins unfasten their holy thread and had some coffee and bread after the long fast. Now they did not belong to their caste any more."[30] The next day, however, about 200 Brahmins, Muslims, and others surrounded the mission house and unsuccessfully tried to extract the young men. On January 6, 1844, missionaries baptized the three young men. Anandarao received a new name, Herrmann Anandarao Kaundinya, after his mentor Herrmann Moegling. On the January 7, tensions simmered in Mangalore because during

> the night, Jacob's [Mukunda Rao] relatives had had the innards and the head of a pig thrown into the tank in front of the main mosque. In India this is regarded as the "password" of the revolt, of the butchering of Christians. The whole town got restless. The soldiers had to be ready for action and the cannons stood at the parade ground ready to be used.[31]

It was Collector Blair who convinced the Muslims that "not the Christians but the Brahmins had polluted their sanctuary," thereby averting an impending disaster. Yet, in passions aroused by the rumor that Christians had desecrated a mosque, one may detect, already in 1844, forebodings of the extraordinary events and alliances that triggered the protests that erupted elsewhere in the subcontinent and that became known as the Indian Mutiny of 1857.

Anandarao's father-in-law, who was an influential man, took this matter to the court, leaving a paper trail of court documents that have been analyzed by the scholar Gauri Viswanathan. As reasons for reclaiming him, petitions submitted by various members of his family cited Anandarao's underage status and mental instability (due to his illness); his civil death (through the loss of his Brahminical status); and the consequent widowhood of his young wife. We do not hear much about these legal battles in the missionary documents. All that we know is that the incident, and the tense moments that ensued, worsened the already poor health of the missionary Moegling. To recuperate, Moegling journeyed to the Nilgiri Hills. He was accompanied by Anandarao and Stephan (called by Moegling his "first black brother"), who was a Tamil boy from the "outcaste" or Pariah community. They were Moegling's companions and *munshis* (language teachers) on the journey.[32]

Records in the Basel Mission's archives show that, from this time until his return to Mangalore a few weeks later, Anandarao recorded an almost daily account of his experience in the Nilgiri Hills in the form of journal extracts written in English, which were sent to Inspector Hoffmann (the director of the mission) in Basel. In all these letters, Anandarao says nothing about the wife whom he had left. Other records suggest that she went to live with her parents, probably like a Brahmin widow, for the next eight years. These letters do indicate, however, that Anandarao wanted to accompany Moegling to Europe. Moegling supported the idea, but the Home Committee did not, expressing concerns about the convert's "spiritual welfare." Disappointed, Anandarao explained that he would have liked to accompany Moegling

> not only because I long to see and to know those dear Friends, who have sent preachers of the Gospel to this country, but also because I am certain that I would learn many, many things in Europe where all people bear at least the name of Christ, and at Basel where our teachers themselves have been educated, and that a stay of some years there would make me much fitter for the service of God than I could otherwise become.[33]

Eventually, the Committee consented to his journey to Europe. In a context where there was a well-established hierarchy between the missionaries and the converted, and where the Committee looked dimly upon the idea of encouraging "native" converts to travel to Europe, what allowed for this relaxation of the rules to include Anandarao? Was it the fact that he was acknowledged as the spiritual son of the missionary Moegling, was it rather Moegling's own "conscious" efforts at living "like" the natives, or was it because of the German academic endorsement of Brahmins as an offshoot of the Indo-Germanic "race"? The last was undoubtedly significant.

Moegling ultimately succeeded in convincing the Committee that Anandarao should go to Basel to be trained as the first "native" missionary to India—something hitherto unprecedented for the Basel Mission in southwest India. The highest status that "natives" could achieve within the hierarchy of the missionary institutions in these locations during this time was generally that of the "catechist." At this time most of the missionaries did not approve of ordaining Indian Christians as pastors.[34]

Nevertheless, in November 1845, Herrmann Anandarao Kaundinya left Mangalore for training in Basel. At the end of his stay the Basel Mission ordained him as the first Indian missionary to be sent to his own "people," that is, to the people who lived in and around the city of Mangalore.

Forging New Communities: The Congregation of "Native Christians" in Mangalore

The caste groups of India presented the Basel missionaries with challenges. The inmates of their boarding schools came entirely from "lower" caste groups. Their very first convert in Mangalore was a fisherman.[35] Soon after they started their work in southwest India it became clear to the Protestant missionaries that most of their converts were going to come from the "lower" rungs of the caste hierarchy, despite dreams of reaching more "higher" social elements.

In 1844, the year of Anandarao's conversion, the missionary C. L. Greiner initiated a process to organize Mangalore's community of "native Christians" more effectively. The process involved having all the adult members of the congregation elect elders who would in turn represent their interests. Greiner also formulated a set of policies and regulations to govern the life of the congregation and met to discuss them with the "native Christians" who accepted their terms.[36] This fascinating document is one of the earliest examples of the negotiation between the members of the first Protestant congregation in this region and the missionaries. It sets out many provisions for organizing the community's life. These included, for example, setting up a special cash reserve for looking after widows and the poor; and scrapping some "cultural" practices, such as playing "devilish music" at weddings, hanging "magical" things (talismans) around the necks of children, or wearing jewelry (among women). The document also provides for the retention of some practices: notably, the wearing of traditional clothes and the exempting of tapping coconut trees for toddy from the rule of "no work" on Sundays. The most remarkable decision, however, involved caste: "There will be no caste distinction in the congregation."[37]

There is a bit of irony in the story of the conversion of Anandarao, whose caste status as a Brahmin continued to afford him prestige among the missionaries, especially when we juxtapose it to these rules governing the first local Christian congregation. It was important for the "ordinary" members to erase memories of caste practices so that they could build a new community of "native" Christians, and a new collective identity. However, as we sift through documents that relate to Anandarao, we see that his identity as an individual, and as a former member of the Brahmin community, remains at the forefront. As Gauri Viswanathan points out in her work *Outside the Fold* (1998), all those who intended to convert to Christianity faced the threat of "loss of caste" in colonial India because they were subject to what was known as "civil death." Civil death—in addition to the "ritual death" observed by families of the high-caste con-verts—translated into a denial of all civil rights to the apostate, including the right to inherit. This was addressed by the passing of the Caste Dis-abilities Removal Act in 1850—an act influenced, to some degree, by the earlier litigation involving Anandarao Kaundinya—which probably made it legally possible for Anandarao later to reclaim his inheritance.[38] It was with this money that he helped Moegling to buy a plot in Coorg District for the members of the Holeya community who had approached the mis-sionaries with a request to establish a school for their children.[39]

Loss of caste may have been less dramatic for converts from the "lower" caste groups, but it was significant to them nonetheless. Former caste members often had no means of sustenance, having lost claims to property or to earlier professions. Hence, within a few years of arriving in Mangalore, the mission set up various industrial units.[40] These created employment opportunities for people who had lost their jobs and also for those whose traditional professions (such as brewing alcoholic toddy, or palm wine) were not entirely acceptable to the missionaries. During the first phase of efforts to create employment for new converts, the missionar-ies had ventured into agriculture but were dissatisfied with the results.[41] In the second phase, which was much more successful, they established handloom weaving units, tile factories, a printing press, and a mechanical workshop, along with an "Industrial Commission" within the mission to oversee them.[42] The missionaries recognized that "cheap English weaving" was replacing the indigenous handloom industry and therefore planned to innovatively create a niche market for their woven products.[43] Later, many non-Christian weavers in the region adapted the innovations that missionaries introduced in the weaving units. Likewise, their tile factories flourished and produced red-clay tiles that are well known even today as "Mangalore tiles." British colonial authorities used such tiles widely in their buildings and they also became a popular item for export to the Middle East and even farther afield.[44]

Following this period of extensive diversification, the Basel Mission attempted to consolidate its work by setting up a joint-stock company in 1882.[45] This grew into a separate wing of the mission called the "Basler Handels-Gesellschaft AG." When World War I started, the Basler Handels-Gesellschaft had thirteen industrial undertakings, including brick factories, weaving and coloring units, and other mechanical units. During the war, the British government in India declared a "Hostile Foreigners (Trading) Order" with the aim of liquidating all these industrial units, which were by then very prolific. During World War I, the Basel Mission was ultimately compelled to transfer these units to new trustees who were actually members of English missionary circles. In hindsight, it is clear that the industrial wing of the Basel Mission had played a crucial role in developing the manufacturing sector of southwest India from the mid-nineteenth century until the outbreak of World War I. The community of "native" Christians benefited; so did the region and its economy as a whole.

The Imagined Relationship between Caste and Race

Returning once more to the issue of Anandarao's conversion, we can see where issues of caste and race intersect. Consider, again, Lakshmi: the Brahmin girl or woman who married Anandarao before his conversion. The customs and traditions of her caste community would have conferred on her the status of a widow once her husband became an apostate. Though Lakshmi was a player in the legal battle for reclaiming

Anandarao, the disruption caused in her life could hardly be captured by the logic of either the personal/spiritual "rebirth" of the individual or that of his own "free" choice to embrace Christianity. When he returned from Europe, Anandarao persuaded Lakshmi to join him. However, after a traumatic process of "cultural conversion" where she had to make the difficult choice between the ways of her ancestors and the new ways of her husband, she died at a young age.[46]

It is in the context of Anandarao's contemplation of remarriage, following Lakshmi's death, that we see the return of the caste issue. He did not think that there were suitable brides for him within the native Christian community, nor in the Protestant congregations of Bombay or Madras. As was the practice with other German missionaries, he wanted a German bride to be sent for him, a proposition he was bold enough to make through his mentor Moegling.[47] A young woman, Marie Reinhardt, was "found suitable" for him; strikingly, she agreed to marry him and "met" him first through correspondence. Defending himself to his future brother-in-law, who opposed their interracial marriage, Anandarao wrote:

> Your branch (*stamm*) wandered towards the north, whereas my branch moved towards the south. Now, after thousands of years, [when] this mutual belonging (*Zusammengehörigkeit*) is made valid through Christianity, the progeny of these old brotherly tribes extend their hands to one another.[48]

It is remarkable that the Basel Mission authorized the marriage of an Indian man to a European woman when the same organization had objected to the marriage of a European missionary to a "black woman" in Africa only a few years before.[49] I suggest, however, that the justification for such racial "hospitality," at a time when perceptions of racial boundaries were growing more rigid, gained credence from the academic discipline of Indology, whose proponents at that time identified Sanskrit as the *Ursprache* of all the languages. Even then, Anandarao's mixed marriage was not an entirely straightforward affair. Nearly a century later, when the Nazis ruled Germany, his descendants in Germany seemed to have become anxious about their mixed ancestry. At that time, in order to protect the family from the impact of Nazi miscegenation laws, the Basel Mission issued letters to several descendants of the Kaundinya family who were living in Germany, asserting that their forebear, Anandarao, was a Brahmin and of the purest Aryan race, so that no racial mixing had actually occurred.[50]

The nineteenth-century Indology prevalent in German universities certainly bore traces of the influence of German Romanticism, but what exactly was its relationship to the Basel Mission? Moegling and Kaundinya, both of whom were influenced by an academic tradition that endorsed the close relationships among caste, race, and language, were also the first to affirm the humanity of the Holeyas, who were considered the lowest of the low within the caste hierarchy of southwest India. (In India today, such people, formerly considered "untouchables," have chosen to call themselves "Dalits.") Like his mentor Moegling, it was in the Coorg District where he later worked as a missionary with his German wife Marie Reinhardt, that Anandarao found his vocation and contributed funds to establish a school for Holeya children. Nevertheless, Indological scholarship, as it developed in this period, exerted an important if unpredictable impact on the missionaries' study of language and culture in southwest India. This brings us to the second major section of this study, which examines the missionaries' roles as scholars who shaped local conceptions of "languages" and "nations."

German Indology, Kannada Linguistics, and the Ethnographic Project

In a "Third Anniversary Discourse" delivered to the Asiatic Society at Calcutta in 1784, William Jones identified an Indo-European family of languages.[51] This "discovery" of the Indo-European languages riveted scholars. Within India itself, this idea energized certain employees of the East India Company who, in their capacity as educators of "natives," had specialized in studying Persian and Sanskrit, the two languages of India's "respectable classes." During the late seventeenth and early eighteenth centuries several of these East India Company "Indologists" (or the broader group to which they belonged, that of "Orientalists") collected rare manuscripts, learned more languages, and extolled the qualities of San-skrit texts.[52] Especially under the leadership of Warren Hastings (Governor General of Bengal, 1773–1785), these efforts enjoyed official patronage.

Meanwhile, Oriental scholarship was flourishing in Europe. In the German states, points out Douglas Timothy McGetchin, the educational system varied from region to region though it was Indology that provided the initial motivation for an emerging sense of "national" culture. The reform in the university system introduced by Alexander von Humboldt (1769–1859) also marked the beginning of the state patronage of Indology in German universities. In order to imagine a unifying nationalist culture for Germany, it was crucial to trace a unique ancestry. "Translating Ancient India" proved to be a very successful tool for the construction of an imagined German unity.[53]

McGetchin shows that many of the German Indologists like Humboldt, August Wilhelm Schlegel, and Franz Bopp had a Romantic attachment to Sanskrit. Humboldt's interest in Indology also cleared the way for founding professorial chairs in Sanskrit in the universities of Bonn and Berlin during the first two decades of the nineteenth century. The study of Sanskrit paved the way, in turn, for the development of comparative linguistics and for speculation about the origin of languages. Yet a basic difference distinguished the classicists, who studied ancient texts in Greek and Latin for their content, from the comparativists, who interpreted ancient society on the basis of their study of the languages. Relating language to culture, and more specifically to race, was central to German Indological studies.[54]

But how indeed was the beginning of Indological Studies in Germany connected to the beginning of the work of the German missionaries in India? Although more research is needed on the question, this essay suggests some preliminary answers. In his analysis of the writing of the Halle missionaries in Tranquebar, Hanco Jürgens suggests that Ziegenbalg's *Gramatica Damilica* (1716) and Niekamp's short version of the "History of the Halle Mission in 'East India'" (1740) already anticipated the "explosion in the Grammar factory"[55] that occurred in the following century. Jürgens points out that Niekamp in 1740 was already mentioning a language called "*Nagaram* or *Dewa-nagaram* (Devanagari) [which] was on par with

Greek, Hebrew and Persian."⁵⁶ However, among German scholars, it was the speech by William Jones at Calcutta in 1784—again, the speech that identified the Indo-European language family—that inspired the more systematic study of Sanskrit, and the explosion of comparative linguistics as an academic discipline.⁵⁷

The first scholar-missionaries sent by the Basel Mission were linked to the University of Tübingen, which became an important center for Indological studies during the nineteenth century. Three of the missionaries of the Basel Mission who went to southwest India, namely, Moegling, Weigle (1816–1855), and Gundert (1813–1893) (who later compiled his Malayalam dictionary), had studied at Tübingen around the time when Indology was gaining prestige as an academic discipline in Germany. Indeed, Rudolph Roth, who taught at Tübingen around this time, was a well-known scholar in Vedic studies.⁵⁸ In other words, these future Basel missionaries received their training in an institution that regarded the study of Indic languages with high esteem. Upon reaching India, they dedicated their lives to studying the local languages, searching for ancient texts, and cataloguing local cultures: they became de facto linguists and ethnographers.

Certainly the Kannada texts compiled, translated, and circulated by the missionaries in southwest India seem to have been well-received by universities and Oriental studies societies in Germany and France. Moegling received an honorary doctorate from the University of Tübingen for his *Bibliotheca Carnatica*, a compilation of several ancient Kannada texts and modern Kannada proverbs that he gathered between 1848 and 1851.⁵⁹ Another missionary, Ferdinand Kittel, received a doctorate *honoris causa* from Tübingen University for his Kannada-English dictionary. Weigle wrote an essay, "On the Canarese Language and Literature," which was found "too scientific and hence not suitable" to be published in a German mission journal, but which finally appeared in the second volume of the *Zeitschrift der deutschen morgenländischen Gesellschaft* (ZDMG), the highly respected journal of the German Oriental Society.⁶⁰

Some of the content-sheets and lists of books that accompany the different issues of ZDMG suggest the interconnectedness between the work of this German society for Oriental studies and the scholarship of the early missionaries like Moegling, Gundert, and Weigle. Moegling's translation of the songs of Purandara Dasa and Kanaka Dasa were published by the ZDMG in 1860.[61] Only twice in his introduction to these songs did Moegling indicate that he was a Christian missionary: once when he showed disappointment that these songs from the "most gifted among a gifted people of India" should be offered to Krishna who, in his view, was a caricature of a "liberator" of godly people; and again, when he compared the spirit that kindled the devotion of Chaitanya in Bengal and the Haridasas in the Kannada-speaking region to the spirit of reform in Europe.[62] Apart from these two instances nothing in his translations would indicate a missionary perspective.

On the ground in southwest India, Moegling went on extensive tours, often on foot, collecting plant specimens and cultural artifacts. He and his students spoke to the local people, wrote down the *sthala purana* or the anecdotal histories of the location, and collected the proverbs known to them. Anandarao's early letters to the mission headquarters in Basel indicate that he often played a role as mediator between the missionary Moegling and the "natives." This ethnographic approach to language strengthened the belief that there was a strong connection between the people, their language, and their culture. The argument that Sanskrit was the original language of all the European languages enabled Anandarao, later on, to justify his belief that there was nothing unusual in his wanting to marry a German woman. Moegling probably shared this view about the Brahmins and the Europeans being a kindred-folk.

The recognition of Sanskrit as either the forerunner or a sibling of the Indo-European family of languages was a result of the contemporary academic predisposition regarding languages and their structures. In Germany, of course, it contributed to theories about race and Aryanism that informed early-twentieth-century popular attitudes. But in southwest India, and in the long run, the linguistic scholarship of the missionaries from Basel contributed less to an Aryan theory of race than to a claim by a region of its Dravidian difference, a difference that marked separation from, rather than connection to, the "Aryans."

Regional Identity: More Support for the "Dravidian Proof"

In 1816 (thirty-two years after William Jones delivered his pathbreaking lecture on the Indo-European languages), British officer Francis Whyte Ellis identified yet another "family"—the Dravidian language family. Drawing upon his research with an Indian scholar studying ancient texts of Tamil grammar, Ellis presented evidence to support the idea of its historical autochthony and to reject the idea of Tamil's—or rather, the Dravidian language family's—derivation from Sanskrit. In a fascinating analysis of nineteenth-century language study in India, Thomas Trautmann calls this text by Francis Whyte Ellis the "Dravidian Proof." I argue that the scholar-missionaries from Basel independently strove to provide further proof for the distinctiveness of the Dravidian family of languages. Missionary Weigle's contribution to the *Zeitschrift der deutschen morgenländischen Gesellschaft* shows that he was thinking along similar lines as Ellis, even though he believed that there was an undeniable connection between the scripts of Kannada and Sanskrit. Based on the difference between the Dekhani (that is, Dravidian) and the Indo-European languages, Weigle proposed his own theory of the encounter between those who spoke Sanskrit and the Dravidian languages.[63] In his conclusion Weigle argued that the language and literature of the Canarese (Kannada-speaking) people deserved "a closer perusal."[64] Though Weigle's research on Kannada is not widely known, the belief in the uniqueness of Kannada language, culture, and heritage has persisted till today.

As the early twenty-first century opened, arguments about the distinctiveness of Kannada culture were continuing to fortify claims raised in Karnataka for official, central-government recognition of the Kannada language as a classical language of India. In 2001 the government of Karnataka installed a statue of Ferdinand Kittel in a traffic island right on Mahatma Gandhi Road, which runs through one of the busiest commercial centers of Bangalore. The statue honored Kittel for his service to Kannada literature and culture, his work in retrieving ancient documents written in Kannada, and, most of all, for his Kannada–English dictionary, which is popularly known as "Kittel's dictionary" and used by people till this day. In a context where regionalism has prompted the renaming of a prominent traffic circle called "Hudson Circle" (named so because of its proximity to the Hudson Memorial Church, built in 1904 in memory of Wesley Missionary Society missionary Josiah Hudson) to be known as "Kittur Rani Chennamma Circle" (named after a queen who opposed the British and fought against them), this gesture of remembering Kittel speaks volumes for public openness toward missionary scholars. Kittel's research certainly paid cultural dividends when, in November 2008, the government of India officially recognized Kannada as a "classical" language—remarkably, just three years after Sanskrit had the same recognition.

Historians today are likely to recognize Kittel as a member of the scholarly tradition of German Indologists.[65] How then, we may ask, did a missionary who had done his training as a seminarian in Basel gain long-term recognition as a German Indologist?[66]

Ferdinand Kittel was a missionary of the Basel Mission who had joined the Basel Mission team in South India in 1853. By 1855, in an ethos of "mutual watching"—used by the Committee for the scrutiny and regulation of missionaries in the "field"[67]—Kittel was found to be a man of his own ideas and will, deemed not fully suited to undertake missionary responsibilities. Indeed, at the beginning of his career as a missionary, Kittel had not even followed simple rules such as sending detailed reports of his daily work to the Home Office. In a letter written to Kittel when he was about twenty-three years old, the director of the mission, Josenhans, had asked him to be mindful of the older gentlemen of the Committee and use appropriate language. He had also gently taken him to task for writing very short quarterly reports and suggested that instead of sending such reports he could describe in detail "a town, a village, a region, a festival, or a profession" in a "natural, refined and objective" language.[68]

Kittel must have taken this suggestion seriously because some of his subsequent letters, which have been reprinted in Wendt's volume *An Indian to the Indians?* (2006), had a strongly ethnographic dimension. Kittel's letters recorded every detail of his observations about the people of the region where he was stationed, their food, and their customs. This early fascination for cultural description clearly helped him while putting together his dictionary, which was published in 1894. Kittel studied classical Kannada grammars and *nighantu* ("dictionaries") and collected samples of spoken Kannada from different regions, thereby using both etymological and ethnographic methodologies for the compilation of the dictionary. In addition to the dictionary, he also edited the classical Kannada Grammar *Shabdamanidarpana* and contributed articles regularly to the journal *Indian Antiquary.* His contributions were on a wide range of issues, including one titled "About Gunpowder," where he speculated on the earliest use of the equivalent of gunpowder in Kannada.[69] In another issue of the journal he responded to the work of the British missionary and scholar of the Tamil language, G. U. Pope (1820–1908); in an item titled "Notes on the South Indian or Dravidian Family of Languages," Kittel argued that Sanskrit contained a few word borrowings from a Dravidian language.[70] This was a rather unusual stance that countered claims for Sanskrit as the *Ursprache,* or origin of all other languages.

Kittel's extraordinary scholarship made him simultaneously a linguist, an ethnographer, and a scholar of comparative religion. But this is not an indication that he stopped thinking like the missionaries of his time. Though he was found to be a poor preacher and was actually pulled out of active missionary service to focus on "literary" work, he could still sound prejudiced in spite of his meticulous study of the Kannada language and its classical texts, such as when he described the "tedious narratives of Krishna" that weighed down certain prayers.[71] It is impressive that even today, at a time of growing Hindu fundamentalism, such demonstrations of prejudice have not diminished the esteem with which more recent generations of Kannada scholars have regarded his scholarship.

The Local Ethnographic Projects

The tradition started by ethnographer-missionaries like Moegling and Kittel is still leaving its mark on the academic milieu of western Karnataka, especially in the coastal districts of Dakshina Kannada and Udupi. The Tulu Lexicon Project that was concluded a few years ago followed Kittel's method of looking not just for word-root etymologies but also for the ethnographic usages specific to different groups. In the preface to the dictionary, the editors acknowledged their debt to the scholarly contributions of the missionaries—and especially to the missionary Männer who compiled the Tulu-English dictionary in 1886—which has inspired new interest in Tulu studies.[72]

The ethnographic project introduced by the missionaries has taken different shapes in this region but it nevertheless persists as the most important academic tool for constructions of the "local." Such constructions are often small-scale, limited to research by groups of college students who document variations in Kannada spoken by specific groups in a given geographic location, or perhaps the performance of a ritual in a particular community. The Regional Resource Centre located in Udupi District has also been involved in the process of documenting folk culture and popular performances such as Yakshagana for many years now.[73]

In sum, the habit of connecting languages with people (such as Aryans or Dravidians on the grand scale) seems to have had a stronger and longer-lasting impact than what we may realize (albeit now more often on the local level). The scholarly legacies of the Basel Mission in Karnataka and southwest India more broadly continue to shape contemporary negotiations around region, language, and identity.

Coda: Legacies of the Basel Mission

The evangelical work of the Basel Mission in southwest India fostered the creation of a small community of "native Christians," whose constituency in Mangalore remains evident. There still exist in Mangalore a number of education institutions, especially primary schools, which the Basel Mission founded long ago. Many of the Basel Mission Christians occupy prominent positions in the city of Mangalore as doctors, educators, businesspeople, and industrialists. Other members of Basel Mission congregations migrated at different times during the twentieth century to Bombay, Bangalore, the Arab Gulf states, and Canada in search of brighter job opportunities, thus creating what we may arguably call a "Basel Mission diaspora." Meanwhile, in 1947, shortly after India achieved independence, many congregations of the Basel Mission joined the Church of South India, which formed from the union of different Protestant denominations that had their roots in mission enterprises. Despite this move toward Protestant ecumenical unity, a distinct community—whose members identify themselves as the Basel Mission Christian community—persists. This is particularly true in the Dakshina Kannada, Udupi, Kodagu, and Dharwad districts of Karnataka, where Protestant Christians take pride in certain cultural practices distinct to themselves.

However, it is not the distinctiveness of these southwest Indian, Basel-Mission Christians that I have aimed to elucidate in this paper. Rather, I have tried to tease out the larger repercussions of the work of the missionaries sent by the Basel Mission, focusing on two issues: the transformations brought about by missionary-native encounters in the way "communities" related to one another; and the transformations that occurred within the local, regional, and global perspectives regarding perceived relationships between language and the cultural identity of a specific region. My intention has not been to draw causal links or provide teleological narratives. I see connections, rather, between transformations within the general intellectual culture of Europe and the "scientific" studies of local cultures and knowledge traditions. The actual experience of living in the mission field along with members of their congregations, the process of engaging with people of other faiths, and the reliance that missionaries placed on local scholars and *munshis* for translation and mediation—all of these together transformed the scholar-missionaries' assumptions and techniques of inquiry, with repercussions for structures of (self-)knowledge in Europe and India. Moreover, these developments together were unexpected—far from the evangelical work that provided the mission's raison d'être. In the case of the Basel Mission, perhaps the most unexpected and most enduring consequence of their local intellectual projects was the impact that they continued to exert in the early twenty-first century on the regional linguistic studies and identitarian politics of the places in southwest India where they began their journey so long ago.

10

The Gospel in Arabic Tongues

British Bible Distribution, Evangelical Mission, and Language Politics in North Africa

Heather J. Sharkey

Yalla, nanzil wa-nabalbil hinak lughathim 'alshan mayafhimush lughat ba'd. Fa-shattathim al-rabb min hinak 'ala washsh kull 'ard. Wa-batalu binayat al-madina. 'Alshan kida ittasammit Babil. Li-anna al-rabb balbal hinak lughat kull al-ard. Wa-min hinak shattathim al-rabb 'ala washsh kull al-ard.

> —Sifr al-Takwin, bil-lugha al-misriyya al-'amma ("The Book of Genesis, in the Common Egyptian Language," 1923), 11:7–9.

Go, let us go down, and there confound their language, that they may not understand one another's speech. So the Lord scattered them abroad from thence upon the face of all the earth: and they left off to build the city. Therefore is the name of it called Babel; because the Lord did there confound the language of all the earth; and from thence did the Lord scatter them abroad upon the face of all the earth.

> —Genesis, 11:7–9 King James Version

Introduction: The Bibles That Flopped?

Founded in 1804, the British and Foreign Bible Society (BFBS) was a Protestant publishing mission that sold Bibles at subsidized prices. Believing that everyone should have access to the Bible in their vernacular languages, and that nothing "should stand between readers and the means of salvation,"[1] the BFBS sponsored massive translation efforts in cooperation with scores of other mission societies. According to its promotional publication *The Gospel in Many Tongues*, the BFBS had by 1939 published full or partial Bible translations in 734 languages.[2] It distributed these globally through missions, churches, and local agencies that supervised "native" colporteurs (male Bible-sellers) and Bible Women. This article considers the social significance of ten variant BFBS scriptures, representing twentieth-century forms of North African Arabic.[3] Six of the ten were translations into forms of colloquial Arabic spoken primarily by Muslims in Morocco, Algeria, Tunisia, the Egyptian Delta, and northern Sudan. Three were in forms of Judeo-Arabic spoken by Jews in Morocco, Tunisia, and Egypt. The tenth and earliest of these North African Arabic texts, published by the BFBS in 1903, was a literary or "classical" Arabic version of the Gospel of Luke that was hand-copied and photographically reproduced in the Maghribi style of Arabic calligraphy, without verse breaks or punctuation, for Muslim readers who had trouble deciphering Arabic print. Circulated for less than a decade, in Tunisia and then in Nigeria, this Tunisian edition of Luke testified to an African Arabic manuscript culture that persisted outside the "Gutenberg galaxy"[4] even as the twentieth century debuted.[5] Among the colloquials, the first two of the nine variants, Gospels of Luke in Algerian Arabic and in the "common Egyptian language," appeared under the BFBS imprint in 1908. The last two, a full Bible in Moroccan Arabic and a full New Testament in a kind of "union" Algerian and Tunisian Arabic, were completed in the late 1950s and published in 1963 and 1965 as decolonization unfolded and as an elderly cohort of missionaries retired.

Many historians and anthropologists have described how Protestant missionary interventions in publishing and translation fostered the emergence of new national identities, print languages, lingua francas, and "language hierarchies."[6] For example, in his classic work of Middle Eastern history, *Arabic Thought in the Liberal Age*, Albert Hourani wrote that the American Protestants of Beirut contributed to the nineteenth-century Arabic *nahda* or literary renaissance—a precursor to pan-Arab nationalism—by helping Syrian Christian intellectuals to develop the Arabic periodical press along with new Arabic print genres like the encyclopedia.[7] In 1997 Sumathi Ramaswamy described how twentieth-century Tamil intellectuals, of various religious persuasions, came to celebrate certain Christian missionaries in a kind of South Indian or Dravidian nationalist hagiography. They celebrated men like the Reverend Robert Caldwell (1814–1891), author of a Tamil comparative grammar, and the Reverend Miron Winslow (1789–1864), author of a Tamil dictionary. "Tamil enthusiasts," Ramaswamy wrote, "and even academics in Tamilnadu today, rarely allege that these missionaries violated Tamil [through their linguistic interventions], though they so accuse other 'foreigners,' such as Brahmans and Aryans from North India."[8] In 2000 J. D. Y. Peel suggested that the Church Missionary Society (CMS) in Nigeria, by hiring local lay evangelists and requiring them to submit reports to London headquarters, encouraged Yoruba-language writing and gave rise to the "first works of the modern Yoruba intelligentsia, which opened up into a diverse literature of cultural self-reflection that continues vigorously down to the present."[9]

The North African Arabic scriptures of the BFBS were not success stories of the same kind. These North African scriptures were all, in the end, rejected or abandoned by their Muslim, Jewish, and Christian target audiences and even by British and American missionaries, so that they are likely to survive today only in archives. They were in vernacular languages that did not evolve into mass-medium, commercially lucrative print languages, and thus they were vernacular editions that did not yield nationalisms in the manner that Benedict Anderson described in *Imagined Communities*.[10] Even the Tunisian "classical" Luke, its manuscript pages photographed for publication, was soon forgotten because it became obsolete, shunted aside by Arabic print.

Yet, this is not a story about Bibles that flopped. Here we have an ephemeral set of volumes whose histories tell us something about who was reading Arabic and how they were doing it at the juncture of oral and literate culture. They also tell us about how poor, barely literate, and disproportionately female readers interacted with a global publishing enterprise through the mediation of missionaries, colporteurs, and Bible Women. This study of the circulation and popular reception of cheap Bibles also yields insights into the political and social history of the Arabic language as well as the evolution of Christian, Muslim, and Jewish identities during an era of Western imperialism.[11]

Searching for the Inside Story

Sadly, these translated scriptures are silent about the very thing for which they were made: private devotion. In *Marking the Hours, the English and Their Prayers* (2006), Eamon Duffy was able to reconstruct some of this "history of intimacy" by examining the jottings and blottings in prayer books, known as "Books of Hours," that were circulated in England between the period from 1240 to 1570, which spanned the transition from manuscript into print culture. In their Books of Hours, men and, more often, women inserted extra prayers and miniature self-portraits; recorded births, deaths, and marriages; added names or scratched out others; defaced certain pictures and texts (in Tudor-era fits of anti-Catholic pique); and so forth. Some volumes made their way through the generations in family bequests; others were sold and adopted into new families. Nearly 800 Books of Hours from England have made their way into libraries, where researchers can now go to see them. Duffy reflected that, "The history of prayer . . . is as difficult to write as the history of sex, and for some of the same reasons. Both activities are intensely personal and in the nature of things not readily accessible to objective analysis."[12] But thanks to the way owners marked up their prayer books (and also, as his book shows, thanks to the way portrait painters like Hans Holbein inserted them into their owners' hands),[13] Duffy was able to speculate on the relationship between Books of Hours and patterns of personal piety.

By contrast, the BFBS's North African Arabic scriptures tell little by themselves. The Bible Society Archives at Cambridge University Library hold one pristine copy of each—a copy for the record. Moreover, from its inception in 1804, the BFBS maintained a firm policy of publishing scriptures "without note or comment" as a way of maintaining amity among diverse Protestant supporters who included both Anglicans and "Dissenters" (e.g., Presbyterians, Methodists, and Baptists).[14] The BFBS allowed no prefaces explaining how the books were translated or for whom—and if missionaries inserted such prefaces in their translations, the BFBS made sure to expunge them.[15] An Egyptian colloquial Arabic edition of the Psalms, published in 1933, is typical in its restraint: the only extraneous text is a note on the inside cover declaring, *"Tab' bi-nafqat al-jami'a al-baritaniyya wal-ajnabiyya li-intishar al-kutub al-muqaddasa"* ("Published at the expense of the British and Foreign Bible Society," or literally, "Published at the expense of the British and foreign society for spreading the holy books").[16]

Outside of the BFBS archives, the odds of survival for these North African versions seem slim. They were produced cheaply, with paper covers, so that they could remain within the means of the poor, and they were also published in the order in which they happened to be translated, one Bible book at a time (e.g., as Luke, Genesis, Matthew, and so on). More importantly, they rendered the scriptures in a language that conveyed a low status. Would the owner of a colloquial Arabic Bible portion have passed the book down to heirs, assuming that the pages neither crumbled nor fell out of their binding? A more likely scenario is that if a Bible owner's wealth and literacy grew, and an interest in the Bible remained, then an upgrading would have occurred, to the Van Dyck Arabic Bible. The latter translation, prepared by American missionaries in Beirut after 1837 in collaboration with a Muslim *shaykh* named Yusuf ibn 'Aql al-Asir al-Husayni, was published by the American Bible Society in New York in 1865, and employed a sufficiently formal Arabic to give an impression of a "classical" pedigree. The Van Dyck Bible was in *fusha*—an Arabic superlative adjective, meaning "most eloquent," which has come to do double-duty as a noun, implying the high literary language.[17] By contrast, colloquial Arabic scriptures were, in the long run, incriminating; they were an embarrassment. Owning a colloquial edition was as good as acknowledging that one's Arabic literacy, like one's education, was limited.

How can we make these claims if the BFBS Bibles, themselves, are so reticent? Fortunately, the BFBS had a fairly elaborate bureaucracy in London. Its translating department and editorial subcommittee kept detailed minutes on BFBS imprints and filed away relevant correspondence, categorized alphabetically by language. The files on Arabic and its variants are thick, so we can see the debates that these colloquial scriptures stirred—at least among the British and American missionaries who maintained close contacts with the BFBS and who interpreted the situation facing Bible culture in North Africa's Islamic societies.

An Arabic Vulgate?

In 1917 Samuel M. Zwemer, the Dutch American missionary who became famous—or infamous—for his work among Muslims,[18] wrote to C. T. Hooper, the British agent for the BFBS in Port Said, insisting that "vulgar" or colloquial Arabic scriptures were a bad idea. Zwemer was referring to the colloquial Egyptian translation of Luke, which the BFBS had published at the request of the British interdenominational Egypt General Mission (EGM) in 1908. Zwemer wrote,

> There is a lack of dignity similar to that which would obtain if the cockney dialect or the vulgarisms of the slums were introduced into the scripture version. As an example, I may quote from the Gospel of Luke, chap. 1, v. 38: "And Mary said, 'I am the female slave of the Lord.'" In the parable of the talents the language is so commonplace my [Muslim] sheikh tells me, that when he was teaching the Gospel to one of the missionaries he could hardly refrain from laughter![19]

Hooper sympathized. In 1909 Hooper had reported to London, "Some of the colporteurs have requested that they be not expected to offer it for sale and one mentions that the people in reading it make fun and say it is the Arabic of the 'comic papers.'"[20] The London office summarized Hooper's subsequent correspondence thus:

> The general opinion and experience of colporteurs is that there is no place for this [colloquial] book, as the Van Dyck edition meets all requirements. It is used by Moslems in support of his [sic] argument that the Christians have changed the [Scriptures]. Unprejudiced natives have said they cannot read it with appreciation. The British Consul at Port Said severely criticized it and expressed his surprise that the B.F.B.S. had taken it up. Mr. H[ooper] is of the opinion that the only place in which it might serve any purpose would be in the hands of Bible women, but even there its use would be very limited. He has

persuaded Mr. Logan [of the EGM] to take over half the edition as he rarely sells a copy.[21]

Hooper was pointing, in part, to a perennial thicket that ensnared Christians in polemical exchanges with Muslims. Muslims argued that Christians (like Jews) had historically tampered with God's revelation in the midst of transmission, inserting human errors. These perceived errors were Islam's raison d'être, leading Muslims to regard the Qur'an, an explicitly and exclusively Arabic text,[22] as the successor to Judeo-Christian religion and as the clarification of God's message for humankind.

Regarding the relationship between Muslims and Christians as one of historic embattlement, missionary critics of colloquial scriptures consistently argued that the use of a poor man's Arabic for the Bible debased Christianity in the eyes of Muslims, who regarded high classical Arabic—like the Arabic of the Qur'an—as the only suitable medium for a message from God. Christian prestige was at stake, they argued, so that translators, publishers, and booksellers needed to take heed of the Bible's place within the framework of Arab-Islamic society.

Even some of the defenders of colloquial scriptures seemed to admit that the language was vulgar in the sense of being both common and ugly. For example, in 1907, George Fischer of the Gospel Missionary Union, a Kansas-based operation that worked in Morocco, wrote to BFBS officials in London explaining why he thought they should make an exception to their policy of publishing "without note or comment." Fischer wanted to include a short preface in front of a Moroccan Arabic version of Luke explaining why the colloquial was warranted. The BFBS minute books summarized his letter thus: "It should be remembered that this was the first book ever published in the Colloquial of Morocco, so far as [Fischer] knows, and that some explanation is felt to be due to the public for printing such grammatical barbarities, instead of offering them the polished diction of the literary language."[23]

The intensity and persistence of the debate over Arabic and "Arabics" perplexed BFBS officials in London, who tried to reconcile their organization's commitment to vernacular Bibles with the cultural hierarchies confronting Christian missionaries in Islamic societies. Officials knew

that the strenuous opposition to colloquial Arabic scriptures, voiced by
missionaries like Zwemer, was matched by equally strenuous arguments
calling for the wider use of such versions.

The Case for Colloquial

In 1914, 1917, and 1922, on the pages of the journal *The Moslem World*
(which Samuel M. Zwemer had founded), Percy P. Smith of the American
Methodist Episcopal Mission (AMEM) in Constantine, Algeria, issued
pleas for literature, and especially biblical literature, that missionaries could
use in "vernacular" or "vulgar" Arabic.[24] From 1910 and until his death in
1932, Smith translated portions of the New Testament that appeared in
successive editions under the BFBS imprint: Algerian Arabic versions of
Luke (1908, 1912, 1929), John (1910, 1921, 1923, 1930), Acts (1913, 1933),
Mark (1931), Matthew (1931), and, posthumously, Romans (1935).[25]

Smith hotly disputed the claims of critics, like Arthur T. Upson, the
British director of the Nile Mission Press (an evangelical publisher in
Cairo that specialized in an auxiliary Christian literature of devotional
tracts, inspirational biographies, and the like), who contended that colloquial Arabic was mere "slang."[26] Smith denied that he was advocating
"some *low-down* kind of Arabic, used only by street vagrants or Eastern
hooligans"; "my plea," he insisted, "was for the use of literature in the Common Speech, the everyday language of both learned and unlearned alike."
Smith pushed on, asking, "What is the living language of the people? Is
it the Literary Arabic, practically the same as that of a thousand years ago,
or is it the Common Speech used by everyone in daily intercourse?" He
expressed hope that "a new departure" could take place in Arabic as in
Modern Greek and Armenian, and challenged, "let the learned classes
make the attempt to use only the literary language in speech, and they
would soon find out the truth of the dictum that in the matter of language
it is the people that rule, not the grammarians and the purists." Smith
added a distinctly Christian element to his plea for the colloquial. "This
[opposition] is due, of course, to the Moslem doctrine that the style of the
Koran is its permanent attesting miracle. It is a bold step, but I certainly
think, a necessary one, that we knock the bottom out of that argument,

by following the Christian tradition of publishing the Word of God in the simple language of the people."[27]

There was another more important reason, besides the theory or principle of "true" vernacular, to favor the Arabic colloquials—or as George Swan of the EGM put it in 1932, to favor Bibles in "the language which is 'understanded [*sic*] of the people.'"[28] That reason was a pattern of illiteracy so pervasive as the twentieth century opened that, in some parts of North Africa, it was the norm among women especially.

"According to the 1897 census [in Egypt]," Beth Baron observed, "eight percent of Egyptian men and 0.2 percent of Egyptian women were literate, by which census takers meant settled Egyptians above the age of seven . . . who could read and write." This minute literacy rate among Egyptian women was nevertheless sufficient to sustain a vibrant women's periodical press beginning in the 1890s.[29] Literacy rates steadily rose, until by the interwar era Egypt could boast an upper- and middle-class reading public whose members followed, and increasingly shaped, nationalist debates.[30] Yet Baron also noted that while male-female literacy rates remained highly uneven, the urban-rural distinction remained starker still. Egyptian literacy flourished in cities and towns, while illiteracy prevailed among the fellaheen in the countryside, a situation, she added, that "was probably exacerbated by the gap between colloquial and literary Arabic."[31]

Illiteracy rates in some other parts of North Africa were higher than in Egypt. In the Arabic-speaking northern Sudan, for example, female literacy was almost nil before the 1930s; even then, the few "modern" girls' schools in the region devoted most curricular hours to domestic arts like embroidery.[32] The Sudan government claimed at independence in 1956 that 4 percent of the female population was literate, relative to 30 percent of men, but these figures are questionable and reflected a sudden burst of government-sponsored school-building for girls.[33] In Algeria, meanwhile, Arabic and Islamic education after the French invasion of 1830 took a beating, leading historians to speculate that Algerian Muslim literacy rates actually dropped as the nineteenth century proceeded.[34] Meanwhile, Morocco's educational infrastructure struggled in the face of poverty, rural underdevelopment, and, probably, language complexity (considering the prevalence or influence of Berber language culture—a situation of linguistic heterogeneity that also affected Sudan and Algeria). By 2004, only some 40 percent of Moroccan women over age fifteen were believed to be literate, relative to nearly 66 percent of men.[35] Of course, among upper-class women and men during the colonial period in North Africa, some achieved literacy in French or English while remaining illiterate in Arabic.[36]

The strongest supporters of colloquial Arabic Bibles were the missionaries who worked among the urban and rural poor and among women— and thus the ones who had close contact with illiterates. Illiteracy was the primary concern that prompted Isabel Scott-Moncrieff, a CMS missionary in Egypt, to write in 1924 to the editorial superintendent of the BFBS in London, urging him to support colloquial Arabic translations.

> No one who has tried to read the Gospels to an audience of fellaheen, or poor women, or school children can have any doubt that the Arabic Bible as now obtainable is largely incomprehensible to them. It is like reading Le Chanson de Roland to a modern French peasant, & *more* remote than Chaucer is from modern day English. You have to stop to translate after each verse. . . . Look at the statistics to find how many Egyptians are literate & you will see that although it looks as if the Bible has been given to the Egyptians, the true fact is that not even the whole of the Gospels have been given to them in their own tongue.[37]

Similar concerns had prompted missionaries in Algeria to call for colloquial scriptures in 1902. One source claimed that missionaries "circulate only an insignificant number of the classical version [meaning the Van Dyck Bible], as it is almost unintelligible to the great mass of Arabs."[38]

Missionaries repeatedly mentioned that the colloquial Bibles were disproportionately used by, and useful for, women. In 1907, for example, the BFBS subagent reported from Casablanca that "the Mogrebi [sic] St. Luke had been specially useful among women, and patients in the Hospital. It was since the publication of this version that the missionaries had the majority of their converts."[39]

In the northern Sudan the connection to women was more obvious still. British CMS missionaries in that region, who by prior agreement with American Presbyterians focused their educational and medical work on females, undertook a translation of the Gospel of Mark that the BFBS published in 1934. Even while granting that many Protestant missionary Bible translations have been "a strangely hit and miss affair,"[40] this CMS version of Mark appears to have been particularly bad—by one account, a "fiasco." Its phrasing was unidiomatic, and missionaries had "Romanized" the text, using Latin print rather than Arabic script to curry favor with British colonial officials (who soon thereafter abandoned a short-lived policy of encouraging Arabic "Romanization").[41] But the BFBS agent in Port Said and the subagent in Khartoum both claimed that, regardless of the merits or faults of this translation, literate northern Sudanese men would never be interested in a colloquial version. Educated northern Sudanese men wanted only "classical" Arabic Bibles, if they wanted them at all, or possibly English Bibles (if they were graduates of the government's Gordon College in Khartoum).

The British CMS missionary R. S. Macdonald speculated that educated Sudanese men might be amenable to an Egyptian colloquial version, given that "the 'office' language of the Sudan is Egyptian [Arabic]," but commented that only the illiterate—including the poor people who came to mission hospital wards—would be willing to have the Bible in colloquial Sudanese Arabic. Macdonald added that the colloquial was particularly critical for Sudanese women, who unlike Sudanese men "could not understand the speech of a native of Egypt."[42] The BFBS agent at Port Said echoed this sentiment, by paraphrasing another CMS missionary who had told him that "the 'Mark,'" referring to the 1934 translation, "is closer to the 'women's talk.'" And indeed, the translators of this Gospel of Mark had been two British women—the "Misses Moore and Jackson"—whose knowledge of Arabic came from encounters with Sudanese females.[43] These comments suggest that just as there could be Muslim Arabics and Jewish Arabics—and, presumably, Christian Arabics—so could Arabic languages vary by sex.

Niche Bibles

Missionaries could agree to disagree on the merits of colloquial Arabic scriptures because the BFBS was willing to publish translations for diverse constituencies. It was willing, in other words, to publish "niche" Bibles.

There were at least five reasons for its continued support of North African Arabic Bibles during the first decades of the twentieth century.

First, the BFBS routinely published scriptures that had been translated by and for one mission for use among one people (with a "people" imagined by missionaries and the BFBS as a unitary language group). In 1927 alone, for example, its new imprints included a Gospel of John in Waja, spoken by 25,000 people in Bauchi province, Nigeria; the Gospel of Mark in Bambatana, the language of Choiseul, one of the Solomon Islands; and a Gospel of Luke in Chihli, a dialect of Mandarin Chinese prepared in the "Wang Chao Peill script" "for peasants who have learnt to read." In that same year, the BFBS Egyptian Agency alone (which was responsible for Egypt, Sudan, Ethiopia, Syria, and Palestine), circulated scriptures in seventy-seven languages, with more than one-fifth of these distributed through thirty-two cooperating mission societies. The BFBS was accustomed to dealing with many missions and to vetting and publishing translations that these missions submitted for use among discrete populations.[44] Thus publishing, say, a colloquial Egyptian Matthew for distribution by just the EGM, or an Algerian Arabic for the AMEM and North Africa Mission (NAM), seemed reasonable to the BFBS.

Second, the example of Judeo-Arabic scriptures, which the BFBS published on behalf of the London Mission to the Jews (LMJ) in versions geared toward Egyptian and Maghribi (and especially Tunisian and Moroccan) speakers, bolstered the case for other Arabic scriptures in the view of BFBS officials in London.[45] Representing forms of Arabic that were written in Hebrew script and that included some distinctive vocabularies and structures (drawn from Hebrew, Aramaic, and other languages), Judeo-Arabic provided examples of written Arabic vernaculars that were socially accepted and very local. In fact, Judeo-Arabic languages or "ethnolects" had a long written and more recently printed tradition within North African Jewish communities and were used for such things as record-keeping, letter-writing, Biblical commentary, and poetry. By the twentieth century there were even some printed Judeo-Arabic romances and folk tales.[46] At Bible House in London, officials filed correspondence for Judeo-Arabic and Muslim Arabic versions together, suggested points of convergence in plans for translations and circulation, and often confused them with each other.[47] The BFBS officials clearly regarded Arabic culture as a plurality to which Judeo-Arabic and Muslim Arabic languages belonged. Of course, as with Muslim forms of Arabic, the BFBS codified or privileged particular Jewish Arabics—for in fact, the Arabic spoken by Jews could vary considerably even from one Moroccan town to another.[48]

Third, the BFBS was willing to publish these versions because missionaries took pains to show that translations were rigorous. They formed advisory committees, prepared drafts, and revised them according to guidelines that the BFBS provided to translators.[49] Even some of the missionaries who criticized colloquial scriptures or declined to distribute them served on these translation committees. This approach sometimes made for a fractious, drawn-out procedure, particularly in the Maghrib, where personality clashes among missionaries seem to have been common, but it was intended to ensure that results would be solid.[50] The situation for translation in North Africa may indeed have been rather different from some other parts of the globe where the BFBS distributed scriptures. Regarding places like Papua New Guinea, the Polynesian Islands, and remote "hill tribe" regions of India, BFBS annual reports occasionally claimed that a particular missionary was one of the only nonnative speakers of a particular language in which he or she had produced a Bible translation.[51] Viewed against this context, the Arabic-speaking world, as a historic center of Islam and of Judeo-Christian culture in antiquity, must have been one of the toughest, most scholastically exacting places for scripture translations in the world.

Fourth, it appears that the colloquial Arabic translations of the BFBS were actually sold—though perhaps not always at the rates the BFBS was led to believe.[52] Editions were small (2,000 to 5,000 copies)[53] but they ran out and were reissued: this was the case, for example, with the Tunisian Judeo-Arabic Daniel (1910, 1922); the Egyptian Luke (1908, 1923, 1929); and the Algerian John (1910, 1921, 1923, 1930).[54] Colporteurs in Egypt may have looked askance at them or found them embarrassing to sell; they may have collected dust on the shelves in Alexandria and Port Said.[55] But some missionaries—joined by some Bible Women, and by colporteurs elsewhere in North Africa—persisted. According to BFBS reports, Egyptians alone took 4,298 copies of colloquial scriptures in

1927, and took 5,600 in 1932, which was described as a year of record sales for Bibles in Egypt.[56] Missionary supporters of colloquial Bibles continued to believe that these works were needed. One of the last entries in the BFBS Editorial Sub-Committee minute books for Arabic, dated 1960, describes a conversation with a missionary named "Marsh" from the Christian Mission to Moslem Lands, who argued that colloquial Arabic scriptures remained important for missionaries in Algeria because the "Classical Version is not understood by the majority of the people," even among those "with a high standard of education."[57] Working with a team, Marsh was translating scriptures into a form of "union" colloquial Arabic that could be used in both Tunisia and Algeria; this was the Algerian-Tunisian New Testament that the BFBS published in 1965, three years after Algeria's independence from France.

Fifth and finally, the BFBS continued to publish these specialized North African scriptures because it maintained, as one of its founding principles, that no language was too humble, and no community too small, remote, or poor, to be worthy of a Bible translation. This belief went to the heart of the British nationalism—and more specifically, of the pluralistic British *Protestant* nationalism[58]—that distinguished the BFBS as an organization and movement. Consider that the BFBS had originally coalesced in 1804 to provide Welsh Bibles to people like Mary Jones, the organization's legendary heroine, a poor young woman who had walked across a mountain in a quest to find scriptures in her own tongue. Asking, "If not for Wales, then why not for the kingdom? Why not for the world?," the founders of the BFBS went on to publish scriptures in Mohawk, a North American language, in 1804, before turning to the British languages of English, Scottish and Irish Gaelic, and Manx, and then moving again overseas.[59] One of its early translations was an 1829 Bible in "Negro-English" prepared for Moravian missionaries who worked among slave communities in Surinam. Some English critics called this "Negro-English" scripture a "degraded travesty of divine revelation" when it first appeared. But the society maintained it and published a new edition as late as 1889, so that "even to this day," wrote William Canton, the society's centennial historian, in 1904, "it is able to lead souls to Christ."[60]

This commitment to vernaculars had a still deeper connection to Britain's Protestant history. If Protestants had not been averse to canonizing great Christians in the Catholic tradition, then the BFBS or one of its affiliates would have surely canonized William Tyndale (ca. 1494–1536), who functioned as the society's unofficial patron saint. Drawing upon the original Hebrew and Greek texts, Tyndale translated the Bible into English, printed his translations in Worms and Antwerp, and in 1535 sent copies to England and Scotland, where ecclesiastical and royal authorities tried to suppress them, staging, in some places, public bonfires of the books. A year later emissaries of King Henry VIII captured Tyndale, convicted him of heresy, and had him strangled and burnt at the stake.[61] In 1925, a year when the society's Egyptian Agency reported a circulation of 105,627 volumes of scripture in seventy-six different languages, the BFBS celebrated Tyndale on the 400th anniversary of his Bible's publication. Its annual report opened by upholding "William Tindale [*sic*]" as "one of the greatest of God's Englishmen. We who speak the tongue that Shakespeare spake owe him an immeasurable debt." His translation, the report continued, "fixed, once and for all, the style and tone of the English Bible" and made it possible for "every ploughboy [to] know the Scriptures."[62] Heeding this history of Britain and the Bible, BFBS executives could not brook the idea that any language—standard England English, "Negro-English," colloquial Arabic in all its varieties, or something else—could be too lowly to carry a message from God.

Conclusion: Lost in the Translation

Tyndale's martyrdom for the cause of English vernacular Bible publishing may have contributed to the founding myth of modern Britain and the BFBS, but it did not quite "translate" for most Arabs. Instead, founding myths in Arabophone North Africa gave a special place to Islam—the religion that enabled the "ethnogenesis" of the Arab peoples, along with the "making of a [new Arab] world."[63] These myths celebrated literary Arabic, with its lexical richness and grammatical clarity, as the language of the Arabs, which God favored for the Qur'an. As the twentieth century opened, moreover, the idea of Arab unity gained popular currency, resting on the premise that one Arabic language could unite peoples from the western Sahara to the Tigris-Euphrates basin, despite the efforts of Western imperial powers to carve up the region.

In the view of many Arab nationalists, Christian missionary efforts to promote regionally distinct colloquial Arabics were just one more way that Britain in particular employed tactics of divide-and-rule.[64] This popular perception toward foreigners and the promotion of colloquial Arabics endured throughout the twentieth century, as the linguistic anthropologist Niloofar Haeri has pointed out. This perception informed postcolonial North African policies toward Arabic-language education, by prompting governments to promote a kind of modern "classical" Arabic while emphasizing the language's connections to the heritage of Islam and the Qur'an.[65] This perception also galvanized those whom Yasir Suleiman, in *A War of Words: Language and Conflict in the Middle East* (2003), has called "Standard Arabic's language defenders." Such "language defenders," Suleiman writes, have interpreted the "smallest whiff of interest in the dialects" as "playing into the hands of those who aim to make the fragmentation of the Arabs a (more) permanent feature of the political scene."[66]

Ironically, the colloquial Arabic Bible translator who became best-known among Arab writers is the one whose translations were rejected by the BFBS. This was Sir William Willcocks (d. 1932), a British hydraulics engineer-turned-born-again-Christian who worked on the Aswan Dam and, earlier, with the British East India Company in the Bengal delta. Among pan-Arab nationalists and Arabic-language purists, Willcocks remains "one of the most 'reviled' figures in the history of the call to use Egyptian Arabic in writing."[67] While retired in Egypt, Willcocks drew upon his own fortune to translate the New Testament into Egyptian Arabic and then to circulate copies for free: he claimed to have distributed more than 42,000 copies of the four Gospels to Egyptians by 1925 alone.[68] But missionaries like W. H. T. Gairdner of the CMS convinced the BFBS not to authorize the Willcocks translations, arguing that they were highly suspect on linguistic and methodological grounds.[69] Willcocks entertained the unusual idea that "The Egyptian language is basically the same language that Christ spoke"—to translate from the colloquial Arabic preface of his translation of the four Gospels![70] In the early twentieth century, Willcocks also broadcast his belief that Egypt's "failure" to embrace its colloquial for writing was connected to Egypt's modern weakness and lack of invention.[71] Willcocks thereby gave credence to the view, common among some postcolonial Arab and Muslim nationalists, that Christian missionaries used psychological weapons as part of the Western imperial assault on Arabs and Muslims, in this case by telling Arabs that they were unimaginative and scientifically feeble in order to make them believe it was so.[72]

One could trace the demise of the colloquial North African Arabic scriptures as follows: The tide began to turn in the 1930s, some thirty years before the last BFBS colloquial Bible appeared. By this time, Muslim antimissionary agitation was reducing the scope of Christian evangelical activities throughout North Africa in general, while the world economic Depression was biting into mission budgets.[73] From Morocco to Sudan, the expansion of mass education and rising literacy rates meant, too, that popular preferences were changing: educated Muslims were buying "classical" Arabic (or in the Maghrib especially, French) Bibles or Bible portions, to the extent that they now bought them at all, while Jews in the Maghribi countries were increasingly opting for Hebrew- and French-language scriptures rather than their Judeo-Arabic counterparts.[74] In a study of the Judeo-Arabic spoken in the Algerian towns of Tlemcen, Aïn-Témouchent, and Constantine, for example, one linguist noted that even before Algerian independence in 1962, "the local Judeo-Arabic, unappreciated, indeed, scorned, was no longer spoken in public, if only by a minority." So rapid and thorough was the demise of Judeo-Arabic, that by the late 1980s, among Algerian Jewish émigrés in France, the best that people under age fifty could do was to "stammer some Arabic words" while "only some people aged sixty years or more could speak (or, to be more precise, understand) the local Arabic."[75]

Decolonization sealed the fate of colloquial scriptures. In Egypt, for example, the EGM, which had done more than any other mission to distribute colloquial versions, found its properties seized and its workers deported in the aftermath of the Suez Crisis in 1956.[76] Missionaries in Morocco, who claimed that the "French police" under the Protectorate

(1912–56) had made colportage "almost impossible,"[77] worried about the broader regional implications of the Suez Crisis and its aftermath. The chief translator of the colloquial Moroccan Bible wrote to the BFBS offices in 1957:

> We have only to reflect on the changes which affected missionary work in Egypt after British rule ended, to realize that there may easily be a hardening up against us in Tunisia and Morocco which are now both Sovereign Moslem States. At the moment it seems possible to get the Bible into North Africa without much difficulty, but what will be the prospects in a few years time?[78]

Eventually Libya banned Bible imports outright, while Algeria banned the import of Arabic Bibles (but not French ones).[79]

Changing laws also made it more difficult for missions to operate. In 1967 the Moroccan government expelled many Christian missionaries, while the Algerian government revoked the legal status of one of the major Protestant missions of the region, the NAM, in 1977.[80] Missionaries worried about the situation in Sudan as well. Christian missions in Sudan went into contraction, first when the government nationalized mission schools in the south in 1957 (one year after independence) and later in 1962, amid civil war, when it expelled foreign missionaries from the country.[81] Finally, in the context of decolonization and the Arab-Israeli conflict, North African Jews dispersed, emigrating to France and Israel above all.[82] The Judeo-Arabic scriptures of the BFBS thus became museum pieces— records of languages that had gone or were going extinct—akin to the society's Bibles in Manx (spoken until the early nineteenth century on Britain's Isle of Man).

At the same time, emphasizing the connections of Arabic to the Islamic heritage and, increasingly, to Arab nationalism, postcolonial governments pursued education policies that confirmed the role of modern standard Arabic (not regional or national dialects) as vehicles for pan-Arab unity. In Algeria and Sudan, Arabization (*ta'rib*) became one casus belli among others for internal civil wars. Ideological battles over language policies reflected deeper debates about whether (or how) the postcolonial state should recognize and promote either unitary or pluralistic visions of national culture.[83] Meanwhile, in Egypt, which was the only North African country to have a substantial Arabic-speaking Christian minority (estimated at some 7 percent of the population),[84] local Christian leaders maintained that the Bible belonged only in *fusha*, the most eloquent version of Arabic. To suggest otherwise, in the heyday of pan-Arab nationalism, would have been to expose local Christians to charges of cultural treason. This said, in private exchanges with BFBS officials, Arab Christian leaders remained adamant in their support for a "classical" Arabic Bible: they wanted a Bible that would be not only the most eloquent possible, but also the most dignified and dignifying. By the 1950s, the BFBS was paying greater heed to Arab Christians, and was therefore turning its attention to an ecumenical movement for revising the Van Dyck "classical" Bible.[85]

If William Canton, the chronicler of the BFBS in 1904, had been alive to write a bicentennial history of the organization in 2004, he might have looked back at these North African Bibles that fizzled, and mused (as he had done with regard to the 1829 "Negro-English" scriptures for Surinam) about how they might have been able to "lead souls to Christ."[86] Did they elicit conversions? Looking back on this record, a social and cultural historian would come back to broader questions about the ways these books changed lives. How did these Bibles, published by a British organization and missionary publisher, involve Arabic-speaking peoples in its enterprise?[87] Did these colloquial Bibles provide stepping-stones to Arabic literacy? What role did they play in the lives of women, the poor, and the unschooled? And how did they affect cultures of reading and influence practices of private (as well as collective) devotion?

But these questions lead the historian to collide with a wall: the sources are beyond reach. To tell this story more fully, the historian needs records that never made their way to the BFBS in London and later to the library at Cambridge University, records that are probably long lost and reduced into dust. These missing records are the logbooks of colporteurs and Bible Women, who toted up sales and jotted down notes on encounters with the individuals who bought these cheap Bibles.[88]

Notes

Bibliography

Index

Notes

1. Introduction: The Unexpected Consequences
of Christian Missionary Encounters

1. See, for example, John L. Comaroff and Jean Comaroff, *Of Revelation and Revolution*, 2 vols. (Chicago: University of Chicago Press, 1991 and 1997); and David M. Gordon, *Nachituti's Gift: Economy, Society, and Environment in Central Africa* (Madison: University of Wisconsin Press, 2006).

2. Rob Norton, "Unintended Consequences," *The Concise Encyclopedia of Economics*, ed. David R. Henderson, Library of Economics and Liberty (2008), http://www.econlib.org/library/Enc/UnintendedConsequences.html (accessed 21 July 2010).

3. Robert K. Merton, "The Unanticipated Consequences of Purposive Social Action," *American Sociological Review* 1, no. 6 (1936): 894–904. See esp. 895 regarding choice and motive.

4. Norton, "Unintended Consequences."

5. For example, see Ken Naito et al., "Unexpected Consequences of a Sudden and Massive Transposon Amplification on Rice Gene Expression," *Nature* 461 (2009): 1130–34; Jessica Mikulski, "Unexpected Consequences of Pump Proton Inhibitor Use in Reflux Disease," *Medical News Today*, 2 November 2009, http://www.medicalnewstoday.com/releases/169467.php (accessed 23 June 2011); Paul Simons, "Weather Eye: Unexpected Consequences of Global Warming," *The Times* (London), 16 July 2008; and Jack Ewing, "Volcanic Ash May Weigh on European Economy," *New York Times*, 18 April 2010.

6. Laura Robson, email communication to author, 1 July 2010.

7. Dana L. Robert, "From Missions to Beyond Missions: The Historiography of American Protestant Foreign Missions since World War II," in *New Directions in American Religious History*, ed. Harry S. Stout and D. G. Hart (New York: Oxford University Press, 1997), 362–93; and Eric Morier-Genoud and Wendy Urban-Mead, "Introduction: A State of the Field," *Social Sciences and Missions*, 24, nos. 2–3 (2011), 145–47. An important reassessment of missionaries vis-à-vis colonial and postcolonial politics appeared in Jean-François Bayart, "Fait missionnaire et politique du ventre: une lecture foucaldienne," *Le Fait Missionnaire* (Lausanne) 6 (1998): 9–38. This article appeared in English

as Jean-François Bayart, "Missionary Activity and the Politics of the Belly," in *Readings in Modernity in Africa*, edited by Peter Geschiere, Birgit Meyer, and Peter Pels (Bloomington: Indiana University Press, 2008), 92–98.

8. J. P. Daughton, *An Empire Divided: Religion, Republicanism, and the Making of French Colonialism, 1880–1914* (Oxford: Oxford University Press, 2006); Alvyn Austin and Jamie S. Scott, eds., *Canadian Missionaries, Indigenous Peoples: Representing Religion at Home and Abroad* (Toronto: University of Toronto Press, 2004); Jeffrey Cox, *The British Missionary Enterprise since 1700* (New York: Routledge, 2008), 3; Susan Thorne, *Congregational Missions and the Making of an Imperial Culture in Nineteenth-Century England* (Stanford: Stanford University Press, 1999); Esther Breitenbach, *Empire and Scottish Society: The Impact of Foreign Missions at Home, c. 1790–c. 1914* (Edinburgh: Edinburgh University Press, 2009); Alison Twells, *The Civilizing Mission and the English Middle Class, 1792–1850* (New York: Palgrave Macmillan, 2009); Ussama Makdisi, *Artillery of Heaven: American Missionaries and the Failed Conversion of the Middle East* (Ithaca: Cornell University Press, 2008); Heather J. Sharkey, *American Evangelicals in Egypt: Missionary Encounters in an Age of Empire* (Princeton: Princeton University Press, 2008).

9. Peggy Levitt, *God Needs No Passport: Immigrants and the Changing American Religious Landscape* (New York: New Press, 2009).

10. Exemplifying this interest in word and image is the work of Paul Landau. See Paul Stuart Landau, *In the Realm of the Word: Language, Gender, and Christianity in a Southern African Kingdom* (Portsmouth, NH: Heinemann, 1995); and his article on missionary uses of the lantern slide, Paul Landau, "The Illumination of Christ in the Kalahari Desert," *Representations* 45 (1994): 26–40. Consider, too, Derek R. Peterson, *Creative Writing: Translation, Bookkeeping, and the Work of Imagination in Colonial Kenya* (Portsmouth, NH: Heinemann, 2004).

11. Kathleen Wilson, ed., *A New Imperial History: Culture, Identity, and Modernity in Britain and the Empire, 1660–1840* (Cambridge: Cambridge University Press, 2004).

12. Steven Vertovec, *Transnationalism* (London: Routledge, 2009), 1.

13. Catherine Hall, *Civilising Subjects: Metropole and Colony in the English Imagination, 1830–1867* (Chicago: University of Chicago Press, 2002); Comaroff and Comaroff, *Of Revelation and Revolution*; Makdisi, *Artillery of Heaven*; Heather J. Sharkey, "American Presbyterians, Freedmen's Missions, and the Nile Valley: Missionary History, Racial Orders, and Church Politics on the World Stage," *Journal of Religious History* 35, no. 1 (2011): 24–42.

14. Anna Johnston, *Missionary Writing and Empire, 1800–1860* (Cambridge: Cambridge University Press, 2003); Andrew Porter, *Religion versus Empire? British Protestant Missionaries and Overseas Expansion, 1700–1914* (New York: Manchester University Press, 2004); Andrew Porter, ed., *The Imperial Horizons of British Protestant Missions, 1880–1914* (Grand Rapids, MI: William B. Eerdmans, 2003); Ryan Dunch, "Beyond Cultural Imperialism: Cultural Theory, Christian Missions, and Global Modernity," *History*

and *Theory* 41 (2002): 301–25; Norman Etherington, ed., *Missions and Empire* (Oxford: Oxford University Press, 2005). An early move in this direction was Brian Stanley, *The Bible and the Flag: Protestant Missions and British Imperialism in the Nineteenth and Twentieth Centuries* (Leicester, UK: Apollos, 1990). A valuable case study is Ryan Dunch, *Fuzhou Protestants and the Making of a Modern China, 1857–1927* (New Haven: Yale University Press, 2001).

15. Ian Tyrrell, *Reforming the World: The Creation of America's Moral Empire* (Princeton: Princeton University Press, 2010); and Elizabeth E. Prevost, *The Communion of Women: Missions and Gender in Colonial Africa and the British Metropole* (Oxford: Oxford University Press, 2010).

16. Johnston, *Missionary Writing*.

17. Daniel R. Headrick, *The Tools of Empire: Technology and European Imperialism in the Nineteenth Century* (New York: Oxford University Press, 1981). Consider, for example, Laura Robson, "Archaeology and Mission: The British Presence in Nineteenth-Century Palestine," paper presented at the conference on "Great Powers in the Holy Land: From Napoleon to the Balfour Declaration," European Institute, Columbia University, 3 April 2009. See, too, Paul S. Landau, "Empires of the Visual: Photography and Colonial Administration in Africa," in *Images and Empires: Visuality in Colonial and Postcolonial Africa*, ed. Paul S. Landau and Deborah D. Kaspin (Berkeley: University of California Press, 2002), 141–71.

18. Patrick Harries, *Butterflies and Barbarians: Swiss Missionaries and Systems of Knowledge in South-East Africa* (Athens: Ohio University Press, 2007); J. D. Y. Peel, *Religious Encounter and the Making of the Yoruba* (Bloomington: Indiana University Press, 2000); Sumathi Ramaswamy, *Passions of the Tongue: Language Devotion in Tamil India, 1891–1970* (Berkeley: University of California Press, 1997).

19. Erick Langer and Robert H. Jackson, eds., *The New Latin American Mission History* (Lincoln: University of Nebraska Press, 1995).

20. Cox, *British Missionary Enterprise*, 16.

21. Stanley H. Skreslet, "Thinking Missiologically about the History of Mission," *International Bulletin of Missionary Research* 31, no. 2 (2007): 59–65, see esp. 60.

22. Dana L. Robert, *Christian Mission: How Christianity Became a World Religion* (Chichester, UK: Wiley-Blackwell, 2009), 118–19, 141. For a sample of recent scholarship on women, gender, and missions, see Inger Marie Okkenhaug, "Introduction: Gender and Missions in the Middle East," *Social Sciences and Missions* 23, no. 1 (2010): 1–6.

23. The literature advancing social theories of conversion has grown. For example, Lewis R. Rambo, *Understanding Religious Conversion* (New Haven: Yale University Press, 1993); Robert W. Hefner, ed., *Conversion to Christianity: Historical and Anthropological Perspectives on a Great Transformation* (Berkeley: University of California Press, 1993); and Andrew Buckser and Stephen D. Glazier, eds., *The Anthropology of Religious Conversion* (Lanham, MD: Rowman & Littlefield, 2003).

24. Norman Etherington, "Recent Trends in the Historiography of Christianity in Southern Africa," *Journal of Southern African Studies* 22, no. 2 (1996): 201–19.

25. Robert, *Christian Mission*, 49.

26. For example, Talal Asad, *Formations of the Secular: Christianity, Islam, Modernity* (Stanford: Stanford University Press, 2003); Michael Gilsenan, *Recognizing Islam: Religion and Society in the Modern Arab World* (New York: Pantheon, 1982); Peter van der Veer, *Imperial Encounters: Religion and Modernity in India and Britain* (Princeton: Princeton University Press, 2001).

27. Chandra Mallampalli, *Christians and Public Life in Colonial South India, 1863–1937: Contending with Marginality* (London: RoutledgeCurzon, 2004).

28. A fascinating study along these lines, about a legal case that occurred in Kenya, is David William Cohen and E. S. Atieno Odhiambo, *Burying SM: The Politics of Knowledge and the Sociology of Power in Africa* (Portsmouth, NH: Heinemann, 1992).

29. Chantal Verdeil, "Jesuits' Encounters with the People of Ottoman Syria: Dependence, Negotiations, and Collaboration," paper presented at the conference on "The Great Powers in the Holy Land: From Napoleon to the Balfour Declaration," European Institute, Columbia University, 3–4 April 2009.

30. R. Pierce Beaver, *American Protestant Women in World Mission: History of the First Feminist Movement in North America*, rev. ed. (Grand Rapids, MI: William B. Eerdmans, 1980); Dana L. Robert, *American Women in Mission: A Social History of Their Thought and Practice* (Macon, GA: Mercer University Press, 1996); Patricia R. Hill, *The World Their Household: The American Woman's Foreign Mission Movement and Cultural Transformation, 1870–1920* (Ann Arbor: University of Michigan Press, 1985).

31. Attention to nineteenth- and early-twentieth-century African-American missionaries abroad is only growing now, too. For example, consider these two biographies of the African American missionary to the Congo, William Sheppard (1865–1927): William E. Phipps, *William Sheppard: Congo's African-American Livingstone*, (Louisville, KY: Geneva Press, 2002); and Pagan Kennedy, *Black Livingstone: A True Tale of Adventure in the Nineteenth-Century Congo* (New York: Viking, 2002).

32. Robert, *Christian Mission*, 51–52.

33. See, for example, Heather J. Sharkey, *Living with Colonialism: Nationalism and Culture in the Anglo-Egyptian Sudan* (Berkeley: University of California Press, 2003).

34. Heather J. Sharkey, "An Egyptian in China: Ahmed Fahmy and the Making of World Christianities," *Church History* 78, no. 2 (2009): 309–26.

35. Robert Eric Frykenberg, *Christianity in India: From Beginnings to the Present* (Oxford: Oxford University Press, 2008).

36. A notable exception is Mrinalini Sebastian, "Reading Archives from a Postcolonial Feminist Perspective: Native Bible Women and the Missionary Ideal," *Journal of Feminist Studies in Religion* 19 (2003): 5–25.

37. Cox, *British Missionary Enterprise*, 16.

38. A wide-ranging study on the global politics of proselytization and missionary overtures is Rosalind I. J. Hackett, ed., *Proselytization Revisited: Rights, Free Markets, and Culture Wars* (London: Equinox, 2008). Two of the contributors to this volume, Stephen Berkwitz and Heather J. Sharkey, also contributed to Hackett's work.

39. Marvin D. Markowitz, *Cross and Sword: The Political Role of Christian Missions in the Belgian Congo, 1908–1960* (Stanford: Hoover Institution Press, 1973), 13–14.

40. See Phipps, *William Sheppard*; and Kennedy, *Black Livingstone*.

41. Adam Hochschild, *King Leopold's Ghost: A Story of Greed, Terror, and Heroism in Colonial Africa* (Boston: Houghton Mifflin, 1998).

42. Andrea Smith, "Soul Wound: The Legacy of Native American Schools," *Amnesty Magazine* (Amnesty International USA), Summer 2003, http://www.amnestyusa.org /amnesty-magazine/summer-2003/soul-wound-the-legacy-of-native-american-schools /page.do?id=1105456 (accessed 20 July 2009).

43. This was Nancy L. Stockdale, who discussed the research for her book, *Colonial Encounters among English and Palestinian Women, 1800–1948* (Gainesville: University Press of Florida, 2007) at the conference on "Missionaries in the Middle East: Rethinking Colonial Encounters," North Carolina State University, 5 May 2007. Beth Baron is also writing a book on the history of orphans and orphanhood in modern Egypt. See her article, Beth Baron, "Comparing Missions: Pentecostal and Presbyterian Orphanages on the Nile," in *American Missionaries in the Middle East: Foundational Encounters*, ed. Mehmet Ali Doğan and Heather J. Sharkey (Salt Lake City: University of Utah Press, 2011), 260–84.

44. Porter, *Religion versus Empire*, 13, regarding missionary "anti-imperialism." In *British Missionary Enterprise*, 36, Cox writes, for example, that a common "defamatory impulse was in constant tension with the genuine Christian universalism of most missionaries, who would not have become missionaries unless they believed in some sense that all human beings, regardless of race or culture, were spiritual equals in the eyes of God."

45. A classic exposition of Christianization-as-modernization appears in Roland Oliver and Anthony Atmore, *Africa since 1800*, 3rd ed. (Cambridge: Cambridge University Press, 1981), 130; and in Roland Oliver, *The Missionary Factor in East Africa* (London: Longmans, Green, 1952). In African studies, a particularly influential work has been Robin Horton, "On the Rationality of Conversion, Parts I and II," *Africa* 45 (1975): 219–35, 373–99. Horton suggested that conversion to Christianity and Islam in Africa reflected and reinforced the deparochialization of local cultures as African men and women became more closely connected to the wider world.

46. Edward W. Said, *Orientalism* (New York: Pantheon Books, 1978).

47. Leela Gandhi, *Postcolonial Theory: A Critical Introduction* (New York: Columbia University Press, 1998), 4, 42, 65.

48. Consider the work of Mrinalini Sebastian, including Sebastian, "Reading Archives," and Mrinalini Sebastian, "Mission without History? Some Ideas for Decolonizing Mission," *International Review of Mission* 93, no. 368 (2004): 75–97.

49. Philip Jenkins, *The Next Christendom: The Coming of Global Christianity* (Oxford: Oxford University Press, 2002); Lamin Sanneh, *Whose Religion Is Christianity? The Gospel beyond the West* (Grand Rapids, MI: William B. Eerdmans, 2003); Sheridan Gilley and Brian Stanley, eds., *World Christianities, c. 1815–1915* (Cambridge: Cambridge University Press, 2006).

50. For an account of the Turkiyya Hasan scandal and its consequences for American Presbyterian missionaries in Egypt, see Sharkey, *American Evangelicals in Egypt.*

51. See Rambo, *Understanding Religious Conversion.*

52. Markowitz, *Cross and Sword,* 15.

53. A promising new study on the role of colonial-era catechists, in this case with reference to what is now Burkina Faso, is: Jean-Marie Bouron, "Être catéchiste en Haute-Volta à la fin de la période coloniale: affirmation d'un personnage prosélyte, transformation d'une personnalité sociale," *Social Sciences and Missions* 23, no. 2 (2010): 187–227.

54. Gilley and Stanley, *World Christianities.*

55. Eamon Duffy, *Marking the Hours, English People and Their Prayers* (New Haven: Yale University Press, 2006), 1.

2. Conflicting Conversions and Unexpected Christianities in Central Africa

1. While the Catholic missions were dominated by the White Fathers, there was a wide range of Protestant influences. For an overview, see Robert Rotberg, *Christian Missionaries and the Creation of Northern Rhodesia, 1880–1924* (Princeton: Princeton University Press, 1965).

2. The argument is further elaborated in the author's new book, David M. Gordon, *Invisible Agents: Spirits in a Central African History* (Athens: Ohio University Press, 2012).

3. Wyatt MacGaffey, "Dialogues of the Deaf: Europeans on the Atlantic Coast of Africa," in *Implicit Understandings: Observing, Reporting and Reflecting on the Encounters between Europeans and Other Peoples in the Early Modern Era,* ed. Stuart B. Schwartz (Cambridge: Cambridge University Press, 1994), 249–67.

4. As first suggested by Thomas O. Beidelman, "Social Theory and Christian Missions in Africa," *Africa: Journal of the International African Institute* 44, no. 3 (1974): 235–49, and considered in detail in his *Colonial Evangelism: A Socio-Historical Study of an East African Mission at the Grassroots* (Bloomington: Indiana University Press, 1982). Since Beidelman's publications, numerous others have conducted studies of missionary engagements, most famously, John L. Comaroff and Jean Comaroff, *Of Revelation and Revolution,* 2 vols. (Chicago: University of Chicago Press, 1991 and 1997).

5. W. V. Stone, Lubwa Annual Report, 1957, C/21, Acc. 7548, Church reports from Africa and Jamaica, National Library of Scotland, Edinburgh (henceforth NLS).

6. The classic account of such African prophetic interventions is B. G. M. Sundkler, *Bantu Prophets in South Africa* (Oxford: Oxford University Press, 1961). Also see more

recent work by Elizabeth Gunner, *The Man of Heaven and the Beautiful Ones of God: Umuntu Wasezulwini Nabantu Abahle Bakankulunkulu: Writings from Ibandla Lamanaz-aretha, a South African Church* (Leiden: Brill, 2002). For political aspects of prophetic Christianity in South Africa, see Clifton Crais, *The Politics of Evil: Magic, State Power, and the Political Imagination in South Africa* (Cambridge: Cambridge University Press, 2002); and Robert R. Edgar and Hilary Sapire, *African Apocalypse: the Story of Nontetha Nkwen-kwe, a Twentieth-Century South African Prophet* (Athens: Ohio University Press, 1999). For a broad survey, see Stephen Ellis and Gerrie ter Haar, *Worlds of Power: Religious Thought and Political Practice in Africa* (New York: Oxford University Press, 2004).

7. For the precolonial Bemba Kingdom, see Andrew Roberts, *A History of the Bemba: Political Growth and Change in North-Eastern Zambia before 1900* (London: Longman, 1973).

8. For the White Fathers in northern Zambia, see Brian Garvey, *Bembaland Church: Religious and Social Change in South Central Africa, 1891–1964* (Leiden: E. J. Brill, 1994).

9. For the history of the Livingstonia Mission in Northern Zambia, see At Ipenburg, *"All Good Men": The Development of the Lubwa Mission, Chinsali, Zambia, 1905–1967* (Frankfurt am Main: Peter Lang, 1996).

10. For the process of allocation, see A 3-10-7 United Free Church Scotland, Living-stone Mission, National Archive of Zambia, Lusaka (henceforth NAZ). Also see, George Prentice, U. Free Church of Scotland, Foreign Mission Committee, *Report on Our Cen-tral African Fields* (n.d. 1922–23?), Acc. 9269, Livingstonia, NLS.

11. Ipenburg, *All Good Men*, 33–47; W. V. Stone, "The Livingstonia Mission and the Bemba," *Bulletin of the Society for African Church History* 2 (1965–68): 311–22.

12. Garvey, *Bembaland Church*, 143.

13. Lubwa Mission Reports 1927, CS 13-2 United Church of Zambia Archives, Min-dolo, Kitwe (henceforth UCZA).

14. Lubwa Mission Reports 1934, CS 13-2, UCZA.

15. Garvey, *Bembaland Church*, 123.

16. Lubwa Mission Reports 1937, CS 13-2, UCZA.

17. Lubwa Mission Reports 1942, CS 13-2, UCZA.

18. Garvey, *Bembaland Church*, 150–54.

19. Tessier to Livinhac, Chilubula, 24 October 1980, as quoted in Garvey, *Bembal-and Church*, 90.

20. Garvey, *Bembaland Church*, 96–97.

21. For Mulolani's movement, see Garvey, *Bembaland Church*, 159–71; L. Oger, "Mutima Church of Emilio Mulolani" (Ilondola, Zambia, n.d., mimeographed).

22. Lubwa Mission Reports 1948, CS 13-2, UCZA.

23. D. J. Cook, "The Influence of the Livingstonia Mission upon the Formation of Welfare Associations in Zambia, 1912–31," in *Themes in the Christian History of Central Africa*, ed. T. Ranger and J. Weller (London: Heinemann, 1975), 98–133, esp. 99.

24. Garvey, *Bembaland Church*, 105–12.

25. Portions of the Bible were translated as early as 1920. Annual reports of the mission contain the books translated into ChiBemba, published, and distributed. For arrival of the completed Bible at Lubwa, see Lubwa Annual Report 1956, Acc. 7548/C17, NLS.

26. Garvey, *Bembaland Church*, 157–58.

27. Audrey I. Richards, "A Modern Movement of Witchfinders," *Africa: Journal of the International African Institute* 8, no. 4 (1935): 448–61. Richards Field Notes, 4/1934, Audrey Richards Files 1/16, London School of Economics (henceforth LSE).

28. Richards, Handwritten Manuscript n.d. (1934?), Audrey Richards Files 1/16, LSE.

29. Cases and Official Correspondence on Bamuchape, in WP 1/14/7, NAZ.

30. Report of Native Clerk Edward Shaba, Ufipa District, 3 March 1934, WP 1/14/7, NAZ.

31. J. Van Sambeek to Audrey Richards, 14/4/1932. Audrey Richards Files 2/15, LSE. For complaints regarding the burning of *mfuba* shrines by Catholics, also see Garvey, *Bembaland Church*, 99.

32. Many blamed Catholic bewitchment for Chief Nkula's death in 1934, since Nkula had initially been reluctant to allow the White Fathers to build the Ilondola Mission. When the colonial administrators expressed a similar reluctance to allow the White Fathers to build their mission, the White Fathers insinuated to the colonial officer that there was some truth to the accusation that they had bewitched and killed Chief Nkula; they dare not be denied the right to build the Ilondola Mission! TS. Fox–Pitt, Mpika to Audrey Richards 21 September 1934, Audrey Richards Files 1/1, LSE. By contrast, consider the White Fathers' mission correspondence on this issue, as found in Garvey, *Bembaland Church*, 127. In addition, the White Fathers were frequently targets of *banyama* vampire rumors (different to *buloshi* witchcraft accusations) covered by Luise White in several publications, including: "Vampire Priests of Central Africa: African Debates about Labor and Religion in Colonial Northern Zambia," *Comparative Studies in Society and History* 35, no. 4 (1993): 746–72; and in her *Speaking with Vampires: Rumor and History in Colonial Africa* (Berkeley: University of California Press, 2000), 175–207.

33. Lenshina's revelation and her early relationship with the Lubwa mission are covered in several interviews: Author interviews with Agnes Mafupa, Lubwa, 12 July 2005; Maggie Nkonde, Chandamali, Chinsali, 9 July 2005. The best contemporary eyewitness account is MacPherson's narrative in Fergus MacPherson, "The Alice Movement in Northern Rhodesia," August 1958, NP 2/12/3, NAZ; Richards Research Notes, 28/8/2957, Audrey Richards Files 1/16, LSE. I have discussed her revelations more thoroughly in David Gordon, "Community of Suffering: Narratives of War and Exile in the Zambian Lumpa Church," in *Recasting the Past: History Writing and Political Work in Modern Africa*, ed. Derek Peterson and Giacomo Macola (Athens: Ohio University Press, 2009), 191–209.

34. White Fathers Hugo F. Hinfelaar and Jean Loup Calmettes closely examine Lumpa hymns in Jean Loup Calmettes, "The Lumpa Sect, Rural Reconstruction, and

Confict," master's thesis, University College of Wales, 1978; and Hugo F. Hinfelaar, *Bemba-Speaking Women of Zambia in a Century of Religious Change* (Leiden: E. J. Brill, 1994), 73–100. The latter portion appeared earlier as Hugo F. Hinfelaar, "Women's Revolt: The Lumpa Church of Lenshina Mulenga in the 1950s," *Journal of Religion in Africa* 21 (1991): 99–129. Influential scholarship on the Lumpa Church includes Andrew Roberts, *The Lumpa Church of Alice Lenshina* (Lusaka: Oxford University Press, 1970); Robert I. Rotberg, "The Lenshina Movement of Northern Rhodesia," *Rhodes-Livingstone Journal* 29 (1961): 63–78; Dorothea Lehmann, "Alice Lenshina Mulenga and the Lumpa Church," in *Christians of the Copperbelt: The Growth of the Church in Northern Rhodesia*, ed. John V. Taylor and Dorothea Lehmann (London: SCM Press, 1961), 248–68; Wim J. van Binsbergen, *Religious Change in Zambia: Exploratory Studies* (London and Boston: Kegan Paul International, 1981), 267–316. Andrew Roberts also published "The Lumpa Church of Alice Lenshina," in *Protest and Power in Black Africa*, ed. R. I. Rotberg and A. A. Mazrui (New York: Oxford University Press, 1970), 515–68.

35. Tour Report No. 5 of 1957, 27 March 1957, NP 3/12/3, NAZ.

36. For the best discussion of numbers, see Calmettes, "Lumpa Sect," 38.

37. "The Alice Movement in Northern Rhodesia" n.d. (1956?); Special Branch, "Report on the Lenshina Movement" n.d. (1959?), 7, NP 3/12/3, NAZ.

38. For smallpox outbreak, see Annandale Hospital, Lubwa, Report 1953, Acc 7548 Foreign Mission Records of the Church of Scotland, NLS; also found in CCAR 13–8 Annandale Hospital Reports, UCZA.

39. The effects of migration of men to urban areas was first discussed in Audrey I. Richards, *Land, Labour, and Diet in Northern Rhodesia* (London: Oxford University Press, 1939); a more recent qualification that focuses on the colonial imposition as a source of alternative agricultural forms is Megan Vaughn and Henrietta L. Moore, *Cutting Down Trees: Gender, Nutrition, and Agricultural Change in the Northern Province of Zambia, 1890–1990* (Portsmouth, NH: Heinemann, 1994).

40. Calmettes, "Lumpa Sect," 115.

41. The rules have been referenced in numerous publications. The first account of them is in a letter to the Governor of Northern Rhodesia, Letter from Alice Lenshina to Governor of NR, 18 April 1957, NP/12/3, NAZ. A similar version, dated 13 December 1957, appears in L. Oger, "The Lenshina Movement in Northern Rhodesia: Religious Sect Founded by Alice Lenshina" (1955–60 [1960?], mimeographed), 26–27. The same version is found in Zambia Government, *Report of the Commission of Enquiry into the Lumpa Church* (Lusaka: Government Printers, 1965), 17.

42. Report on DC Visit to Kasomo, 10 August 1956, NP 3/12/3, NAZ.

43. Ibid.

44. Ilondola Annual Report, 1955–56, White Fathers Archives, Zambia (henceforth WFA).

45. Report on DC Visit to Kasomo, 10 August 1956, NP 3/12/3, NAZ.

46. For blessing of seeds and harvest, see L. Oger, "Lenshina Movement," 14.

47. "I call on you, come and enter; In the house of Seed," "Namwita seni mwingile; Munganda ya lubuto." In Calmettes, "Lumpa Sect," 24.

48. DC, Chinsali, Report to PC, Kasama, 4 April 1957, NP 3/12/3, NAZ.

49. Religious Organization Reports, August 1956, NP 3/12/13, NAZ.

50. Kayambi Mission to Lord Bishop, Ilondola Mission Diary, 1/4/1955; "The statue of Our lady of the Rosary was stolen from Ilondola," in Ilondola Misson Diary, 6 September 1955, 5/WF/MD/63, WFA.

51. DC to Sec. Native Affairs, 22 June 1957, NP 3/12/3, NAZ. For "Rosary Campaigns," see Chalabesa Annual Report, 1955–56, Calmettes Box 7, WFA.

52. Chalabesa Annual Report 1955–56, Calmettes Box 7, WFA.

53. Garvey, *Bembaland Church*, 177.

54. Abercorn Vicariate, Circular No. 4 April 1957, as quoted in Calmettes, "Lumpa Sect," 25.

55. CCAR Minutes of Presbytery 1956, 9. As quoted and discussed in Calmettes, "Lumpa Sect," 124–25.

56. For Kakokota's accusation, see Garvey, *Bembaland Church*, 176. Based on Ilondola Diary, 11–12 September 1956, 5/WF/MD/63, WFA. For subsequent sentencing of Petros and the colonial official perspective, see "Report on Religious Organisation/Lenshina," 1956, NP 3-12-3, NAZ.

57. Calmettes, "Lumpa Sect," 133–34.

58. The attack on teachers and witchcraft accusations against them is discussed in Calmettes, "Lumpa Sect," 143–44.

59. W. V. Stone, Lubwa Annual Report 1957, C/21, Acc. 7548, Church reports from Africa and Jamaica, NLS.

60. Author interviews with Jennifer Ngandu, Lusaka, 25 March 2005; Stephanie Nguni, Chiponya, 19 July 2005.

61. For the war, see David Gordon, "Rebellion or Massacre? The UNIP-Lumpa Conflict Revisited," in *One Zambia, Many Histories: Towards a History of Post-Colonial Zambia*, ed. Jan-Bart Gewald, Marja Hinfelaar, and Giacomo Macola (Leiden: Brill, 2008), 45–76.

3. Church versus Country: Palestinian Arab Episcopalians, Nationalism, and Revolt, 1936–39

1. For a useful comparison of the Great Revolt and the first *intifada*, see especially Kenneth W. Stein, "The Intifada and the 1936–39 Uprising: A Comparison," *Journal of Palestine Studies* 19, no. 4 (1990): 66–67. On the revolt more broadly, see especially Ted Swedenburg, *Memories of Revolt: The 1936–1939 Rebellion and the Palestinian National Past* (Fayetteville: University of Arkansas Press, 2003); Weldon Matthews, *Confronting an*

Empire, Constructing a Nation: Arab Nationalists and Popular Politics in Mandate Palestine (London and New York: I. B. Tauris, 2006); Ylana Miller, *Government and Society in Rural Palestine, 1920–1948* (Austin: University of Texas Press, 1985); Ellen Fleischmann, *The Nation and Its "New" Women: The Palestinian Women's Movement, 1920–1948* (Berkeley: University of California Press, 2003); Bayan Nuwayhid al-Hut, *Qiyadat wa-al-mu'assasat al-siyasiyya fi Filastin 1917–1948* (Beirut: n.p., 1981); Issa Khalaf, *Politics in Palestine: Arab Factionalism and Social Disintegration, 1939–1948* (Albany: State University of New York Press, 1991); W. F. Abboushi, "The Road to Rebellion: Arab Palestine in the 1930's," *Journal of Palestine Studies* 6, no. 3 (spring 1977): 23–46; Ann Mosely Lesch, *Arab Politics in Palestine, 1917–1939: The Frustration of a Nationalism Movement* (Ithaca: Cornell University Press, 1979); Rashid Khalidi, *Palestinian Identity: The Construction of Modern National Consciousness* (New York: Columbia University Press, 1997); Gershon Shafir, *Land, Labor and the Origins of the Israeli-Palestinian Conflict, 1882–1914* (Berkeley: University of California Press, 1996); and Kamil Khillah, *Filastin wa-al-intidab al-baritani, 1922–1939* (Beirut: Munazzamat al-Tahrir al-Filastiniyya, 1974).

2. Cited in Michael Oren, *Power, Faith and Fantasy: America in the Middle East, 1776 to the Present* (New York: W. W. Norton, 2007), 91. See also Mehmet Ali Doğan and Heather J. Sharkey, eds., *American Missionaries in the Middle East: Foundational Encounters* (Salt Lake City: University of Utah Press, 2011).

3. This was a common pattern for European missionaries throughout the Middle East; in Lebanon, Syria, Egypt, and elsewhere, Protestant missionaries quickly turned their attention to local indigenous Christian populations. See, for instance, Joseph Grabill, *Protestant Diplomacy and the Near East: Missionary Influence on American Policy, 1810–1927* (Minneapolis: University of Minnesota Press, 1971); A. L. Tibawi, *American Interests in Syria, 1800–1901: A Study of Education, Literary and Religious Work* (Oxford: Clarendon Press, 1966); *British Interests in Palestine, 1800–1901: A Study of Religious and Educational Enterprise* (London: Oxford University Press, 1971); and Sharkey, *American Evangelicals in Egypt.*

4. Palestinian Arab converts objected strongly to being called "Anglicans," as they were adamant that their church was not British but Palestinian. Consequently, I have distinguished here between British Anglicans in Palestine and Palestinian Arab Episcopalians.

5. See, for instance, Minutes of Palestine Native Church Council (henceforth PNCC), Jerusalem, 20 October 1936, Church Missionary Society Archives, Birmingham, UK (henceforth CMS), G2/P3/1.

6. Stewart to Davidson, 6 June 1936, Lambeth Palace Archives, London, UK (henceforth LPA), Lang Papers 52.

7. The Peel Commission was a Royal Commission of Inquiry appointed in the aftermath of the strike to investigate the causes of violence in Palestine and advise the British government on a course of action. Headed by Lord Robert Peel, it was the first body

to recommend the partition of Palestine into an Arab and a Jewish state. The report was published as Palestine Royal Commission, *Report of the Palestine Royal Commission* (London: Her Majesty's Stationery Office, 1937).

8. A particular source of outrage was the assigning of the Galilee, which was almost entirely Arab, to the proposed Jewish state.

9. Most of the members of the AHC were deported to the Seychelles; Hajj Amin al-Husayni escaped to Beirut.

10. One seminal work on Palestinian nationalism suggests that the revolt sparked major hostility toward Christians, manifested in attacks on Christian villages as well as less serious incidences of forcing Christian women to wear the veil and making Christians observe their day of rest on Fridays; see Yehoshua Porath, *The Palestinian Arab National Movement: From Riots to Rebellion, 1929–1939* (London: F. Cass, 1977), 269–71. But a more recent study based on oral sources notes that no evidence of sectarian tensions emerged in interviews with participants in the revolt, suggesting that Muslim-Christian tensions were elided as a nationalist historiography of the revolt emerged among Palestinians. See Swedenburg, *Memories of Revolt*, 89–90.

11. PNCC to Lang, 6 June 1936, LPA, Lang Papers 52.

12. The nationalist organization based around the Husayni family was known as the *majlisiyyun* because of Hajj Amin al-Husayni's position as head of the Supreme Muslim Council. The other major political faction in mandate Palestine, headed by the Nashashibi family, was known as the *mu'arida*, the opposition.

13. Izzat Tannous, *The Palestinians: A Detailed Documented Eyewitness History of Palestine under British Mandate* (New York: I.G.T., 1988), 179.

14. Ghawri [Ghori] to Ormsby-Gore, 6 June 1936, Colonial Office, National Archives, London UK (henceforth CO) 733/312/1.

15. Lambeth Palace to Stewart, June 1936, LPA, Lang Papers 52.

16. Cash to Marmura, 30 June 1936, CMS, G2/Pd/1.

17. Graham Brown to Jerusalem and East Mission (henceforth JEM), 15 October 1936, JEM, 61/1; see also Rafiq Farah, *In Troubled Waters: A History of the Anglican Diocese in Jerusalem 1841–1998* (Leicester, UK: Christians Aware, 2002), 111.

18. Bishop to Hooper, 6 June 1936, CMS, G2/P/1.

19. Minutes of PNCC meeting Jerusalem, 24 September 1937, CMS, G2/P3/1.

20. Graham Brown to Lang, 28 July 1937, LPA, Lang Papers 52.

21. *Filastin*, 24 July 1937; *Palestine Post*, 22 July 1937.

22 Ibid.

23 See, for instance, Taufik Canaan, *The Palestine Arab Cause* (Jerusalem: Modern Press, 1936); and Taufik Canaan, *Conflict in the Land of Peace* (Jerusalem: Syrian Orphanage Press, 1936).

24. Canaan, *Palestine Arab Cause*, 16.

25. Tannous, *Palestinians*, 183.

26. Stefan Wild, "Judentum, Christentum und Islam in der palastinensischen Poesie," *Die Welt des Islams* 23 (1984): 262n6.

27. Graham Brown to Lang, 28 July 1937, JEM, 60/1/2.

28. "Some Christian Considerations in Regard to the Partition Problem," by Graham Brown, Warburton, Bridgeman and Stewart, 1937, JEM, 65/4.

29. Graham Brown to Lang, 15 January 1937, LPA, Lang Papers 52.

30. Lang to Francis, 9 September 1937, LPA, Lang Papers 52.

31. Swedenburg, *Memories of Revolt*, xxi.

32. For an examination of the British military approach to the revolt, see Charles Townshend, "In Defence of Palestine: Insurrection and Public Security, 1936–1939," *English Historical Review* 103, no. 409 (1988): 917–49.

33. Minutes of PNCC meeting, Jaffa, 3 April 1938, CMS, G2/P3/1.

34. The appearance of some anti–Christian pamphlets around villages involved in the revolt led the British to think Christians were being targeted as part of a *jihad*. "The Christians are not afraid of the educated Moslem or the Effendi class who live in the towns," Graham Brown wrote to the Peel Commission in 1937, "but they have come to realize that the zeal shown by the fellahin in the late disturbances was religious and fundamentally in the nature of a Holy War against a Christian Mandate and against Christian people as well as against the Jews." See Graham Brown to Peel Commission, 12 January 1937, LPA, Lang Papers, 52. This extravagant claim reflected the continuing British commitment to the idea that religious affiliation always trumped every other kind of loyalty among Palestinian Arabs. It might also be noted that this view has been repeated by a number of modern scholars; see, for instance, Yehoshua Porath, *The Emergence of the Palestinian Arab National Movement, 1918–1929* (London: F. Cass, 1974); Porath, *Palestinian Arab National Movement*; and Daphne Tsimhoni, "The Arab Christians and the Palestinian Arab National Movement During the Formative Stage," in *The Palestinians and the Middle East Conflict*, ed. Gabriel Ben-Dor (Ramat Gan: Turtledove, 1978), 90. See also her "The Status of the Arab Christians under the British Mandate in Palestine," *Middle Eastern Studies* 20, no. 4 (1984): 166–92, and "The Greek Orthodox Patriarchate of Jerusalem during the Formative Years of the British Mandate in Palestine," *Asian and African Studies* 12 (1978): 77–122.

35. Marmura to Lang, 12 August 1937, LPA, Lang Papers 52.

36. Graham Brown, "Notes of conversations with leading Arab Christians in Jerusalem," January 1937, LPA, Lang Papers 52.

37. Saba to Warren, October 1946, CMS, G2/P3/1.

38. CMS Palestine Mission Report on Moslem Evangelism, Conference 1936, CMS, G2/P/2.

39. Minutes of PNCC Standing Committee Meeting, 10 August 1938, JEM 21/3.

40. Minutes of PNCC meeting Nazareth, 27 April 1947, CMS, G2/P3/1.

41. Minutes of PNCC meeting Jaffa, 9 May 1943, CMS, G2/P3/1.

42. Minutes of PNCC meeting Nazareth, 30 April 1947, CMS, G2/P3/1.

43. Memo by Hooper on interview with Suleiman Tannus, London, 31 December 1946, CMS, G2/P3/1.

44. Graham Brown, "Notes of Conversations with Leading Arab Christians in Jerusalem," January 1937, LPA, Lang Papers 52.

45. Marmura to Lang, 12 August 1937, LPA, Lang Papers 52.

46. Graham Brown, "Notes of Conversations with leading Arab Christians in Jerusalem," January 1937, LPA, Lang Papers 52.

47. Riah Abu El-Assal, *Caught in Between: The Story of an Arab Palestinian Christian Israeli* (London: SPCK, 1999), 52. Abu El-Assal suggests that Saba did this at the instigation of the local district commissioner.

48. It went from 29,350 to 10,982, according to Daphne Tsimhoni, *Christian Communities in Jerusalem and the West Bank since 1948: An Historical, Social and Political Study* (Westport, CT: Praeger, 1993), 19; see also Bernard Sabella, "Palestinian Christian Emigration from the Holy Land," *Proche-Orient Chrétien* 41 (1991): 74–85, esp. 75.

49. Bernard Sabella, "Socio-Economic Characteristics and Challenges to Palestinian Christians in the Holy Land," in *Palestinian Christians: Religion, Politics and Society in the Holy Land*, ed. Anthony O'Mahony (London: Melisende, 1999), 84. For further discussions of Palestinian Christian emigration, see also Sabella's "Palestinian Christian Emigration"; and "The Emigration of Christian Arabs: Dimensions and Causes of the Phenomenon," in *Christian Communities in the Arab Middle East: The Challenge of the Future*, ed. Andrea Pacini (Oxford: Clarendon Press, 1998), 127–54.

50. Nurit Yaffe, *The Arab Population of Israel 2003* (Jerusalem: Central Bureau of Statistics, 2003). The Palestinian Arab population of Israel constitutes approximately 20% of the population (about 1.3 million people). Most of the Palestinian Christian population is now concentrated in the Galilee region.

51. Sabella, "Palestinian Christian Emigration," 74. See also one of the few case studies of the Palestinian diaspora in Latin America, Nancie L. Solien González, *Dollar, Dove, and Eagle: One Hundred Years of Palestinian Migration to Honduras* (Ann Arbor: University of Michigan Press, 1993), 10.

52. Bernard Sabella, "Palestinian and Arab Christians: The Challenges Ahead," Sami Hadawi Memorial Lecture, Amman, Jordan, 22 September 2004 (many thanks to the author for providing me with this text). Of course, this category includes other Middle Eastern Christians besides Palestinians.

53. It is worth noting that the pattern of persistent Arab Christian emigration goes beyond Palestine and extends throughout the Middle East. For a useful examination of the demographics of Middle Eastern Christianity after 1945, see especially Philippe Fargues, "Demographic Islamization: Non-Muslims in Muslim Countries," *SAIS Review* 21, no. 2 (2001): 103–16, and Philippe Fargues, "The Arab Christians of the Middle East: A Demographic Perspective," in *Christian Communities in the Arab Middle East*, ed.

Andrea Pacini (Oxford and New York: Clarendon Press, 1998), 48–66; and Youssef Courbage and Philippe Fargues, *Chrétiens et juifs dans l'Islam arabe et turc* (Paris: Fayard, 1992).

4. Missionaries and Ethnography in the Service of Litigation: Hindu Law and Christian Custom in India's Deccan, 1750–1863

1. This chapter defines the Deccan broadly as the plateau region extending from the Maratha country to Hyderabad and its vicinity, and southward into Bangalore, Mysore, and other interior districts of peninsular India.

2. Bellary city was located in Bellary District, one of four "Ceded Districts" (the others being Anantapur, Cuddapah, and Kurnool).

3. Mrinalini Sebastian addresses related notions of missionary "knowledge systems" and their consequences in her essay "The Scholar-Missionaries of the Basel Mission in Southwest India: Language, Identity, and Knowledge in Flux," in this volume.

4. Recent contributions to the study of Protestant conversion in South Asia include Christopher Harding, *Religious Transformation in South Asia: The Meanings of Conversion in Colonial Punjab* (Oxford: Oxford University Press, 2008); R. E. Frykenberg, ed., *Christians and Missionaries in India: Cross-Cultural Communication since 1500* (Grand Rapids, MI: Eerdmans, 2003); and Geoffrey A. Oddie, *Religious Conversion Movements in South Asia: Continuities and Change, 1800–1900* (London: Taylor & Francis, 1997).

5. Protestant attitudes toward caste, he argues, tended to become more accommodating by the late nineteenth and early twentieth centuries as missionaries contended increasingly with mass conversions. See D. M. Forrester, *Caste and Christianity: Attitudes and Policies on Caste of Anglo-Saxon Protestant Missions* (London: Curzon Press, 1980), 53ff.

6. For a fascinating study of Catholic interactions with indigenous knowledge systems, see Ines Zupanov, *Disputed Mission: Jesuit Experiments and Brahminical Knowledge in Seventeenth Century India* (Oxford: Oxford University Press, 2000).

7. In this respect, missionaries functioned like imperial rulers, whose transformative agendas often gave way to the imperatives of survival through adaptation.

8. Discussions of the role of missionaries as knowledge producers include Nicolas Dirks, *Castes of Mind: Colonialism and the Making of Modern India* (Princeton: Princeton University Press, 2001); Lata Mani, *Contentious Traditions: The Debate on Sati in Colonial India* (Berkeley: University of California Press, 1998); and Geoffrey Oddie, *Imagined Hinduism: British Protestant Missionary Constructions of Hinduism, 1793–1900* (Thousand Oaks, CA: Sage, 2006).

9. Dirks, *Castes of Mind*, 21–24.

10. J. A. Dubois, *Letters on the State of Christianity in India, in which the Conversion of the Hindus Is Considered as Impracticable* (London: Paternoster Row, 1823).

11. Ralph Wardlaw, *Memoir of the Late Rev. John Reid, M.A., of Bellary, East Indies: Comprising Incidents of the Bellary Mission for a Period of Eleven Years, 1830 to 1840* (Glasgow: James Maclehose, 1845), 129.

12. Bellary District Records, Tamil Nadu Archives, Chennai (henceforth BDR), 421, 105–10. Hands had to persuade the original occupants of the land to sell it to him. Somehow, he acquired the funds to buy it from them.

13. From the Revenue Department to the Collector at Bellary, 9 November 1811. Grant of ground to Mr. John Hands. BDR, 390, 55–58, 67–69.

14. W. Francis, *Madras District Gazetteers: Bellary* (Madras: Government Press, 1904), 56. Hands's translations are kept at the Oriental and India Office Collection (henceforth OIOC) of the British Library.

15. Wardlaw, *Memoir of the Late Rev. John Reid*, 137ff.

16. Personal Letters of John Hands, School of Oriental and African Studies (henceforth SOAS) Special Collections Room, South India, Canarese, 1817-25, box 1, folder 3, jacket C. It was not unusual in the mission field for understaffed Anglican churches to employ a Dissenting preacher to conduct services. Author interview with M. Sabapathy, retired minister at Trinity Church, Bellary, 20 December 2006. Sabapathy has written a B.D. thesis on John Hands, Union Theological College, Bangalore.

17. According to another London Missionary Society (henceforth LMS) report, Cowl Bazaar "contains a population equal to Bellary itself. A mixed multitude, generally camp followers. They are mostly Malabars, and of course speak the Canarese . . . Hands preached to the Canarese in chapel on Sunday mornings, when about ten adults and 70 children attend. He also preaches occasionally in a schoolroom in the town, when 70 or 80 persons gather to hear. He also meets the native converts weekly, at his own house, for conversation and prayer." "Letter of the Rev. D. Tyerman and G. Bennet, Esq. Report of Deputation to South Seas," *Transactions of the London Missionary Society* (hereafter, *Transactions*), October 1828, SOAS Special Reading Room.

18. Wardlaw, *Memoir of the late Rev. John Reid*, 124.

19. Ibid., 131–37.

20. "A Sub Collector May Not Act as a Missionary," Minutes of Sir Thomas Munro and William Thackeray, President of the Board of Revenue, concerning the removal of John Allen Dalzell from the post of Sub-Collector of Bellary owing to his excessive zeal for propagating Christianity among the native population, November 1822–July 1825; 1681, OR/F/4/27324, OIOC, British Library.

21. Ibid., 1690.

22. Debates over discourses of choice, coercion, and inducement persist in the current scholarship on conversion in India. See David Gilmartin, "Divine Displeasure and Muslim Elections: The Shaping of Community in Twentieth Century Punjab," in *The Political Inheritance of Pakistan*, ed. D. A. Low (London: Macmillan Academic and Professional LTD, 1991), 106–29.

23. But their protest soon subsided, and numbers increased until the classroom had to be enlarged. Wardlaw, *Memoir of the Late Rev. John Reid*, 131.

24. "Extracts from the Journal of Mr. William Reeve, Missionary at Bellary," in *Transactions* 1 (1816–19): 243.

25. Ibid., 244.

26. "Extracts from a Journal of Mr. John Hands, Missionary at Bellary," 26 September 1817, in *Transactions* (April 1820): 419–20.

27. Ibid., 419.

28. Ibid., 419–20.

29. *Transactions* (April 1820): 420–23.

30. He also provided details of an instance of *sati* that had occurred in Mysore in the previous year.

31. Kate Brittlebank describes how the festival was important enough to compel even the Muslim Tipu Sultan to observe it during his reign. See Brittlebank, "Assertion," in *The Eighteenth Century in Indian History: Evolution or Revolution?*, ed. P. J. Marshall (New Delhi: Oxford University Press, 2005), 268–92.

32. "Extracts from a Journal of Mr. John Hands, Missionary at Bellary," *Transactions* (April 1820): 422; *Transactions* (July 1820): 452.

33. Francis, *Madras District Gazetteers: Bellary*, 62.

34. Sanjay Subrahmanyam, *Penumbral Visions: Making Polities in Early Modern South Asia* (New Delhi: Oxford University Press, 2001), 65.

35. Ibid., 66.

36. Ibid.

37. Subrahmanyam bases his description on the account given by the Jesuit Joachim Dias, who lived in the Hassan district of western Mysore. The account provides details about the complex eighteenth century politics in Mysore and surrounding regions. Ibid., 74.

38. Ibid., 86.

39. Dubois has long been associated with the book *Hindu Manners, Customs and Ceremonies* (Oxford: Clarendon Press, 1906). Sylvia Murr has shown how Dubois had substantially plagiarized a manuscript from the 1760s written by Père Gaston-Laurent Coeurdoux. Later, he added his own material to it. The ethnographic information contained in this work was prized by the government as vital to the administration of Indian society. See Dirks, *Caste of Mind*, 21.

40. J. A. Dubois, *Description of the Character, Manners and Customs of the People of India and of Their Institutions, Religious and Civil*, translation from the French manuscript (London: Longman, Hurst, Rees, Orme, & Brown, 1817): 108–9. As much as this is a plagiarized manuscript, the views resemble those that Dubois states in his *Letters on the State of Christianity*.

41. Dubois, *Description of Character*, 111.

42. Ibid., 117.

43. Dubois, *Letters on the State of Christianity*, 11.

44. Ibid., 74.

45. Ibid., 100.

46. Ibid., 69.

47. James Hough, *A Reply to the Letters of the Abbe Dubois on the State of Christianity in India* (London: L. B. Seeley & Sons, 1824), 102–3.

48. Ibid., 40.

49. "Extract of a Letter from Mr. John Hands, Missionary at Bellary, dated Nundihall, August 8, 1822, addressed to the Secretary," *Quarterly Chronicle of Transactions of the London Missionary Society in the Years 1820–1824* 2 (London, 1825): 392–93.

50. "Extracts from a Journal of Mr. John Hands, Missionary at Bellary," 26 September 1817, *Transactions* (April 1820): 421.

51. Ibid.

52. "Extracts from a Journal of Mr. John Hands, Missionary at Bellary," *Transactions* (July 1820): 449–50.

53. A *sudra* is a member of the lowest of the fourfold caste order, consisting of servants of various kinds.

54. Anonymous, *Memoir of the late Rev. Samuel William Flavel, of the Bellary Mission* (Bellary: Mission Press, 1848), 10–13.

55. Ibid., 21–24.

56. Hands refers to Flavel in his journal. His papers also include Flavel's own detailed account of his life, conversion and call to Christian work. See the Papers of John Hands, 3 August 1831, box 3, folder 2, jacket A, SOAS Archives.

57. *Memoir of Samuel William Flavel*, 127.

58. The clusters of documents pertaining to *Abraham v. Abraham—Cases with Judgments, Privy Council Decision of Abraham v. Abraham* (1863)—are in a box stored in the Oriental and India Office Collection (OIOC) of the British Library. OIOC, *the Civil Court of Bellary, Abraham v. Abraham*, no. 200. Deposition of Plaintiff's 73rd witness. Reverend William Howell, aged nearly 68 years, a Protestant, a Pensioned Missionary, of European descent, and residing at Poonamalee. 19 October 1857, 257.

59. Ibid. By the time Charlotte had filed the case in 1854, John Hands was long retired in England. His contact with the family, however, had not ceased entirely. In 1840, the Abrahams' eldest son, Charles Henry, went to England to study law. At the time, Francis Abraham had contacted Hands to look after Charles and help him acclimate to life in England.

60. OIOC, *In the Civil Court of Bellary, Abraham v. Abraham*, no. 156. Deposition of Plaintiff's 3rd witness. Mr. Frederick Seymour, son of Stephen Newton Seymour, and Protestant, a retired warrant officer. 9 January 1858, 151.

61. Wardlaw, *Memoir of Rev. John Reid*, 133.

62. Chris Bayly notes that transformations of bodily practices and rising levels of uniformity in dress were among the effects of modernity upon many world cultures. The uniformity involved not only the adoption of Western clothes but also the need for people to "represent themselves publicly in a similar way." Concern about *when* the Abraham brothers had adopted Western dress predated developments described by Bayly by at least fifty years. C. A. Bayly, *The Birth of the Modern World, 1780–1914* (Oxford: Blackwell, 2004), 13.

63. OIOC, *Abraham v. Abraham*, no. 196. Testimony of Plaintiff's 68th witness, General William Cullen, aged 72 years, a Protestant, belonging to the Madras Artillery, and residing at Travancore. 4 November 1857: 239. Francis himself dated the change of dress to 1818 or 1819. OIOC, *Abraham v. Abraham*, no. 162. Testimony of Francis Abraham, son of Abraham, a Protestant, aged 44 years. 21 December 1857, 157. A Muslim witness, Booden Saib, claims to have seen Francis as a young boy dressed in an English "frock," suggesting that he followed Matthew's lead in adopting Western clothes. OIOC, *Abraham v. Abraham*, no. 180. Plaintiff's 45th witness, Booden Saib, son of Mahomed Oomer, caste Sheik, Sect Haneefa, aged 57 years, civil record keeper, and residing at Bellary. *Translation* (23 January 1858): 194.

64. OIOC, *Abraham v. Abraham*, no. 200. Testimony of Reverend William Howell, 255.

65. OIOC, *Abraham v. Abraham*, no. 189. Deposition of Plaintiff's 58th witness, 29 September 1857. Reverend John Guest, aged 44 years, a Protestant, a Clergyman, an East Indian, and residing at Veprey in Madras, 211.

66. "Could the defendant plead Hindu law if he were to commit bigamy?" she posed in her opening statement. OIOC, *Abraham v. Abraham*, 13.

67. OIOC, *Abraham v. Abraham*, Testimony of John Guest, 210.

68. Little is known more generally about the origins of Roman Catholics in Bellary. According to one source, from 1733, French Jesuits from the Mysore Mission began making visits to Bellary. By the end of the eighteenth century, missionaries from Goa seem to have played a more active role. From 1775 to 1784, Joachim de Souza visited Bellary from his station in Pepally. During these years, the Catholic presence in Bellary and surrounding regions came under the authority of the Padroado Real (the mission backed by the Portuguese state, and patronized by the Vatican). Fr. Sylvester McGoldrick, *Bellary Mission* (Buckingham, UK: Franciscan Missionary Union, 1960), 207. See also Mathew Walsh, *Our Fathers in India: An Account of the Mission of Bellary, South India* (London: The Friary, 1931), 29. Walsh dates the arrival of Catholics to the 16th century, when Portuguese Franciscans had visited the region.

69. McGoldrick, *Bellary Mission*, 207–8. Perozy remained in Bellary for some years after Doyle replaced him. He continued to interact with members of the Abraham family. Fredrick Seymour, a Protestant witness who had known Matthew from the days of his employment at Bellary's arsenal, stated that he encountered Perozy during his periodic

visits to the Abraham home. OIOC, *Abraham v. Abraham*, Testimony of Frederick Seymour, 153.

70. In 1868, he established an orphanage with an adjoining school. Originally this was intended only for European and Anglo-Indian children; but later, Indian children were admitted in increasing numbers. McGoldrick, *Bellary Mission*, 208.

71. C. R. Brackenbury, *Madras District Gazetteers: Cuddapah* (Madras: Government Press, 1915), 56.

72. Francis, *Madras District Gazetteers: Bellary*, 55. Such Indian designations for priests was not unusual. Two Carmelite priests during the eighteenth century received similar designations: a Father Felix was called "Baggiananda" (father of happiness) and a Father John Paradisi was called "Rajendra" (father of the kingdom). Matthew Walsh, *Our Fathers in India: An Account of the Mission of Bellary, South India* (London: The Friary, 1931), 31.

73. There is no record of Francis joining the LMS chapel, but one may presume that he did so since he was his brother's younger dependent at the time.

74. On the Vellalars, see Dennis Hudson, *Protestant Origins in India: Tamil Evangelical Christians, 1706–1835* (Grand Rapids, MI: Eerdmans, 2000). Note that any of the four principal castes or *varnas*, Brahmin, Kshaitrya, Vaisya, and Sudra, are subdivided into numerous *jatis*.

75. OIOC, *Before the Civil Court of Madura, Abraham v. Abraham*, no. 398. Deposition of Defendant's 82nd witness, Murrya Sowriah Pillay, son of Davasagoyum Pillay, a Vellalen by caste, a Roman Catholic by religion, aged 35 years, a Natam, and cultivator by occupation, and residing at Ilpamullanoor, Madura. 2 October 1857, 503.

76. OIOC, *Before the Civil Court of Guntur, Abraham v. Abraham*, no. 378. Deposition of Defendant's 59th witness, Govindoo Rayannah, son of Marriannah, caste Balja, religion Christian, aged 39 years, occupation cultivator, residing at Mutloor, Pratipad Talook, Zillah Guntoor, 23 September 1857, 460–61.

77. By then colonial authorities had long assumed that Christian converts had forfeited their rights to inheritance under Hindu law, precisely because of their inability to perform funeral rites for deceased elders. See Mallampalli, *Christians and Public Life*, chapter 2.

78. OIOC, *In the Civil Court of Bellary, Abraham v. Abraham*, no. 338. Deposition of Defendant's 1st witness. Reverend P. Doyle, son of Nicholas Doyle, aged 42 years, Roman Catholic Chaplain and residing at Bellary. 18 February 1858, 392.

79. Ibid., 393.

80. OIOC, *Judgment on the Appeal of Abraham v. Abraham, from the Sudder Diwani Adalat at Madras; heard by the Lords of the Judicial Committee of the Privy Council. February 1863. Judgment delivered 13th June, 1863*, 15.

81. Edmund F. Moore, *Reports of Cases Heard and Determined by the Judicial Committee and the Lords of H.M. Most Honourable Privy Council, on Appeal from the Supreme*

and Sudder Dewaney Courts in the East Indies, vol. 9 (London: V. and R. Stevens, 1863) (commonly and henceforth known as *Moore's Indian Appeals*).

82. See *Abraham v. Abraham*, in *Moore's Indian Appeals*, 9 (1863): 257–59.

83. Gauri Viswanathan places this case in the context of other landmark conversion-related cases in her book, *Outside the Fold: Conversion, Modernity and Belief* (Princeton: Princeton University Press, 1998).

5. Hybridity, Parody, and Contempt: Buddhist Responses to Christian Missions in Sri Lanka

1. See, for example, the comments on the centrality of the 1873 debate between monks and missionary in Panadure, Sri Lanka in Donald S. Lopez Jr., *A Modern Buddhist's Bible: Essential Readings from East and West* (Boston: Beacon Press, 2002), 3.

2. The adoption of Buddhism by most inhabitants in the island is said to have followed an earlier Buddhist "mission" led by a group of monks from India around the third century BCE. All signs suggest that the king and his subjects quickly embraced Buddhism, such that by the beginning of the Common Era, the vast majority of the island's inhabitants were devotees of the "Three Jewels" (i.e., the Buddha, the Dharma, and the Sangha). From this point onward, Sri Lankans periodically endeavored to spread the Buddhist religion toward lands overseas. Further, the Islamic religion established in the island by traders has historically refrained from seeking to convert other people to Islam.

3. Wilhelm Geiger, trans., *The Mahāvaṃsa: Or the Great Chronicle of Ceylon* (reprint, Oxford: Pali Text Society, 2001), 55.

4. For examples of critical views of Christian missions in Sri Lanka, see C. Gaston Perera, *The Portuguese Missionary in 16th and 17th Century Ceylon: The Spiritual Conquest* (Colombo: Vijitha Yapa, 2009); and M. U. de Silva, "Suppression of Buddhism and Aspects of Indigenous Culture under the British," *Journal of the Royal Asiatic Society of Sri Lanka* 49 (2004): 15–52. A more positive view is found in S. G. Perera's *The Jesuits in Ceylon (In the XVI and XVII Centuries)* (New Delhi: Asian Educational Services, 2004).

5. See Antony Fernando, "Understanding the 'Sinhala-Buddhist' Movement in Sri Lanka," *Journal of Dharma* 20, no. 2 (1995): 208.

6. For instance, a recent and ongoing team of Sri Lankan scholars have organized themselves under the name "The Portuguese Encounter Group" and have begun to hold conferences that focus on the harm caused by Portuguese colonialism and research Buddhist and Hindu temples allegedly razed by Portuguese troops. At the same time, the Portuguese themselves have apparently done little to discourage such one-sided views of their history in Sri Lanka. The Portuguese diplomatic mission in Colombo closed in 1974, and Portugal has not pursued an active program of political or cultural engagement with Sri Lanka. See Jorge Manuel Flores, *Hum Curto Historia de Ceylan: Five Hundred Years of Relations Between Portugal and Sri Lanka* (Lisbon: Fundação Oriente, 2000), 130–31.

7. Alan Strathern, *Kingship and Conversion in Sixteenth–Century Sri Lanka: Portuguese Imperialism in a Buddhist Land* (Cambridge: Cambridge University Press, 2007), 87.

8. C. R. Boxer, "'Christians and Spices': Portuguese Missionary Methods in Ceylon 1518–1658," *History Today* 8 (1958): 348.

9. See K. D. Paranavitana, "Suppression of Buddhism and Aspects of Indigenous Culture under the Portuguese and the Dutch," *Journal of the Royal Asiatic Society of Sri Lanka* (n.s.) 49 (2004): 1–14.

10. A. V. Suraweera, *Rājāvaliya* (Ratmalana, Sri Lanka: Sarvodaya Vishva Lekha, 2000), 76.

11. Quoted in Paranavitana, "Suppression of Buddhism," 4. It should be noted that what is often called the *Cūḷavaṃsa* actually comprises later additions appended to the earlier chronicle called the *Mahāvaṃsa*.

12. In addition, Michael Roberts has studied a number of war-poems (*haṭana*) and concluded that the majority of them tend to depict European colonialists dichotomously as hostile, even demonic forces compared to the benevolent Buddhist community of the local inhabitants. See Michael Roberts, *Sinhala Consciousness in the Kandyan Period 1590s to 1815* (Colombo: Vijitha Yapa, 2004).

13. S. G. Perera, Society of Jesuits (hereafter SJ), and M. E. Fernando, *Alagiyawanna's Kustantinu Haṭana* (Colombo: Catholic Press, 1932), x–xi.

14. Boxer estimates that the Portuguese converted no more than 10 percent of the island's inhabitants to Catholicism. See Boxer, "'Christians and Spices,'" 346. Recent census data suggests that the number of all Christians in Sri Lanka remains just under 10 percent.

15. Alagiyavanna's poetry is the subject of my next monograph project, tentatively titled: *Buddhist Poetry and Portuguese Colonialism in Early Modern Sri Lanka* (under consideration).

16. Charles Hallisey, "Works and Persons in Sinhala Literary Culture," in *Literary Cultures in History: Reconstructions from South Asia*, ed. Sheldon Pollock (Berkeley: University of California Press, 2003), 790–91.

17. I heard this folk legend in June 2006 from Herbert Kumar Alagiyawanna, a Sri Lankan author who is descended from the famous early modern poet.

18. Perera and Fernando, *Alagiyawanna's Kustantinu Haṭana*, vii. Doubts about the composition of *Subhāṣitaya* in 1611 are expressed chiefly because it abuts Alagiyavanna's conversion around 1612. This objection, however, is mainly based on the (debatable) conclusion that the poet had become a faithful Catholic by this time.

19. P. E. Pieris, *The Ceylon Littoral 1593*, reprinted in Paulus Edward Pieris, *Sir Paul E. Pieris' Selected Writings* (New Delhi: Navrang, 1995), 9.

20. The striking similarities between *Kustantīnu Haṭana* and Alagiyavanna's other works have been documented in Perera and Fernando, *Alagiyawanna's Kustantinu Haṭana*, xiv–xxiv.

21. Ibid., vv. 1–3.

22. Ibid., v. 126.

23. Ibid., v. 80.

24. Ibid., v. 22.

25. For similar arguments about the "harmonization" of Christianity and Sinhala culture in Alagiyavanna's work, see W. L. A. Don Peter, *Lusitanian Links with Lanka* (Ragama, Sri Lanka: W. L. A. Don Peter, 1979), 69.

26. Recent fieldwork on Sinhala Catholicism notes that despite the heightened emphasis on distinct religious identities in contemporary Sri Lanka, many Sinhala Catholics continue to visit Buddhist shrines and to draw on Buddhist ideas of asceticism and demons to supplement their religious worldview. See R. L. Stirrat, *Power and Religiosity in a Post-Colonial Setting: Sinhala Catholics in Contemporary Sri Lanka* (Cambridge: Cambridge University Press, 1992), 150.

27. Homi Bhabha, *The Location of Culture* (reprint, London: Routledge, 2008), 159–63.

28. R. F. Young and G. S. B. Senanayaka, *The Carpenter-Heretic: A Collection of Buddhist Stories about Christianity from 18th-Century Sri Lanka* (Colombo: Karunaratne & Sons, 1998), 14–15. Even some Portuguese officials, churchmen, and chroniclers in the seventeenth century recognized and bemoaned the "tyrannies" that some of their countrymen inflicted on the local inhabitants. See, for example, V. Perniola, *The Catholic Church in Sri Lanka: The Portuguese Period, Volume II, 1566 to 1619* (Dehiwala, Sri Lanka: Tisara Publishers, 1991), 316.

29. Young and Senanayaka, *Carpenter-Heretic*, 17–18.

30. Ibid., 11.

31. Ibid., 87.

32. Ibid., 92.

33. James C. Scott, *Domination and the Arts of Resistance: Hidden Transcripts* (New Haven: Yale University Press, 1990), 117–18.

34. K. D. Somadasa, ed., *Catalogue of the Hugh Nevill Collection of Sinhalese Manuscripts in the British Library*, vol. 2 (London: British Library and Pali Text Society, 1989), 65.

35. Elizabeth J. Harris, *Theravāda Buddhism and the British Encounter: Religious, Missionary and Colonial Experience in Nineteenth Century Sri Lanka* (London: Routledge, 2006), 53.

36. Young and Senanayaka, *Carpenter-Heretic*, 6.

37. Stephen C. Berkwitz, "Resisting the Global in Buddhist Nationalism: Venerable Soma's Discourse of Decline and Reform," *Journal of Asian Studies* 67, no. 1 (2008), 90–91.

38. Kitsiri Malalgoda, *Buddhism in Sinhalese Society 1750–1900: A Study of Religious Revival and Change* (Berkeley: University of California Press, 1976), 228–30.

39. Moves to establish Buddhist schools to counter the missionary institutes were slow and halting for several decades. Only in the latter part of the nineteenth century, with the assistance of Colonel Henry Steel Olcott and the Ceylon branch of the Theosophical Society that he founded, did efforts to establish Buddhist schools meet with success. For an account of the influence of Colonel Olcott on Ceylon, see Stephen R. Prothero, *The White Buddhist: The Asian Odyssey of Henry Steel Olcott* (Bloomington: Indiana University Press, 1996).

40. See, for example, Beth Baron's essay, "The Port Said Orphan Scandal of 1933: Colonialism, Islamism, and the Egyptian Welfare State," in this volume.

41. H. L. Seneviratne, *The Work of Kings: The New Buddhism in Sri Lanka* (Chicago: University of Chicago Press, 1999), 28–31.

42. Ibid., 34–35.

43. Ananda Guruge, ed., *The Return to Righteousness: A Collection of Speeches, Essays and Letters of the Anagarika Dharmapala* (Colombo: Department of Cultural Affairs, 1991), 512, 524–25.

44. Buddhist Committee of Enquiry, *The Betrayal of Buddhism: An Abridged Version of the Report of the Buddhist Committee of Inquiry* (Balangoda, LK: Dharmavijaya Press, 1956), 124.

45. Nira Wickremasinghe, *Sri Lanka in the Modern Age: A History of Contested Identities* (Honolulu: University of Hawai'i Press, 2005), 184.

46. See Heather J. Sharkey's essay, "The Gospel in Arabic Tongues: British Bible Distribution, Evangelical Mission, and Language Politics in North Africa," in this volume.

47. Buddhist Committee of Enquiry, *The Betrayal of Buddhism,* 5–7.

48. Walpola Rahula, *The Heritage of the Bhikkhu: A Short History of the Bhikkhu in Educational, Cultural, Social, and Political Life,* trans. K. P. G. Wijayasurendra (New York: Grove Press, 1974), 21–22.

49. Wickremasinghe, *Sri Lanka in the Modern Age,* 186.

50. Berkwitz, "Resisting the Global," 94–95.

51. Chamika Munasinghe, *Apē Dharma Katikāvata* (Imbulgoda, Sri Lanka: Senarath Publishers, 2004), 37–38.

52. Ibid., 38.

53. Ibid.

54. For an insightful discussion into the critiques of Christian proselytism by the Hindu nationalist Hindutva movement, see Kalyani Devaki Menon, "Converted Innocents and Their Trickster Heroes: The Politics of Proselytizing in India," in *The Anthropology of Religious Conversion,* ed. Andrew Buckser and Stephen D. Glazier (Lanham, MD: Rowman & Littlefield, 2003), 41–53. An important treatment of the logic that guides the politics of Hindutva may be seen in Sumit Sarkar, "Indian Nationalism and the Politics of Hindutva," in *Making India Hindu: Religion, Community, and the Politics*

of Democracy in India, ed. David Ludden (Philadelphia: University of Pennsylvania Press, 1996), 270–93.

55. Seneviratne, *The Work of Kings*, 159.

56. Munasinghe, *Apē Dharma Katikāvata*, 40.

57. Berkwitz, "Resisting the Global," 92.

58. Munasinghe, *Apē Dharma Katikāvata*, 43.

59. Gananath Obeyesekere, "Religious Symbolism and Political Change in Ceylon," in *The Two Wheels of Dhamma: Essays on the Theravada Tradition in India and Ceylon*, ed. Bardwell L. Smith (Chambersburg, PA: America Academy of Religion, 1972), 61–62.

60. John C. Holt, "Protestant Buddhism?" *Religious Studies Review* 17, no. 4 (1991): 309–10. See also Anne M. Blackburn's critique of the assumptions within the concept of "Protestant Buddhism" in her *Locations of Buddhism: Colonialism and Modernity in Sri Lanka* (Chicago: University of Chicago Press, 2010), 197–201.

61. Seneviratne, *Work of Kings*, 41. A more detailed discussion of the idea of "Protestant Buddhism" may be found in Richard Gombrich and Gananath Obeyesekere, *Buddhism Transformed: Religious Change in Sri Lanka* (Princeton: Princeton University Press, 1988).

62. Munasinghe, *Apē Dharma Katikāvata*, 47.

63. Ibid.

64. As of August 2011, *The World Factbook* of the U.S. Central Intelligence Agency estimated that 6.2% of Sri Lanka's population was Christian. Although most available statistics do not break the Christian population down into specific denominations, newspaper reports and informal interviews with residents often point to an increasingly visible presence of Charismatic Christians in the island.

65. For a discussion of the contemporary debates over Christian proselytization in Sri Lanka, see Stephen C. Berkwitz, "Religious Conflict and the Politics of Conversion in Sri Lanka," in *Proselytization Revisited: Rights Talk, Free Markets and Culture Wars*, ed. Rosalind I. J. Hackett (London: Equinox, 2008), 199–229.

66. On the colonial construction of discrete religious and ethnic identities in Sri Lanka, see Nira Wickremasinghe, *Ethnic Politics in Colonial Sri Lanka* (New Delhi: Vikas, 1995).

6. The Port Said Orphan Scandal of 1933: Colonialism, Islamism, and the Egyptian Welfare State

1. For brief accounts of the Turkiyya Hassan affair or its context, see B. L. Carter, "On Spreading the Gospel to Egyptians Sitting in Darkness: The Political Problem of Missionaries in Egypt in the 1930s," *Middle Eastern Studies* 20, no. 4 (October 1984): 24; Umar Ryad, "Muslim Responses to Missionary Activity in Egypt: With a Special Reference to the Al-Azhar High Corps of 'Ulama (1925–1935)," in *New Faith in Ancient Lands:*

Western Missions in the Middle East in the Nineteenth and Early Twentieth Centuries, ed. Heleen Murre-van den Berg (Leiden: Brill, 2006), 291–92; Heather J. Sharkey, *American Evangelicals in Egypt: Missionary Encounters in an Age of Empire* (Princeton: Princeton University Press, 2008), 124–29; and Khalid Naʿim, *Tarikh Jamʿiyyat muqawamat al-tansir al-misriyya (1927–33)* (Cairo: Kitab al-Mukhtar, 1987).

2. See, for example, works by Ellen Fleischmann, Inger Marie Okkenhaug, Mehmet Ali Dogan, Cemal Yetkiner, Carolyn Goffman, and Betty Anderson.

3. See, for example, Heather J. Sharkey, "Muslim Apostasy, Christian Conversion, and Religious Freedom in Egypt: A Study of American Missionaries, Western Imperialism, and Human Rights Agendas," in *Proselytization Revisited: Rights, Free Markets, and Culture Wars,* ed. Rosalind I. J. Hackett (London: Equinox, 2008), 139–66.

4. Lewis R. Rambo, *Understanding Religious Conversion* (New Haven: Yale University Press, 1993), 5.

5. On the legal consequences of conversion in India, see Chandra Mallampalli's essay, "Missionaries and Ethnography in the Service of Litigation: Hindu Law and Christian Custom in India's Deccan, 1750–1863," in this volume; and also Gauri Viswanathan, *Outside the Fold: Conversion, Modernity and Belief* (Princeton: Princeton University Press, 1998).

6. Beth Baron, "Orphans and Abandoned Children in Modern Egypt," in *Interpreting Welfare and Relief in the Middle East,* ed. Nefissa Naguib and Inger Marie Okkenhaug (Leiden: Brill, 2008), 13–34; and Beth Baron, "Comparing Missions," 260–84.

7. Brynjar Lia, *The Society of the Muslim Brothers in Egypt: The Rise of an Islamic Mass Movement, 1928–1942* (Reading, UK: Ithaca Press, 1998); Richard P. Mitchell, *The Society of the Muslim Brothers* (1969; reprint, Oxford: Oxford University Press, 1993).

8. U.S. National Archives, RG 59, State Department (henceforth SD), 883.00/768, Enclosure 1, Maria Ericsson to Turkya, 8 September 1932.

9. U.S. National Archives, RG 84, SD 350/37/13/04, Egypt, Port Said Consulate, Strictly Confidential Files, Horace Remillard, American Consul, Port Said, to William Jardine, American Minister, Cairo, 26 June 1933, "The So-Called 'Missionary Incident' at Port Said." Thanks to Craig Daigle for helping me to decipher the U.S. National Archives and thus locate this report.

10. Presbyterian Historical Society (henceforth PHS), RG 209, Box 26, Folder 12, *al-Siyasa,* 14 June 1933. The American Mission subscribed to a press translation service, which summarized articles of interest in the Arabic press for the missionary and foreign communities; members of the Mission also worked as translators. In cases where the original Arabic and English have been compared, the translation has been found to be reliable. In cases where the original Arabic is not accessible, the translations provide an important record.

11. Sharkey, *American Evangelicals in Egypt,* 259.

12. PHS, RG 209, Folder 12, quote from *al-Balagh,* 16 June 1933, *Kawkab al-Sharq,* 21 June 1933.

13. U.S. National Archives, RG 59, SD, 883.00/768, Enclosure 1, Maria Ericsson to Turkya, 8 September 1932.

14. Ibid.

15. Ibid.

16. U.S. National Archives, RG 59, SD 883.00/768, A. W. Keown-Boyd, Ministry of the Interior, European Department, to George Swann, Chairman of the Inter-Mission Council of Egypt, 14 June 1933; PHS, RG 209, Box 26, Folder 12, *al-Balagh*, 16 June 1933.

17. Ibid.

18. PHS, RG 209, Box 26, Folder 12, *al-Siyasa*, 20 June 1933.

19. Sharkey, *American Evangelicals in Egypt*, chapter 4.

20. PHS, RG 209, Box 26, Folder, *al-Jihad*, 12 June 1933.

21. *Al-Ahram* (Cairo), 13 June 1933, 1.

22. "A Port Said Missionary Incident," *Egyptian Gazette*, 15 June 1933, 4.

23. U.S. National Archives, RG 59, SD 883.404/43, Enclosure 4, Keown Boyd to George Swan, 1 July 1933, 2.

24. Ibid., 1.

25. "70,000 Guinea," *al-Fath* (Cairo) 7, no. 350, 28 Safar 1352/22 June 1933, 7; "The Port Said Missionary Incident: Minister of Interior's Statement," *Egyptian Gazette*, 16 June 1933, 6.

26. PHS, RG 209, Box 26, Folder 38, Letter from C. C. Adams, American Mission in Egypt, Cairo, to Dr. Anderson, Philadelphia, 26 June 1933, 1–2; U.S. National Archives, RG 59, SD 883.404/43 W. M. Jardine to Secretary of State, 8 July 1933, 7; John R. Mott, ed., *Conferences of Christian Workers among Moslems 1924* (New York: International Missionary Council, 1924), 98.

27. "70,000 Guinea," *al-Fath*; "The Port Said Missionary Incident," *Egyptian Gazette*, 6.

28. PHS, RG 209, Box 26, Folder 12, *al-Balagh*, 16 June 1933, 8.

29. PHS, RG 209, Box 26, Folder 38, Letter from C. C. Adams, American Mission in Egypt, Cairo, to Dr. Anderson, Philadelphia, 26 June 1933, 4; Box 26, Folder 12, *Kawkab al-Sharq*, 23 June 1933, 24.

30. PHS, RG 209, Box 26, Folder 12, *Kawkab al-Sharq*, 22 June 1933; *al-Siyasa*, 23 June 1933.

31. PHS, RG 209, Box 26, Folder 12, *al-Jihad*, 24 June 1933.

32. PHS, RG 209, Box 26, Folder 38, Letter from C. C. Adams to Dr. Anderson, 26 June 1933, 1.

33. Ibid.

34. U.S. National Archives, RG 84, SD 350/37/13/03, Egypt, Port Said Consulate, vol. 82, J. Rives Childs, Second Secretary of Legation, Cairo, to Horace Remillard, American Consul, Port Said, 22 June 1933.

35. U.S. National Archives, RG 84, SD 350/37/13/04, Egypt, Port Said Consulate, Alice Marshall, Acting Principal, Salaam Mission Girls School and Orphanage, Port Said, to American Consul, Port Said, 24 June 1933; Horace Remillard, American Consul, Port Said, to Alice Marshall, 26 June 1933.

36. U.S. National Archives, RG 84, SD 350/37/13/04, Horace Remillard to William Jardine, 26 June 1933, "The So-Called 'Missionary Incident' at Port Said," 2.

37. Ibid., 2–3.

38. Ibid., 3–4.

39. Ibid., 5.

40. Ibid., 4.

41. Ibid., 2.

42. Ibid., 6.

43. PHS, RG 209, Box 26, Folder 38, C. C. Adams, American Mission in Cairo, 26 June 1933, to Rev. W. B. Anderson, Philadelphia.

44. U.S. National Archives, RG 59, SD 883.404/43, Enclosure 3, Swan to Keown-Boyd, Cairo, 26 June 1933.

45. Helmi Pekkola, *Jumalan Poluilla Islamin Eramaassa* (Porvoo, Finland: Werner Soderstrom Osakeyhitio, 1934), 7. I am very grateful to Merja Jutila, who translated sections of the work from Finnish to English.

46. Ibid., 218.

47. Ibid., 219–21.

48. Ibid., 221.

49. Ibid., 222.

50. Ibid.

51. U.S. National Archives, RG 59, SD 883.00/768, A. W. Keown-Boyd to George Swann, 14 June 1933; PHS, RG 209, Box 26, Folder 12, *al-Balagh*, 16 June 1933.

52. Pekkola, *Jumalan Poluilla Islamin Eramaassa*, 222.

53. U.S. National Archives, RG 59, SD 883.404/43, Enclosure 4, Keown-Boyd to Swan, Cairo, 1 July 1933.

54. Pekkola, *Jumalan Poluilla Islamin Eramaassa*, 218.

55. "al-Mujrim al-Akbar," *al-Fath* 7, no. 350, 22 June 1933, 8.

56. Ibid.

57. PHS, RG 209, Box 26, Folder 37, *al-Balagh*, 1 July 1933.

58. "Turkiyya Hassan," *al-Fath* 8, no. 353, 13 July 1933, 3.

59. Pekkola, *Jumalan Poluilla Islamin Eramaassa*, 224.

7. Robert Moffat and the Invention of Christianity in South Africa

1. See Clifton Crais, *White Supremacy and Black Resistance in Precolonial South Africa* (Cambridge: Cambridge University Press, 1992), 89; and Alan Lester, *Imperial*

Networks, Creating Identities in Nineteenth-Century South Africa and Britain (London: Routledge, 2001), for illuminating discussions here.

2. Paul S. Landau, *Popular Politics in the History of South Africa, 1400 to 1948* (New York: Cambridge University Press, 2010), 77.

3. Moffat to Alexander Moffat, 25 February 1822, in Isaac Schapera, ed., *Apprenticeship at Kuruman: Being the Journals and Letters of Robert and Mary Moffat, 1820–1828* (London: Chatto and Windus, 1951), 56–57; also cited by William Worger, "Parsing God: Conversations about the Meaning of Words and Metaphors in Nineteenth Century Southern Africa," *Journal of African History* 42, no. 3 (2001): 433. For "place of fish," a fine recent treatment is Nancy Schmidt, *Environmental Power and Injustice, A South African History* (Cambridge: Cambridge University Press 2003), 34ff.

4. Read's story is well told by Elizabeth Elbourne, *Blood Ground: Colonialism, Missions, and the Contest for Christianity in the Cape Colony and Britain, 1799–1853* (Montreal: Queen's University Press, 2002), 218–27; and by Doug Stuart, "'Of Savages and Heroes': Discourses of Race, Nation and Gender in the Evangelical Missions to Southern Africa in the Nineteenth Century," Ph.D. diss., University of London, Institute of Commonwealth Studies, 1994; Julia Wells, "The Scandal of James Read and the Taming of the London Missionary Society by 1820," *South African Historical Journal* 42 (2000): 136–60.

5. Several biographies of Moffat exist, including those by his son and wife, but most importantly, see Robert Moffat, *Missionary Labours and Scenes in Southern Africa* (London: R. Carter, 1843, and London: John Snow, 1846); Schapera, *Apprenticeship at Kuruman*; J. P. R. Wallis, ed., *The Matabeleland Journals of Robert Moffat, 1829–60* (London: Chatto and Windus, 1945); and Steve de Gruchy, "The Alleged Political Conservatism of Robert Moffat," in *The London Missionary Society in Southern Africa, 1799–1999*, ed. John de Gruchy, (Athens: Ohio University Press, 2000), 17–36, who lists more material on 194.

6. Martin Legassick, "The Griqua, the Sotho-Tswana, and the Missionaries, 1789 to 1840: The Politics of a Frontier Zone," Ph.D. diss., University of California–Los Angeles, History, 1969, 288 especially.

7. Janet Hodgson, "A Battle for Sacred Power: Christian Beginnings among the Xhosa," in *Christianity in South Africa: a Political, Social & Cultural History*, ed. Richard Elphick and Rodney Davenport (Cape Town: David Philip, 1997), 70. The Reverend Shaw quoted in Crais, *White Supremacy*, 101; "no idea of a spiritual" is from Samuel Broadbent, *Narrative of the Introduction of Christianity among the Baralong* (London: Wesleyan Mission House, 1865), 81–84 (January 1823); Moffat, *Apprenticeship*, 49, 264; and see Paul S. Landau, "Transformations in Consciousness," *The Cambridge History of South Africa*, vol. 1, ed. Carolyn Hamilton, Bernard K. Mbenga, and Robert Ross (Cambridge: Cambridge University Press, 2010), 392–448.

8. Moffat, *Apprenticeship*, 83, from 25 May 1823. Karel Schoeman, ed., *The Mission at Griquatown, 1800–1821* (Griquatown: Griqua Toerisme Veren/National Book Printers, 1997), 30 quoting Anderson.

9. See Henry Bredekamp and Robert Ross, *Missions and Christianity in South African History* (Johannesburg: University of Witwatersrand Press, 1995); Richard Elphick and Rodney Davenport, eds., *Christianity in South Africa* (Cape Town: David Philip, 1997); and John L. Comaroff and Jean Comaroff, *Of Revelation and Revolution*, 2 vols. (Chicago: University of Chicago Press, 1991 and 1997); for further context, J. D. Y. Peel, "For Who Hath Despised the Day of Small Things? Missionary Narratives and Historical Anthropology," *Comparative Studies in Society and History* 37, no. 3 (1995): 581–607; Peter Van der Veer, "Introduction," in Peter van der Veer, ed., *Conversion to Modernities: the Globalization of Christianity* (New York: Routledge, 1996), 1–23; and Gabriel Setiloane, *The Image of God among the Sotho-Tswana* (Rotterdam: Balkema, 1975).

10. Schapera, *Apprenticeship*, 253 (Moffat, Monday, 21 May 1827).

11. Ibid., and other material from this section: 241–60, 4 April to 11 June 1827.

12. Ibid., 241, entry for 5 April.

13. Neil Parsons, personal communication on Kurrechane and Kaditshwene.

14. Schapera, *Apprenticeship*, 266–67: Robert Moffat to Mary Moffat, Dithakong, 11 May 1827.

15. S. M. Molema, *Chief Moroka: His Life, His Times and His People* (Cape Town: Methodist Publishing House, 1951) in the 1920s gave Bogachu's father as Motlhware, a repeated family name, who was "Moroka's half-uncle," 146.

16. Thomas Arbousset and François Daumas, *Narrative of an Exploratory Tour of the North-East of the Colony of the Cape of Good Hope* (Cape Town: A. S. Robertson, 1846), 212; and Norman Etherington, *The Great Treks: The Transformation of Southern Africa, 1815–54* (London: Pearson Education, 2001), 137–38.

17. Schapera, *Apprenticeship*, 244; Moffat, *Missionary Labours*, 248ff., 10 April 1827.

18. Schapera, *Apprenticeship*, 246, 15 April.

19. Ibid., 141.

20. Robert to Mary Moffat, "Chuin," 25 April 1827, Schapera, *Apprenticeship*, 264.

21. Ibid., 256, 25 April. Other missionaries set up missions with the people of *ha-rotse* or *Bahurutshe* as it came to be written.

22. Ibid., 256, 25 April.

23. Cory Library, Rhodes University, Grahamstown, MS 1116, ms. Journals of the Rev. Francis Owen, signed 24 June 1839 (thanks to Sandy Rowoldt-Shell).

24. Moffat, in Schapera, *Apprenticeship*, 281–82.

25. Hoyt Alverson, *Mind in the Heart of Darkness: Value and Self-Identity among the Tswana of Southern Africa* (New Haven: Yale University Press, 1978), 125–26; Moffat, *Missionary Labours*, 257–58; Wesleyan Methodist Missionary Society Archives, SOAS, Journal of the Rev. Shrewsbury, 1829, fiche 69, box 301; and see David Chidester, *Savage Systems: Colonialism and Comparative Religion in Southern Africa* (Cape Town: University of Cape Town Press, 1996), esp. 156, 132.

26. See Landau, *Popular Politics in the History of South Africa*.

27. Ibid., chap. 4.

28. Drawing on Robert Moffat, "Mahuku a Morimo" (not "Marimo" as given in the catalogue), Kuruman Press, 1842, and "Mahuku a Morimo mo puon ea Secuana," 1847 (H 259), at the SOAS Senate House Library, London.

8. Missionaries and the Making of Colonial Notables: Conversions to Modernity in Eritrea and Ethiopia, 1890–1935

1. *Manuale d'industrie, arti e mestieri ad uso degli indigeni nelle due lingue italiano e tigrignà per cura della missione cattolica/Maṣeḥafe ṭebaben śerāḥen belhāt-nageden* (Asmara: Tipografia Francescana, 1914), 6. This volume appears to have been written by a missionary priest, Ezechio da Iseo, who was working under the direction of Camilo Carrara. See Giuseppe Puglisi, *Chi è dell' Eritrea?: Dizionario biografico* (Asmara: Agenzia Regina, 1952), 120.

2. Ibid., 8.

3. Galdino da Mezzana, *La missione Eritrea affidata ai frati minori cappucini di Milano* (Milan: Lanzani, 1912), 21.

4. Ethiopian Manuscript Microfilm Library (EMML) 1470, Addis Ababa University and Hill Monastic Manuscript Library, St. John's College, Collegeville, Minnesota.

5. EMML 1470, 142.

6. Bahru Zewde, *Pioneers of Change in Ethiopia: The Reformist Intellectuals of the Early Twentieth Century* (Oxford: James Currey, 2002).

7. Ibid., 49–52; Nicole Denise Saulsberry, "The Life and Times of Woldeab Woldemariam, 1905–1995," Ph.D. diss., Stanford University, 2001, 62–70.

8. Gustav Arén, *Envoys of the Gospel in Ethiopia: In the Steps of the Evangelical Pioneers, 1898–1936* (Stockholm: EFS Förlaget, 1999); and Karl Johan Lundström and Ezra Gebremedhin, *Kenisha: The Roots and Development of the Evangelical Church of Eritrea, 1866–1935* (Trenton, NJ: Red Sea Press, 2011).

9. Benedict Anderson, *Imagined Communities: Reflections on the Origins and Spread of Nationalism*, 2nd rev. ed. (London: Verso, 2002).

10. Partha Chatterjee, *Nationalist Thought and the Colonial World: A Derivative Discourse?* (London: Zed Books, 1986), 22.

11. Peter van der Veer, ed., *Conversion to Modernities: the Globalization of Christianity* (New York: Routledge, 1996).

12. "Land Tenure in Eritrea," in *Encyclopaedia Aethiopica* (henceforth abbreviated AE), vol. 3 (Wiesbaden: Harrassowitz Verlag, 2007), 500–501.

13. Irma Taddia, *L'Eritrea colonia, 1890–1952: Paesaggi, stutture, uomini del colonialismo* (Milan: Franco Angelli, 1986); Tekeste Negash, *Italian Colonialism in Eritrea, 1882–1941: Policies, Praxis, and Impact* (Stockholm: Almqvist, 1987); Jonathan Miran, *Red Sea Citizens: Cosmopolitan Society and Cultural Change in Massawa* (Bloomington: Indiana

University, 2009); Uoldelul Chelati Dirar, "Colonialism and the Construction of National Identities: The Case of Eritrea," *Journal of East African Studies* 1, no. 2 (2007): 256–76; and "Colonialism," in *AE*, vol. 1 (Wiesbaden: Harrassowitz Verlag, 2007), 774–79.

14. For an overview, see "Colonial History of Eritrea," in *AE*, vol. 2: 359–65.

15. Portuguese Jesuits and other Catholic missionaries had worked in the region in the sixteenth and seventeenth centuries, but the Ethiopian emperor Fāsiladas expelled them in the 1630s.

16. Mezzana, *La missione Eritrea*, 9; and "Lazarists," in *AE*, vol. 3, 526–27.

17. For overviews, see Uoldelul Chelati Dirar, "Church-State Relations in Colonial Eritrea: Missionaries and the Development of Colonial Strategies (1869–1911)," *Journal of Modern Italian Studies* 8, no. 3 (2003): 391–410; and "Missions," in *AE*, vol. 3, 979–81. A detailed Catholic mission history is Metodio Da Nembro, *Missione dei Minori Cappuccini in Eritrea (1894–1952)* (Rome: Biblioteca Seraphico–Capuccina, 1953).

18. The Waldensians are an Italian Protestant minority with late medieval origins. Following the Reformation, they allied themselves with the mainline Protestant churches. Some of the Swedes took great interest in the tradition of their Italian brethren: see *Missions-Tidning* (henceforth *MT*), 15 November 1926, 315–17. Waldensian-SEM relations are outlined in Lundström and Gebremedhin, *Kenisha: The Roots and Development of the Evangelical Church of Eritrea*, 211–13.

19. *MT*, 15 August 1926, 221–22. Tron's career is discussed in Lundström and Gebremedhin, *Kenisha: The Roots and Development of the Evangelical Church of Eritrea*, 365–66.

20. *Missions-Tidning Budbäraren* (henceforth *MTB*), 28 June 1931, 340–41.

21. *MT*, 15 November 1926, 317.

22. Mezzana, *La missione Eritrea*, 77–78.

23. Jonas Iwarson and Alessandro Tron, *Notizie storiche e varie sulla Missione Evangelica Svedese dell'Eritrea, 1866–1916* (Asmara: Swedish Evangelical Mission, 1918), 24.

24. Ibid., 41.

25. Cited in Lundström and Gebremedhin, *Kenisha: The Roots and Development of the Evangelical Church of Eritrea*, 304.

26. Mezzana, *La missione Eritrea*, 33.

27. Ibid., 63. For a later estimate, see Da Nembro, *Missione dei Minori Cappuccini*, 481. The Capuchins opened more schools after 1930, when they acquired schools of some expelled Swedish missionaries: ibid., 193–94, including fn. 61.

28. Jonathan Miran, "Missionaries, Education, and the State in the Italian Colony of Eritrea," in *Christian Missionaries and the State in the Third World*, ed. Holger Bernt Hansen and Michael Twaddle (Athens: Ohio University Press, 2002), 121–35; Berhane Teklehaimanot, "Education in Eritrea during the European Colonial Period," *Eritrean Studies Review* 1, no. 1 (1996): 1–22.

29. Dirar, "Church-State Relations," 391–410.

30. Mezzana, *La missione Eritrea*, 18.

31. Carrara, *Manuale d'industrie*.

32. For examples, see ibid., preface; and Tekeste Negash, "The Ideology of Colonialism: Educational Policy and Praxis in Eritrea," in *Italian Colonialism*, ed. Ruth Ben-Ghiat and Mia Fuller (New York: Palgrave-Macmillan, 2005), 112–13.

33. See for example the patriotic and even bellicose sentiments expressed by Carrara following the conquest of Libya, which he described as vengeance for the Italian defeats at Adwa and elsewhere: Mezzana, *La missione Eritrea*, 29–30.

34. Miran, "Missionaries," 129–32. The Lateran Accords resolved the question of the relationship between the Vatican and the Italian state, in part by granting sovereignty to the former and making Catholicism the "sole" religion of Italy. For a parallel discussion of the French Third Republic, see J. P. Daughton, *An Empire Divided: Religion, Republicanism, and the Making of French Colonialism, 1880–1914* (Oxford: Oxford University Press, 2006).

35. Evangeliska Fosterlandsstiftelsen (Swedish Evangelical Mission), *Berhān yeḥun sebekat zāntā wédo nehezebi 'ityoṗyā/Sia la Luce! Prediche, racconti, e spiegazioni edificanti per il popolo etiopico* (Asmara: Tipografia della Missione Svedese, 1912), 23–25. See also Iwarson and Tron, *Notizie storiche e varie sulla Missione Evangelica Svedese dell'Eritrea*, which as an Italian-language publication seems aimed at potentially skeptical Italian audiences.

36. Evangeliska Fosterlandsstiftelsen (Swedish Evangelical Mission), *Consigli ai maestri e programma d'insegnamento* (Asmara: Tipografia della Missione Svedese, 1917), preface.

37. Iwarson and Tron, *Notizie storiche e varie sulla Missione Evangelica Svedese dell'Eritrea*, 28–29 and 13–15. In 1906, the Italian traveler Renato Paoli voiced a similar objection to the teaching of German at a Swedish mission school: Renato Paoli, *Nella colonia Eritrea* (Milan: Fratelli Treves, 1908), 181–87. See also the discussion of this issue in Miran, "Missionaries," 125–27.

38. Lundström and Gebremedhin, *Kenisha: The Roots and Development of the Evangelical Church of Eritrea*, 365–71.

39. Iwarson and Tron, *Notizie storiche e varie sulla Missione Evangelica Svedese dell'Eritrea*," 19.

40. Lundström and Gebremedhin, *Kenisha: The Roots and Development of the Evangelical Church of Eritrea*, 360.

41. Ibid., 365–71.

42. Johannes Launhardt, *Evangelicals in Addis Ababa (1919–1991): With Special Reference to the Ethiopian Evangelical Church Mekane Yesus and the Addis Ababa Synod* (Münster: Lit Verlag, 2004), 34–35; and Zewde, *Pioneers of Change in Ethiopia*, 35–78.

43. Lundström and Gebremedhin, *Kenisha: The Roots and Development of the Evangelical Church of Eritrea*, 368.

44. Arén, *Envoys of the Gospel in Ethiopia*, 453–536; Launhardt, *Evangelicals in Addis Ababa*, 70–88; and Lundström and Gebremedhin, *Kenisha: The Roots and Development of the Evangelical Church of Eritrea*, 410–25. See also Ernst Bauerochse, *A Vision Finds Fulfillment: Hermannsburg Mission in Ethiopia* (Berlin: Lit Verlag, 2008), 26–27.

45. For an overview, see "Education," in *AE*, vol. 2, 228–37.

46. Many Christian elites had a limited interest in reading and writing: "Çäwa," in *AE*, vol. 1, 703.

47. European missionaries were not always supportive of local language literacy: according to former student Yaqob Walda Maryam, the instructors at his Catholic mission school in Ethiopia burned Amharic and Oromo books in the 1930s: Yaqob Walda Maryam, *Brief Autobiography and Selected Articles* (Addis Ababa: Artistic Printing Press, 2003), 22.

48. Giuseppe Fumagalli, *Bibliografia etiopica: catalogo descrittivo e ragionato degli scritti pubblicati dalla invenzione della stampa fino a tutto il 1891* (Milan: Ulrico Hoepli, 1893), 271.

49. For an overview of Ethiopian printing during this same period, see "Printing," in *AE*, vol. 4, 217–18.

50. Iwarson and Tron, *Notizie storiche e varie sulla Missione Evangelica Svedese dell'Eritrea*, 36–39; Da Nembro, *Missione dei Minori Cappuccini*, 475–79. Complete surveys of the Eritrean mission press publications can be found in Stephen Wright, *Ethiopian Incunabula* (Addis Ababa: n.p., 1967).

51. For a summary, see "Berhan yekun," *AE*, vol. 1, 535.

52. Saulsberry, "The Life and Times of Woldeab Woldemariam,"62–70; John Bunyan, *Magedi krestyān*, trans. Teresa de Pertis and Bairu Okbit (Asmara: Missione Evangelica, 1934); Iwarson and Tron, *Notizie storiche e varie sulla Missione Evangelica Svedese dell'Eritrea*, 37. For a detailed discussion of the operations of a mission press, see Mezzana, *La missione Eritrea*, 72–76.

53. Renato Paoli, *Nella colonia Eritrea*, 202; Pier Ludovico Occhini, *Viaggi, una gita nell'Eritrea, ricordi dell'Italia irredenta* (Città di Castello: S. Lapi, 1908), 174–75. Items from one such library are now preserved in Uppsala University Library. See for example the Amharic edition of Pilgrim's Progress that contains a list of borrowers: John Bunyan, *Yakrestiyān manged kazih 'ālam wada zlālam ḥeywat yamiwased*, trans. Gabra Giyorgis Tarfa and Martin Flad (Monkullo, Eritrea: EFS, the Religious Tract Society, and the London Society for Promoting Christianity among the Jews, 1892).

54. Lundström and Gebremedhin, *Kenisha: The Roots and Development of the Evangelical Church of Eritrea*, 464.

55. Arén, *Envoys of the Gospel in Ethiopia*, 254–55. In 1906, Renato Paoli met a young Eritrean student of the Swedish Mission school with a remarkable number of books in Arabic, Tigre, Tigrinya, and German: Paoli, *Nella colonia Eritrea*, 175–76.

56. Gabra Heywet Bāykadāñ's work was published serially in the 1920s, and as the editor of *Berhānnā Salām* newspaper, Gabra Krestos Takla Hāymānot contributed a number of articles.

57. Ḥeruy Walda Śelāsé, *Ba'ityoṗyā yamigaleñ yamaṣāḥefet quṭer* (Addis Ababa: n.p., 1911/12) and *Ba'ityoṗyā yamigañu bage'eznā bāmāriñā qwānqwā yataṣāfā yamaṣāḥafet kātālog* (Addis Ababa: Tafari Makonen Press, 1927/8). These publication dates reflect a translation from the Ethiopian calendar.

58. Irma Taddia and Uoldelul Chelati Dirar, "Constructing Colonial Power and Political Collaboration in Colonial Eritrea," in *Personality and Political Culture in Modern Africa: Studies Presented to Professor Harold G. Marcus*, ed. Melvin Page, Stephanie Beswick, Tim Carmichael, and Jay Spaulding (Boston: Boston University African Studies Center, 1998), 30.

59. Berhanou Abebbe, *Hāymānot abaw qadamot: La foi des pères anciens* (Stuttgart: Steiner Verlag, 1986), 10.

60. Irma Taddia, "Correspondence as a New Source for African History: Some Evidence from Colonial Eritrea," *Cahiers des études africaines* 157 (2000). See also Tim Carmichael, "Bureaucratic Literacy, Oral Testimonies, and the Study of Twentieth Century Ethiopian History," *Journal of African Cultural Studies* 18, no. 1 (June 2006): 23–42. An excellent example of this trend is the work taken to be the first secular piece of Amharic literature, the 1864/65 work *Maṣḥafa ćawātā śegāwi wamanfasāwi (Book of Secular and Spiritual Diversions)* by Zannab, the personal secretary of Tewodros II and a Protestant through his contacts with the CMS mission of the mid-nineteenth century. This work is mentioned in *AE*, vol. 1, 703.

61. Cited in Saulsberry, "The Life and Times of Woldeab Woldemariam," 92.

62. On varieties of resistance, see Tekeste Negash, *No Medicine for the Bite of a White Snake: Notes on Nationalism and Resistance in Eritrea, 1890–1940* (Uppsala: University of Uppsala, 1986); Dirar, "Colonialism and the Construction"; and Taddia, *L'Eritrea colonia*, esp. 209–79. See also Roy Pateman, "Eritrean Resistance during the Italian Occupation," *Journal of Eritrean Studies* 2 (1989): 13–24. Events in Ethiopia are summarized in *Pioneers of Change in Ethiopia*, 201–7.

63. I borrow the useful phrase "living with colonialism" from Heather J. Sharkey, *Living with Colonialism: Nationalism and Culture in the Anglo-Egyptian Sudan* (Berkeley: University of California Press, 2003).

64. Irma Taddia and Uoldelul Chelati Dirar, "Essere acani nell'Eritrea italiana," in *Adua: Le ragioni di una sconfitta*, ed. Angelo del Boca (Rome: Laterza, 1997), 231–53; Miran, *Red Sea Citizens*, 183–216. See also the parallel case of Fuga communal identity and institutions of governance, described in Teclehaimanot Gebreselassie, "The Low-Caste Fuga Occupational Group under the Italian Administration in the Horn of Africa," *Northeast African Studies* (n.s.) 10, no. 3 (2003): 33–44.

65. Puglisi, *Chi è dell' Eritrea?*, 25. This example and those that follow come from this biographical dictionary of Eritrean notables. The descriptive detail of Puglisi's entries suggests that some of the subjects contributed to the production of their own biographies. The examples have been selected from among many similar entries in order to illustrate the trend.

66. Puglisi, *Chi è dell' Eritrea?*, 143.

67. Ibid., 158.

68. Ibid., 24.

69. Bairu Tafla, *Troubles and Travels of an Eritrean Aristocrat: A Presentation of Kantibā Gilāmikā'él's Memoirs* (Aachen: Shaker Verlag, 2007).

70. Mezzana, *La missione Eritrea*, 50.

71. Puglisi, *Chi è dell' Eritrea?*, 143.

72. Ibid., 118.

73. Ibid., 223.

74. Ibid., 145.

75. Ibid., 203. Haylé Tuku, Hagos Negusé, and Mohamed Saleh Hamid Hamden all used their education to pursue similar kinds of professional careers. See Puglisi, *Chi è dell' Eritrea?*, 145 and 160.

76. Mezzana, *La missione Eritrea*, 26.

77. Negash, *No Medicine for the Bite of a White Snake*, 43.

78. Benjamin Lawrance, Emily Lynn Osborn, and Richard Roberts, "Introduction: African Intermediaries and the 'Bargain' of Collaboration," in *Intermediaries, Interpreters, and Clerks: African Employees in the Making of Colonial Africa* (Madison: University of Wisconsin, 2006), 4. See also Frances Karttunen, *Between Worlds: Interpreters, Guides, and Survivors* (New Brunswick, NJ: Rutgers University, 1994).

79. Lawrance et al., "Introduction: African Intermediaries and the 'Bargain' of Collaboration," 20.

80. For an example of this view, see Mesfin Araya, "Eritrea 1941–52: The Failure of the Emergence of the Nation State: Towards a Clarification of the Eritrean Question in Ethiopia," Ph.D. diss., CUNY Graduate Faculty, 1988, 53–54.

81. This short biography is based on Gabra Mikā'él Germu, *Dagyāt Bāhtā Hāgos Saganayeti (Dağazmāč Bāhtā Hāgos [of] Saganayeti)* (Asmara: n.p., 1997).

82. Puglisi, *Chi è dell' Eritrea?*, 146.

83. Richard Pankhurst, personal correspondence with author, 23 January 2009.

84. For one of many examples in the Institute of Ethiopian Studies collection, see the copy of Tāyya Gabra Māryām (Ed.), *Maṣeḥafe sewāsew yage'ez qwānqwā mamāryā yamaṣeḥaf magelaċā* (Menkulu, Eritrea: Swedish Mission Press, 1889), with Gabra Mikā'él's signature on the frontispiece.

85. Gabra Mikā'el Germu, *Dagyāt Bāhtā Hāgos and Blātā Gabra 'Egzi'abhér Gilay Sā'edā Krestyān (Blātā Gabra 'Egzi'abhér Gilay of Sā'edā Krestyān)*, unpublished

manuscript in Tigrinya (n.d.). See also his newspaper articles, which include a critique of customary law and land tenure in *Nāy 'Éretrā sāmonāwi gāzéṭā (Eritrean Weekly News)*, 13 October 1944, and "Gabra 'Egzi'abhér Hāmāsanāy," *Ethiopia* (1961). I am grateful to Irma Taddia and Bairu Tafla for providing me with information on these works.

86. EMML 1467. Portions of this work appear to have been derived from another work in his private library. See EMML 1472, n. by Getatchew Haile.

87. It is telling that his work ends before the victory of Menilek's armies at the battle of Adwa, the "resounding protest" of colonialism. For other early historical assessments of Menilek, see Zewde, *Pioneers of Change in Ethiopia*, 141–58.

88. For a succinct summary of these, see Richard Reid, "The Trans-Mereb Experience: Perceptions of the Historical Relationship between Eritrea and Ethiopia," *Journal of Eastern African Studies* 1, no. 2 (2007): 238–55.

89. EMML 1470, 158.

90. Ibid. For the consequences of this turning point, see EMML 1470, 161.

91. His account appears to be the earliest historical treatment of this subject, and it is particularly valuable as a record of how the first generation of colonial Eritrean intellectuals began to perceive their own history in unique terms. The autobiography of Kantiba Gilamikā'él is also significant in this respect.

92. For one example of this charge, see Donald Crummey, "The Politics of Modernization: Protestant and Catholic Missionaries in Modern Ethiopia," in *The Missionary Factor in Ethiopia*, ed. Samuel Rubenson, Getatchew Haile, and Aasulv Laude (New York: Peter Lang, 1998), 85–99.

93. Dirar, "Church-State Relations," 406.

94. See for example his discussion of "heartbreaking scenes" at the mission school, Mezzana, *La missione Eritrea*, 33–35.

95. Ibid., 84.

96. This phenomenon has been particularly well studied in the SEM context by Arén, Lundström, and Gebremedhin. It is significant that indigenous converts were often the main targets of antimission Orthodox Christian sentiment.

97. See helpful discussion of this in Porter, *Religion versus Empire?*, esp. 316–30.

98. See the case of Gabra Baraki, cited on p. 168.

99. A number of his Eritrean contemporaries made similar choices, such as Fesseha Giyorgis and Gabra 'Egzi'ābhér Gilāy.

9. The Scholar-Missionaries of the Basel Mission in Southwest India: Language, Identity, and Knowledge in Flux

1. This paper would never have been written if the Rev. Dr. C. L. Furtado had not long ago given me a photocopy of the story of Lakshmi Kaundinya, the wife of Anandarao. I am extremely grateful to him for sharing this precious material, and for encouraging

me to delve into the archives of the Basel Mission. I am also grateful to the librarian and principal of Karnataka Theological College, Mangalore, who allowed me access to Basel Mission material several years ago. The former archivist of Basel Mission, Dr. Paul Jenkins, went out of his way to help a researcher from the Third World make the best use of the wealth of information available in the archival collections of Mission 21 at Basel. My thanks to him and the present archivist, Dr. Guy Thomas.

2. Regarding the history of the region's Christian communities, see Mathias A. Mundadan, *History of Christianity in India*, vol. 1 (Bangalore: Theological Publications in India, 1984); and Vijaya Kumar, *Ecumenical Co-operation of the Missions in Karnataka* (Delhi: Indian Society for the Promotion of Christian Knowledge, 2005).

3. See again Kumar, *Ecumenical Co-operation*, regarding details of the changing British-German relationship in India.

4. For a parallel discussion, see Chandra Mallampalli's essay, "Missionaries and Ethnography in the Service of Litigation: Hindu Law and Christian Custom in India's Deccan, 1750–1863," in this volume, as well as Gauri Viswanathan, *Outside the Fold: Conversion, Modernity and Belief* (Princeton: Princeton University Press, 1998).

5. For a postcolonial reading of "mission" and a more detailed analysis of Anandarao's conversion see my article, Mrinalini Sebastian, "Mission without History?: Some Ideas for Decolonizing Mission," *International Review of Mission* 93, no. 368(2004): 75–96.

6. The term "languages and nations" is drawn from Thomas R. Trautmann's seminal work, *Languages and Nations: The Dravidian Proof in Colonial Madras* (Berkeley: University of California Press, 2006).

7. Jon Miller, *Missionary Zeal and Institutional Control: Organizational Contradictions in the Basel Mission on the Gold Coast, 1828–1927* (Grand Rapids, MI: Eerdmans, 2003), 14.

8. In the Indian context the word "communalism" often carries a negative connotation. I persist in using it, however, to indicate the centrality of the "community of believers" to the worldview of the Pietists, and to many other newly formed Protestant groups at this time.

9. Jaroslav Pelikan, "Pietism," in *Dictionary of the History of Ideas*, ed. Philip P. Wiener, vol. 3 (New York: Charles Scribner's Sons, 1973), 493–95.

10. For further information on the education model of Halle and Francke's collection of natural objects and other artifacts in the *Kunst-und Naturalienkammer* and the influence of this educational model on two Indian intellectuals, see Indira Viswanathan Peterson, "Tanjore, Tranquebar, and Halle: European Science and German Missionary Education in the Lives of Two Indian Intellectuals in the Early Nineteenth Century," in *Christians and Missionaries in India: Cross-Cultural Communication since 1500*, ed. Robert Eric Frykenberg (Grand Rapids, MI: Eerdmans, 2003), 93–126.

11. Originally written in Latin, *Christianopolis* represented a Christian republic where Christian faith inspired a life of communism, teaching of the children in faith and

the sciences, and caring of the old, the sick, and the widows. For an English translation, see Felix Emil Held, trans., *Christianopolis: An Ideal State of the Seventeenth Century, translated from the Latin of Johann Valentin Andreae* (New York: Oxford University Press, 1914). Erich Beyreuther, *Geschichte des Pietismus* (Stuttgart: J. F. Steinkopf Verlag, 1978) considers *Christianopolis* an important influence on Pietist thinking.

12. Mark Larrimore, "Orientalism and Antivoluntarism in the History of Ethics: On Christian Wolff's 'Oratio de Sinarum Philosophia Practica,'" *Journal of Religious Ethics* 28, no. 2 (2000): 189–219.

13. Edward W. Said, *Orientalism* (New York: Pantheon, 1978).

14. For this reason the Basel Mission remained willing to cooperate with other mission societies, for example, by supplying missionaries for the work of the British Anglican Church Missionary Society (CMS) in Egypt during the first half of the nineteenth century. See Paul Sedra, *From Mission to Modernity: Evangelicals, Reformers and Education in Nineteenth-Century Egypt* (London: I. B. Tauris, 2011).

15. Paul Jenkins, *Texte und Documente: Kurze Geschichte der Basler Mission* (Basel: Basler Mission, 1989).

16. Miller, *Missionary Zeal*, 7.

17. Ibid., 15–16.

18. For a less acrimonious but still polemical discussion between the missionary and the "guru" of the Lingayat tradition in North Karnataka, see Herrmann Moegling, "Herrmann Mögling's diary of a brief visit to Hubli in 1838," in *Journeys and Encounters: Religion, Society and the Basel Mission in North Karnataka, 1837–1852: Translations and Summaries from Published Materials in German*, ed. Jennifer and Paul Jenkins, http://www.library.yale.edu/div/fa/Karnataka.htm, accessed 10 January 2011.

19. Amitav Ghosh, in "The Slave of MS. H.6," *Subaltern Studies VII*, ed. Partha Chatterjee and Gyanendra Pandey (Delhi: Oxford University Press, 1993), 159–220, investigates one of the earliest known references to the town of Mangalore, and to a slave who came from there, in an eleventh-century letter written by a Jewish merchant in Aden to a colleague who then lived in Mangalore. Ghosh's search for details about "Bomma," the slave mentioned in Geniza MS. H.6 of the National and University Library, Jerusalem, inspired his book *In an Antique Land* (Delhi: Ravi Dayal, 1992).

20. Wilhelm Schlatter, *Geschichte der Basler Mission 1815–1915, mit besonderer Berücksichtigung der ungedruckten Quelle; II Band: Die Geschichte der Basler Mission in Indien und China* (Basel: Verlag der Basler Missionsbuchhandlung, 1916), 17.

21. The apparent discrepancy in population figures is created by the fact that one pertains to the District and the other to the city of Mangalore.

22. Anandarao Kaundinya, *Die Lebensgeschichte des H. Anandaraja Kaundinya* (Basel: Die evangelische Missionsgesellschaft zu Basel, 1853), 4, Archives of Basel Mission, Basel, Switzerland (henceforth BM), in Mission 21, C–1.3. Most of Kaundinya's writings are in German as he learned to speak and write the language fluently while he was in Basel.

23. Herrmann Gundert, "Hermann Moegling," trans. Christoph Steinweg and Elisabeth Steinweg-Fleckner, in *Hermann Moegling*, ed. Albrecht Frenz (Kottayam, India: DC Books, 1997), 90.

24. The missionaries misrepresented this worship of the Bhutas as "devil-worship."

25. It is hard to miss references to this "famous" conversion in the reports and other written documents of the Basel Mission. Gauri Viswanathan has analyzed the conversion of Anandarao Kaundinya based entirely on a reading of the official British court documents in her book *Outside the Fold* (1998). She also points out that the novel *The Outcaste*, by F. E. (Fanny Emily) Penny (1912), was inspired by this story. For more on the conversion, education, and career of Anandarao, see also my article, M. Sebastian, "Mission without History?" Regarding the conversion and death of his wife Lakshmi, see Jayakiran Sebastian, "The Baptism of Death: Rereading the Life and Death of Lakshmi Kaundinya," *Mission Studies* 28 (2011): 26–53. Anandarao's conversion and the publication in 1850 by Moegling of *Eerarru Patrike*, which contains an exchange of letters between Anandarao and his brother-in-law, is the focus of analysis of another essay: Parinitha [Shetty, *sic*], "Conversion, Contestation and Community: Missionary Dialogues," in *Zukunft im Gedenken/Future in Remembrance*, ed. Albrecht Frenz and Stefan Frenz (Norderstedt, Germany: Books on Demand GmbH, 2007), 132–52. In her appraisal of the pedagogic practices and educational institutions of the Basel Mission in Mangalore, Parinitha Shetty includes the case of Anandarao Kaundinya as an example of gradual conversion through "Christian" education. Even though missionaries described his conversion as a sudden transformation, it was "the result of a long and complex process, located largely within the mission school, of both reconstituting the prospective convert's understanding of the self and giving shape to his own subjective spiritual longings." Parinitha Shetty, "Missionary Pedagogy and Christianisation of the Heathens: The Educational Institutions Introduced by the Basel Mission in Mangalore," *Indian Economic and Social History Review* 45, no. 4 (2008): 509–51, see esp. 538.

26. This letter sent to Inspector Hoffmann of Basel Mission is written in English. Correspondence in English, Anandarao Kaundinya, Archives of BM, C-1.3.

27. Gundert, "Herrmann Moegling," 131–32.

28. Her age is mentioned in the petition that she filed in the court, asking for Anandarao's return to his family. See Viswanathan, *Outside the Fold*, 95.

29. Gundert, "Herrmann Moegling," 134.

30. Ibid.

31. Ibid.

32. Moegling seems to have taken a liking to these two young men and wanted to bring them to Basel. Anandarao's journals suggest that relations between Anandarao and Stephan were sometimes tense, but it is not clear if perceptions of their caste differentials were at play. In a letter sent home, Moegling comments that Herrmann (Anandarao) still had "some of the typical Brahmin pride—without knowing that himself—and Stephan, a

born Tamil Pariah—has still some of the pride of ordinary people who feel raised above their standing." See Gundert, "Herrmann Moegling," 136. This story of the high-caste and the "outcast" Christian converts does not proceed far because Stephan subsequently died of chickenpox.

33. Letter dated 7 January 1845, to Inspector Hoffman of Basel Mission (BM) Archives C 1.3.

34. For example, Moegling's senior colleague Hebich was staunchly opposed to such a move.

35. The first convert Abraham Manju joined the Mission in 1837 along with his daughter. He was a fisherman who had learnt about Christianity already in Calicut through a Tamil-Christian. Schlatter, *Geschichte der Basler Mission*, 20.

36. See the Appendix to the Report of Basel Mission, *Dreissigsten Jahresbericht der evangelischen Missionsgesellschaft zu Basel*, printed annual report of BM, 1845, 133–41.

37. Appendix to the Report of Basel Mission, *Dreissigsten Jahresbericht der evangelischen Missionsgesellschaft zu Basel*, printed annual report of BM, 1845, 139.

38. Viswanathan, *Outside the Fold*, 90, is of the opinion that the legal case against the conversion of Anandarao "marks precisely that point of transition between a policy of deliberate nonintervention and the enactment of legal measures to protect converts like Ananda against the imposition of caste disabilities." In fact, she even hints that there is a connection between this case and the draft of the Lex Loci Act published in 1845. This was the precursor to the Caste Disabilities Removal Act of 1850. Anandarao seems to have gained from the passing of this act. In a letter to the Committee written in 1852, Anandarao indicated that his wife Lakshmi preserved the documents of the property that he inherited. For details see Albrecht Frenz, *Freiheit hat Gesicht/Future in Remembrance: Anandapur-Eine Begegnung zwischen Kodagu und Baden-Wütemberg, Briefe, Berichte und Bilder versehen mit Einleitung, biografischen Skizzen und Anhang von Albrecht Frenz* (Stuttgart: Staatsanzeiger Verlag, 2003), 44.39. For details of the work among the Holeyas of Coorg see M. Sebastian, "Mission without History?" Anandarao bought the land for a coffee plantation that aimed to provide employment for the Holeyas who had decided to join Christianity. According to Schlatter, *Geschichte der Basler Mission*, 83, the plantation was almost ruined because of an insect attack in 1870. Though this was not an economically profitable project, it provided space for the resettlement of those people who were once the bonded laborers of the Coorgi landlords. The place continues to be called "Anandapura," a name selected by Moegling in honor of Anandarao Kaundinya. The special bilingual publication, Albrecht Frenz and Stefan Frenz, eds., *Zukunft in Gedenken/ Future in Remembrance* (Stuttgart: Staatsanzeiger Verlag, 2003), includes several contributions on Anandapura, Kaundinya, his German wife Marie Reinhardt, Moegling, Weigle, Pauline (widow of Weigle, later married to Moegling), and Kittel.

40. Kumar, *Ecumenical Co-operation*; Karl Rennstich, *Handwerker-Theologen und Industrie-Brueder als Botschafter des Friedens: Entwicklungshilfe der Basler Mission im*

19. Jahrhundert (Stuttgart: Evangelischer Missionsverlag im Christlichen Verlagshaus Gmbh, 1985); Jaiprakash Raghaviah, *Basel Mission Industries in Malabar and South Canara, 1834–1914: A Study of Its Social and Economic Impact* (New Delhi: Gian Publishing House, 1990).

41. Rennstich, *Handwerker-Theologen und Industrie-Brueder*, 111.

42. Raghaviah, *Basel Mission Industries*, 28.

43. Ibid., 31.

44. Somerset Playne, comp., *Southern India: Its History, People, Commerce, and Industrial Resources* (London: Foreign and Colonial Compiling and Publishing Co., 1914–1915 [*sic*]), 514.

45. Henry S. Wilson, "Basel Mission's Industrial Enterprise in South Kanara and Its Impact between 1834 and 1914," *Indian Church History Review* 14, no. 2 (1980): 90–104.

46. J. Sebastian, "The Baptism of Death"; Veena Maben, "Pauline Moegling: An Exceptional Mission Woman," in Frenz and Frenz, *Zukunft im Gedenken*, 324–43.

47. It was common for the Basel missionaries to get their brides sent from the homeland. In most cases these women only met their future husbands upon their arrival in India. For details see Dagmar Konrad, *Missionsbrauete: Pietistinnen des 19 Jahrhunderts in der Basler Mission* (Muenster: Waxmann Verlag, 2001).

48. Wilhelm Stamm, "Herrmann Anandarao Kaundinya: Zur 100-jaehrigen Wiederkher seines Tauftags, 6 Januar 1844," *Evangelisches Missionsmagazin* 1944 (Basel: Verlag der Basler Missionsbuchhandlung, 1945), 47; translation mine.

49. See Miller, *Missionary Zeal*. Johannes Zimmermann, a missionary of the Basel Mission in Africa, married a black woman Catherine Mulgrave in 1850 and then informed the Committee in Basel about the marriage. By marrying a non-European he had broken the rule of the Mission of not entertaining "too-familiar" relationships with the Africans. More importantly, by not seeking permission from the Committee before marriage he had breached the mission's marriage rules. Strikingly, the Committee reconciled itself to this fact. However, Miller notes that the mission refused to accept two other interracial marriages involving Africans (or descendants of Africans) in the 1880s. This reinforces my argument about the relationship between caste and race that theoretically made Brahmins and the Europeans siblings.

50. Basel Archives, Kaundinya File, BV, 316.

51. Trautmann, *Languages and Nations*, 13–41.

52. On the different positions held by Orientalists and Anglicists regarding suitable education for "natives," see Lynn Zastoupil and Martin Moir, eds., *The Great Indian Education Debate: Documents Relating to the Orientalist-Anglicist Controversy, 1781–1843* (Richmond, UK: Curzon, 1999).

53. Douglas McGetchin, Peter K. J. Park, and Damodar SarDesai, eds., *Sanskrit and "Orientalism": Indology and Comparative Linguistics in Germany, 1750–1958* (New Delhi: Manohar, 2004).

54. Douglas T. McGetchin, "The Sanskrit Reich: Translating Ancient India for Modern Germans, 1790–1914," Ph.D. diss., University of California–San Diego, 2002, 155.

55. In *Languages and Nations*, Trautmann uses this term to describe the extensive work on comparative grammar undertaken during the nineteenth century.

56. Hans Jürgens, "German Indology *avant la lettre*: The Experiences of the Halle Missionaries in Southern India, 1750–1810," in *Sanskrit and Orientalism*, 41–82, esp. 57.

57. Trautmann, *Languages and Nations*, 13–41.

58. Heidrun Brueckner, "Ferdinand Kittel in the Context of 19th Century German Indology," in *A Dictionary with a Mission: Papers of the International Conference on the Occasion of the Centenary Celebrations of Kittel's Kannada-English Dictionary*, ed. William Madtha et al. (Mangalore: Karnataka Theological Research Institute, 1998), 103–27.

59. Albrecht Frenz, "Linguists' Correspondence," in *Hermann Moegling*, 244–67, see esp. 247. Among texts collected and given to Tübingen University are Lakshmisha's *Jaiminibharata*, a collection of *Daasarapadagalu*, Bhimakavi's *Basavapurana*, Kumaravyasa's *Kannadabharata*, Virupaksha Pandita's *Cannabasavapurana*, and a collection of Kannada proverbs called *Kannadagadegalu*. Frenz indicates that the State Library of Württemberg has, in addition to the above-mentioned works, extracts from the Mahabharata.

60. The essay was published as "Ueber canaresische Sprache und Literatur," *Zeitschrift der Deutschen morgenlaendischen Gesellschaft* (henceforth ZDMG), vol. 3 (1848), 257–84, and has been translated by Karen Scherer into English as "On the Canarese Language and Literature," in *Herrmann Moegling*, 268–91. The author emphasized historical linkages between southwest India and East Africa, through oceanic trade.

61. Moegling, "Lieder Kanaresischer Sänger," ZDMG (1860): 502–16. In *Freiheit hat Gesicht*, Albrecht Frenz has included translations of these songs and a few others by Moegling, Gottfried Weigle and his wife Pauline. Some of these translations were printed as early as 1850.

62. Moegling, "Lieder Kanaresischer Sänger," 502, 505.

63. Weigle suggests that it was more likely that the Sanskrit-speaking people traveled to the south by sea rather than over the mountains. Scherer, "On the Canarese Language and Literature."

64. Ibid., 291.

65. Brueckner, "Ferdinand Kittel," 103–27; George Baumann, "A Few Intellectual Predecessors of Ferdinand Kittel in 19th Century Tuebingen," in *A Dictionary with a Mission*, 128–43.

66. For more on Kittel in the organizational context of Basel Mission, see Paul Jenkins, "Ferdinand Kittel in the Context of the Basel Mission as Organisation," in *An Indian to Indians?*, ed. Reinhard Wendt (Wiesbaden, DE: Harrassowitz Verlag, 2006), 195–210.

67. Miller, *Missionary Zeal*, 110.

68. Letter by Inspector Josenhans, 25 January 1855, cited in Wendt, *An Indian to Indians?*, 15.

69. See Sulochana S. Murthy, "Rev. F. Kittel: Literature Survey," in *A Dictionary with a Mission*, 243–44.

70. Madtha et al., *A Dictionary with a Mission*, 238–39. For the involvement of missionaries such as G. U. Pope and Robert Caldwell in linguistic studies in Tamil see Vincent Y. Kumaradoss, *Robert Caldwell: A Scholar-Missionary in Colonial South India* (Delhi: ISPCK, 2007); and Sumathi Ramaswamy, *Passions of the Tongue: Language Devotion in Tamil India, 1891–1970* (Berkeley: University of California Press, 1997).

71. Srinivasa Havanur, "Kittel's Dictionary as Used by Scholars Like M. Govinda Pai," in *A Dictionary with a Mission*, 57–64, see esp. 62.

72. U. P. Upadhyaya, *Tulu Lexicon: Tulu-Kannada-English Dictionary*, 6 vols. (Udupi, Karnataka: Rashtrakavi Govinda Pai Samshodhana Kendra, 1988).

73. Yakshagana is a form of folk dance and an important component of popular culture in the districts of Dakshina Kannada, Udupi, and Uttara Kannada in South India. It was popularized by the Kannada novelist Shivarama Karanth.

10. The Gospel in Arabic Tongues: British Bible Distribution, Evangelical Mission, and Language Politics in North Africa

1. Leslie Howsam, *Cheap Bibles: Nineteenth-Century Publishing and the British and Foreign Bible Society* (Cambridge: Cambridge University Press, 1991), xiii. The two most important histories of the British and Foreign Bible Society (henceforth BFBS) in the twentieth century are James Moulton Roe, *A History of the British and Foreign Bible Society, 1905–1954* (London: British and Foreign Bible Society, 1965); and Stephen Batalden, Kathleen Cann, and John Dean, eds., *Sowing the Word: The Cultural Impact of the British and Foreign Bible Society, 1804–2004* (Sheffield, UK: Sheffield Phoenix Press, 2004).

2. British and Foreign Bible Society, *The Gospel in Many Tongues: Specimens of the 734 languages in which the British and Foreign Bible Society has published or circulated some portion of the Word of God* (London: British and Foreign Bible Society, 1939).

3. By "variant" I mean here language set, e.g., Egyptian Arabic (specifically, the form spoken primarily by Muslims in the Delta) as one variant in which several books of the Bible eventually appeared.

4. Marshall McLuhan, *The Gutenberg Galaxy: The Making of Typographic Man* (Toronto: University of Toronto Press, 1962).

5. This 1903 Tunisian Luke has nothing inside to identify it as a BFBS imprint, judging from the copy in the Bible Society Archives at Cambridge University Library (henceforth CUL BSA). Copies of this edition were requested for a Lagos mission bookshop in 1912: "Very few of the Mohammedans in Nigeria can read the ordinary printed Arabic, but they are quite familiar with classical Arabic *in script*." Claude W. Wakeman

to Dr. Kilgour, Chingford, 20 July 1912, in CUL BSA/E3/3/21/1: Translations Dept. Correspondence, Arabic: Tunisian. On the Maghribi style of Arabic script, and on what distinguished it from other forms of Arabic calligraphy, see Sheila Blair, "Arabic Calligraphy in West Africa," in *The Meanings of Timbuktu*, ed. Shamil Jeppie and Souleymane Bachir Diagne (Cape Town: HSRC Press, 2008), 60–75.

6. See Joseph Errington, "Colonial Linguistics," *Annual Review of Anthropology* 30 (2001): 19–39.

7. Albert Hourani, *Arabic Thought in the Liberal Age, 1798–1939* (London: Oxford University Press, 1962). A new edition appeared in 1983.

8. Sumathi Ramaswamy, *Passions of the Tongue: Language Devotion in Tamil India, 1891–1970* (Berkeley: University of California Press, 1997), 190.

9. J. D. Y. Peel, *Religious Encounter and the Making of the Yoruba* (Bloomington: Indiana University Press, 2000), 11.

10. Benedict Anderson, *Imagined Communities: Reflections on the Origins and Spread of Nationalism*, 2nd rev. ed. (London: Verso, 2002).

11. A model for this kind of history is Ami Ayalon, *Reading Palestine: Printing and Literacy, 1900–1948* (Austin: University of Texas Press, 2004).

12. Eamon Duffy, *Marking the Hours, English People and Their Prayers* (New Haven: Yale University Press, 2006) , ix, 3.

13. See, for example, Duffy, *Marking the Hours*, illustration #42, 56.

14. Howsam, *Cheap Bibles*, 5–7.

15. Cambridge University Library holds a 1905 Egyptian colloquial Luke, *Injil Luka* (translated by John Gordon Logan of the Egypt General Mission, henceforth EGM, and printed by the American mission press in Boulaq, Cairo), which was published three years before securing the BFBS imprint. This 1905 EGM version included a short preface in Arabic, but the BFBS 1908 edition did not. Likewise, American missionaries of the Gospel Missionary Union in Morocco had included an explanatory note in a 1904 (pre-BFBS) edition of a "Moorish" Luke, explaining that the text was not in "grammatical Arabic" but rather "the Arabic spoken in Morocco," so that, with the "love and mercy of God," "it may be understood by all." BFBS authorities later removed it. CUL BSA E.S.C. Minute Cards, vol. 1, "Arabic: Moorish or Magrabi [*sic*]," entries for 25 May 1904; 3 October 1906; and 31 August 1907.

16. *Safr al-Mazamir, bil-lugha al-misriyya al-ʿamma*, Tabʾ bi-nafqat al-jamiʾa al-baritaniyya wal-ajnabiyya li-intishar al-kutub al-muqaddasa 1933. Identification of the BFBS as the publisher was the only note the BFBS wanted. The 1921 Algerian edition of the Gospel of Luke was missing even that. Editorial Superintendent to E. G. Steven of Depot Biblique, Tangier, Morocco, 6 September 1922, in CUL BSA E3/3/16/2: Translation Dept., Correspondence, Arabic (All Varieties).

17. John Alexander Thompson, *The Major Arabic Bibles: Their Origin and Nature* (New York: American Bible Society, 1956), 20–27.

18. Heather J. Sharkey, "Arabic Antimissionary Treatises: Muslim Responses to Christian Evangelism in the Modern Middle East," *International Bulletin of Missionary Research* 28, no. 3 (2004): 112–18.

19. Zwemer to Hooper, Cairo, 11 December 1917, in CUL BSA/E3/3/16/1: Translation Department, Correspondence, Arabic (All Varieties).

20. CUL BSA E.S.C. Minute Cards, Vol. 1, "Arabic," 12 May 1909.

21. Ibid., 28 July 1909.

22. See Qur'an 43:3.

23. CUL BSA E.S.C. Minute Cards, vol. 1, "Arabic: Moorish or Magrabi," 31 August 1907.

24. Percy Smith, "A Plea for Literature in Vernacular Arabic," *Moslem World* 7, no. 4 (1917): 333–42; "Another Plea for Literature in Vernacular Arabic," *Moslem World* 9, no. 4 (1919): 351–62; and "A Plea for the Use of Versions of Scripture and of Other Literature in the Vulgar Arabic," *Moslem World* 4, no. 1 (1914): 52–63.

25. In publishing Luke and John, Smith picked up work that had been started by Eric Nystrom (d. 1907), a Swedish evangelical missionary. CUL BSA E.S.C. Minute Cards, vol. 1, "Arabic: Versions for Algeria," 31 August 1907.

26. Writing under the pseudonym Abdul-Fady, Arthur T. Upson published *Arabic Simplified Parts I–X (Lessons 1–200)* (Cairo: Nile Mission Press, n.d. [1917]); and *High Lights in the Near East: Reminiscences of Nearly 40 Years' Service* (London: Marshall, Morgan & Scott, 1936).

27. Rev. Percy Smith, A.M.E.M. Constantine, Algeria, "A Further Plea and Justification for Literature in the Vernacular Arabic," typescript, 1919, in CUL BSA/E3/3/16/1: Translation Department, Correspondence, Arabic (All Varieties).

28. George Swan, *Lacked Ye Anything?: A Brief Story of the Egypt General Mission*, rev. ed. (London: Egypt General Mission, 1932), 53–54. Swan mentions that the EGM's effort to produce colloquial Bible translations began with a version of Luke in 1903.

29. Beth Baron, *The Women's Awakening in Egypt: Culture, Society, and the Press* (New Haven: Yale University Press, 1994); and *Egypt as a Woman: Nationalism, Gender, and Politics* (Berkeley: University of California Press, 2005), 12.

30. Israel Gershoni and James Jankowski, *Redefining the Egyptian Nation, 1930–1945* (Cambridge: Cambridge University Press, 1995), xiv.

31. Beth Baron, "Readers and the Women's Press in Egypt," *Poetics Today* 15, no. 2 (1994): 217–40. See especially 220.

32. Heather J. Sharkey, "Christians among Muslims: the Church Missionary Society in the Northern Sudan," *Journal of African History* 43 (2002): 51–75.

33. Lilian Sanderson, "The Development of Girls' Education in the Northern Sudan, 1898–1960," *Pedagogica Historica* 8 (1968): 120–21. The first government girls' secondary school had opened in Sudan in 1949 with 67 students. Sudan Government,

Report by the Governor-General on the Administration, Finance, and Conditions of the Sudan in 1949 (Khartoum: Sudan Government, 1951), 141.

34. John Ruedy, *Modern Algeria: The Origins and Development of a Nation* (Bloomington: Indiana University Press, 1992), 103.

35. UNESCO Institute for Statistics, "UIS Statistics in Brief: Morocco," available at http://stats.uis.unesco.org/ (accessed 6 March 2008). These are 2004 figures.

36. See, for example, Baron, "Readers and the Women's Press," 221–22.

37. Miss I. Scott Moncrieff to Kilgour, n.d. [April 1924], in CUL BSA/E3/3/16/3: Translation Department, Correspondence, Arabic (All Varieties). Some missionaries argued then and later that the rift between colloquial and literary Arabic was not quite so wide, or rather, that bridges could be built by promoting a simplified modern literary Arabic. Arthur T. Upson took this view. Later, a similar assumption informed the rural adult literacy projects supported by the American Presbyterians and the Coptic Evangelical (Presbyterian) Organization for Social Service (henceforth CEOSS). See, for example, Marjorie Dye, Davida Finney, Adib Galdas, and Samuel Habib, *Literacy– The Essential Skill* (New York: Committee on World Literacy and Christian Literature, 1964).

38. CUL BSA E.S.C. Minute Cards, vol. 1, "Arabic: Versions for Algeria," 25 June 1902.

39. CUL BSA E.S.C. Minute Cards, vol. 1, "Arabic: Moorish or Magrabi," 4 September 1907.

40. Noel Malcolm, "Comenius, Boyle, Oldenburg, and the Translation of the Bible into Turkish," *Church History and Religious Culture* 87 (2007): 327–62, see esp. 327.

41. E. W. G. Hudgell [to Kilgour?], report, "Sudanese Colloquial (Roman Type) Arabic 'Mark,'" 7 March 1930, in CUL BSA/E3/3/24/1: Translations Department Correspondence, Arabic: Sudan Colloquial. On the missionary "Romanization" of Sudanese Arabic, see Heather J. Sharkey, "Christians among Muslims"; and Sharkey, "Sudanese Arabic Bibles and the Politics of Translation," *Bible Translator*, Technical Papers, 62, no. 1 (2011): 37–45.

42. R. S. Macdonald to Dr. Kilgour, CMS mission, Akol, southern Sudan, 24 May 1930, in CUL BSA/E3/3/24/1: Translations Department Correspondence, Arabic: Sudan Colloquial.

43. Hudgell to Kilgour, "Sudanese Colloquial (Roman Type) Arabic 'Mark,'" 7 March 1930, and Hudgell to Kilgour, Port Said, 9 July 1930, in CUL BSA/E3/3/24/1: Translations Department Correspondence, Arabic: Sudan Colloquial.

44. British and Foreign Bible Society, *The Hundred and Twenty-Third Report of the British and Foreign Bible Society for the Year Ending March MCMXXVII* (London: Bible House, 1927), 2–3, 115–17.

45. The literature on British missions to North African Jews is meager. The major survey of the LMJ appeared in 1908, two years before the BFBS published its first

Tunisian Judeo-Arabic scripture. W. T. Gidney, *The History of the London Society for Promoting Christianity amongst the Jews, from 1809 to 1908* (London: London Society for Promoting Christianity amongst the Jews, 1908). See also R. Attal, "Les missions protestantes anglicanes en Afrique du Nord et leurs publications en judéo-arabe a l'intention des juifs," *Revue des études juives* 132, no. 1 (1973): 95–118.

46. Benjamin H. Hary, *Multiglossia in Judeo-Arabic* (Leiden: E. J. Brill, 1992), 72–78.

47. Confusion started around 1911 when the BFBS published a Judeo-Arabic translation for Tunisia, and called it "Tunisian" in the records; another Tunisian version—but a version based on the dialect of Muslims—appeared soon thereafter, and the BFBS had to find ways of distinguishing these texts in its records. For the next few years, BFBS officials tried to clarify the situation by variously calling the Judeo-Arabic version "Tunisian Yiddish," "Tunisian (Hebrew characters)," "North African Yiddish," and "Judeo-Tunisian," before settling finally in 1914 on "Judeo-Arabic of North Africa." However, the last term still managed to produce confusion vis-à-vis the Moroccan and Egyptian Judeo-Arabic versions! CUL BSA/E3/3/21/1: Translations Department Correspondence, "Arabic: Tunisian," April 1910–August 1912; and CUL BSA E.S.C. Minute Cards, vol. 1, "Arabic."

48. Jeffrey Heath, *Jewish and Muslim Dialects of Moroccan Arabic* (London: RoutledgeCurzon, 2002).

49. British and Foreign Bible Society, *Rules for the Guidance of Translators, Revisers, & Editors, working in connection with the British and Foreign Bible Society* (London: British and Foreign Bible Society, 1906). The BFBS periodically published revisions of these rules.

50. Problems like these beset the Moroccan Bible translation that Eric Fisk and several colleagues completed in 1953, though BFBS officials in London (who were by this time reluctant to publish a Bible for a very small market) grudgingly admitted that its translation was rigorous. CUL BSA/E3/3/23/1: Translations Department Correspondence, Arabic: North African Colloquial, 1955–58.

51. How many missionaries, for example, could have advised the Lutheran duo, "Messrs. E. Schnabel and U. Keysser," who translated Luke and the Epistles to the Thessalonians into "Kate," the language of "a Papuan hill tribe dwelling in the hinterland of Finschafen"? *Hundred and Twenty-Third Report of the BFBS*, 3. Likewise, how many could have advised Rev. C. E. Fox of the Melanesian Mission, when after twenty years residence on San Cristoval in the Solomon Islands, he completed the translation of the four Gospels and Acts in the "Arosi dialect" spoken in the western part of that island? British and Foreign Bible Society, *The Hundred and Eighteenth Report of the British and Foreign Bible Society for the Year Ending March MCMXXII* (London: Bible House, 1922), 3.

52. The BFBS representative for the Maghrib visited Tunis in 1924 and saw a depot stacked with copies of Judeo-Arabic translations: he speculated that the translator, Guiz (whom other sources identify as a former Jewish rabbi-turned-Christian) was persuading the BFBS to publish because he wanted fees from translation. Extract from the Rev. W.

H. Rainey to Boughton, Madrid, 8 July 1924, in CUL BSA/E3/3/16/3: Translation Department, Correspondence, Arabic (All Varieties).

53. The 1908 Egyptian Luke was apparently issued in a run of 2,000. CUL BSA E.S.C. Minute Cards, vol. 1, Arabic, 1 June 1910. In 1922 Swan of the EGM suggested a print run of 5,000 each for a revised Egyptian Luke and an Egyptian Genesis; an Algerian Gospel (presumably Percy Smith's translation of John) was printed around that time in a 5,000 print run. Extract of letter from J. Gordon Logan, EGM, 13 May 1922, and Robert Steven to Kilgour, Tangier, 10 May 1922, in CUL BSA/E3/3/16/2: Translation Department, Correspondence, Arabic (All Varieties).

54. I identified these versions by searching the Cambridge University Library catalogue by author, using the name of the chief translator for each edition.

55. CUL BSA E.S.C. Minute Cards, vol. 1, "Arabic," 12 May 1909, 28 July 1909, and 1 June 1910.

56. BFBS, *Hundred and Twenty-Third Report of the BFBS*, 117; "Stress, But Progress," *The Bible in the World* (June 1932): 91–94.

57. CUL BSA E.S.C. Minute Cards, vol. 1, Arabic: Algerian-Tunisian, entry on letter from L. R. Stedeford, Algiers, 18 February 1960.

58. Linda Colley, for example, calls Protestantism one of the "main cements of Great Britain" and key to its "invention"; she also emphasizes that it was distinctly pluralistic. Linda Colley, *Britons: Forging the Nation, 1707–1837*, 2nd ed. (New Haven: Yale University Press, 2005), 8, 18, 53–54.

59. John A. Patten, *These Remarkable Men: The Beginnings of World Enterprise* (London: Lutterworth Press, 1945); and Roger Steger, "'Without Note or Comment': Yesterday, Today, and Tomorrow," in *Sowing the Word*, 67.

60. William Canton, *The Story of the Bible Society* (London: John Murray, 1904), 202.

61. David Daniell, *William Tyndale: A Biography* (New Haven: Yale University Press, 1994).

62. British and Foreign Bible Society, *The Hundred and Twenty-First Report of the British and Foreign Bible Society for the Year Ending March MCMXXV* (London: Bible House, 1925), 1, 115.

63. Patricia Crone, *Meccan Trade and the Rise of Islam* (Princeton: Princeton University Press, 1987); Albert Hourani, *A History of the Arab Peoples* (Cambridge, MA: Harvard University Press, 1991).

64. Regarding the divisions that the British wrought in Palestine, for example, see Laura Robson's essay, "Church versus Country: Palestinian Arab Episcopalians, Nationalism, and Revolt, 1936–39," in this volume; and her book, *Colonialism and Christianity in Mandate Palestine* (Austin: University of Texas Press, 2011).

65. Niloofar Haeri, "Form and Ideology: Arabic Sociolinguistics and Beyond," *Annual Review of Anthropology* 29 (2000): 61–87; and Haeri, *Sacred Language, Ordinary People: Dilemmas of Culture and Politics in Egypt* (New York: Palgrave Macmillan, 2003).

66. Yasir Suleiman, A *War of Words: Language and Conflict in the Middle East* (Cambridge: Cambridge University Press, 2003), 82.

67. Suleiman, A *War of Words*, 66. Willcocks is reviled in works like Naffusa Zakariya Sa'id, *Tarikh al-da'wa ila al-'ammiyya wa-athruha fi Misr* (Alexandria: Dar Nashr al-Thaqafa, 1964), 17 and elsewhere; and Nabil 'Abd al-Hamid Sayyid Ahmad, *al-Ajanib wa-athruhum fi al-mujtama' al-misri, min sanat 1882 ila sanat 1992* 2 (Damietta, EG: Maktabat Nansi, 2004), 169–70. See also Heather J. Sharkey, "Christian Missionaries and Colloquial Arabic Printing," *Journal of Semitic Studies*, supplement 15: *History of Printing and Publishing in the Languages and Countries of the Middle East*, ed. Philip Sadgrove, published by Oxford University Press on behalf of the University of Manchester (2004), 131–49.

68. Extract from Mr. Athanassian to Dr. Kilgour, 14 December 1925, in CUL BSA/ E3/3/16/3: Translation Department, Correspondence, Arabic (All Varieties).

69. W. H. T. Gairdner to George Swan, 13 February 1925, in CUL BSA/E3/3/16/3: Translation Department, Correspondence, Arabic (All Varieties). Willcocks nevertheless sent the BFBS some copies, and these are now in CUL: the Gospels of Matthew and Mark, as *al-Arba' Bashayir bil-lugha a-misriyya, al-qism al-awlani: Bashayir Matta wa-Murqus*, trans. Sir William Willcocks (Cairo: Nile Mission Press, 1924); and the Acts of the Apostles, as *al-Khabr al-Tayyib Bita' Yasu' al-Masih, aw al-Injil bil-lugha al-'misriyya [no. 5], A'mal al-Rusul*, trans. Sir William Willcocks (Cairo: Nile Mission Press, 1926).

70. Willcocks, in the preface to *al-Arba' Bashayir bil-lugha a-misriyya*, 6: "Al-lugha al-misriyya taqriban hiya dhat al-lugha illi itakallim biha al-masih."

71. Suleiman, A *War of Words*, 67.

72. See Sharkey, "Arabic Anti-Missionary Treatises." Strikingly, Umar Farrukh, whom Yasir Suleiman describes as a fervent "language defender" against Arabic dialects (see 74), coauthored the most influential Arab nationalist critique of Christian missionaries. This was Mustafa Khalidi and 'Umar Farrukh, *al-Tabshir wa'l-isti'mar fi al-bilad al-'arabiyya*, 2nd ed. (Beirut: n.p., 1957).

73. See Heather J. Sharkey, *American Evangelicals in Egypt: Missionary Encounters in an Age of Empire (Princeton: Princeton University Press, 2008).*

74. References to these trends are scattered in the society's annual reports, which include commentaries and Bible sales figures.

75. Moshe Bar-Asher, *La composante hebraïque du judeo-arabe algerien (communautés de Tlemcen et Aïn-Témouchent)* (Jerusalem: Hebrew University, 1992), 14, 144–45.

76. On the impact of the Suez Crisis on missions in Egypt, see Sharkey, *American Evangelicals in Egypt*; and Sharkey, "Empire and Muslim Conversion: Historical Reflections on Christian Missions in Egypt," *Islam and Christian-Muslim Relations* 16, no. 1 (2005): 43–60.

77. Eric Fisk to W. J. Bradnock, 29 July 1956, in CUL BSA/E3/3/23/1: Translations Department Correspondence, Arabic: North African Colloquial.

78. Eric Fisk to W. J. Bradnock, Penrith, Cumberland, 5 June 1957, in CUL BSA/E3/3/23/1: Translations Department Correspondence, Arabic: North African Colloquial.

79. Communication by email from John Dean, formerly of the BFBS and the United Bible Societies, 3 April 2008.

80. Unable to acquire residency and work permits to stay in Algeria, the North African Mission eventually moved its base to southern France where there was a large Maghribi émigré community. Francis R. Steele, *Not in Vain: The Story of the North Africa Mission* (Pasadena: William Carey Library, 1981), 66–78.

81. Heather J. Sharkey, "Missionary Legacies: Muslim-Christian Encounters in Egypt and Sudan during the Colonial and Postcolonial Periods," in *Muslim-Christian Encounters in Africa*, ed. Benjamin F. Soares (Leiden: Brill, 2006), 57–88.

82. See, for example, Joel Beinin, *The Dispersion of Egyptian Jewry* (Berkeley: University of California Press, 1998).

83. Hafid Gafaïti, "The Monotheism of the Other: Language and De/Construction of National Identity in Postcolonial Algeria," and Djamila Saadi-Mokrane, "The Algerian Linguicide," in *Algeria in Others' Languages*, ed. Anne-Emanuelle Berger (Ithaca: Cornell University Press, 2002), 19–43 and 44–58; Heather J. Sharkey, "Arab Identity and Ideology in Sudan: The Politics of Language, Ethnicity, and Race," *African Affairs* 107, no. 426 (2008): 21–43.

84. Maurice Martin, "Statistiques chrétiennes d'Égypte," *Travaux et Jours* (Beirut) 24 (1967): 65–75.

85. Papers on the Van Dyck revision are in CUL BSA/E3/3/18: Arabic Translation Papers, 1949–57.

86. Canton, *Bible Society*, 202. There was, in fact, a bicentennial volume, a fascinating collection of essays on the BFBS in London, Britain, and abroad. This is Batalden, Cann, and Dean, *Sowing the Word.*

87. A compelling attempt to retrieve this history of local Christians, in the South Indian context, is found in M. Sebastian, "Reading Archives from a Postcolonial Feminist Perspective."

88. Colporteurs and Bible Women did keep records, and showed these to British agents, who used them to compile reports. A few remarkable accounts from Egypt survive, dating from 1869 to 1871; these are from a German-speaking colporteur named Schlotthauer who described his Bible-selling ventures in Lower Egypt. The Rev. A. Thomson translated and recorded portions of them verbatim into his agent's book. This was from a period when the BFBS itself participated more heavily in manuscript culture! See, for example, "Book distribution in Egypt during 1870 by Mr. Schlotthauer, rec. August 14, 1871," in CUL BSA Agent's Book, no. 133, Rev. A. Thomson (1871). In December 2007, Kathleen Cann of Cambridge University Library told me that some logbooks of Viennese colporteurs were discovered in an Austrian library; these have since been sent to Cambridge. Maybe others survive elsewhere?

Bibliography

Archival Sources

Basel Mission Archives, Basel, Switzerland (BM)

Bellary District Records, Tamil Nadu Archives, Chennai, India (BDR)

British Library, Oriental and India Office Collection, London, United Kingdom (OIOC)

Cambridge University Library, Bible Society Archives, Cambridge, United Kingdom (CUL BSA)

Church Missionary Society Archives, Birmingham, United Kingdom (CMS)

Colonial Office, National Archives, London, United Kingdom (CO)

Cory Library, Rhodes University, Grahamstown, South Africa

Ethiopian Manuscript Microfilm Library, Addis Ababa University and Hill Monastic Manuscript Library, St. John's College, Collegeville, Minnesota (EMML)

Jerusalem and East Mission Archives, Middle East Centre, St. Antony's College, Oxford, United Kingdom (JEM)

Lambeth Palace Archives, London, United Kingdom (LPA)

London School of Economics Archives, London, United Kingdom (LSE)

National Archive of Zambia, Lusaka, Zambia (NAZ)

National Library of Scotland, Edinburgh, United Kingdom (NLS)

Presbyterian Historical Society, Philadelphia, Pennsylvania (PHS)

School of Oriental and African Studies, Special Collections, University of London, London, United Kingdom (SOAS)

United Church of Zambia Archives, Mindolo, Kitwe, Zambia (UCZA)

United States National Archives, State Department Records, Washington, D.C. (SD)

White Fathers Archives, Lusaka, Zambia (WFA)

Archived Periodicals

al-Ahram (Cairo)
The Bible in the World (London)
Egyptian Gazette (Cairo)
al-Fath (Cairo)
Filastin (Jaffa)
Missions-Tidning (Stockholm)
Missions-Tidning Budbäraren (Stockholm)
Palestine Post (Jerusalem)
Transactions of the London Missionary Society (London)

Works Cited

Abboushi, W. F. "The Road to Rebellion: Arab Palestine in the 1930's." *Journal of Palestine Studies* 6, no. 3 (spring 1977): 23–46.

Abdul-Fady [Arthur T. Upson]. *Arabic Simplified Parts I–X (Lessons 1–200)*. Cairo: Nile Mission Press, n.d. [1917].

———. *High Lights in the Near East: Reminiscences of Nearly 40 Years' Service*. London: Marshall, Morgan & Scott, 1936.

Abebbe, Berhanou. *Hāymānot abaw qadamot: La foi des pères anciens*. Stuttgart: Steiner Verlag, 1986.

Abu El-Assal, Riah. *Caught in Between: The Story of an Arab Palestinian Christian Israeli*. London: SPCK, 1999.

Ahmad, Nabil 'Abd al-Hamid Sayyid. *al-Ajanib wa-athruhum fi al-mujtama' al-misri, min sanat 1882 ila sanat 1992*. Vol. 2. Damietta, Egypt: Maktabat Nansi, 2004.

Alverson, Hoyt. *Mind in the Heart of Darkness: Value and Self-Identity among the Tswana of Southern Africa*. New Haven: Yale University Press, 1978.

Anderson, Benedict. *Imagined Communities: Reflections on the Origin and Spread of Nationalism*. 2nd rev. ed. London: Verso, 1991.

Anonymous. *Memoir of the Late Rev. Samuel William Flavel, of the Bellary Mission*. Bellary: Mission Press, 1848.

Araya, Mesfin. "Eritrea 1941–52: The Failure of the Emergence of the Nation State: Towards a Clarification of the Eritrean Question in Ethiopia." Ph.D. diss., CUNY Graduate Faculty, 1988.

Arbousset, Thomas, and François Daumas. *Narrative of an Exploratory Tour of the North-East of the Colony of the Cape of Good Hope.* Cape Town: A. S. Robertson, 1846.

Arén, Gustav. *Envoys of the Gospel in Ethiopia: In the Steps of the Evangelical Pioneers, 1898–1936.* Stockholm: EFS Förlaget, 1999.

Asad, Talal. *Formations of the Secular: Christianity, Islam, Modernity.* Stanford: Stanford University Press, 2003.

Attal, R. "Les missions protestantes anglicanes en Afrique du Nord et leurs publications en judéo-arabe a l'intention des juifs.'" *Revue des études juives* 132, no. 1 (1973): 95–118.

Austin, Alvyn, and Jamie S. Scott, eds. *Canadian Missionaries, Indigenous Peoples: Representing Religion at Home and Abroad.* Toronto: University of Toronto Press, 2004.

Ayalon, Ami. *Reading Palestine: Printing and Literacy, 1900–1948.* Austin: University of Texas Press, 2004.

Bar-Asher, Moshe. *La composante hebraïque du judeo-arabe algerien (communautés de Tlemcen et Aïn-Témouchent).* Jerusalem: Hebrew University, 1992.

Baron, Beth. "Readers and the Women's Press in Egypt." *Poetics Today* 15, no. 2 (1994): 217–40.

———. *The Women's Awakening in Egypt: Culture, Society, and the Press.* New Haven: Yale University Press, 1994.

———. *Egypt as a Woman: Nationalism, Gender, and Politics.* Berkeley: University of California Press, 2005.

———. "Orphans and Abandoned Children in Modern Egypt." In *Interpreting Welfare and Relief in the Middle East,* edited by Nefissa Naguib and Inger Marie Okkenhaug. Leiden: Brill, 2008, 13–34.

———. "Comparing Missions: Pentecostal and Presbyterian Orphanages on the Nile." In *American Missionaries in the Middle East: Foundational Encounters,* edited by Mehmet Ali Doğan and Heather J. Sharkey. Salt Lake City: University of Utah Press, 2011, 260–84.

Basler Mission (Basel Mission). *Dreissigsten Jahresbericht der evangelischen Missionsgesellschaft zu Basel.* Basel: Basler Mission, 1845.

Batalden, Stephen, Kathleen Cann, and John Dean, eds. *Sowing the Word: The Cultural Impact of the British and Foreign Bible Society, 1804–2004.* Sheffield, UK: Sheffield Phoenix Press, 2004.

Bauerochse, Ernst. *A Vision Finds Fulfillment: Hermannsburg Mission in Ethiopia*. Berlin: Lit Verlag, 2008.

Baumann, George. "A Few Intellectual Predecessors of Ferdinand Kittel in 19th Century Tuebingen." In *A Dictionary with a Mission: Papers of the International Conference on the Occasion of the Centenary Celebrations of Kittel's Kannada-English Dictionary*, edited by William Madtha et al. Mangalore: Karnataka Theological Research Institute, 1998, 128–43.

Bayart, Jean-François. "Fait missionnaire et politique du ventre: une lecture foucaldienne." *Le Fait Missionnaire* (Lausanne) 6 (1998): 9–38.

———. "Missionary Activity and the Politics of the Belly." In *Readings in Modernity in Africa*, edited by Peter Geschiere, Birgit Meyer, and Peter Pels. Bloomington: Indiana University Press, 2008, 92–98.

Bayly, C. A. *The Birth of the Modern World, 1780–1914*. Oxford: Blackwell, 2004.

Beaver, R. Pierce. *American Protestant Women in World Mission: History of the First Feminist Movement in North America*. Rev. ed. Grand Rapids, MI: William B. Eerdmans, 1980.

Beidelman, Thomas O. "Social Theory and Christian Missions in Africa." *Africa: Journal of the International African Institute* 44, no. 3 (1974): 235–49.

———. *Colonial Evangelism: A Socio-Economic Study of an East African Mission at the Grassroots*. Bloomington: Indiana University Press, 1982.

Beinin, Joel. *The Dispersion of Egyptian Jewry*. Berkeley: University of California Press, 1998.

"Berhan yekun." In *Encyclopaedia Aethiopica*, edited by Siegbert Uhlig et al. Vol. 1. Wiesbaden: Harrassowitz Verlag, 2007, 535.

Berkwitz, Stephen C. "Resisting the Global in Buddhist Nationalism: Venerable Soma's Discourse of Decline and Reform." *Journal of Asian Studies* 67, no. 1 (2008): 73–106.

———. "Religious Conflict and the Politics of Conversion in Sri Lanka." In *Proselytization Revisited: Rights Talk, Free Markets and Culture Wars*, edited by Rosalind I. J. Hackett. London: Equinox, 2008, 199–229.

Beyreuther, Erich. *Geschichte des Pietismus*. Stuttgart: J. F. Steinkopf Verlag, 1978.

Bhabha, Homi. *The Location of Culture*. Reprint ed. London: Routledge, 2008.

van Binsbergen, Wim J. *Religious Change in Zambia: Exploratory Studies*. London: Kegan Paul International, 1981, 267–316.

Blackburn, Anne M. *Locations of Buddhism: Colonialism and Modernity in Sri Lanka*. Chicago: University of Chicago Press, 2010.

Blair, Sheila. "Arabic Calligraphy in West Africa." In *The Meanings of Timbuktu*, edited by Shamil Jeppie and Soulaymane Bachir Diagne. Cape Town: HSRC Press, 2008, 60–75.

Bouron, Jean-Marie. "Être catéchiste en Haute-Volta à la fin de la période coloniale: affirmation d'un personnage prosélyte, transformation d'une personnalité sociale." *Social Sciences and Missions* 23, no. 2 (2010): 187–227.

Boxer, C. R. "'Christians and Spices': Portuguese Missionary Methods in Ceylon 1518–1658." *History Today* 8 (1958): 346–54.

Brackenbury, C. R. *Madras District Gazetteers: Cuddapah.* Madras: Government Press, 1915.

Bredekamp, Henry, and Robert Ross. *Missions and Christianity in South African History.* Johannesburg: University of Witwatersrand Press, 1995.

Breitenbach, Esther. *Empire and Scottish Society: The Impact of Foreign Missions at Home, c. 1790–c. 1914.* Edinburgh: Edinburgh University Press, 2009.

British and Foreign Bible Society. *Rules for the Guidance of Translators, Revisers, and Editors, Working in Connection with the British and Foreign Bible Society.* London: British and Foreign Bible Society, 1906.

———. *The Hundred and Eighteenth Report of the British and Foreign Bible Society for the Year Ending March MCMXXII.* London: Bible House, 1922.

———. *The Hundred and Twenty-First Report of the British and Foreign Bible Society for the Year Ending March MCMXXV.* London: Bible House, 1925.

———. *The Hundred and Twenty-Third Report of the British and Foreign Bible Society for the Year Ending March MCMXXVII.* London: Bible House, 1927.

———. *The Gospel in Many Tongues: Specimens of the 734 Languages in Which the British and Foreign Bible Society Has Published or Circulated Some Portion of the Word of God.* London: British and Foreign Bible Society, 1939.

Brittlebank, Kate. "Assertion." In *The Eighteenth Century in Indian History: Evolution or Revolution?*, edited by P. J. Marshall. New Delhi: Oxford University Press, 2005, 268–92.

Broadbent, Samuel. *Narrative of the Introduction of Christianity among the Baralong.* London: Wesleyan Mission House, 1865.

Brueckner, Heidrun. "Ferdinand Kittel in the Context of 19th Century German Indology." In *A Dictionary with a Mission: papers of the International Conference on the Occasion of the Centenary Celebrations of Kittel's Kannada-English Dictionary*, edited by William Madtha et al. Mangalore: Karnataka Theological Research Institute, 1998, 103–27.

Buckser, Andrew, and Stephen D. Glazier, eds. *The Anthropology of Religious Conversion.* Lanham, MD: Rowman & Littlefield, 2003.

Buddhist Committee of Enquiry. *The Betrayal of Buddhism: An Abridged Version of the Report of the Buddhist Committee of Inquiry.* Balangoda, Sri Lanka: Dharmavijaya Press, 1956.

Bunyan, John. *Yakrestiyān manged kazih 'ālam wada zlālam ḥeywat yamiwased*, translated by Gabra Giyorgis Tarfa and Martin Flad. Monkullo, Eritrea: EFS, the Religious Tract Society, and the London Society for Promoting Christianity among the Jews, 1892.

———. *Magedi krestyān*, translated by Teresa de Pertis and Bairu Okbit. Asmara: Missione Evangelica, 1934.

Calmettes, Jean Loup. "The Lumpa Sect, Rural Reconstruction, and Confict." Master's thesis, University College of Wales, 1978.

Canaan, Taufik. *Conflict in the Land of Peace.* Jerusalem: Syrian Orphanage Press, 1936.

———. *The Palestine Arab Cause.* Jerusalem: Modern Press, 1936.

Canton, William. *The Story of the Bible Society.* London: John Murray, 1904.

Carmichael, Tim. "Bureaucratic Literacy, Oral Testimonies, and the Study of Twentieth Century Ethiopian History." *Journal of African Cultural Studies* 18, no. 1 (June 2006): 23–42.

Carter, B. L. "On Spreading the Gospel to Egyptians Sitting in Darkness: The Political Problem of Missionaries in Egypt in the 1930s." *Middle Eastern Studies* 20, no. 4 (October 1984): 18–36.

"Çäwa." In *Encyclopaedia Aethiopica*, vol. 1 , edited by Siegbert Uhlig et al. Wiesbaden: Harrassowitz Verlag, 2007, 703.

Central Intelligence Agency, United States Government. *The World Factbook.* https://www.cia.gov/library/publications/the-world-factbook/. Accessed 9 August 2011.

Chatterjee, Partha. *Nationalist Thought and the Colonial World: A Derivative Discourse?* London: Zed Books, 1986.

Chidester, David. *Savage Systems: Colonialism and Comparative Religion in Southern Africa.* Cape Town: University of Cape Town Press, 1996.

Cohen, David William, and E. S. Odhiambo Atieno. *Burying SM: The Politics of Knowledge and the Sociology of Power in Africa.* Portsmouth, NH: Heinemann, 1992.

Colley, Linda. *Britons: Forging the Nation, 1707–1837.* 2nd ed. New Haven: Yale University Press, 2005.

"Colonial History of Eritrea." In *Encyclopaedia Aethiopica*. Vol. 2, edited by Siegberg Uhlig et al. Wiesbaden: Harrassowitz Verlag, 2007, 359–65.

"Colonialism." In *Encyclopaedia Aethiopica*. Vol. 1, edited by Siegberg Uhlig et al. Wiesbaden: Harrassowitz Verlag, 2007, 774–79.

Comaroff, John L., and Jean Comaroff. *Of Revelation and Revolution*. 2 vols. Chicago: University of Chicago Press, 1991 and 1997.

Cook, D. J. "The Influence of the Livingstonia Mission upon the Formation of Welfare Associations in Zambia, 1912–1913." In *Themes in the Christian History of Central Africa*, edited by T. Ranger and J. Weller. London: Heinemann, 1975, 98–133.

Courbage, Youssef, and Philippe Fargues. *Chrétiens et juifs dans l'Islam arabe et turc*. Paris: Fayard, 1992.

Cox, Jeffrey. *The British Missionary Enterprise since 1700*. New York: Routledge, 2008.

Crais, Clifton. *White Supremacy and Black Resistance in Precolonial South Africa*. Cambridge: Cambridge University Press, 1992.

———. *The Politics of Evil: Magic, State Power, and the Political Imagination in South Africa*. Cambridge: Cambridge University Press, 2002.

Crone, Patricia. *Meccan Trade and the Rise of Islam*. Princeton: Princeton University Press, 1987.

Crummey, Donald. "The Politics of Modernization: Protestant and Catholic Missionaries in Modern Ethiopia." In *The Missionary Factor in Ethiopia*, edited by Samuel Rubenson, Getatchew Haile, and Aasulv Laude. New York: Peter Lang, 1998, 85–99.

Daniell, David. *William Tyndale: A Biography*. New Haven: Yale University Press, 1994.

Daughton, J. P. *An Empire Divided: Religion, Republicanism, and the Making of French Colonialism, 1880–1914*. Oxford: Oxford University Press, 2006.

Dirar, Uoldelul Chelati. "Church-State Relations in Colonial Eritrea: Missionaries and the Development of Colonial Strategies (1869–1911)." *Journal of Modern Italian Studies* 8, no. 3 (2003): 391–410.

———. "Colonialism and the Construction of National Identities: The Case of Eritrea." *Journal of East African Studies* 1, no. 2 (2007): 256–76.

Dirks, Nicholas. *Castes of Mind: Colonialism and the Making of Modern India*. Princeton: Princeton University Press, 2001.

Doğan, Mehmet Ali, and Heather J. Sharkey, eds. *American Missionaries in the Middle East: Foundational Encounters*. Salt Lake City: University of Utah Press, 2011.

Don Peter, W. L. A. *Lusitanian Links with Lanka*. Ragama, Sri Lanka: W. L. A. Don Peter [self-published], 1979.

Dubois, J. A. *Description of the Character, Manners and Customs of the People of India and of Their Institutions, Religious and Civil*. London: Longman, Hurst, Rees, Orme, & Brown, 1817.

————. *Letters on the State of Christianity in India, in Which the Conversion of the Hindus Is Considered as Impracticable*. London: Paternoster Row, 1823.

————. *Hindu Manners, Customs and Ceremonies*. Oxford: Clarendon Press, 1906.

Duffy, Eamon. *Marking the Hours, English People and Their Prayers, 1240–1570*. New Haven: Yale University Press, 2006.

Dunch, Ryan. *Fuzhou Protestants and the Making of a Modern China, 1857–1927*. New Haven: Yale University Press, 2001.

————. "Beyond Cultural Imperialism: Cultural Theory, Christian Missions, and Global Modernity." *History and Theory* 41 (2002): 301–25.

Dye, Marjorie, Davida Finney, Adib Galdas, and Samuel Habib. *Literacy—The Essential Skill*. New York: Committee on World Literacy and Christian Literature, 1964.

Edgar, Robert R., and Hilary Sapire. *African Apocalypse: the Story of Nontetha Nkwenkwe, a Twentieth-Century South African Prophet*. Athens: Ohio University Press, 1999.

"Education." In *Encyclopaedia Aethiopica*. Vol. 2, edited by Siegbert Uhlig et al. Wiesbaden: Harrassowitz Verlag, 2007, 228–37.

Elbourne, Elizabeth. *Blood Ground: Colonialism, Missions, and the Contest for Christianity in the Cape Colony and Britain, 1799–1853*. Montreal: Queen's University Press, 2002.

Ellis, Stephen, and Gerrie ter Haar. *Worlds of Power: Religious Thought and Political Practice in Africa*. New York: Oxford University Press, 2004.

Elphick, Richard, and Rodney Davenport, eds. *Christianity in South Africa: A Political, Social and Cultural History*. Cape Town: David Philip, 1997.

Errington, Joseph. "Colonial Linguistics." *Annual Review of Anthropology* 30 (2001): 19–39.

Etherington, Norman. "Recent Trends in the Historiography of Christianity in Southern Africa." *Journal of Southern African Studies* 22, no. 2 (1996): 201–19.

————. *The Great Treks: The Transformation of Southern Africa, 1815–54*. London: Pearson Education, 2001.

Etherington, Norman, ed. *Missions and Empire*. Oxford: Oxford University Press, 2005.

Evangeliska Fosterlandsstiftelsen (Swedish Evangelical Mission). *Berhān yeḥun sebekat zāntā wédo nehezebi 'ityoṗyā/Sia la Luce! Prediche, racconti, e spiegazioni edificanti per il popolo etiopico*. Asmara: Tipografia della Missione Svedese, 1912.

———. *Consigli ai maestri e programma d'insegnamento*. Asmara: Tipografia della Missione Svedese, 1917.

Ewing, Jack. "Volcanic Ash May Weigh on European Economy." *New York Times*, 18 April 2010.

Farah, Rafiq. *In Troubled Waters: A History of the Anglican Diocese in Jerusalem 1841–1998*. Leicester, UK: Christians Aware, 2002.

Fargues, Philippe. "The Arab Christians of the Middle East: A Demographic Perspective." In *Christian Communities in the Arab Middle East*, edited by Andrea Pacini. Oxford: Clarendon Press, 1998, 48–66.

———. "Demographic Islamization: Non-Muslims in Muslim Countries." *SAIS Review* 21, no. 2 (2001): 103–16.

Fernando, Antony. "Understanding the 'Sinhala-Buddhist' Movement in Sri Lanka." *Journal of Dharma* 20, no. 2 (1995): 207–22.

Fleischmann, Ellen. *The Nation and Its "New" Women: The Palestinian Women's Movement, 1920–1948*. Berkeley: University of California Press, 2003.

Flores, Jorge Manuel. *Hum Curto Historia de Ceylan: Five Hundred Years of Relations between Portugal and Sri Lanka*. Lisbon: Fundação Oriente, 2000.

Forrester, D. M. *Caste and Christianity: Attitudes and Policies on Caste of Anglo-Saxon Protestant Missions*. London: Curzon Press, 1980.

Francis, W. *Madras District Gazetteers: Bellary*. Madras: Government Press, 1904.

Frenz, Albrecht, ed. *Hermann Moegling*. Kottayam, India: DC Books, 1997.

———. "Linguists' Correspondence." In *Hermann Moegling*, edited by Albrecht Frenz. Kottayam, India: DC Books, 1997, 244–67.

———. *Freiheit hat Gesicht/Future in Remembrance: Anandapur—Eine Begegnung zwischen Kodagu und Baden-Wütemberg, Briefe, Berichte und Bilder versehen mit Einleitung, biografischen Skizzen und Anhang von Albrecht Frenz*. Stuttgart: Staatsanzeiger Verlag, 2003.

Frenz, Albrecht, and Stefan Frenz, eds. *Zukunft in Gedenken/Future in Remembrance*. Stuttgart: Staatsanzeiger Verlag, 2003.

Frykenberg, Robert Eric. *Christians and Missionaries in India: Cross-Cultural Communication since 1500*. Grand Rapids, MI: Eerdmans, 2003.

————. *Christianity in India: From Beginnings to the Present.* Oxford: Oxford University Press, 2008.

Fumagalli, Giuseppe. *Bibliografia etiopica: catalogo descrittivo e ragionato degli scritti pubblicati dalla invenzione della stampa fino a tutto il 1891.* Milan: Ulrico Hoepli, 1893.

Gafaïti, Hafid. "The Monotheism of the Other: Language and De/Construction of National Identity in Postcolonial Algeria." In *Algeria in Others' Languages*, edited by Anne-Emanuelle Berger. Ithaca, NY: Cornell University Press, 2002, 19–43.

Gandhi, Leela. *Postcolonial Theory: A Critical Introduction.* New York: Columbia University Press, 1998.

Gabra Mikā'él Germu. "Gabra 'Egzi'abhér Hāmāsanāy." *Ethiopia* (1961).

————. *Dagyāt Bāhtā Hāgos Saganayeti (Daǧazmāč Bāhtā Hāgos [of] Saganayeti).* Asmara: n.p., 1997.

————.*Dagyāt Bāhtā Hāgos and Blātā Gabra 'Egzi'abhér Gilay Sā'edā Krestyān (Blātā Gabra 'Egzi'abhér Gilay of Sā'edā Krestyān).* Unpublished manuscript in Tigrinya (n.d.).

Garvey, Brian. *Bembaland Church: Religious and Social Change in South Central Africa, 1891–1964.* Leiden: E. J. Brill, 1994.

Gebreselassie, Teclehaimanot. "The Low-Caste Fuga Occupational Group under the Italian Administration in the Horn of Africa." *Northeast African Studies* (n.s.) 10, no. 3 (2003): 33–44.

Geiger, Wilhelm, trans. *The Mahāvaṃsa: Or the Great Chronicle of Ceylon.* Oxford: Pali Text Society, 2001.

Gershoni, Israel, and James Jankowski. *Redefining the Egyptian Nation, 1930–1945.* Cambridge: Cambridge University Press, 1995.

Ghosh, Amitav. *In an Antique Land.* Delhi: Ravi Dayal, 1992.

————. "The Slave of MS. H.6." In *Subaltern Studies*, edited by Partha Chatterjee and Gyanendra Pandey. Vol. 7. Delhi: Oxford University Press, 1993, 159–220.

Gidney, W. T. *The History of the London Society for Promoting Christianity amongst the Jews, from 1809 to 1908.* London: London Society for Promoting Christianity amongst the Jews, 1908.

Gilmartin, David. "Divine Displeasure and Muslim Elections: The Shaping of Community in Twentieth Century Punjab." In *The Political Inheritance of Pakistan*, edited by D. A. Low. London: Macmillan Academic and Professional LTD, 1991, 106–29.

Gilley, Sheridan, and Brian Stanley, eds. *World Christianities, c. 1815–1915.* Cambridge: Cambridge University Press, 2006.

Gilsenan, Michael. *Recognizing Islam: Religion and Society in the Modern Arab World.* New York: Pantheon, 1982.

Gombrich, Richard, and Gananath Obeyesekere. *Buddhism Transformed: Religious Change in Sri Lanka.* Princeton: Princeton University Press, 1988.

González, Nancie L. Solien. *Dollar, Dove, and Eagle: One Hundred Years of Palestinian Migration to Honduras.* Ann Arbor: University of Michigan Press, 1993.

Gordon, David M. *Nachituti's Gift: Economy, Society, and Environment in Central Africa.* Madison: University of Wisconsin Press, 2006.

———. "Rebellion or Massacre? The UNIP-Lumpa Conflict Revisited." In *One Zambia, Many Histories: Towards a History of Post-Colonial Zambia,* edited by Jan-Bart Gewald, Marja Hinfelaar, and Giacomo Macola. Leiden: Brill, 2008, 45–76.

———. "Community of Suffering: Narratives of War and Exile in the Zambian Lumpa Church." In *Recasting the Past,* edited by Derek Peterson and Giacomo Macola. Athens: Ohio University Press, 2009, 191–209.

———. *Invisible Agents: Spirits in a Central African History.* Athens: Ohio University Press, 2012.

Grabill, Joseph. *Protestant Diplomacy and the Near East: Missionary Influence on American Policy, 1810–1927.* Minneapolis: University of Minnesota Press, 1971.

de Gruchy, Steve. "The Alleged Political Conservatism of Robert Moffat." In *The London Missionary Society in Southern Africa, 1799–1999,* edited by John de Gruchy. Athens: Ohio University Press, 2000, 17–36.

Gundert, Herrmann. "Hermann Moegling." Translated by Christoph Steinweg and Elisabeth Steinweg-Fleckner. In *Hermann Moegling,* edited by Albrecht Frenz. Kottayam, IN: DC Books, 1997, 90–136.

Gunner, Elizabeth. *The Man of Heaven and the Beautiful Ones of God: Umuntu Wasezulwini Nabantu Abahle Bakankulunkulu: Writings from Ibandla Lamanazaretha, a South African Church.* Leiden: Brill, 2002.

Guruge, Ananda, ed. *The Return to Righteousness: A Collection of Speeches, Essays and Letters of the Anagarika Dharmapala.* Colombo: Department of Cultural Affairs, 1991.

Hackett, Rosalind I. J., ed. *Proselytization Revisited: Rights, Free Markets, and Culture Wars.* London: Equinox, 2008.

Haeri, Niloofar. "Form and Ideology: Arabic Sociolinguistics and Beyond." *Annual Review of Anthropology* 29 (2000): 61–87.

———. *Sacred Language, Ordinary People: Dilemmas of Culture and Politics in Egypt.* New York: Palgrave Macmillan, 2003.

Hall, Catherine. *Civilising Subjects: Metropole and Colony in the English Imagination, 1830–1867.* Chicago: University of Chicago Press, 2002.

Hallisey, Charles. "Works and Persons in Sinhala Literary Culture." In *Literary Cultures in History: Reconstructions from South Asia,* edited by Sheldon Pollock. Berkeley: University of California Press, 2003, 689–746.

Harding, Christopher. *Religious Transformation in South Asia: The Meanings of Conversion in Colonial Punjab.* Oxford: Oxford University Press, 2008.

Harries, Patrick. *Butterflies and Barbarians: Swiss Missionaries and Systems of Knowledge in South-East Africa.* Athens: Ohio University Press, 2007.

Harris, Elizabeth J. *Theravāda Buddhism and the British Encounter: Religious, Missionary and Colonial Experience in Nineteenth Century Sri Lanka.* London: Routledge, 2006.

Hary, Benjamin H. *Multiglossia in Judeo-Arabic.* Leiden: E. J. Brill, 1992.

Havanur, Srinivasa. "Kittel's Dictionary as Used by Scholars Like M. Govinda Pai." In *A Dictionary with a Mission: Papers of the International Conference on the Occasion of the Centenary Celebrations of Kittel's Kannada-English Dictionary,* edited by William Madtha et al. Mangalore: Karnataka Theological Research Institute, 1998, 57–64.

Headrick, Daniel R. *The Tools of Empire: Technology and European Imperialism in the Nineteenth Century.* New York: Oxford University Press, 1981.

Heath, Jeffrey. *Jewish and Muslim Dialects of Moroccan Arabic.* London: RoutledgeCurzon, 2002.

Hefner, Robert W., ed. *Conversion to Christianity: Historical and Anthropological Perspectives on a Great Transformation.* Berkeley: University of California Press, 1993.

Held, Felix Emil, trans. *Christianopolis: An Ideal State of the Seventeenth Century, translated from the Latin of Johann Valentin Andreae.* New York: Oxford University Press, 1914.

Hill, Patricia R. *The World Their Household: The American Woman's Foreign Mission Movement and Cultural Transformation, 1870–1920.* Ann Arbor: University of Michigan Press, 1985.

Hinfelaar, Hugo F. "Women's Revolt: The Lumpa Church of Lenshina Mulenga in the 1950s." *Journal of Religion in Africa* 21 (1991): 99–129.

————. *Bemba-Speaking Women of Zambia in a Century of Religious Change.* Leiden: E. J. Brill, 1994.

Hochschild, Adam. *King Leopold's Ghost: A Story of Greed, Terror, and Heroism in Colonial Africa.* Boston: Houghton Mifflin, 1998.

Hodgson, Janet. "A Battle for Sacred Power: Christian Beginnings among the Xhosa." In *Christianity in South Africa: A Political, Social and Cultural History,* edited by Richard Elphick and Rodney Davenport. Cape Town: David Philip, 1997: 68–88.

Holt, John C. "Protestant Buddhism?" *Religious Studies Review* 17, no. 4 (1991): 307–12.

Horton, Robin. "On the Rationality of Conversion, Parts I and II." *Africa* 45 (1975): 219–35, 373–99.

Hough, James. *A Reply to the Letters of the Abbe Dubois on the State of Christianity in India.* London: L. B. Seeley & Sons, 1824.

Hourani, Albert. *Arabic Thought in the Liberal Age, 1798–1939.* London: Oxford University Press, 1962.

————. *A History of the Arab Peoples.* Cambridge: Harvard University Press, 1991.

Howsam, Leslie. *Cheap Bibles: Nineteenth-Century Publishing and the British and Foreign Bible Society.* Cambridge: Cambridge University Press, 1991.

Hudson, Dennis. *Protestant Origins in India: Tamil Evangelical Christians, 1706–1835.* Grand Rapids, MI: Eerdmans, 2000.

al-Hut, Bayan Nuwayhid. *Qiyadat wa-al-mu'assasat al-siyasiyya fi Filastin.* Beirut: n.p., 1981.

Ipenburg, At. *"All Good Men": The Development of the Lubwa Mission, Chinsali, Zambia, 1905–1967.* Frankfurt am Main: Peter Lang, 1996.

Iwarson, Jonas, and Alessandro Tron. *Notizie storiche e varie sulla Missione Evangelica Svedese dell'Eritrea, 1866–1916.* Asmara: Swedish Evangelical Mission, 1918.

Jenkins, Paul. *Texte und Documente: Kurze Geschichte der Basler Mission.* Basel: Basler Mission, 1989.

————. "Ferdinand Kittel in the Context of the Basel Mission as Organisation." In *An Indian to Indians?*, edited by Reinhard Wendt. Wiesbaden: Harrassowitz Verlag, 2006, 195–210.

Jenkins, Philip. *The Next Christendom: The Coming of Global Christianity.* Oxford: Oxford University Press, 2002.

Johnston, Anna. *Missionary Writing and Empire, 1800–1860.* Cambridge: Cambridge University Press, 2003.

Jürgens, Hans. "German Indology *avant la lettre*: The Experiences of the Halle Missionaries in Southern India, 1750–1810." In *Sanskrit and "Orientalism": Indology and Comparative Linguistics in Germany, 1750–1958*, edited by Douglas McGetchin, K. J. Park, and Damodar SarDesai. New Delhi: Manohar, 2004, 41–82.

Karttunen, Frances. *Between Worlds: Interpreters, Guides, and Survivors*. New Brunswick, NJ: Rutgers University, 1994.

Kaundinya, Anandarao. *Die Lebensgeschichte des H. Anandaraja Kaundinya*. Basel: Die evangelische Missionsgesellschaft zu Basel, 1853.

Kennedy, Pagan. *Black Livingstone: A True Tale of Adventure in the Nineteenth-Century Congo*. New York: Viking, 2002.

Khalaf, Issa. *Politics in Palestine: Arab Factionalism and Social Disintegration, 1939–1948*. Albany: State University of New York Press, 1991.

Khalidi, Mustafa, and 'Umar Farrukh. *al-Tabshir wa'l-isti'mar fi al-bilad al-'arabiyya*. 2nd ed. Beirut: n.p., 1957.

Khalidi, Rashid. *Palestinian Identity: The Construction of Modern National Consciousness*. New York: Columbia University Press, 1997.

Khillah, Kamil. *Filastin wa-al-intidab al-Baritani, 1922–1939*. Beirut: Munazzamat al-Tahrir al-Filastiniyya, 1974.

Konrad, Dagmar. *Missionsbraeute: Pietistinnen des 19 Jahrhunderts in der Basler Mission*. Muenster: Waxmann Verlag, 2001.

Kumar, Vijaya. *Ecumenical Co-operation of the Missions in Karnataka*. Delhi: Indian Society for the Promotion of Christian Knowledge, 2005.

Kumaradoss, Vincent Y. *Robert Caldwell: A Scholar-Missionary in Colonial South India*. Delhi: Indian Society for the Promotion of Christian Knowledge, 2007.

"Land Tenure in Eritrea." In *Encyclopaedia Aethiopica*, vol. 3, edited by Siegbert Uhlig et al. Wiesbaden: Harrassowitz Verlag, 2007, 500–501.

Landau, Paul Stewart. "The Illumination of Christ in the Kalahari Desert." *Representations* 45 (1994): 26–40.

———. *In the Realm of the Word: Language, Gender, and Christianity in a Southern African Kingdom*. Portsmouth, NH: Heinemann, 1995.

———. "Empires of the Visual: Photography and Colonial Administration in Africa." In *Images & Empires: Visuality in Colonial and Postcolonial Africa*, edited by Paul S. Landau and Deborah D. Kaspin. Berkeley: University of California Press, 2002, 141–71.

———. *Popular Politics in the History of South Africa, 1400 to 1948*. New York: Cambridge University Press, 2010.

———. "Transformations in Consciousness." In *The Cambridge History of South Africa*, edited by Carolyn Hamilton, Bernard K. Mbenga, and Robert Ross. Vol. 1. Cambridge: Cambridge University Press, 2010, 392–448.

Langer, Erick, and Robert H. Jackson, eds. *The New Latin American Mission History*. Lincoln: University of Nebraska Press, 1995.

Larrimore, Mark. "Orientalism and Antivoluntarism in the History of Ethics: On Christian Wolff's 'Oratio de Sinarum Philosophia Practica.'" *Journal of Religious Ethics*, 28, no. 2 (2000): 189–219.

Launhardt, Johannes. *Evangelicals in Addis Ababa (1919–1991): With Special Reference to the Ethiopian Evangelical Church Mekane Yesus and the Addis Ababa Synod*. Münster: Lit Verlag, 2004.

Lawrance, Benjamin, Emily Lynn Osborn, and Richard Roberts. "Introduction: African Intermediaries and the 'Bargain' of Collaboration." In *Intermediaries, Interpreters, and Clerks: African Employees in the Making of Colonial Africa*, edited by Benjamin Lawrance, Emily Lynn Osborn, and Richard Roberts. Madison: University of Wisconsin, 2006, 3–34.

"Lazarists." In *Encyclopaedia Aethiopica*. Vol. 3, edited by Siegbert Uhlig et al. Wiesbaden: Harrassowitz Verlag, 2007, 526–27.

Legassick, Martin. "The Griqua, the Sotho-Tswana, and the Missionaries, 1789 to 1840: The Politics of a Frontier Zone." Ph.D. diss., University of California–Los Angeles, History, 1969.

Lehmann, Dorothea. "Alice Lenshina Mulenga and the Lumpa Church." In *Christians of the Copperbelt: The Growth of the Church in Northern Rhodesia*. London: SCM Press, 1961, 248–68.

Lesch, Ann Mosely. *Arab Politics in Palestine, 1917–1939: The Frustration of a Nationalism Movement*. Ithaca, NY: Cornell University Press, 1979.

Lester, Alan. *Imperial Networks, Creating Identities in Nineteenth-Century South Africa and Britain*. London: Routledge, 2001.

Levitt, Peggy. *God Needs No Passport: Immigrants and the Changing American Religious Landscape*. New York: New Press, 2009.

Lia, Brynjar. *The Society of the Muslim Brothers in Egypt: The Rise of an Islamic Mass Movement, 1928–1942*. Reading, UK: Ithaca Press, 1998.

Lopez, Donald S., Jr. *A Modern Buddhist's Bible: Essential Readings from East and West*. Boston: Beacon Press, 2002.

Lundström, Karl Johan, and Ezra Gebremedhin. *Kenisha: The Roots and Development of the Evangelical Church of Eritrea, 1866–1935.* Trenton, NJ: Red Sea Press, 2011.

Maben, Veena. "Pauline Moegling: An Exceptional Mission Woman." In *Zukunft im Gedenken/Future in Remembrance,* edited by Albecht Frenz and Stefan Frenz. Norderstedt, Germany: Books on Demand GmbH, 2007, 324–43.

MacGaffey, Wyatt. "Dialogues of the Deaf: Europeans on the Atlantic Coast of Africa." In *Implicit Understandings: Observing, Reporting and Reflecting on the Encounters between Europeans and Other Peoples in the Early Modern Era,* edited by Stuart B. Schwartz. Cambridge: Cambridge University Press, 1994, 249–67.

Makdisi, Ussama. *Artillery of Heaven: American Missionaries and the Failed Conversion of the Middle East.* Ithaca, NY: Cornell University Press, 2008.

Malalgoda, Kitsiri. *Buddhism in Sinhalese Society 1750–1900: A Study of Religious Revival and Change.* Berkeley: University of California Press, 1976.

Malcolm, Noel. "Comenius, Boyle, Oldenburg, and the Translation of the Bible into Turkish." *Church History and Religious Culture* 87 (2007): 327–62.

Mallampalli, Chandra. *Christians and Public Life in Colonial South India, 1863–1937: Contending with Marginality.* London: RoutledgeCurzon, 2004.

Mani, Lata. *Contentious Traditions: The Debate on Sati in Colonial India.* Berkeley: University of California Press, 1998.

Manuale d'industrie, arti e mestieri ad uso degli indigeni nelle due lingue italiano e tigrignâ per cura della missione cattolica/ Maṣeḥafe ṭebaben śerāḥen belhātnageden. Asmara: Tipografia Francescana, 1914.

Markowitz, Marvin D. *Cross and Sword: The Political Role of Christian Missions in the Belgian Congo, 1908–1960.* Stanford: Hoover Institution Press, 1973.

Martin, Maurice. "Statistiques chrétiennes d'Égypte." *Travaux et Jours* (Beirut) 24 (1967): 65–75.

Māryām, Tāyya Gabra, ed. *Maṣeḥafe sewāsew yage'ez qwānqwā mamāryā yamaṣeḥaf magelaćā.* Menkulu, Eritrea: Swedish Mission Press, 1889.

Maryam, Yaqob Walda. *Brief Autobiography and Selected Articles.* Addis Ababa: Artistic Printing Press, 2003.

Matthews, Weldon. *Confronting an Empire, Constructing a Nation: Arab Nationalists and Popular Politics in Mandate Palestine.* London: I. B. Tauris, 2006.

McGetchin, Douglas T. "The Sanskrit Reich: Translating Ancient India for Modern Germans, 1790–1914." Ph.D. diss., University of California–San Diego, 2002.

McGetchin, Douglas, Peter K. J. Park, and Damodar SarDesai, eds. *Sanskrit and "Orientalism": Indology and Comparative Linguistics in Germany, 1750–1958*. New Delhi: Manohar, 2004.

McGoldrick, Sylvester. *Bellary Mission*. Buckingham, UK: Franciscan Missionary Union, 1960.

McLuhan, Marshall. *The Gutenberg Galaxy: The Making of Typographic Man*. Toronto: University of Toronto Press, 1962.

Menon, Kalyani Devaki. "Converted Innocents and Their Trickster Heroes: The Politics of Proselytizing in India." In *The Anthropology of Religious Conversion*, edited by Andrew Buckser and Stephen D. Glazier. Lanham, MD: Rowman & Littlefield, 2003, 41–53.

Merton, Robert K. "The Unanticipated Consequences of Purposive Social Action." *American Sociological Review* 1, no. 6 (1936): 894–904.

da Mezzana, Galdino. *La missione Eritrea affidata ai frati minori cappucini di Milano*. Milan: Lanzani, 1912.

Mikulski, Jessica. "Unexpected Consequences of Pump Proton Inhibitor Use in Reflux Disease." *Medical News Today* (November 2009), http://www.medical newstoday.com/releases/169467.php, accessed 8 April 2013.

Miller, Jon. *Missionary Zeal and Institutional Control: Organizational Contradictions in the Basel Mission on the Gold Coast, 1828–1927*. Grand Rapids, MI: Eerdmans, 2003.

Miller, Ylana. *Government and Society in Rural Palestine, 1920–1948*. Austin: University of Texas Press, 1985.

Miran, Jonathan. "Missionaries, Education, and the State in the Italian Colony of Eritrea." In *Christian Missionaries and the State in the Third World*, edited by Holger Bernt Hansen and Michael Twaddle. Athens: Ohio University Press, 2002, 121–35.

———. *Red Sea Citizens: Cosmopolitan Society and Cultural Change in Massawa*. Bloomington: Indiana University Press, 2009.

"Missions." In *Encyclopaedia Aethiopica*, vol. 3, edited by Siegbert Uhlig et al. Wiesbaden: Harrassowitz Verlag, 2007, 3:979–981.

Mitchell, Richard P. *The Society of the Muslim Brothers*. Oxford: Oxford University Press, 1993.

Moegling, Hermann. "Lieder Kanaresischer Sänger." *Zeitschrift der Deutschen morgenländischen Gesellschaft* (1860): 502–16.

———. "Herrmann Möegling's Diary of a Brief Visit to Hubli in 1838." In *Journeys and Encounters: Religion, Society and the Basel Mission in North*

Karnataka, 1837–1852: Translations and Summaries from Published Materials in German, edited by Jennifer and Paul Jenkins, http://www.library.yale.edu/div/fa/Karnataka.htm, accessed 10 January 2011.

Moffat, Robert. *Missionary Labours and Scenes in Southern Africa*. London: R. Carter, 1843, and London: John Snow, 1846.

Molema, S. M. *Chief Moroka: His Life, His Times and His People*. Cape Town: Methodist Publishing House, 1951.

Moore, Edmund F. *Reports of Cases Heard and Determined by the Judicial Committee and the Lords of H. M. Most Honourable Privy Council, on Appeal from the Supreme and Sudder Dewaney Courts in the East Indies*. Vol. 9. London: V. & R. Stevens, 1864.

Morier-Genoud, Eric, and Wendy Urban-Mead. "Introduction: A State of the Field." *Social Sciences and Missions* 24, nos. 2–3 (2011): 145–47.

Mott, John R., ed. *Conferences of Christian Workers among Moslems 1924*. New York: International Missionary Council, 1924.

Munasinghe, Chamika. *Apē Dharma Katikāvata*. Imbulgoda, Sri Lanka: Senarath Publishers, 2004.

Mundadan, Mathias A. *History of Christianity in India*. Vol. 1. Bangalore: Theological Publications in India, 1984.

Murthy, Sulochana S. "Rev. F. Kittel: Literature Survey." In *A Dictionary with a Mission: Papers of the International Conference on the Occasion of the Centenary Celebrations of Kittel's Kannada-English Dictionary*, edited by William Madtha et al. Mangalore: Karnataka Theological Research Institute, 1998, 243–44.

Na'im, Khalid. *Tarikh Jam'iyyat muqawamat al-tansir al-misriyya (1927–33)*. Cairo: Kitab al-Mukhtar, 1987.

Naito, Ken, et al. "Unexpected Consequences of a Sudden and Massive Transposon Amplification on Rice Gene Expression." *Nature* 461 (2009): 1130–34.

da Nembro, Metodio. *Missione dei Minori Cappuccini in Eritrea (1894–1952)*. Rome: Biblioteca Seraphico-Capuccina, 1953.

Negash, Tekeste. *No Medicine for the Bite of a White Snake: Notes on Nationalism and Resistance in Eritrea, 1890–1940*. Uppsala: University of Uppsala, 1986.

———. *Italian Colonialism in Eritrea, 1882–1941: Policies, Praxis, and Impact*. Stockholm: Almqvist, 1987.

———. "The Ideology of Colonialism: Educational Policy and Praxis in Eritrea." In *Italian Colonialism*, edited by Ruth Ben-Ghiat and Mia Fuller. New York: Palgrave Macmillan, 2005, 109–20.

Norton, Rob. "Unintended Consequences." *The Concise Encyclopedia of Economics*, edited by David R. Henderson. Library of Economics and Liberty (2008), http://www.econlib.org/library/Enc/UnintendedConsequences.html, accessed 21 July 2010.

Obeyesekere, Gananath. "Religious Symbolism and Political Change in Ceylon." In *The Two Wheels of Dhamma: Essays on the Theravada Tradition in India and Ceylon*, edited by Bardwell L. Smith. Chambersburg, PA: America Academy of Religion, 1972, 58–78.

Occhini, Pier Ludovico. *Viaggi, una gita nell'Eritrea, ricordi dell'Italia irredenta*. Città di Castello: S. Lapi, 1908.

Oddie, Geoffrey A. *Religious Conversion Movements in South Asia: Continuities and Change, 1800–1900*. London: Taylor & Francis, 1997.

———. *Imagined Hinduism: British Protestant Missionary Constructions of Hinduism, 1793–1900*. Thousand Oaks, CA: Sage, 2006.

Oger, L. "Mutima Church of Emilio Mulolani." Ilondola, Zambia, mimeograph, n.d.

———. "The Lenshina Movement in Northern Rhodesia: Religious Sect Founded by Alice Lenshina." 1955–60, mimeograph (1960?).

Okkenhaug, Inger Marie. "Introduction: Gender and Missions in the Middle East." *Social Sciences and Missions* 23, no. 1 (2010): 1–6.

Oliver, Roland. *The Missionary Factor in East Africa*. London: Longmans, Green, 1952.

Oliver, Roland, and Anthony Atmore. *Africa since 1800*. 3rd ed. Cambridge: Cambridge University Press, 1981.

Oren, Michael. *Power, Faith and Fantasy: America in the Middle East, 1776 to the Present*. New York: W. W. Norton, 2007.

Palestine Royal Commission. *Report of the Palestine Royal Commission*. London: Her Majesty's Stationery Office, 1937.

Paoli, Renato. *Nella colonia Eritrea*. Milan: Fratelli Treves, 1908.

Paranavitana, K. D. "Suppression of Buddhism and Aspects of Indigenous Culture under the Portuguese and the Dutch." *Journal of the Royal Asiatic Society of Sri Lanka* (n.s.) 49 (2004): 1–14.

Pateman, Roy. "Eritrean Resistance during the Italian Occupation." *Journal of Eritrean Studies* 2 (1989): 13–24.

Patten, John A. *These Remarkable Men: The Beginnings of World Enterprise*. London: Lutterworth, 1945.

Peel, J. D. Y. "For Who Hath Despised the Day of Small Things? Missionary Narratives and Historical Anthropology." *Comparative Studies in Society and History* 37, no. 3 (1995): 581–607.

———. *Religious Encounter and the Making of the Yoruba*. Bloomington: Indiana University Press, 2000.

Pekkola, Helmi. *Jumalan Poluilla Islamin Eramaassa*. Porvoo, Finland: Werner Soderstrom Osakeyhitio, 1934.

Pelikan, Jaroslav. "Pietism." In *Dictionary of the History of Ideas*, edited by Philip P. Wiener. Vol. 3. New York: Charles Scribner's Sons, 1973, 493–95.

Penny, F. E. *The Outcaste*. London: Chatto & Windus, 1912.

Perera, C. Gaston. *The Portuguese Missionary in 16th and 17th Century Ceylon: The Spiritual Conquest*. Colombo: Vijitha Yapa, 2009.

Perera, S. G. *The Jesuits in Ceylon (in the XVI and XVII Centuries)*. New Delhi: Asian Educational Services, 2004.

Perera, S. G., and M. E. Fernando. *Alagiyawanna's Kustantinu Haṭana*. Colombo: Catholic Press, 1932.

Perniola, V. *The Catholic Church in Sri Lanka: The Portuguese Period, Volume II, 1566 to 1619*. Dehiwala, Sri Lanka: Tisara, 1991.

Peterson, Derek R. *Creative Writing: Translation, Bookkeeping, and the Work of Imagination in Colonial Kenya*. Portsmouth, NH: Heinemann, 2004.

Peterson, Indira Viswanathan. "Tanjore, Tranquebar, and Halle: European Science and German Missionary Education in the Lives of Two Indian Intellectuals in the early Nineteenth Century." In *Christians and Missionaries in India: Cross-Cultural Communication since 1500*, edited by Robert Eric Frykenberg. Grand Rapids, MI: Eerdmans, 2003, 93–126.

Phipps, William E. *William Sheppard: Congo's African-American Livingstone*. Louisville, KY: Geneva Press, 2002.

Pieris, P. E. *The Ceylon Littoral 1593*. Reprinted in Paulus Edward Pieris, *Sir Paul E. Pieris' Selected Writings*. New Delhi: Navrang, 1995.

Playne, Somerset, comp. *Southern India: Its History, People, Commerce, and Industrial Resources*. London: Foreign and Colonial Compiling and Publishing Co., 1914–1915.

Porath, Yehoshua. *The Emergence of the Palestinian Arab National Movement, 1918–1929*. London: F. Cass, 1974.

———. *The Palestinian Arab National Movement: From Riots to Rebellion, 1929–1939*. London: F. Cass, 1977.

Porter, Andrew, ed. *The Imperial Horizons of British Protestant Missions, 1880–1914*. Grand Rapids, MI: William B. Eerdmans, 2003.

———. *Religion versus Empire? British Protestant Missionaries and Overseas Expansion, 1700–1914*. New York: Manchester University Press, 2004.

Prevost, Elizabeth E. *The Communion of Women: Missions and Gender in Colonial Africa and the British Metropole*. Oxford: Oxford University Press, 2010.

"Printing." In *Encyclopaedia Aethiopica*, edited by Siegbert Uhlig et al. Vol. 4. Wiesbaden: Harrassowitz Verlag, 2007, 4:217–18.

Prothero, Stephen R. *The White Buddhist: The Asian Odyssey of Henry Steel Olcott*. Bloomington: Indiana University Press, 1996.

Puglisi, Giuseppe. *Chi è dell' Eritrea?: Dizionario biografico*. Asmara: Agenzia Regina, 1952.

Raghaviah, Jaiprakash. *Basel Mission Industries in Malabar and South Canara, 1834–1914: A Study of Its Social and Economic Impact*. New Delhi: Gian, 1990.

Rahula, Walpola. *The Heritage of the Bhikkhu: A Short History of the Bhikkhu in Educational, Cultural, Social, and Political Life*. Translated by K. P. G. Wijayasurendra. New York: Grove Press, 1974.

Ramaswamy, Sumathi. *Passions of the Tongue: Language Devotion in Tamil India, 1891–1970*. Berkeley: University of California Press, 1997.

Rambo, Lewis R. *Understanding Religious Conversion*. New Haven: Yale University Press, 1993.

Ranger, T., and J. Weller, eds. *Themes in the Christian History of Central Africa*. London: Heinemann, 1975.

Reid, Richard. "The Trans-Mereb Experience: Perceptions of the Historical Relationship between Eritrea and Ethiopia." *Journal of Eastern African Studies* 1, no. 2 (2007): 238–55.

Rennstich, Karl. *Handwerker-Theologen und Industrie-Brueder als Botschafter des Friedens: Entwicklungshilfe der Basler Mission im 19. Jahrhundert*. Stuttgart: Evangelischer Missionsverlag im Christlichen Verlagshaus Gmbh, 1985.

Richards, Audrey I. "A Modern Movement of Witchfinders." *Africa: Journal of the International African Institute* 8, no. 4 (1935): 448–61.

———. *Land, Labour, and Diet in Northern Rhodesia*. London: Oxford University Press, 1939.

Robert, Dana L. *American Women in Mission: A Social History of Their Thought and Practice*. Macon, GA: Mercer University Press, 1996.

———. "From Missions to Beyond Missions: The Historiography of American Protestant Foreign Missions since World War II." In *New Directions in American Religious History*, edited by Harry S. Stout and D. G. Hart. New York: Oxford University Press, 1997, 362–93.

———. *Christian Mission: How Christianity Became a World Religion*. Chichester, UK: Wiley-Blackwell, 2009.

Roberts, Andrew. "The Lumpa Church of Alice Lenshina. In *Protest and Power in Black Africa*, edited by R. I. Rotberg and A. A. Mazrui. New York: Oxford University Press, 1970, 515–68.

———. *The Lumpa Church of Alice Lenshina*. Lusaka: Oxford University Press, 1970.

———. *A History of the Bemba: Political Growth and Change in North-Eastern Zambia before 1900*. London: Longman, 1973.

Roberts, Michael. *Sinhala Consciousness in the Kandyan Period 1590s to 1815*. Colombo: Vijitha Yapa, 2004.

Robson, Laura. "Archaeology and Mission: The British Presence in Nineteenth-Century Palestine." Paper presented at the conference on "Great Powers in the Holy Land: From Napoleon to the Balfour Declaration," The European Institute, Columbia University, 3 April 2009.

———. *Colonialism and Christianity in Mandate Palestine*. Austin: University of Texas Press, 2011.

Roe, James Moulton. *A History of the British and Foreign Bible Society, 1905–1954*. London: British and Foreign Bible Society, 1965.

Rotberg, Robert. "The Lenshina Movement of Northern Rhodesia." *Rhodes-Livingstone Journal* 29 (1961): 63–78.

———. *Christian Missionaries and the Creation of Northern Rhodesia, 1880–1924*. Princeton: Princeton University Press, 1965.

Ruedy, John. *Modern Algeria: The Origins and Development of a Nation*. Bloomington: Indiana University Press, 1992.

Ryad, Umar. "Muslim Responses to Missionary Activity in Egypt: With a Special Reference to the Al-Azhar High Corps of 'Ulama (1925–1935)." In *New Faith in Ancient Lands: Western Missions in the Middle East in the Nineteenth and Early Twentieth Centuries*, edited by Heleen Murre-van den Berg. Leiden: Brill, 2006, 281–307.

Saadi-Mokrane, Djamila. "The Algerian Linguicide." In *Algeria in Others' Languages*, edited by Anne-Emanuelle Berger. Ithaca, NY: Cornell University Press, 2002, 44–58.

Sabella, Bernard. "Palestinian Christian Emigration from the Holy Land." *Proche-Orient Chrétien* 41 (1991): 74–85.

———. "The Emigration of Christian Arabs: Dimensions and Causes of the Phenomenon." In *Christian Communities in the Arab Middle East: The Challenge of the Future*, edited by Andrea Pacini. Oxford: Clarendon Press, 1998, 127–54.

———. "Socio-Economic Characteristics and Challenges to Palestinian Christians in the Holy Land." In *Palestinian Christians: Religion, Politics and Society in the Holy Land*, edited by Anthony O'Mahony. London: Melisende, 1999, 82–95.

———. "Palestinian and Arab Christians: The Challenges Ahead." Sami Hadawi Memorial Lecture, Amman, Jordan, 22 September 2004.

Sa'id, Naffusa Zakariya. *Tarikh al-da'wa ila al-'ammiyya wa-athruha fi Misr*. Alexandria: Dar Nashr al-Thaqafa, 1964.

Said, Edward W. *Orientalism*. New York: Pantheon, 1978.

Sanderson, Lilian. "The Development of Girls' Education in the Northern Sudan, 1898–1960." *Pedagogica Historica* 8 (1968): 120–52.

Sanneh, Lamin. *Whose Religion Is Christianity? The Gospel beyond the West*. Grand Rapids, MI: William B. Eerdmans, 2003.

Sarkar, Sumit. "Indian Nationalism and the Politics of Hindutva." In *Making India Hindu: Religion, Community, and the Politics of Democracy in India*, edited by David Ludden. Philadelphia: University of Pennsylvania Press, 1996, 270–93.

Saulsberry, Nicole Denise. "The Life and Times of Woldeab Woldemariam, 1905–1995." Ph.D. diss., Stanford University, 2001.

Schapera, Isaac, ed. *Apprenticeship at Kuruman: Being the Journals and Letters of Robert and Mary Moffat, 1820–1828*. London: Chatto & Windus, 1951.

Scherer, Karen, trans. "On the Canarese Language and Literature." In *Hermann Moegling*, edited by Albrecht Frenz. Kottayam, India: DC Books, 1997, 268–91.

Schlatter, Wilhelm. *Geschichte der Basler Mission 1815–1915, mit besonderer Berücksichtigung der ungedruckten Quelle; II Band: Die Geschichte der Basler Mission in Indien und China*. Basel: Verlag der Basler Missionsbuchhandlung, 1916.

Schmidt, Nancy. *Environmental Power and Injustice, A South African History*. Cambridge: Cambridge University Press 2003.

Schoeman, Karel, ed. *The Mission at Griquatown, 1800–1821*. Griquatown: Griqua Toerisme Veren/National Book Printers, 1997.

Scott, James C. *Domination and the Arts of Resistance: Hidden Transcripts.* New Haven: Yale University Press, 1990.

Sebastian, J. Jayakiran. "The Baptism of Death: Rereading the Life and Death of Lakshmi Kaundinya." *Mission Studies* 28 (2011): 26–53.

Sebastian, Mrinalini. "Reading Archives from a Postcolonial Feminist Perspective: Native Bible Women and the Missionary Ideal." *Journal of Feminist Studies in Religion* 19, no. 1 (2003): 5–25.

———. "Mission without History? Some Ideas for Decolonizing Mission." *International Review of Mission* 93, no. 368 (2004): 75–97.

Sedra, Paul. *From Mission to Modernity: Evangelicals, Reformers and Education in Nineteenth-Century Egypt.* London: I. B. Tauris, 2011.

Śelāsé, Ḥeruy Walda. *Ba'ityop̄yā yamigaleñ yamaṣāḥefet quṭer.* Addis Ababa, 1911/12.

———. *Ba'ityop̄yā yamigañu bage'eznā bāmāriñā qwānqwā yataṣāfā yamaṣāḥafet kātālog.* Addis Ababa: Tafari Makonen Press, 1927/8.

Seneviratne, H. L. *The Work of Kings: The New Buddhism in Sri Lanka.* Chicago: University of Chicago Press, 1999.

Setiloane, Gabriel. *The Image of God among the Sotho-Tswana.* Rotterdam: Balkema, 1975.

Shafir, Gershon. *Land, Labor and the Origins of the Israeli-Palestinian Conflict.* Berkeley: University of California Press, 1996.

Sharkey, Heather J. "Christians among Muslims: the Church Missionary Society in the Northern Sudan." *Journal of African History* 43 (2002): 51–75.

———. *Living with Colonialism: Nationalism and Culture in the Anglo-Egyptian Sudan.* Berkeley: University of California Press, 2003.

———. "Arabic Anti-Missionary Treatises: Muslim Responses to Christian Evangelism in the Modern Middle East." *International Bulletin of Missionary Research* 28, no. 3 (2004): 112–18.

———. "Christian Missionaries and Colloquial Arabic Printing." *Journal of Semitic Studies,* supp. 15: *History of Printing and Publishing in the Languages and Countries of the Middle East,* edited by Philip Sadgrove. Published by Oxford University Press on behalf of the University of Manchester, 2004, 131–49.

———. "Empire and Muslim Conversion: Historical Reflections on Christian Missions in Egypt." *Islam and Christian-Muslim Relations* 16, no. 1 (2005): 43–60.

———. "Missionary Legacies: Muslim-Christian Encounters in Egypt and Sudan during the Colonial and Postcolonial Periods." In *Muslim-Christian Encounters in Africa*, edited by Benjamin F. Soares. Leiden: Brill, 2006, 57–88.

———. *American Evangelicals in Egypt: Missionary Encounters in an Age of Empire*. Princeton: Princeton University Press, 2008.

———. "Arab Identity and Ideology in Sudan: The Politics of Language, Ethnicity, and Race." *African Affairs* 107, no. 426 (2008): 21–43.

———. "Muslim Apostasy, Christian Conversion, and Religious Freedom in Egypt: A Study of American Missionaries, Western Imperialism, and Human Rights Agendas." In *Proselytization Revisited: Rights, Free Markets, and Culture Wars*, edited by Rosalind I. J. Hackett. London: Equinox, 2008, 139–66.

———. "An Egyptian in China: Ahmed Fahmy and the Making of World Christianities." *Church History* 78, no. 2 (2009): 309–26.

———. "American Presbyterians, Freedmen's Missions, and the Nile Valley: Missionary History, Racial Orders, and Church Politics on the World Stage." *Journal of Religious History* 35, no. 1 (2011): 24–42.

———. "Sudanese Arabic Bibles and the Politics of Translation." *Bible Translator*, Technical Papers, 62, no. 1 (2011): 37–45.

Shetty, Parinitha. "Conversion, Contestation and Community: Missionary Dialogues." In *Zukunft im Gedenken/Future in Remembrance*, edited by Albecht Frenz and Stefan Frenz. Norderstedt, Germany: Books on Demand GmbH, 2007, 132–52.

———. "Missionary Pedagogy and Christianisation of the Heathens: The Educational Institutions Introduced by the Basel Mission in Mangalore." *Indian Economic and Social History Review* 45, no. 4 (2008): 509–51.

de Silva, M. U. "Suppression of Buddhism and Aspects of Indigenous Culture under the British." *Journal of the Royal Asiatic Society of Sri Lanka* 49 (2004): 15–52.

Simons, Paul. "Weather Eye: Unexpected Consequences of Global Warming." *The Times* (London), 16 July 2008, http://www.thetimes.co.uk/tto/weather/article2033737.ece, accessed 8 April 2013.

Skreslet, Stanley H. "Thinking Missiologically about the History of Mission." *International Bulletin of Missionary Research* 31, no. 2 (2007): 59–65.

Smith, Andrea. "Soul Wound: The Legacy of Native American Schools," *Amnesty Magazine* (Amnesty International USA), Summer 2003, http://www.amnestyusa.org/amnesty-magazine/summer-2003/soul-wound-the-legacy-of-native-american-schools/page.do?id=1105456, accessed 20 July 2009.

Smith, Percy. "A Plea for the Use of Versions of Scripture and of Other Literature in the Vulgar Arabic." *Moslem World* 4, no. 1 (1914): 52–63.

———. "A Plea for Literature in Vernacular Arabic." *Moslem World* 7, no. 4 (1917): 333–42.

———. "Another Plea for Literature in Vernacular Arabic." *Moslem World* 9, no. 4 (1919): 351–62.

Somadasa, K. D., ed. *Catalogue of the Hugh Nevill Collection of Sinhalese Manuscripts in the British Library.* Vol. 2. London: British Library and Pali Text Society, 1989.

Stamm, Wilhelm. "Herrmann Anandarao Kaundinya: Zur 100-jaehrigen Wiederkher seines Tauftags, 6. Januar 1844." *Evangelisches Missionsmagazin 1944.* Basel: Verlag der Basler Missionsbuchhandlung, 1945, 47.

Stanley, Brian. *The Bible and the Flag: Protestant Missions and British Imperialism in the Nineteenth and Twentieth Centuries.* Leicester, UK: Apollos, 1990.

Steele, Francis R. *Not in Vain: The Story of the North Africa Mission.* Pasadena, CA: William Carey Library, 1981.

Steger, Roger. "'Without Note or Comment': Yesterday, Today, and Tomorrow." In *Sowing the Word: The Cultural Impact of the British and Foreign Bible Society, 1804–2004,* edited by Stephen Batalden, Kathleen Cann, and John Dean. Sheffield, UK: Sheffield Phoenix Press, 2004, 63–80.

Stein, Kenneth W. "The Intifada and the 1936–39 Uprising: A Comparison." *Journal of Palestine Studies* 19, no. 4 (1990): 64–85.

Stirrat, R. L. *Power and Religiosity in a Post-Colonial Setting: Sinhala Catholics in Contemporary Sri Lanka.* Cambridge: Cambridge University Press, 1992.

Stockdale, Nancy L. *Colonial Encounters among English and Palestinian Women, 1800–1948.* Gainesville: University Press of Florida, 2007.

Stone, W. V. "The Livingstonia Mission and the Bemba." *Bulletin of the Society for African Church History* 2 (1965–68): 311–22.

Strathern, Alan. *Kingship and Conversion in Sixteenth-Century Sri Lanka: Portuguese Imperialism in a Buddhist Land.* Cambridge: Cambridge University Press, 2007.

Stuart, Doug. "'Of Savages and Heroes': Discourses of Race, Nation and Gender in the Evangelical Missions to Southern Africa in the Nineteenth Century." Ph.D. diss., University of London, Institute of Commonwealth Studies, 1994.

Subrahmanyam, Sanjay. *Penumbral Visions: Making Polities in Early Modern South Asia.* New Delhi: Oxford University Press, 2001.

Sudan Government. *Report by the Governor-General on the Administration, Finance, and Conditions of the Sudan in 1949.* Khartoum: Sudan Government, 1951.

Suleiman, Yasir. *A War of Words: Language and Conflict in the Middle East.* Cambridge: Cambridge University Press, 2003.

Sundkler, B. G. M. *Bantu Prophets in South Africa.* Oxford: Oxford University Press, 1961.

Suraweera, A. V. *Rājāvaliya.* Ratmalana, Sri Lanka: Sarvodaya Vishva Lekha, 2000.

Swan, George. *Lacked Ye Anything?: A Brief Story of the Egypt General Mission.* Rev. ed. London: Egypt General Mission, 1932.

Swedenburg, Ted. *Memories of Revolt: The 1936–1939 Rebellion and the Palestinian National Past.* Fayetteville: University of Arkansas Press, 2003.

Taddia, Irma. *L'Eritrea colonia, 1890–1952: Paesaggi, stutture, uomini del colonialismo.* Milan: Franco Angelli, 1986.

———. "Correspondence as a New Source for African History: Some Evidence from Colonial Eritrea." *Cahiers des études africaines* 157 (2000): 109–34.

Taddia, Irma, and Uoldelul Chelati Dirar. "Essere africani nell'Eritrea italiana." In *Adua: Le ragioni di una sconfitta,* edited by Angelo del Boca. Rome: Laterza, 1997, 231–53.

———. "Constructing Colonial Power and Political Collaboration in Colonial Eritrea." In *Personality and Political Culture in Modern Africa: Studies Presented to Professor Harold G. Marcus,* edited by Melvin Page, Stephanie Beswick, Tim Carmichael, and Jay Spaulding. Boston: Boston University African Studies Center, 1998, 23–36.

Tafla, Bairu. *Troubles and Travels of an Eritrean Aristocrat: A Presentation of Kantibā Gilāmikā'él's Memoirs.* Aachen: Shaker Verlag, 2007.

Tannous, Izzat. *The Palestinians: A Detailed Documented Eyewitness History of Palestine under British Mandate.* New York: I. G. T., 1988.

Teklehaimanot, Berhane. "Education in Eritrea during the European Colonial Period." *Eritrean Studies Review* 1, no. 1 (1996): 1–22.

Thompson, John Alexander. *The Major Arabic Bibles: Their Origin and Nature.* New York: American Bible Society, 1956.

Thorne, Susan. *Congregational Missions and the Making of an Imperial Culture in Nineteenth-Century England.* Stanford: Stanford University Press, 1999.

Tibawi, A. L. *American Interests in Syria, 1800–1901: A Study of Education, Literary and Religious Work.* Oxford: Clarendon Press, 1966.

————. *British Interests in Palestine, 1800–1901: A Study of Religious and Educational Enterprise.* London: Oxford University Press, 1971.

Townshend, Charles. "In Defence of Palestine: Insurrection and Public Security, 1936–1939." *English Historical Review* 103, no. 409 (1988): 917–49.

Trautmann, Thomas R. *Languages and Nations: The Dravidian Proof in Colonial Madras.* Berkeley: University of California Press, 2006.

Tsimhoni, Daphne. "The Arab Christians and the Palestinian Arab National Movement During the Formative Stage." In *The Palestinians and the Middle East Conflict,* edited by Gabriel Ben-Dor. Ramat Gan, Israel: Turtledove, 1978, 73–98.

————. "The Greek Orthodox Patriarchate of Jerusalem during the Formative Years of the British Mandate in Palestine." *Asian and African Studies* 12 (1978): 77–122.

————. "The Status of the Arab Christians under the British Mandate in Palestine." *Middle Eastern Studies* 20, no. 4 (1984): 166–92.

————. *Christian Communities in Jerusalem and the West Bank since 1948: An Historical, Social and Political Study.* Westport, CT: Praeger, 1993.

Twells, Alison. *The Civilizing Mission and the English Middle Class, 1792–1850.* New York: Palgrave Macmillan, 2009.

Tyrrell, Ian. *Reforming the World: The Creation of America's Moral Empire.* Princeton: Princeton University Press, 2010.

UNESCO Institute for Statistics. "UIS Statistics in Brief: Morocco," available at http://stats.uis.unesco.org/, accessed 6 March 2008.

Upadhyaya, U. P. *Tulu Lexicon: Tulu-Kannada-English Dictionary.* 6 vols. Udupi, Karnataka, India: Rashtrakavi Govinda Pai Samshodhana Kendra, 1988.

Upson, Arthur T. Cited in *Arabic Simplified Parts I–X (Lessons 1–200).* Cairo: Nile Mission Press, n.d. [1917].

————. Cited in *High Lights in the Near East: Reminiscences of Nearly 40 Years' Service.* London: Marshall, Morgan & Scott, 1936.

Vaughn, Megan, and Henrietta L. Moore. *Cutting Down Trees: Gender Nutrition and Agricultural Change in the Northern Province of Zambia, 1890–1990.* Portsmouth, NH: Heinemann, 1994.

van der Veer, Peter, ed. *Conversion to Modernities: the Globalization of Christianity.* New York: Routledge, 1996.

————. *Imperial Encounters: Religion and Modernity in India and Britain.* Princeton: Princeton University Press, 2001.

Verdeil, Chantal. "Jesuits' Encounters with the People of Ottoman Syria: Dependence, Negotiations, and Collaboration." Paper presented at the conference on "The Great Powers in the Holy Land: From Napoleon to the Balfour Declaration," European Institute, Columbia University, 3–4 April 2009.

Vertovec, Steven. *Transnationalism*. London: Routledge, 2009.

Viswanathan, Gauri. *Outside the Fold: Conversion, Modernity and Belief.* Princeton: Princeton University Press, 1998.

Wallis, J. P. R., ed. *The Matabeleland Journals of Robert Moffat, 1829–60*. London: Chatto & Windus, 1945.

Walsh, Matthew. *Our Fathers in India: An Account of the Mission of Bellary, South India*. London: The Friary, 1931.

Wardlaw, Ralph. *Memoir of the Late Rev. John Reid, M.A., of Bellary, East Indies: Comprising Incidents of the Bellary Mission for a Period of Eleven Years, 1830 to 1840*. Glasgow: James Maclehose, 1845.

Weigle, Gottfried. "Ueber canaresische Sprache und Literatur." *Zeitschrift der Deutschen morgenlaendischen Gesellschaft*, 3 (1848): 257–84.

Wells, Julia. "The Scandal of James Read and the Taming of the London Missionary Society by 1820." *South African Historical Journal* 42 (2000): 136–60.

Wendt, Reinhard, ed. *An Indian to Indians?* Wiesbaden: Harrassowitz Verlag, 2006.

White, Luise. "Vampire Priests of Central Africa: African Debates about Labor and Religion in Colonial Northern Zambia." *Comparative Studies in Society and History* 35, no. 4 (1993): 746–72.

———. *Speaking with Vampires: Rumor and History in Colonial Africa*. Berkeley: University of California Press, 2000.

Wickremasinghe, Nira. *Ethnic Politics in Colonial Sri Lanka*. New Delhi: Vikas, 1995.

———. *Sri Lanka in the Modern Age: A History of Contested Identities*. Honolulu: University of Hawai'i Press, 2005.

Wild, Stefan. "Judentum, Christentum und Islam in der palastinensischen Poesie." *Die Welt des Islams* 23 (1984): 259–97.

Willcocks, William, trans. *al-Arba' Bashayir bil-lugha a-misriyya, al-qism al-awlani: Bashayir Matta wa-Murqus*. Cairo: Nile Mission Press, 1924.

———. *al-Khabr al-Tayyib Bita' Yasu' al-Masih, aw al-Injil bil-lugha al-'misriyya [no. 5], A'mal al-Rusul*. Cairo: Nile Mission Press, 1926.

Wilson, Henry S. "Basel Mission's Industrial Enterprise in South Kanara and Its Impact between 1834 and 1914." *Indian Church History Review* 14, no. 2 (1980): 90–104.

Wilson, Kathleen, ed. *A New Imperial History: Culture, Identity, and Modernity in Britain and the Empire, 1660–1840.* Cambridge: Cambridge University Press, 2004.

Worger, William. "Parsing God: Conversations about the Meaning of Words and Metaphors in Nineteenth Century Southern Africa." *Journal of African History* 42, no. 3 (2001): 417–47.

Wright, Stephen. *Ethiopian Incunabula.* Addis Ababa: 1967.

Yaffe, Nurit. *The Arab Population of Israel 2003.* Jerusalem: Central Bureau of Statistics, 2003.

Young, R. F., and G. S. B. Senanayaka. *The Carpenter-Heretic: A Collection of Buddhist Stories about Christianity from 18th-Century Sri Lanka.* Colombo: Karunaratne & Sons, 1998.

Zambia Government. *Report of the Commission of Enquiry into the Lumpa Church.* Lusaka: Government Printers, 1965.

Zastoupil, Lynn, and Martin Moir, eds. *The Great Indian Education Debate: Documents Relating to the Orientalist-Anglicist Controversy, 1781–1843.* Richmond, UK: Curzon, 1999.

Zewde, Bahru. *Pioneers of Change in Ethiopia: The Reformist Intellectuals of the Early Twentieth Century.* Oxford: James Currey, 2002.

Zupanov, Ines. *Disputed Mission: Jesuit Experiments and Brahminical Knowledge in Seventeenth Century India.* Oxford: Oxford University Press, 2000.

Index

Abdul-Fady. *See* Upson, Arthur T.

"About Gunpowder" (Kittel), 200

Abraham, Charles Henry, 242n59

Abraham, Daniel Vincent, 94

Abraham, Francis: conversion of, 84–85; John Hands and, 242n59; as Hindu, 87; testimony of, 94, 243n63; Viswanathan on, 95; witnesses for, 68–69, 89–93

Abraham, Matthew, 16–17, 24, 67–68; clothing worn by, 85–86, 243nn62–63; conversion, 81–87, 88–89; conversion narrative of, 83–87; Doyle and, 88–89, 244n73; as East Indian, 69. *See also Abraham v. Abraham*

Abraham v. Abraham (India, 1863), 17, 67–96; appeal of, 94; conversions and, 17, 69, 81–87, 88–89, 96, 244n77; cultural transformation and, 83–87; depositions from, 84–87; East Indians and, 68–69; ethnographic writings and, 71–82; John Hands and, 82–87, 96, 242n59; Hindu Law and, 67, 68, 87, 243n66, 244n77; missionary knowledge systems and, 68, 70, 239n3, 239n7; Fulgence Perozy and, 88, 243–44n69; verdict for, 93–96; Viswanathan on, 94–95, 245n83; Western clothing and, 85–86, 243nn62–63; witnesses for Charlotte,

68–69, 84–87, 89, 94, 243n63; witnesses for Francis, 68–69, 89–93

Abu El-Assal, Riah, 238n47

Adams, C. C., 130–31, 133

African elites, 31, 44–45, 48

African teachers, 34–35, 36–37

Africa Orientale Italiana, 165

Afrikaner, Jonker, 149

agency, 7, 12, 139

AHC (Arab Higher Committee), 54–55, 239n9

Alagiyavanna, 103–7, 119–20, 246nn17–18, 246n20

Alagiyawanna, Herbert Kumar, 246n17

Alexander, Michael Solomon, 52

Algeria: Arabization (*ta'rib*) in, 220; Bible translations for, 204, 212, 216, 219, 220, 273n53; literacy in, 211; NAM in, 220, 275n80

'Almedom, Mesghenna, 169

'Alula, 172

AMEM (American Methodist Episcopal Mission), 210

American Bible Society, 207

American Methodist Episcopal Mission (AMEM), 210

American Peniel Mission, 132

American Presbyterians, 13, 124, 126, 130, 134, 212, 230n50

American University of Beirut, 53

186–90, 192–93, 264n25, 264–65n32, 265n38; Dravidian languages and, 198–200; early history of, 180–81; ethnographic research and, 177, 181, 194–97, 199–201; first conversion by, 190, 265n35; hierarchy of, 181–82; Indology and, 177; interracial marriage and, 193, 266n49; legacies of, 201–2; local cultures and beliefs and, 185–86, 190–91, 264n24; long-term impact of, 177–78, 200–201; mission compounds, 182–83; Pietism and, 20–21, 178, 181, 263n14; principles of, 182; religious and intellectual context of, 179–83; scholar-missionaries of, 177, 182, 194–97, 202

Basler Handels-Gesellschaft AG, 192

Belgian Congo (1908–1960), 12–13

beliefs, non-Christian. *See* local cultures and beliefs

Bellary, India: *Abraham v. Abraham* and, 67–68; Catholics in, 87–89, 243–44n69, 243n68; Hands in, 72–77; location of, 239n2; schools in, 72, 74, 240n12, 241n23; Sub Collector of, 73, 240n20; Tamil Christians and, 83

Bemba, 15–16, 32–33, 34–35

Benedict XIV, 78–79

Berber language, 211–12

Berhān Yehun, 166

Berlin Treaty (1885–86), 34

Betrayal of Buddhism, The (Sri Lanka, 1956), 25

BFBS. *See* British and Foreign Bible Society

Bhutas, 185–86, 264n24

Biancheri, Lorenzo, 165

Bible translations, 23, 203–21; Bantu language, 141, 142, 152–53; ChiBemba language, 37–38, 232n25;

classical Arabic, 204, 207, 221; demise of, 217–21, 274n72, 274n74; English, 217; extraneous text in, 206–8, 269n16; French language, 219; Hindustani language, 75; Judeo-Arabic language, 204, 214–15, 219, 220, 271–72n45, 272n47; Kannada language, 72, 81; language expertise of missionaries and, 215, 272n51; Lenshina movement on, 45; Negro-English, 216–17, 221; for niche Bibles, 213–17; sales of, 215, 272–73n52, 273n53; sellers of, 204, 215, 219–20, 221, 275n88; for Tunisia, 205, 215; Welsh, 216. *See also* colloquial Arabic Bibles

Bible Women, 204, 215, 221, 275n88

Bibliotheca Carnatica (Moegling), 196

Billavas, 185–86

Bishop, Eric, 57

Blair (Collector of Mangalore), 187

boarding schools, 181, 190

bodily practices, 85–86, 91–92, 243n62

Bogachu (Chief), 145, 146, 147–48, 152–53, 254n15

bogologo (the past), 150

Bomma (slave), 263n19

Book of Counsel (*Yemeṣehaf maker*) (Gabra Mikā'él), 171

Book of Gabra Mika'él Germu (*Zemeṣehaf Zegabra Mikā'él Germu*), 171

Books of Hours, 206

Booth (Judge), 132

born-again Christians, 48, 218

Boxer, C. R., 246n14

Brahmins, 76–79, 94, 178, 184, 186–90. *See also* caste system

bribery, 102

Cowl Bazaar, India, 72, 88, 240n17,
244n70
Cox, Jeffrey, 229n44
Cūḷavaṃsa (Minor Chronicle), 102,
246n11
culture: Buddhist, 105, 120; Hindu,
71–82, 86–87, 89–92; language and,
195; of literacy, 19–20. *See also* local
cultures and beliefs

Da Carbonara, Michele, 161
da Iseo, Ezechia, 157, 159, 255n1
Dalzell, John Allen, 240n20
Daniel, Book of, 215
Dasara festival, 76, 241n31
Dayananda (father of mercy), 88,
244n72
death: Bantu language and, 149, 150;
Buddhist god of, 110; Christian mis-
sionary understandings of, 19, 145,
148–49; civil and ritual forms of, 24,
188, 191
Debab ʻAraya, 172, 173
Deccan region, 67, 239n1
decolonization, 16, 21, 23, 31, 204,
219–20
demons, 108, 110, 246n12
de Pertis, Nicola, 161–62
de Sá de Noronha, Constantino, 105, 106
Devanagari language, 195–96
Dharmapala, Anagarika, 25, 112–13,
115, 116
Dias, Joachim, 77–78, 241n37
Difaqane region, 147, 154
al-Din al-Khatib, Muhibb, 136
Dirar, Uoldelul Chelati, 163, 166–67
Dirks, Nicolas, 71
Dissenters, 72, 85, 88, 206, 240n16
Diutlwileng (Chief), 146

divine incarnation (*avatāraya*), 110
"Do Not Fear the People of the Temple"
("Mwitina Bena Itempele"), 44
doubters, pragmatic, 141
Doyle, Patrick: *Abraham v. Abraham*
and, 70–71, 88–89, 92–93, 244n73;
background of, 87–88, 96, 244n70,
244n72
Dravidian languages, 20, 198–200, 205,
267n63
Dubois, Jean Antoine, 70–71, 76–82, 83,
96, 241n39
Duffy, Eamon, 206
Dupont (Bishop), 32, 34
Dutch colonialism, 100, 107–8, 115

East India Company, 71, 73, 74, 88, 194
East Indians, 68–69, 84, 87. *See also*
Abraham v. Abraham
education, 12, 21, 34, 36, 37, 51, 53,
65, 112, 157–59, 162, 163, 167, 170,
179, 181, 182, 211, 219–20. *See also*
schools
Eerarru Patrike (Moegling), 264n25
EGM (Egypt General Mission), 208,
211, 219–20, 270n28, 273n53
Egypt: antimissionary movement in,
129, 135, 138; Bible translations
for, 203, 204, 208, 215–16, 218, 221,
269n15, 273n53; Capitulations,
127; colonialism in, 122, 123, 127;
colporteurs in, 275n88; Constitution of 1923, 122; conversions in,
122–23; freedom of religion in, 127;
Judeo-Arabic language in, 204; literacy in, 211; missionary encounters
in, 22, 24, 122–23; Muslim identity
in, 18. *See also* Port Said orphan
scandal

Taddia, Irma, 166–67

Taklahāymānot, 172

al-Takwin, Sifr, 203

tali, 80

Tamil Brahmins, 69

Tamil Christians, 72–73, 77, 83

Tamil language, 198, 200, 205

Tannus, 'Izzat, 56, 59

Tannus, Suleiman, 64

target audience, 3, 23, 205

ta'rib (Arabization), 220

Tārik 'it ālyānā'ityopya. See History of Italy and Ethiopia (Gabra Mikā'él)

Tavernier, Jean Baptiste, 103–4, 107

Tāye Gabra Māryām, 159

teachers, African, 34–35, 36–37

Telugu Christians, 92–93

temple (*itempile*), 43

textbooks, 157, 163, 164, 255n1, 257n33

Thackeray, William, 240n20

Al-thawra al-kubra. See Great Revolt (Palestine, 1936–1939)

theologians, 139–41

Theosophical Society, 248n39

Third Anniversary Discourse (Asiatic Society at Calcutta), 194

This Is the Last Talk I Will Give (*Mē Mama Karana Avasan Kathāvayi*) (Soma), 111, 114–17

Thom, George, 142

Thomson, A., 275n88

Three Jewels of Buddhism, 105–6

Tigrinya language, 164, 165, 170

tile factories, 191, 192

Tipu Sultan, 74–75, 79, 241n31

Tombo (land register), 103, 104, 105

traditional beliefs. *See* local cultures and beliefs

translations. *See* Bible translations; song translations

transnationalism, 5, 6, 183

Trautmann, Thomas R., 198, 262n6

Tron, Alesandro, 161

Tshidi, 147

Tulu language, 176, 177, 178, 185, 200–201

Tulu Lexicon Project, 200–201

Tunisia: Bible translations for, 205, 215; Judeo-Arabic language in, 204, 272n47; Maghribi calligraphy style in, 204, 268–69n5

Turkiyya Hasan affair. *See* Port Said orphan scandal

Tyndale, William, 217

ubuloshi. See witchcraft (*ubuloshi*)

Ufipa district, 39–40

"Unanticipated Consequences of Purposive Social Action, The" (Merton), 2

undivided families, 90–91, 94

United Nations, 64

United Presbyterian Church of North America, 124

universalism, 229n44

University of Halle, 180

University of Pennsylvania symposium (2008), 4

University of Tübingen, 196

Upson, Arthur T., 210, 270n26, 271n37

utopianism, 20–21

Vaḍu Tīrthaka Maḷasohonpreta Kathāva (Story of the Carpenter-Heretic Cemetery Ghost), 107–11

vampire rumors, 232n32

Van Dyck Arabic Bible, 207, 212, 221

Vatican, Lateran Accords (1929), 164, 257n34